COUNTY LOUTH
and the
IRISH REVOLUTION
1912–1923

Donal Hall has written and lectured widely on the Great War and the revolutionary period in Co. Louth; he is the author of *World War I and nationalist politics in County Louth, 1914–1920* (2005), 'The unreturned army': *County Louth Dead in the Great War* (2005) and (with Brendan Hall) *The Louth Rifles 1877–1908* (2000).

Martin Maguire is Senior Lecturer and Director of the BA (Hons) Digital Humanities in the Department of Humanities at Dundalk IT. He is the author of *The Civil Service and the Revolution in Ireland 1912–38: 'Shaking the Blood-stained Hand of Mr Collins'* (2009) and has published extensively on the history of Irish Protestantism.

COUNTY LOUTH
and the
IRISH REVOLUTION
1912–1923

EDITORS

DONAL HALL & MARTIN MAGUIRE

IRISH ACADEMIC PRESS

First published in 2017 by
Irish Academic Press
10 George's Street
Newbridge
Co. Kildare
Ireland
www.iap.ie

978-1-911024-56-9 (paper)
978-1-911024-57-6 (cloth)
978-1-911024-58-3 (Kindle)
978-1-911024-59-0 (Epub)
978-1-911024-60-6 (PDF)

British Library Cataloguing in Publication Data
An entry can be found on request

Library of Congress Cataloging in Publication Data
An entry can be found on request

Interior design by www.jminfotechindia.com
Typeset in Minion Pro 11.5/14.5 pt
Cover design by edit+ www.stuartcoughlan.com

Cover/jacket front: Group of Irish Volunteers and Cumann na mBan, Dundalk,
1921. Mary McHugh, middle front (courtesy of Barbara McCourt).
Cover/jacket back: Millmount, Drogheda, Co. Louth, after bombardment,
July 1922 (courtesy of Old Drogheda Society).

Printed in by TJ International Ltd, Padstow, Cornwall.

Contents

Co. Louth, 1912–1923, Key Locations

Omeath

★ Ravensdale Park (burned)

Carlingford

Greenore

☆ *Annaskeagh House (burned)*

Cavananore House (burned) ☆   Falmore Hall ★

Ballymascanlon House ★
◆ *Ballymascanlon*
★ Bellurgan House

Castletown House ★   ★ Castletown Castle
◆ *BridgeSt*
DUNDALK   ◆ *Quay St*
◆ *Anne St*

Stephenstown House ★   ◆ *Blackrock*

Louth   Fane Valley ★   ★ Clermont Park (burned)

◆

Knock Abbey (burned) ★

Tallanstown

Glyde   ◆ *Gilbertstown*
Court ★
Louth Hall ★   ★ Corbollis House

Reaghstown ◆   CASTLEBELLINGHAM
Castlebellingham
Lisrenny House ★   ★ The Crescent
Bellingham Castle ★
Braganstown House ★   ★ Milestown House (burned)

★ Williamstown House

☆ *Ballygassan House (burned)*

★ Red House   ★ Drumcashel House
★ Drumcar House   Dunany House ★
ARDEE   *Ardee*
Ardee House ★   ★ Charleville House
★ Richardstown Castle

◆ *Dunleer*
DUNLEER   ★ Barmeath Castle
★ Rathescar

★ Smarmore   ★ Rokeby Hall
Castle
★ Stone House   ◆ *Clogherhead*

★ Oriel Temple   Piperstown   ★ Blackhall
House ★
COLLON   *Collon*   ★ Rath House

TERMONFECKIN
★ Monasterboice House   Carstown   ★ Newtown House,
House   Termonfeckin

Newtown House, ★   ★ Beaulieu House
Townley Hall ★   Drogheda
Westgate
DROGHEDA   ◆ *South Quay*

───── Major roads
++++++++ Railways
◆ *RIC Stations*
★ **Big Houses**
☆ *Other Houses*

Map courtesy of Jean Young.

Introduction
County Louth and the Irish Revolution, 1912–1923

The history of the revolutionary period (1912–23) is often imagined as the history of an idealistic national response to the struggle between the IRA and the British State for popular legitimacy. County Louth has been marginal to popular and academic study of that history due to the comparatively low level of armed activity in the county during the period, and that few personalities emerged from the county that made an impact on the national stage. The experiences of Belfast-born Sean MacEntee, who received a death sentence for his activities, dominates the narrative where the participation of the Louth Volunteers in the 1916 Rising is noted at all. The War of Independence is usually glossed over, while the primary focus in the Civil War is generally Frank Aiken from Co. Armagh, and his efforts to keep the 4th Northern Division of the IRA out of the conflict. The future political careers of both MacEntee and Aiken were founded on their activities in Co. Louth, yet the context from which they drew those reputations has remained largely unexamined.

It is by examining the experience of those in the quieter and more marginal areas that a different but no less true evaluation of the national revolution can be made, as the drumbeat of distant conflict transformed lives and communities in a less violent but no less complete manner. The local experience, when subject to close scrutiny, is seen as less idealistic and more pragmatic. Actions were taken, which were influenced less by the national ideal than by deep local traditions and antagonisms. Taking Co. Louth as a geographical area and looking at the local activism of the IRA, but also beyond the actions of the IRA, this book evaluates the experience of revolution by those such as labour, RIC men, republican women, cultural activists, the Big House families, the railway workers and owners. Increasingly, for all these social groups, events were shaped by the developing reality of partition that transformed a marginal county into a borderland, creating a zone of new violence and banditry.

Donal Hall's opening chapter on politics and revolution is an exploration of the persistence of factionalism and the resilience of Redmondite nationalism. He concludes with an analysis of the overriding power of localism that coloured all expressions of nationalism, whether constitutional or revolutionary, in Co. Louth. Cumann na mBan is the subject of Ailbhe Rogers' chapter. She narrates in rich detail the activism of the Co. Louth women, who began as auxiliaries to the Irish Volunteers but rose to the developing tempo of the revolution in organisations for the dependants of the 1916 dead and prisoners, in mobilising opposition to conscription, and in support for the IRA through the War of Independence and the Civil War. She concludes by briefly considering these women's reaction to the position of women in the patriarchal and conservative society that emerged from the revolution.

Martin Maguire looks at the strong urban and rural labour tradition that Co. Louth had nurtured and its enduring culture of trade unionism in field and factory. He shows how 'Red Flag' Dundalk and Drogheda in 1919 looked to the revolution in Petrograd for inspiration rather than to that of Easter 1916. The imposition of partition fatally weakened labour as Co. Louth found itself becoming a border county at the edge of the newly emerging state. Policing the county in the period of revolution and after is the subject of Brendan McAvinue's chapter. He shows that the RIC had good relations with the people and it took a lot of persuasion by the IRA, along with the banditry of the Black and Tans, to end those good relations. As the RIC retreated to secure barracks, the task of policing a fractious community had to be taken on by the Republican Police, albeit relucantly. As the Civil War threatened to unleash social disorder and unrestrained banditry, experiments in local policing were attempted. McAvinue concludes with the consolidation of the new Garda Síochána as the accepted police force of the community.

Fiona Fearon's chapter documents the luxuriant culture of local dramatics in Co. Louth that embraced the townspeople, the military garrison and the rural villages. She shows the growth of a new nationalist culture expressed in drama, details the political and ideological battles to define Irishness through drama, and analyses how the performers and the audience found each other. Peter Rigney turns his unparallelled expertise on the history of the Irish railways to the experience of Co. Louth. Midway between Belfast and Dublin, and caught between loyalism and republicanism, the Great Northern Railway (GNR) struggled to maintain a service. Dundalk, formerly at the centre of the network and the key location of the GNR engineering works, emerged out of the revolution on a frontier. However, he concludes that, rather than partition, it was the development of road transport, competing with the railways, that did most to undermine the GNR.

County Louth, as Jean Young writes in her chapter, had a relatively significant 'Big House' presence. She details the decline of the Big House families through the operation of the Land Acts, the attrition of the Great War on the male line, and the incendiarism of the Civil War. Her chapter charts the end of the economic, social and cultural life of the Big House and the end of landlordism in one county. John McCullen details the unique case of a man wrongly arrested in the sweep after 1916 and his attempts to sue the responsible District Inspector of the RIC. His case illustrates the dubious legality of the post-1916 repression under martial law and the utterly chaotic police reponse locally. The defending barrister for the wronged man was the sharp-tongued and acerbic T.M. Healy.

Conor McNamara forensically explores the intersection between political, sectarian and communal violence in the escalating war between the IRA commanded by Aiken and the B-Specials in the border areas, culminating in the killing of six Protestants at Altnaveigh in June 1922. The Civil War in Drogheda, as is shown by Mal Martin in his chapter, was triggered by a purely local incident in which the killing of an RIC constable led to Drogheda becoming a battlefield between the National Army and the Anti-Treaty forces in a replication of the fighting in Dublin City. Don Johnston considers the case of Charles Gyles, a Protestant working class man and First World War veteran, who joined the new National Army and was assassinated on the street in Dundalk. The reluctance of the National Army and the authorities to pursue his killers and the resulting bitterness sown in his surviving family is documented in detail.

Seamus Bellew details the culture of memorials and inscription that commemorates the dead of the world war, the veterans of the 1916 Rising and the War of Independence. He notes the recent incorporation of the dead of the world war in official commemorations but queries the, as yet, unresolved challenge of incorporating the Civil War dead. Lorraine McCann, the Co. Louth archivist, takes us through the process of compiling the names of those who mobilised in 1916 in the county, detailing in a model of best research the sources and how to interpret them.

The editors wish to acknowledge the inspiration and support of the County Louth Archaeological and Historical Society, Dundalk Institute of Technology and Louth County Council. Special thanks to Bernadette Fennell, the co-ordinator of County Louth's 1916 commemorations, and to Conor Graham and Fiona Dunne of Irish Academic Press. It is our hope that this volume of essays will inspire further research into the local experience of national revolution.

Donal Hall & Martin Maguire,
January 2017

1

Politics and Revolution in County Louth, 1912–1923

Donal Hall

In 1914, Co. Louth was politically nationalist. Since 1885, the county had returned two nationalist members of the Irish Parliamentary Party (IPP) to parliament for the North Louth and South Louth constituencies. County Louth nationalists were already riven by factionalism when they were further bitterly divided with the fall of Parnell in 1891. In the general election of 1892, Tim Healy and Dr Daniel Ambrose, both anti-Parnellites, were returned for the North Louth and South Louth constituencies respectively, with a combined vote of 4,719, while the pro-Parnellite candidates could only summon up 2,695 votes between them.[1] Anti-Parnellites held both seats in the 1895 and 1900 elections. The IPP then united behind a new leader, John Redmond, a Parnellite. The member for South Louth, Joseph Nolan, supported Redmond, but Tim Healy for North Louth remained aloof. Healy was returned as MP for North Louth in 1906 and in the first election of 1910. In the second election of 1910, Healy lost his seat to the Redmondite IPP candidate Richard Hazleton. That result was overturned in the courts, and in the 1911 by-election the seat reverted to a pro-Healyite, Augustine Roche.

The United Irish League (UIL), which controlled the selection of IPP candidates for election, was founded in 1898, and by 1916 had twenty-five branches in Louth, with over 2,000 members, although it was generally moribund.[2] Alongside the UIL was the Ancient Order of Hibernians (AOH) Bord of Éireann group that, on the one hand, provided muscular street support for the IPP and, on the other, administered sickness and unemployment benefit for its members after the passing of the National

Insurance Act of 1911. The AOH established a branch in Dundalk in August 1907 and by 1916 had twenty-three branches in Co. Louth, with 1,900 members.[3] In September 1907, a branch of a rival breakaway organisation of the AOH, the Irish-American Alliance, John Boyle O'Reilly Division, alternatively known as the Knights of Hibernia (KOH), was set up in Dundalk. By 1916, it had three branches in Co. Louth, with a membership of over 500.[4] Also, in 1907, a branch of Sinn Féin was founded in Dundalk under the stewardship of William D'arcy and Patrick Hughes, the latter a rates collector with Dundalk Urban District Council (UDC) and Louth County Council.

The Ulster Volunteer Force (UVF) was founded in January 1913 to oppose, by force of arms if necessary, the introduction of Home Rule in Ireland. In response to the growing threat from the UVF, the Irish Volunteers, Óglaigh na hÉireann, was founded in Dublin on 25 November 1913 to defend Home Rule. At a meeting in the Dundalk Town Hall on Sunday, 1 February 1914, the feasibility of establishing the first corps of the Irish Volunteers in Co. Louth was considered. The meeting was presided over by Matthew Comerford, town clerk. Patrick Hughes acted as secretary to the meeting.[5] Present were representatives from various Catholic and nationalist organisations:

AOH (Bord of Éireann): Peter Toner, Ed Duffy and P Green.
KOH (John Boyle O'Reilly Division): P.J. Clarke, Owen Grant,
    Patrick Baxter.
Young Ireland Society: J. McKinley, Peter Ward.
Sinn Féin: T. Clifford, J. Murtagh, J. Jameson.
Emmet Band: M. Dobbs, P. Walmsley.
Hearts of Oriel: M. McGowan, T. Rourke.
Catholic Young Men's Society: N. McCourt, P. Gilmore, P. Markey.
John Dillon Gaelic Football Club: Mr Lennon and Mr Crilly.

The first enrolment meeting in Co. Louth was held in Dundalk at the athletic grounds on Sunday, 22 February 1914. Matthew Comerford proclaimed that the Irish Volunteers had the full support of every nationalist organisation in the town and 'several hundred men' were enrolled.[6] On 31 March 1914, a preliminary meeting was held in Drogheda in the Mayoralty Rooms, with a view to establishing the Irish Volunteers in that town. The meeting was presided over by P. Clinton, and the following committee was appointed: J.B. Connolly, town clerk; P. Clinton, president, AOH; T.V. McQuillan, town commissioner; J. Clarke, president, Tredagh Football Club; with F. Clare, J. Carroll, J. Carr and W. Elliott.

The *Drogheda Independent* of 9 May 1914 reported that a branch of the Irish Volunteers was formally launched in Drogheda on 8 May. Several thousand persons were reported to have attended and were addressed by Eoin MacNeill and Tom Kettle MP. The inaugural meeting held in the Mall, was preceded by a procession of the AOH; Irish National Foresters; Workman's Total Abstinence Society; Mell Total Abstinence Society; Pioneer Total Abstinence Society; St Mary's Total Abstinence Society, Drogheda Branch; Gaelic League; and the Gaelic Athletic Association. Also noted to be present were Aldermen L.J. Elcock CC, James McCarthy JP CC, Dr W. Bradley JP, A.J. McQuillan, JP TC, T.V. McQuillan, TC, M.A. Casey, editor, *Drogheda Independent*, J. McGolrick, J. Byrne, J. Tynan, Wes Bradley, Robert May, O'Gogarty, Joe Carr, Secretary, J. Keeley, J. Doherty, Peter Lynch JP, J. Lochrin, C. McInerney, Peter Clinton (President AOH), Frank Clarke, J. Smith, C. Nulty, Laurence Stanley TC, J Berril TC, J.J. Clarke TC, L. Carroll, P. Weldon SSO, PP Kesley JP, J.S. Kelly TC, P. Kelly, F. Byrne TC, Ald. T.M. McCullagh, T. McCabe, Walter O'Gorman, Thomas Kealey, George Lee, P.D. McIvor. The *Dundalk Democrat* of 2 May 1914 reported that on 29 April a meeting was held in Ardee, addressed by William Doran JP CC, J.T. Dolan, and P.J. McMahon with a view to 'reorganising' the Irish Volunteers 'on a firmer basis' in that area, with 'close on a hundred young men formally enrolled in the ranks'.

On the night of 24 April 1914, the UVF caused a sensation by landing large quantities of arms in Larne, Bangor and Donaghadee. The Ulster gun-running provided the impetus to expand the organisation of the Irish Volunteers in Louth. The police reported that the AOH, although for some time opposed to the Volunteers, 'feel that the Ulster movement has been allowed to go too far and that a counter-move is necessary'. By the end of May 1914, membership of the Irish Volunteers in Louth stood at 1,898.[7] The highpoint of the organisation in Louth occurred on 12 July 1914, when the principal feature of the annual feis in Castlebellingham was a parade by the Louth Irish Volunteers. The event was organised by the Gaelic League and planned as a propaganda event. On the day, an appreciative audience of some 10,000 witnessed a march-past by 2,000 Volunteers from Louth. The proceedings were filmed and newsreels were still being shown of the event as late as December 1914[8] (see Table 1: Organisation of Co. Louth Irish Volunteers, August 1914).

In the first week of July 1914, a brief report in the *Dundalk Democrat* noted the 'shocking tragedy' of the assassination of Franz Ferdinand, the heir to the throne of Austria, and of his wife Sophie, in Serbia.[9] On 1 August, the *Dundalk Democrat* noted that intermeshing treaties, which ensnared the major powers and smaller countries, made it seem likely that a European war would break out. In a startling misreading of the situation, the *Democrat* opined that 'it is not regarded as probable that [the British foreign minister, Sir Edward Grey] will do anything to embroil his country in a war that does not concern her'.[10] Three days later, on 4 August, Britain formally declared war on Germany and Austria. Redmond's reaction to the imminent threat of war was to pledge, on 3 August 1914, the services of the Irish Volunteers for the defence of Ireland and urged the British government to concentrate her army on attacking Germany. This pledge was, according to the *Dundalk Democrat*, 'a splendid day's work for Ireland'.[11]

The *Dundalk Examiner* took an altogether different view: 'There was nothing dignified but a great deal that was obsequious in Mr Redmond's statement and Ireland has surrendered her just line of defence without price or promise of requital.'[12] A garrison battalion of the Royal Field Artillery was mobilised and marched out of Dundalk army barracks on the night of 20 August 1914. Friends and a company of buglers from the Volunteers escorted the soldiers to the train station. The *Dundalk Examiner* furiously referred to the buglers as 'excrescences on the Volunteer movement … who had turned out to do honour to a regiment of British soldiers whose companions in arms a few weeks ago ruthlessly shot down unarmed men, women and children in the streets of Dublin'.[13]

The presence of the buglers at the parade also infuriated Patrick Hughes and some others of the Dundalk Irish Volunteers. On 27 August, a meeting of the Dundalk Corps heard a report that the Organising Committee had voted seven to four to dispense with the services of the bugling instructor. The Corps overturned the decision by 115 votes to 66. The seven members of the Organising Committee who had originally voted for expulsion, James Hughes, Patrick Hughes, James Ward, Bernard Kelly, Owen Grant, Sean MacEntee and P. O'Dubhtaigh, resigned, as did Tom Hearty. Seamus McGuill recounted how, during the argument, older political divisions came to the fore, 'some of the committee … stated they would have no Healyite or Sinn Féin element in the corps … This naturally caused a split in the Dundalk Corps'.[14]

John Redmond's Woodenbridge speech of 20 September 1914, encouraging the Irish Volunteers to enlist in the British Army, was headlined 'Mr Redmond's Latest Treason' by the *Dundalk Examiner*. In Drogheda, where about 500 men were on the rolls of the Irish Volunteers, a meeting was called to propose a resolution asking the Volunteers to give Redmond's policy enthusiastic support. The proposal was overwhelmingly passed, only one man being heard to dissent.[15] The 'Redmondite' Volunteers, became known as the National Volunteers and established a new organisation headquarters in Dublin. On 7 October, by a vote of six to four, the Dundalk Volunteers decided to affiliate to the National Volunteers.[16]

With the split in September 1914, a breakaway provisional committee of Irish Volunteers was established under Eoin MacNeill. Public meetings in support of the provisional committee were held in Grange, Cooley, on 11 October, presided over by P. Donnelly, and in Ardee on 15 October, presided over by P.J. McMahon. Patrick Hughes set about affiliating the Irish Volunteers in Co. Louth to the new provisional committee and to that end called a meeting in the town hall in Dundalk on Sunday, 18 October 1914, that was attended by about twenty-four people. When word of the meeting got out, the building was surrounded and attacked by members of the AOH. The *Dundalk Democrat* condemned the meeting as 'a convocation of cranks and sham extremists who will not speak for the National Volunteers or for the men who throughout the country have sustained Ireland's constitutional fight for freedom for the past thirty-five years'.[17]

There was more friction between the two factions in the following weeks. According to one account the people of Dundalk were generally 'most hostile to the Irish Volunteers'.[18] Another reported that on occasions stones were fired at Irish Volunteers while on route marches.[19] On Sunday, 25 October 1914, a convention was held in Dublin of the Volunteers who had broken with Redmond, and it was reported that Patrick Hughes (Dundalk), P.J. McMahon (Ardee) and P. Donnelly (Cooley) were present. This convention formally established the Irish Volunteers as an independent organisation body separate from the National Volunteers.[20]

Following reorganisation, membership of the Irish Volunteers in Louth remained low. Their activities were not recorded in monthly RIC reports until October 1915, and as late as February 1916, the County Inspector stated that the Irish Volunteers had little influence or support within the county. Membership barely exceeded 200 by March 1916, mostly in the Dundalk area.[21] Although drilling and marching took place in both Dundalk and Drogheda, the quality and quantity of weaponry in their hands was poor. After the Volunteer split, the National Volunteers had retained the weaponry with the result that, approaching Easter 1916, the bulk of the Irish Volunteers were armed with shotguns and revolvers. Innovations of dubious quality increased the supply of arms and equipment. Volunteer Arthur Greene described how Sean MacEntee had procured some lead and, at the Volunteer drill hall in Dundalk, both Greene and John Kieran spent long hours converting the lead into buckshot for shotgun cartridges.[22] Bayonets were also manufactured from garden shears and adapted for fitting to shotguns.

The secretive Military Council of the Irish Republican Brotherhood (IRB) had decided that a nationwide armed rebellion would take place, with German support, at Easter 1916. Patrick Hughes was informed and, recognising his own limited capabilities in military matters, requested assistance. Donal O'Hannigan from Limerick was instructed by Sean McDermott to take charge of the Louth/Meath, South Down, South Armagh and South Monaghan area. O'Hannigan's instructions from Patrick Pearse were to muster his men with the Meath Volunteers at the Hill of Tara in Co. Meath at 7 p.m. on Easter Sunday, to read the Proclamation of the Irish Republic and then to proceed to Blanchardstown where they were to cut the railway line. They were to remain *in situ* as part of a ring of Volunteers around the city. O'Hannigan questioned the convenience of Tara as a location but was told by Pearse that for historical reasons the Proclamation of the Republic had to be read there.[23]

Volunteers were instructed to mobilise, in full gear and with three days of provisions, at Dundalk, Drogheda and Ardee on Easter Sunday morning for route marches. Figures differ in various reports, but between 100 and 120 barely trained and poorly armed Volunteers mobilised in Dundalk and marched towards Ardee at 10 a.m. At Gilbertstown they were joined by a contingent of about ten men from Dunleer and continued to Ardee where rifles and ammunition in the possession of the National Volunteers were acquired. The Drogheda Volunteers, meanwhile, under the command of Philip Monahan, having mobilised and set out towards Slane, were intercepted by Dr Bradley of Drogheda, who informed them of Eoin MacNeill's order countermanding the mobilisation. The Drogheda march was cancelled and the men dispersed. The Dundalk Volunteers continued to Slane where Sean MacEntee caught up with them and informed them of the countermanding orders.

The activities of the Louth Irish Volunteers in 1916 are detailed elsewhere in this book. The active involvement of former National Volunteers, during and after the rebellion, in security operations on the side of the British army was an illustration of the unbridgeable gap that had emerged between these former comrades. Matthew Comerford, Dundalk town clerk and secretary of the National Volunteers, voluntarily surrendered fifty rifles to the military authorities that had remained in the custody of the National Volunteers in Dundalk. Seamus McGuill noted that Comerford, 'for his treachery to Ireland, was honoured by the British Government with the title OBE shortly after Easter Week'.[24] The Home Defence Corps, a short-lived local militia which contained many ex-National Volunteers, was mobilised and set up checkpoints in and around Dundalk. According to the RIC, the National Volunteers in Drogheda also gave assistance to the security forces.

On 4 May, about sixty-three suspected participants and sympathisers were arrested around the county. Sean MacEntee, Frank Martin, Denis Leahy and James Sally were tried and found guilty by Court Martial for the murder of Constable McGee at Castlebellingham and all but Sally were condemned to death. MacEntee's sentence was commuted to penal servitude for life, Martin's and Leahy's to ten years and Sally was sentenced to five years. Patrick Hughes escaped arrest, and remained 'on the run' until January 1922, as did Donal O'Hannigan (see Table 2: Arrests and detentions, 1916).

Police reports for August and September 1916 indicated increased signs of disloyalty following the release of some rebel prisoners, particularly in Drogheda where the wearing of Sinn Féin badges was prevalent among young men and women. Police in Ardee had put in 'stringent measures' to prevent the recurrence of telegraph poles being painted in Sinn Féin colours.[25] As more prisoners were released during 1917, the Volunteers became more active. In April 1917, three companies of Volunteers were established in Dundalk, the first attempt formally to organise the Volunteers since the rebellion one year before. Peter Kieran described how route marches began around Dundalk in April and how, some days after a march to Louth village, nine of their men were arrested and received varying gaol sentences, 'leading to riotous clashes with the RIC'.[26] A police report for July described how J. MacEntee, P. McMahon, J. Walsh and J. Murray addressed meetings in Clogherhead, Dunleer and Drogheda, the speeches being 'of a violent and disloyal nature'.[27]

In September 1917, membership of the Irish Volunteers was estimated by the Royal Irish Constabulary (RIC) at 234.[28] The military situation on the allied side in Europe at the end of 1917 was precarious. The great autumn offensive by the British had failed, the French army was paralysed by mutinies, and Russia had abandoned the war after a revolution in October. Reinforced by armies released from the Russian front, the early success of the German spring offensive in 1918 caused manpower shortages in the British army that led in turn to the introduction of the Conscription Bill on 9 April 1918, extending conscription to Ireland for the first time.

The conscription threat was met with a storm of protest and outrage both inside and outside of parliament. In Drogheda, 'men of all creeds and classes rushed to join the Irish Volunteers. Members of the Ancient Order of Hibernians, who previously were our bitterest enemies, sought admission and joined the Volunteers as did many Unionists'.[29] The Dundalk Irish Volunteers also received a big influx of recruits, and with the three existing companies in Dundalk, eleven other companies were established in the rural hinterland of Dundalk.[30] By July 1918, it became clear that the introduction of conscription was, for the time being, on hold, and the enthusiasm of many recent recruits for the Volunteers evaporated. Despite that falling off, membership of the Volunteers in Louth increased from 289 in January 1918 to 870 by January 1919.[31]

In October 1918, following the death of James Toal, Seamus McGuill was appointed commanding officer of the Dundalk Volunteers and Head Centre of the IRB in Louth (see Table 3: Organisation of Co. Louth Irish Volunteers, 1918: Dundalk Battalion).[32] Irish Republican Army (IRA) companies tended to operate independently of each other and in an effort to improve co-ordination and increase efficiency, a county-wide brigade structure was introduced in 1920, which was shortly afterwards divided into a two-brigade structure: North Louth and South Louth. (See Table 4: Reorganisation of Co. Louth IRA Brigades, 1920).

The 1916 Rising is usually taken to be the tipping point that led to the terminal decline in support for the IPP. However, this was not the case in Co. Louth or in the region generally. Support for Redmond remained strong in Louth, and in February 1916, only weeks before the Easter Rising, a by-election in North Louth went in his favour. The vote divided along the traditional IPP/Healyite lines and P.J. Whitty won the seat for the IPP, with 2,299 votes against his opponent Bernard Hamill, who received 1,810 votes. This was a significant victory for the IPP and Redmond. After the Rising, Sinn Féin won four by-elections in a row, and the feeling was that the IPP was a spent force.[33]

However, in February 1918, after a bruising and sometimes violent campaign, for which the AOH and Sinn Féin drew in supporters from all over the country, the IPP held the seat in a by-election in South Armagh, soundly defeating the Sinn Féin candidate. The continued popularity of the IPP in the region was shown in the results of the general election of December 1918. In Louth, there was a straight contest between the IPP candidate, Richard Hazleton, and the Sinn Féin candidate, J.J. O'Kelly. The profile of the Irish electorate in 1918 had changed in two major ways from preceding elections: first, all males over the age of twenty-one could vote for the first time, and second, voting rights had been granted to women over the age of thirty for the first time.

On top of these factors, all Co. Louth was now a single constituency. The increase in the electorate, the change in constituency boundaries, and the strength of the continued antipathy between Redmondites and Healyites made the outcome in the constituency a difficult one to predict. In Drogheda on 25 November, Fr Michael O'Flanagan, acting president of Sinn Féin, addressed a gathering of 1,200 people, after which considerable uproar was caused when attempts were made to interrupt a Hazleton meeting. Two days later in Dundalk, two companies of Irish Volunteers carrying hurleys paraded and drilled close to the town hall in which Hazleton was holding a meeting. The police opinion was that the parades were a means of testing the waters to see how far they would be allowed to go.[34] On polling day, O'Kelly received a mere 255 votes more than Hazleton, out of a total poll of 21,285. The closeness of the vote reflected previous electoral contests in North Louth, and raises questions as to the role of localism rather than constitutional matters in the determination of how votes were cast in Louth in 1918.[35]

The immediate consequence of the December 1918 elections was the establishment of a separatist Sinn Féin-dominated parliament, Dáil Éireann, in Dublin. Comprising solely of the seventy-three successful Sinn

Féin candidates, it started setting up a parallel underground government designed to wrestle state control away from Dublin Castle. Perhaps the most significant and successful initiative that the Dáil government undertook was to receive the official recognition of most urban and county councils a full year before the Anglo-Irish Truce in July 1921 put a halt to the armed conflict. [36]

Town and borough elections were held in January 1920 that yet again confirmed the finely balanced nature of Co. Louth politics. There were twenty-one seats in the Dundalk Urban Council. Sinn Féin won six seats, the IPP won eight, the remainder going to two 'Nationalist and Labour' candidates, two to Labour, and three to independents. In the elections to Drogheda Corporation, Sinn Féin did well, winning twelve out of the twenty-four seats, while the IPP Nationalists only managed to take four seats. The Chamber of Commerce took four seats and various independents and labour interests took the rest. The urban local elections when taken together show that Sinn Féin had taken eighteen out of forty-five seats. By agreeing pacts with the independents, Sinn Féin gained control of local government in Dundalk and Drogheda, the two largest urban centres in the county.

The rural local elections held in June 1920 were a disaster for the IPP, which took only six seats, while Sinn Féin took seventeen, and others took five. [37] By June 1920, Sinn Féin could claim to be the political party with the greatest support base in Co. Louth, but the IPP or its adherents, with members of smaller parties and independents, remained a visible and substantial opposition. Local authorities in Co. Louth – Drogheda Corporation, Dundalk UDC, Ardee town commissioners and Louth County Council – all chose in turn to recognise the authority of Dáil Éireann, the underground government of the Republic of Ireland. Dundalk UDC was, however, ambivalent, and restored recognition of the Local Government Board (LGB) in January 1921 to secure a sizeable grant from the LGB to address the high level of unemployment in the town. On the other hand, Dundalk UDC refused to draw down LGB grants to finance the construction of new housing.[38]

It was alleged that during the War of Independence, the IRA in Co. Louth lacked aggressive spirit. Patrick Casey from Newry was in no doubt. In referring to an unsuccessful ambush in February 1921 at Plaster, to the north of Dundalk, he stated:

although this operation took place near Dundalk, few men from that town took part. I know of none. It is also true to say that, taking them by and large, the men of north Louth took little if any part in the fight for Independence. It was necessary to take men from all parts of Armagh and Down to do the work that should have been done by the Dundalk men.

Later after the Truce, he witnessed IRA Chief of Staff Richard Mulcahy

slating ... officers of the North Louth Brigade for their complete inactivity in the War of Independence. The officers of North Louth specially picked out for the lecture were [name redacted] and [name redacted]. I am sure that their faces were red to get such a castigation in front of all the officers from Armagh and South Down.[39]

James McGuill, one-time Officer Commanding, Dundalk Battalion IRA, recalled:

The military operations in County Louth were not as numerous as was the case in some of the Southern areas ... When headquarters recommended attacks on RIC Barracks we made plans to carry out our instructions but we were faced with a scarcity of rifles so we decided to attack three armed patrols of the RIC ... For one reason or another the disarming of those patrols were postponed on at least two occasions and on the third night ... we had the misfortune of losing one of our best men – Thomas Mulholland.[40]

In the south of the county, the situation was no better:

[In 1919,] the men in charge of the [Drogheda] Volunteers did not appear inclined to push the militant side of the Volunteers movement and ... the Volunteer organisation in our area dropped into a state of inertia which rapidly developed into a state of disorganisation in which men who really desired to take a militant part in the freedom effort could do very little in the matter. ... A state of apathy took possession on the rank and file in the organisation which soon became almost dead to all appearances.[41]

Unlike the rest of the country, where active or passive support from much of the population could be assured, during the War of Independence 1919–21, the IRA in Ulster operated in a hostile environment. Frank Aiken from Camlough, Co. Armagh had, by 1921, despite being only twenty-three years old, acquired for himself a reputation for aggression and ruthlessness, coupling large-scale operations such as attacks on RIC stations in Newtownhamilton and Camlough with smaller-scale attacks and assassinations. To improve its own efficiency, the IRA was reorganised into divisional groupings in March/April 1921. South Louth units were absorbed into the 1st Eastern Division, which also included South Meath and north Co. Dublin. North Louth IRA units, along with those from South Armagh and South Down and East Tyrone, were combined to make up the 4th Northern Division, led by Frank Aiken. The combined strength of the IRA in Co. Louth, comprising local elements of the 4th Northern and 1st Eastern Division at the time of the Truce in July 1921, was 632.

The IRA was not, despite this reorganisation, in good condition. The lack of armaments was a constant problem and Aiken himself recalled that at the time of the truce in July 1921 he had only thirty-three rifles for his entire Division.[42] In July 1922, at the outbreak of the Civil War, the IRA had 704 men on its rolls. One year later, at the end of the Civil War, the effects of organisational splits and the aggressive security policies of the Irish Government were evident on the IRA in Louth whose membership (combined with South Meath – separate figures not available) was reduced to 110 men with only 24 on active service and 320 in gaol (see Table 5: Reorganisation of Co. Louth IRA, 1921–2).

The Great War had not ended in November 1918. Officially it was suspended by an armistice, pending agreement on a series of peace treaties between all the warring parties. It was with trepidation that the British Government realised that, once the treaties were agreed and the war was officially over, it was obliged to reactivate the 1914 Home Rule Act that had been suspended for the duration of the war. A cabinet committee under Walter Long, a former leader of the Unionist Party, was established to find a solution. In October 1919, the Long committee proposed that there should be a new Government of Ireland Bill establishing two Irish parliaments for both southern and northern Ireland, accompanied by a Council of Ireland to encourage future Irish unity. The Government of Ireland Act received the royal assent on 23 December 1920, and came into effect on 3 May 1921.

General elections under a new proportional representation single transferable vote system (PRSTV) were due to be held for the two parliaments in Ireland. In fact, no polling took place for the Dublin parliament, as the number of candidates nominated equated with the number of seats to be filled. One hundred and twenty-four Sinn Féin candidates were deemed to be elected, and four Unionists from Dublin. County Louth was part of a five-seat Louth/Meath constituency. Three of those elected had their power base mainly in Co. Louth. J.J. O'Kelly (Ó Ceallaigh), was the outgoing Co. Louth representative, Peter Hughes was a Sinn Féin member of Dundalk UDC first elected as a Redmondite councillor in 1905. James Murphy from Drogheda was the Sinn Féin chairman of the Louth County Council. The Dáil decided that the May elections would be used to elect a new assembly and any deputy elected would be regarded as members of Dáil Éireann.[43] The Second Dáil finally assembled after the Truce, on 16 August 1921. The Dublin parliament envisaged by the Government of Ireland Act met once only, on 14 January 1922, to approve the formation of the Provisional Government under the Treaty.

The 1921 reorganisation triggered an increase in IRA activity in the county. On Sunday, 10 April 1921, a party of Ulster Special Constabulary who were attending religious services in Creggan, Co. Armagh, was ambushed by the IRA made up of units of Aiken's men, including some from Dundalk. One constable was killed and three others injured.[44] A group of RIC men cycling to mass was ambushed at Greenore on 10 May 1921, and nearby, on 13 May, an IRA volunteer, John Magee, was shot and killed. Castletown Mount House, which housed the archive of the Louth Archaeological Society, was burned on 17 June, and an attempt was made to burn nearby Castletown Castle on the same night.

Constable William Campbell was shot and killed in Dundalk also on 17 June and, in retaliation a few hours later, two brothers, Patrick and John Watters, were shot and killed in Quay Street, Dundalk. RIC Constable Alex McDonald disappeared without trace from Dundalk on 21 June, and three days later, in an operation planned and implemented by Aiken himself, a troop train returning from the official opening of the Belfast Parliament was derailed at Adavoyle on the Louth/Armagh border. Four men and eighty horses were killed.

Other significant attacks occurred when members of Drogheda IRA raided trains in pursuit of the Belfast Boycott on 9 May and 16 June, roads were blocked on 29 May, and two coastguard stations near Laytown were attacked and destroyed as was another at Clogherhead on 22 June.[45] On 29 June, the police station at Clogherhead was destroyed.[46]

During May and June 1921, the British government moved to a position where it was willing to engage in peace discussions with Sinn Féin, and on 24 June invitations were sent to de Valera and James Craig to negotiations in London.[47] A truce was agreed with Sinn Féin representatives on 9 July 1921 to come into force two days later, on 11 July 1921. Under the threat from Britain of an immediate resumption of war, on 6 December 1921, the Irish plenipotentiaries, duly accredited under the authority of the Irish government as appointed by the Dáil, signed a treaty establishing the Irish Free State as a self-governing dominion within the British Commonwealth. The Sinn Féin party split over the Anglo-Irish Treaty, the main issues of contention being the continued subordination of the new state to the British crown, as represented by the pledge of fidelity to the King, and by the office of the Governor General representing the crown.

The continuance of a separate state in six counties of north-east Ulster played little part in the debates, as it was confidently hoped that a Boundary Commission, established under the Treaty, would cede so much territory to the Irish Free State to leave Northern Ireland unsustainable. After a bitter and divisive debate, the Dáil voted on 7 January 1922 to ratify the Treaty by a small majority of sixty-four votes to fifty-seven.[48]

Of the three Co. Louth TDs, only Sean O'Ceallaigh made a significant contribution to the Treaty debates, and only O'Ceallaigh opposed the Treaty settlement in the Dáil vote. The principal reason for O'Ceallaigh's opposition to the Treaty was the oath of fidelity, 'this Oath … [intensifies] the accursed union against which we have never ceased to protest and which we shall never cease to detest and to loathe … I am opposed to this declaration of fidelity to an alien King because it is an outrage on the memory of our martyred comrades'.[49] Hughes and Murphy remained mostly silent during the debates, voted in support of the Treaty and in doing so, by accident or design, reflected the feeling of the majority of the electorate of Co. Louth.

Under the terms of the Anglo-Irish Treaty, the Provisional Government was required to hold a general election to a new Dáil that would debate and approve the constitution of the Irish Free State. Campaigning for a new general election began in March 1922. The electorate had the unfamiliar experience of seeing the once monolithic

Sinn Féin organisation split in all but name. Arthur Griffith at a meeting in Dundalk on 12 March 1922 stated:

> the great majority of the men who were for the Treaty were the men who bore the brunt of the fight. The bulk of the fighting men of Ireland were with them. They were not out to humbug the people, they were not out for a name or a label; they fought for reality ... not a name but a reality, and that was for Ireland and for the Irish people.[50]

At the same meeting, James Murphy TD (Teachta Dála - member of Dáil Éireann) from Drogheda, explained that he supported the Treaty because there was no rational alternative. He recognised that the Treaty was not a final settlement, but a weapon to be used in the achievement of freedom.[51] The anti-Treaty side had their turn on 2 April 1921, when a public meeting in Dundalk was addressed by Éamon de Valera, Cathal Brugha and Erskine Childers. De Valera was of course the main speaker and in his address, he attacked the 'stepping stone' to freedom argument put forward by the pro-Treaty faction:

> the man who tells you (that) you have achieved freedom to achieve freedom, when he knows you have not, is capable of telling you other things equally untrue ... If the nation had full liberty to choose its own course it would choose absolutely to be an isolated Republic. It was a queer doctrine when its two principal apostles differed. Mr Griffith told them they had got it and Mr Collins said they had not, but they had the freedom to achieve it ... They had not got either independence or the freedom to achieve it, and if they gave up their right to achieve it then they became a slave people.[52]

Polling took place on 16 June 1922 under PRSTV. There were six candidates for the five seats in the Louth/Meath constituency. Four of the candidates were pro-Treaty Sinn Féin – Edmund Duggan, Peter Hughes, Justin McKenna, and James Murphy. One was anti-Treaty Sinn Féin, Sean (J.J.) O'Kelly. Cathal O'Shannon, who stood as a Labour candidate, supported the Treaty (See Table 6: Dáil Éireann election, June 1922, first preference votes in Louth–Meath). O'Shannon, Duggan, O'Kelly, Hughes and Murphy were all elected (one Labour, three pro-Treaty Sinn Féin, one anti-Treaty Sinn Féin). In the constituency of Louth/Meath, out of

36,501 valid votes cast, 30,768 or 84.2 per cent of first preference votes were in favour of candidates that supported the Treaty. The surprising result of this election was that Cathal O'Shannon, who had practically no local profile, topped the poll with twice the quota. O'Shannon himself speculated that while he got most of his votes from labour interests, a sizeable vote went his way in protest against the panel system agreed between pro-Treaty and anti-Treaty Sinn Féin.[53]

The results showed overwhelming support for the Treaty, and that esoteric arguments about the meaning of the oath of fidelity, or even partition when it was infrequently raised, counted for very little amongst the general electorate. Despite the apparent presence of a protest vote that worked to his favour, O'Shannon's campaign for improvements in housing, land distribution, jobs and schooling attracted greater support than the constitutional niceties that beset the pro- and anti-Treaty factions of Sinn Féin. The election of June 1922, and the course of the subsequent brief civil war, indicated the acceptance of the Treaty in its essentials by the majority of the electorate.[54]

Once the Dáil voted for the acceptance of the Treaty, the Provisional Government moved to oversee the transition to independence. That government set about formalising the organisation of the IRA into a uniformed disciplined force, and in January 1922, recruiting began for a new National Army. The IRA still existed as an organisation, however, under the control of a general headquarters (GHQ), with chief of staff, Eoin O'Duffy, and the minister for defence, Richard Mulcahy, answerable to the Dáil. The IRA effectively split in March 1922, with a breakaway group setting up its own headquarters in Dublin, eventually taking over the Four Courts. Some units of the IRA in Louth went with the breakaway executive – the garrison in Millmount, Drogheda, and the 1st Brigade 4th Northern, the latter comprising mostly of North Louth men. The majority of the 4th Northern, including Aiken himself, comprising units drawn from Northern Ireland, continued to take their orders from the Provisional Government and the GHQ until after the outbreak of the Civil War.

Millmount was attacked and taken by the National Army on 4 July 1922. Aiken's avowed aim was to remain neutral in the conflict and was preparing to abandon his outposts and dump arms when on 15 July 1922, Dundalk army barracks, which housed Aiken and most of his men, was attacked and captured by the 5th Northern Division from Co. Monaghan under the command of General Dan Hogan.[55] Not all of Aiken's men went into captivity, in fact a substantial portion joined the National Army. John McCoy, Adjutant of the 4th Northern, was in Dublin at the time of Hogan's attack and recalled having to go into hiding when he returned to Dundalk as the town was being patrolled by men who had changed sides. On 17 July, Sergeant George Laverty, one of those who changed sides, was shot and killed in a pub in Church Street, Dundalk, and in the aftermath, former 4th Northern Division men, now in the National Army, and armed, carried out an aggressive search for the perpetrators.

As a further indication of the number of men who decamped to the National Army, contemporaneous reports note the difficulties in dealing with a group of 124 men formerly of the 4th Northern Division who were shipped off to the Curragh for induction and training.[56]

Aiken extracted revenge on Hogan on 17 August 1922 when he retook Dundalk by force, and held it for three days while he and his men systematically removed vast amounts of military stores. Yet it was another two months before Aiken was to subscribe officially to the anti-Treaty side, and when he did, the operational area of the 4th Northern Division was extended to include South Louth, Co. Cavan, Monaghan South, Mid-Armagh and South Down. Despite the resources available to him, there were no further significant offensive operations carried out by Aiken, for which he was severely criticised in an internal IRA report, which Aiken dismissed with barely concealed contempt.[57] Aiken carried out an inspection of the area and his report of January 1923 noted that the IRA in Co. Louth now consisted of the Dundalk Battalion, which had a membership of sixty men (including ten Fianna boys), and Drogheda, part of the Boyne Brigade (North Meath and South Louth), had twenty-four men.[58]

A further report in March 1923 recorded no significant difference, but added the detail that the Boyne Brigade had forty rifles and one machine-gun while the Dundalk Battalion had fifty rifles and three machine-guns. At this stage, according to the IRA's own intelligence, the National Army had in total 1,350 men stationed at Dundalk, Omeath, Greenore, Mountpleasant, Kellystown, Dromin, Dunleer, Ardee and Drogheda.[59] The strength of the IRA in Louth by the end of the Civil War shows how unequal the contest had become (see Table 7: Strength of Co. Louth IRA, July 1923). The IRA could barely muster eighty men, while 320 of their numbers were incarcerated, and would remain so until the government decided otherwise.[60] With the death of Liam Lynch on 10 April 1923, Frank Aiken, the last and most reluctant IRA divisional commander to commit to the anti-Treaty side, was appointed Chief of Staff of the IRA. On 27 April, he issued instructions to suspend all offensive operations. One month later, following unsuccessful attempts by de Valera to negotiate, through intermediaries, a peace deal with the Irish Government, Aiken issued a dump arms order on 27 May 1923, ending the Civil War.

A general election was called for August 1923. As historian John Regan put it, for the first time, the pro-Treaty position would be put before the electorate in material and legislative terms and 'it offered a little something to everyone who broadly accepted the Treaty'.[61] The outgoing government promised to complete the transfer of land, emphasised the importance of agriculture, housing for workers and reform of education, justice and the Poor Law. Five candidates were nominated for the three seats in Co. Louth in 1923. These were, for Cumann na nGaedheal, the outgoing TDs, Peter Hughes and James Murphy; for Labour, outgoing TD, Cathal O'Shannon; for Sinn Féin, Frank Aiken; and for the Farmers' Party, Patrick McGee. It was anticipated that O'Shannon was in danger as he had drawn a great part of his support from Co. Meath in the previous election which was now lost to him.[62] The *Democrat* noted in relation to Aiken's candidature that 'Mr F. Aiken is the strongest man the Republican party could put up – though naturally the association of his name with certain despicable events of last year will tell against him amongst those who do not belong to his party'.[63]

Aiken was Chief of Staff of the IRA and was to remain so until the end of 1925. As he was liable to be arrested on sight, he made no public appearances during the election campaign. The election itself went off quietly, with no untoward incidents reported. The lack of excitement in the elections in Louth reflected the national trend, where the percentage poll was around 60 per cent. (See Table 8: Dáil Éireann election, August 1923, first preference votes in Co. Louth). The collapse of O'Shannon's vote had been anticipated. As had been noted in the previous year's election, O'Shannon had drawn some of his support from both factions of Sinn Féin. Coupled with the loss of Co. Meath support, and the polarising effect of the recently ended Civil War, the loss of his seat was probably inevitable.

There was no surprise that Aiken took a seat. However, it was not anticipated that he would top the poll. It was reasoned that he obtained few votes in the south of the county, and that a solid part of his support came from the Cooley Peninsula, where farmers had been badly hit by lack of access to British markets for their produce.[64] Although Aiken received the highest number of first preference votes, the electorate continued to support pro-Treaty parties by a proportion of almost three to one, as they had in the election that immediately preceded the outbreak of the Civil War. After the August 1923 elections, out of 153 Dáil seats, Cumann na nGaedheal held sixty-three seats while the abstentionist Sinn Féin held forty-four seats. The largest party in opposition in the Dáil was the Farmers' Party that held fifteen seats, while the Labour Party and Independents held fourteen seats each. The combined opposition in the Dáil could only muster forty-three seats between them, which gave the Cumann na nGaedheal government a comfortable working majority of twenty in any Dáil vote.

Despite its success, the August 1923 elections were the high-water mark of support for Sinn Féin. Results from nine by-elections held in March 1925 have been held up as an indicator of the party's decline as they only managed to take two seats, while the government party took seven.[65] Any hopes of an electoral breakthrough were shattered when, in local elections, Sinn Féin received only 11 per cent of first-preference votes.[66] From this relative failure in 1925 in local and by-elections, many in Sinn Féin saw that the republican cause could not be advanced by abstentionism. Others in Sinn Féin disagreed, and, following the inevitable split, Fianna Fáil, the Republican Party, was founded in May 1926. The declared intention of Fianna Fáil was to enter the Dáil, after the general election of June 1927, without taking the oath of fidelity to the British monarch. They failed in this endeavour. Following the assassination of Kevin O'Higgins in August 1927, legislative changes required all election candidates to swear to take the oath if elected. Fianna Fáil deputies, including Frank Aiken, bowed to the inevitable, took the oath and took their seats, and thus the democratic foundations of the state were finally stabilised. The growth of Fianna Fáil coincided with the end of Peter Hughes' political career. Appointed Minister for Defence in the aftermath of the Army Mutiny of 1924, Hughes lost his seat in June 1927, ironically not to a Fianna Fáil candidate, but to James Coburn, running for a briefly resurgent Redmondite party, the Irish National League.

To follow the trajectory of success or failure in the uncertain years from 1912, it is useful to look at the careers of Patrick and Peter Hughes,

Sean MacEntee and Frank Aiken. Patrick Hughes was, in the words of one contemporary witness, 'looked upon as the leader in Dundalk in everything that tended towards the complete independence of this country from outside influence'.[67] Through his energy, and frequently his pocket, he built up a cadre of volunteers who mobilised and tried their best to carry out the impractical orders given to them for the 1916 Rising. On the run until the Dáil voted to accept the Treaty in January 1922, his health was broken by the strain of living for five years in safe houses. He was distressed by the outbreak of the Civil War and took no part in it. Elected as a non-party member of the Dundalk UDC in 1925, on the foundation of Fianna Fáil he became one of its local leading lights, closely identified with Frank Aiken.

Patrick Hughes was elected Chairman of Dundalk UDC in 1932, and when, in the following year, Frank Aiken as Minister for Defence established the Volunteer Force as an alternative military force to the National Army or the IRA, where young men with Republican ideals could have military training, he was appointed to one of the local recruiting committees. He was not financially secure, due in part to his personal generosity, and, although he supported others in their applications for pensions under the Military Services Act, it was not until November 1935 that he applied for a pension for himself. He died from a heart attack on 2 February 1936 leaving a wife and three children, and it took two years for a decision to be made that Patrick Hughes was entitled to a reduced pension. Two years after that, in 1940, £108 arrears of the pension dating back to 1934 were paid in full to his widow.

Peter Hughes, his brother, was a stalwart of the IPP on Dundalk UDC. He broke with the party in early 1916 because he was refused the nomination as by-election candidate.

After the 1916 Rising, Peter Hughes's sympathy for the prisoners provided him with a platform to relaunch himself as an advocate for the separatist cause. He remained in the inner circles of Sinn Féin and later Cumann na nGaedheal. Although he supported the Treaty, he was sufficiently respected by both sides that Frank Aiken used him as a go-between with the government at the outbreak of the Civil War. Despite this, in January 1922, the IRA made three attempts to kidnap or assassinate Peter Hughes.[68] In February 1923, an effort was made to burn his house and business in Park Street, Dundalk. He became Minister for Defence in the aftermath of the Army Mutiny of 1924, but lost his Dáil seat to a resurgent Redmondite candidate in the June 1927 election, which effectively ended his political career. He was chairman of the Army Pensions Board for a time, and chaired a committee that made recommendations in 1932 to the Hospitals Trust on the disbursement of sweepstake funds. He unsuccessfully tried again for the Dáil in the 1932 general election and thereafter quit politics and ran a successful dairy business for many years. When he died, in 1954, his funeral was attended by people representing all shades of political opinion, including W.T. Cosgrave, former President of the Executive Council from 1922 to 1932, and Frank Aiken.

Sean MacEntee's activities with the Louth Volunteers and in the GPO in Dublin in 1916 established a sound foundation for his future political career.[69] He had little to do with Co. Louth thereafter, and eventually returned to his native Belfast in 1919 where he became Vice-Brigadier of the Belfast Brigade of the IRA, a position which earned him few plaudits because of his 'pacifist' views.[70] He took the anti-Treaty side in the fighting in Dublin at the outbreak of the Civil War, and was later arrested and interned. A founder member of Fianna Fáil, he was a highly influential member of the front bench, and held a number of Ministerial posts, including Minister for Finance, where he is chiefly remembered for his deeply conservative economic policies.

Frank Aiken's emergence as an aggressive guerrilla leader also brought him into the inner circles of the revolutionary movement. Like MacEntee, he was founder member of Fianna Fail, and dominated Co. Louth politics for fifty years, although he lived in Dublin, until his retirement in 1973. He held a number of senior front bench positions, including Minister for Defence and Minister for External Affairs, making significant contributions to national and international politics. It is ironic that Aiken and MacEntee, who were not native to Co. Louth, would derive a long-term benefit from their association with the county during the revolutionary period, while the Hughes brothers, who devoted many years to the nationalist and separatist cause, would eventually view national politics from the sidelines.

The trajectory of the most mythologised organisation of the period, the Irish Volunteers/IRA, was even more variable. In mid-1914, the strength of the Irish Volunteers in Louth was just under 5,000, most of whom fell away at the outbreak of the Great War. Thanks to stalwart effort by all involved, a small band participated in the 1916 Rising, one of the few outside of Dublin that managed to carry out the duties assigned to it. The energy of the formative years dissipated, and when the War of Independence had run its course in 1921, the Louth IRA was accused of lacking aggressive spirit. Conflict visited Louth during the Civil War where the opposing sides, the National Army and the IRA, both claimed the mantle of the Volunteers who fought in 1916 and 1919–21.

While the National Army was victorious and the IRA soundly defeated, the tragedy was that the killings, executions, assassinations and destruction inflicted on the population of Co. Louth were essentially an aside that made no impact whatsoever on the overall course or result of the Civil War. Frank Aiken, operating from the borderlands of Louth and Armagh, was a late and reluctant participant in the Civil War, and a severe critic of republican military strategy. He was initially reluctant to hand over command of what remained of the 4th Northern Division to take on a more senior role on the anti-Treaty side. After an unforeseeable sequence of events, Aiken, the eternal outsider, accepted the position of Chief of Staff of the IRA. Within weeks and as a result of astute political manoeuvring on his part, he ordered the ceasefire that ended the bitter conflict he had striven to avoid. For the twenty-four men of the 4th Northern Division still on active service, and for their 320 interned comrades, it was time to recognise that they had been militarily defeated.[71]

Table 1. Organisation of Co. Louth Irish Volunteers,
August 1914

Dundalk

No. 1 Company. President: M. Comerford; Secretaries: J. Ward, O. Hanratty; Treasurers: P. Toner, Patrick Hughes; Committee: M. Carr, E. Donnelly, W. Russell

No. 2 Company. President: M. Comerford; Secretaries: J. Ward, P. O'Dubhthaigh; Treasurers: P. Toner, M. Comerford; Committee: Patrick J Roe, J. J. Martin, O. Grant

No. 3 Company. President: M. Comerford; Secretaries: J. Ward, P. O'Dubhthaigh; Treasurers: M. Comerford: James Hughes; Committee: B. J. Roe, James Hughes, J. McEntee.

No. 4 Company. President: Patrick Hughes; Secretaries: J. Ward, J. McGuinness (Park Street); Treasurers: M. Comerford, P. Toner; Committee: A. Kerley, P. Darcy, M. Hartigan.

Table 1. *Continued.*

No. 5 Company. President: M. Comerford: Secretaries: J. Ward, P. O'Dubhthaigh; Treasurers: Patrick O'Connell, M. Comerford; Committee: Patrick O'Connell, Peter J. Roe, Thomas Duffy

No. 6 Company: President: M. Comerford; Secretaries: H. Smyth, James Hughes; Treasurers: P. Toner, D. O'Connell; Committee: Leo Ward, John Ballintine, W. Keating.

No. 7 Company. President: M. Comerford; Secretaries: J. Ward, J. Hughes; Treasurers: D. O'Connell, P. Toner; Committee: B. Watters, T. Hughes, T. Keogh

No. 8 Company. President: Patrick Hughes; Secretaries: J. Ward, Patrick Hughes; Treasurers: P. O'Dubhthaigh, M. Comerford; Committee: P. Walsh, Felix McQuillan, John McGuill.

Companies were formed in Drogheda as follows:

A Company: Chord Road, North Strand, Greenhills, Newfoundwell, Scarlet Street, Hand Street, Nun's Walk, Laurence Street.

B Company: St Mary's and outlying districts.

C Company: Freeschool Lane, William Street, Magdalene Street, Sunday's Gate, North Road, Windmill Lane.

D Company: West Street, Shop Street, Stockwell Lane, Trinity Street and Mell.

Reports exist of branches being established in:

Kilsaran (17 May). Addressed by Mr Magee and Mr McMahon.

Lordship (17 May).

Jenkinstown (24 May). Presided by Dr Blake, Present James Connolly JP, J.H. Macardle JP CC; James O'Hanlon, Patrick Rice JP Dundalk; James Hughes, President AOH Dundalk; P. Toner, President AOH Dundalk Division; P. O'Connell CC, JJ Martin. Addressed by P.H. Pearse, BA, BL, Central Executive.

Blackrock (24 May). T.J. Byrne JP CC presided, other speakers, Thomas Soraghan RDC, P.J. Murphy RDC, James H. Murphy Solicitor; C.S. Whitworth; J. Synott; James Hughes.

Reaghstown (24 May) Presided over by Peter Hoey, addressed by Mr Faulkner and Mr Neary.

Dunleer (31 May) Presided over by James McGrane JP, Joseph Nolan MP, Dr W.J. Bradley and Thomas Faulkner.

Kilkerley (31 May).

Stabannon (early June).

Also, a Ladies Nursing Ambulance Corps was established in Stabannon on 7 June, with twenty members enrolled, The committee consisted of Miss M. Byrne, Charleville, M.A. Landy, M. Byrne, Drumgoolstown, M.T. Clarke, M. Culligan and R. Matthews.

Louth (7 June), presided over by Mr J.F. Murphy.

Knockbridge (14 June).

Table 1. *Continued.*

Carlingford (14 June).

Omeath (14 June).

Cooley (14 June).

Tallanstown (14 June).

Dromin and Philipstown (14 June).

Committee, J. Magee, DC President, P. Tenanty VP, T. Brennan DC; J. Bellew; J.P. O'Callaghan Hon Sec; P. Philips, Thos Carroll, J.J. Meehan. Philipstown, J. Dogette, D. Flanagan' L.J. Jordan.

Darver (29 June).

On 9 June, a county executive of the Irish Volunteers was established with the aim of perfecting the organisation in the county. The Volunteers were reorganised into battalions as follows:

Castlebellingham, Darver, with Dromiskin; Dunleer, Grangebellew, Togher, with Annagassan; Louth, Knockbridge, Kilkerley, with Castlering; Dundalk, Blackrock, with Kilcurry; Stabannon, Dromin, with Ardee; Reaghstown, Tallanstown, with Killanny; Omeath with Carlingford, half battalion; Drogheda; Tullyallen, Collon, with Monasterboice; Termonfeckin with Clogherhead.

Table 2. Arrests and detentions, 1916

The men listed below were arrested in the days immediately following the surrender in Dublin on 29 April 1916. They were held locally, in Dundalk Gaol and in Millmount Barracks, Drogheda, before being moved to Richmond Barracks, Dublin. Some were released after a few days while the majority were moved to prisons in Britain. Where a prison in indicated, the column headed 'Interned on' is the date on which they were received into the British prisons.

Surname	First name	From	Prison	Interned on	Released by	Notes
Atkinson	William	Dundalk	Wakefield	13 May 1916	20 July 1916	
Barrett	John	Dundalk	Stafford	8 May 1916	23 Dec 1916	
Bateson	Frank	Drogheda			12 May 1916	
Berrill	P.J.	Dundalk	Knutsford	2 June 1916	23 Dec 1916	
Burke	Thomas	Drogheda	Wandsworth	9 May 1916	20 July 1916	
Butterly	John	Dunleer	Wakefield	2 June 1916		
Butterly	James	Dunleer		5 May 1916		
Carr	Joseph	Drogheda	Wandsworth	9 May 1916	22 May 1916	

Table 2. *Continued.*

Casey	Patrick	Dundalk	Stafford	8 May 1916	23 Dec 1916	
Clifford	Peter	Dundalk	Glasgow	20 May 1916	2 Aug. 1916	
Conroy	James Sr	Dundalk			12 May 1916	
Conroy	James Jr	Dundalk			12 May 1916	
Donnelly	Patrick	Carlingford	Wandsworth	2 June 1916	23 Dec 1916	
Farrelly	James	Ardee	Wandsworth	9 May 1916		
Ferguson	Michael	Cooley	Wandsworth	2 June 1916	23 Dec 1916	
Finnegan	John	Dundalk	Wakefield	13 May 1916	20 July 1916	
Finnegan	Joseph	Drogheda	Wandsworth	9 May 1916		
Gavin	Thomas	Drogheda			12 May 1916	
Greene	Arthur	Dundalk			12 May 1916	
Hall	Samuel	Dundalk	Wakefield	13 May 1916	20 July 1916	
Halpenny / Halpin	Peter	Dundalk	Stafford	8 May 1916	23 Dec 1916	
Halpin	Thomas	Drogheda	Wandsworth	9 May 1916		
Hamill	Thomas	Dundalk	Wakefield	13 May 1916	20 July 1916	
Hanratty	James	Dundalk	Wakefield	13 May 1916	23 Dec 1916	
Harkin	Michael	Drogheda			29 May 1916	
Hastings	John	Drogheda	Wandsworth	9 May 1916		
Hearty	Thomas	Dundalk	Knutsford	16 June 1916	20 July 1916	
Jennings	James	Dundalk	Lewes	20 May 1916	2 Aug 1916	
Keenan	Michael	Drogheda	Wandsworth	9 May 1916		
Kelly	Thomas	Dunleer	Wakefield	2 June 1916		
Kelly	James	Dunleer	Wakefield	2 June 1916		
Kerr	Patrick	Dundalk	Wakefield	13 May 1916	2 Aug 1916	
Lalor / Lawlor	Fintan	Drogheda			12 May 1916	
Layng	Joseph	Dunleer	Wakefield	2 June 1916	23 Dec 1916	
Leahy	Denis	Dundalk	Lewes	May 1916	17 June 1917	Court Martial, 10 yrs
Martin	Frank	Dundalk	Lewes	April 1916	17 June 1917	Court Martial, 10 yrs
Matthews	Thomas	Ardee	Wandsworth	9 May 1916	July 1916	
McCrave	Thomas	Dundalk	Knutsford	16 June 1916	23 Dec 1916	

Table 2. *Continued.*

MacEntee	Sean	Dundalk	Lewes	April 1916	17 June 1917	Court Martial, Life
McGeough	Owen	Dundalk	Wakefield	13 May 1916	20 July 1916	
McGrane	Thomas	Dundalk	Wandsworth	9 May 1916		
McGuill	Joseph	Dundalk	Wakefield	13 May 1916	23 Dec 1916	
McMahon	Philip J.	Ardee		15 May 1916		Court Martial, 5 yrs
McQuillan	Philip	Dundalk	Wakefield	13 May 1916	2 Aug 1916	
McQuillan	William	Drogheda	Richmond	3 May 1916	8 May 1916	
McTaggart	Thomas	Dundalk	Wandsworth	9 May 1916	29 May 1916	
Monaghan	J.P.	Drogheda		May 1916		
Munster	Thomas	Drogheda	Wakefield	6 May 1916	22 May 1916	
Murphy	Peadar	Dundalk	Stafford	1 May 1916	23 Dec 1916	
Necy	Frank	Dundalk	Knutsford	2 June 1916	23 Dec 1916	
O'Byrne	Thomas	Dundalk	Lewes	20 May 1916	2 Aug 1916	
O'Hanlon	J.	Cooley	Richmond	30 May 1916	23 Dec 1916	
O'Kiely	John	Drogheda			12 May 1916	
O'Neill	Arthur	Dundalk	Wakefield	13 May 1916	23 Dec 1916	
O'Neill	Felix	Dundalk	Knutsford	2 June 1916	20 July 1916	
Quinn	John	Dundalk				Court Martial, 3 yrs
Reynolds	Michael	Dundalk		15 May 1916		Court Martial, 5 yrs
Rynne / Wrenne	William	Ardee			2 June 1916	
Sally	James	Dundalk	Lewes	April 1916	June 1917	Court Martial, 5 yrs
Sharkey	J.	Dundalk	Stafford	8 May 1916	23 Dec 1916	
Tuite	Daniel	Dundalk	Wakefield	13 May 1916	2 Aug 1916	
Waller	Joseph	Dundalk	Stafford	8 May 1916	23 Dec 1916	
Walsh	Laurence J.	Drogheda	Wakefield	13 May 1916	2 June 1916	

Source: *1916 Rebellion Handbook* (Dublin, 1917; republished 1998) and *Dundalk Examiner* May–December 1916.

Table 3. Organisation of Co. Louth Irish Volunteers, 1918:
Dundalk Battalion

Unit	Commanding Officer
Dundalk 'A' Company	Joseph McGuill
Dundalk 'B' Company	M. O'Callaghan
Dundalk 'C' Company	Philip McQuillan
Ravensdale	Thomas Callan
Cooley	Michael Ferguson
Omeath	Patrick Oakes
Bridge-A-Crinn	Matthew Lynch
Sheelagh	Thomas Luckey
Blackrock	Joseph Cotter
Knockbridge	Joseph McKenna
Killanny	Frank Byrne
Inniskeen	Owen Meegan
Louth	P. Murtagh

Source: MA, BMH, WS353, 'Seamus McGuill', p. 38.

Table 4. Reorganisation of Co. Louth IRA Brigades, 1920

In mid-1920, there was a county-wide reorganisation with the IRA organised into North Louth and South Louth Brigades.

County Staff appointed were:

Commandant: Philip Monahan (Drogheda).

Vice Commandant: Laurence Walsh (Drogheda).

Adjutant: James McGuill (Dundalk).

Quartermaster: James E Murphy (Drogheda).

North Louth Staff were:

Officer Commanding: James McGuill.

Adjutant: Sean Gormley.

Quartermaster: Thomas Callan.

Table 5. Reorganisation of Co. Louth IRA, July 1921–2

In March 1921, a further reorganisation took place. North Louth, from Castlebellingham northwards, became part of the newly formed 4th Northern Division, areas south of that line became part of the 1st Eastern Division. There were three Brigades of the 4st Northern Division.

No. 1 Brigade, 1st Battalion: Louth from Castlebellingham to Dundalk.

No. 1 Brigade, 2nd Battalion: Louth from Dundalk northwards.

No. 1 Brigade, 3rd and 4th Battalions: South Armagh area.

No. 2 Brigade, 4th Northern Division: Co. Down area.

No. 3 Brigade, 4th Northern Division: Central and North Armagh area.

The following are the units of the 4th Northern Division in Co. Louth at the time of the Truce (11 July 1921) and the outbreak of the Civil War (June 1922).

4th Northern Division GHQ staff

	March 1921	July 1921	April 1922	July 1922
Officer Commanding	Frank Aiken	Frank Aiken	Frank Aiken	Frank Aiken
Adjutant	John McCoy	Seamus Monaghan	John McCoy	John McCoy
Quartermaster	Sean Quinn	Sean Quinn	Thomas Rogers	Padraig Quinn
Engineering		Seamus McGauran	Seamus Goodfellow	Ivor Monaghan
Training		Thomas McPolin	Thomas McPolin	Andy O'Hare
Chemist			Sean McGauran	Ned Fitzpatrick
Transport			Peter Boyle	Peter Boyle
Signals				Jerry Tipping
Intelligence Officer				Michael O'Hanlon
Medical Services				Dr. James McKee

Source: MA, MA-MSPC-RO-423, 4th Northern Division GHQ, Frank Aiken memo, 26 Jul. 1937.

North Louth Battalion Headquarters, July 1921

GHQ Organiser	Patrick McKenna
Officer Commanding	Sean Gormley
Vice Officer Commanding	Felix Dawe
Adjutant	Seamus Kennedy
Quartermaster	Thomas Conlon
Intelligence Officer	Eugene Sweeney
Engineering	Denis Barret

Source: MA, MA-MSPC-RO-425, 'Dundalk Area, North Louth Battn., 4th Nor. Div. IRA'.

Table 5. *Continued.*

1st Brigade 4th Northern Division (North Louth)

Unit	O/C 11 July 1921	No of men	O/C 1 July 1922	No. of men
1 Brigade	Not formed		Patrick McKenna	
1st North Louth Battalion	Sean Gormley		Seamus Kennedy	
Dundalk 'A' Company	Thomas McCrave	131	Joseph Larrissey	122
Dundalk 'B' Company	Not formed		Sean Lynch	43
Blackrock/Haggardstown	Michael White	24	Michael White	16
C'Bellingham/Dromiskin		20	Martin O'Donnell	21
Louth/Knockbridge	Frank Conlon	33		
Knockbridge			Joseph McKenna	24
Louth			Frank Conlon	20
2nd North Louth Battalion			Felix Dawe	
Dundalk 'C' Company	Owen Clifford	97	Sean Toal	103
Omeath	Patrick Oakes	13		
Cooley	James Boyle	78	Peter Thornton	70
Lordship			Harry Johnston	62
Ravensdale	Thomas Brannigan	16	Patrick McDermott	25
Kilcurry			Edward Bailey	71
Dromintee (Co. Armagh)	Peter McAteer	65	Peter McAteer	97
Ballsmill (Co. Armagh)	Frank Donnelly	8		
Crossmaglen (Co. Armagh)			James Quigley	67

Source: MA, 4th Northern Division, North Louth Battalion, 11 July 1921, MA/MSPC/RO/424; 4th Northern Division, 1st Brigade GHQ, MA/MSPC/RO/425; 4th Northern Division, 1st Brigade, 1st Battalion, 1 July 1922, MA/MSPC/RO/426; 4th Northern Division, 1st Brigade, 2nd Battalion (Dundalk), 1 July 1922, MA/MSPC/RO/427.

Table 5. *Continued.*

9th Brigade 1st Eastern Division (South Louth)

Unit	O/C 11 July 1921	No of men	O/C 7 July 1922	No. of men
1st Eastern Division				
9th Brigade	Eugene Kavanagh	145	Joseph O'Higgins	78
1st Battalion (Drogheda)	Patrick Murray		Thomas Clarke	
'A' Company	Benny Higgins	34	Robert McCabe	30
'B' Company	Patrick Matthews	31	George Owens	26
'C' Company	Thomas Morgan	14	Thomas Morgan	8
'D' Company	John Brady	23	John Brady	3
'E' Company	John McEvoy	14	Non-existent	0
'F' Company	William Tuite	11	Joe Carolan	5
'G' Company (Slane)	Vincent Gerrard	9	J Marry	6
'H' Company (Slane)	J Ledwidge	9	Non-existent	
2nd Battalion (Dunleer)	Michael Alwill		Michael Alwill	
'A' Company	James Brennan	22	James Brennan	13
'B' Company	Michael Butterly	26	Michael Butterly	17
'C' Company	Peter Mooney	17	Non-existent	0
3rd Battalion (Ardee)	Owen Doherty			
Ardee Company	Peter Kealy	14	Richard Murphy	9
Smarmore (incl Collon)	John Halligan	14	Included with Ardee	
Churchtown	With 3rd Meath Brigade		Frank Rafferty	16
Barley Hill (Meath)	With 3rd Meath Brigade		John Byrne	18
Meath Hill (Meath)	With 3rd Meath Brigade		Eugene Foster Roskey	11
Drumcondrath (Meath)			Francis Watters	15

Source: MA, 1st Eastern Division, 9th Brigade (South Louth) GHQ, MA/MSPC/RO/525; 1st Eastern Division, 9th Brigade (South Louth), 1st Battalion (Drogheda), MA/MSPC/RO//526; 1st Eastern Division, 9th Brigade (South Louth), 2nd Battalion (Dunleer), MA/MSPC/RO/527; 1st Eastern Division, 9th Brigade (South Louth) 3rd Battalion (Ardee), MA/MSPC/RO//528.

Table 5. *Continued.*

Estimated Total Strength of Louth IRA, July 1921/July 1922

Unit	11 July 1921	1 July 1922
1st North Louth Battalion	208	246
2nd North Louth Battalion	204	331
North Louth Subtotal	412	577
1st Battalion (Drogheda)	127	72
2nd Battalion (Dunleer)	65	30
3rd Battalion Ardee	28	25
South Louth Subtotal	220	127
Total Louth Subtotal	632	704
Including Armagh and Meath Units	91	214
Totals	723	918

Source: Derived from the two preceding tables.

Table 6. Dáil Éireann election, June 1922, first preference
votes in Louth–Meath

Number of Seats	5
Candidates	6
Electorate	63,000
Valid votes	36,501
Quota	6,084
Cathal O'Shannon (Labour)	13,994
Edmund Duggan (Pro Treaty Sinn Féin)	6,990
J.J. O'Kelly (anti-Treaty Sinn Féin)	5,733
Peter Hughes (pro-Treaty Sinn Féin)	4,282
Justin McKenna (pro-Treaty Sinn Féin)	2,135
James Murphy (pro-Treaty Sinn Féin)	3,367

Source: Brian M Walker (ed.), *Parliamentary election results in Ireland, 1918–92* (Dublin, 1992), p. 106; *DD*, 24 June 1922. Walker does not record the figure for the total valid poll, which has been extracted from local newspaper reports.

Table 7. Strength of Co. Louth IRA, July 1923

	1st Brigade (North Louth)	6th Brigade (South Louth and North Meath)	Totals
On Roll	50	60	110
On Service	12	12	24
In Gaol	200	120	320
Rifles etc.	23	18	41
Small Arms	13	13	26
Thompson Sub-machine Guns	1	1	2
Ammunition	8,244	5,740	13,984
Grenades	190 (174 home-made)	40 (36 home-made)	230 (214 home-made)
Explosives	312.5 lb	112 lb	424.5 lb

Source: UCDA, Twomey Papers, P69/35(207-209), D/O to C/S, 21 July 1923.

Table 8. Dáil Éireann election, August 1923, first preference votes in Co. Louth

Number of Seats	3
Candidates	5
Electorate	39,120
No. of votes cast	25,476
Percentage poll	65%
Spoiled votes	970
Valid votes	24,506
Quota	6,127
Frank Aiken (Sinn Féin)	6,651 (E)
Peter Hughes (Cumann na nGaedheal)	5,798 (E)
James Murphy (Cumann na nGaedheal)	5,663 (E)
Patrick McGee (Farmers' Party)	3,877
Cathal O'Shannon (Labour)	2,517

Source: Brian M Walker (ed.), *Parliamentary election results in Ireland, 1918–92* (Dublin, 1992), p. 113; *DD*, 1 Sept. 1923. Walker states that the electorate was 38,548, while the *Dundalk Democrat* states that the electorate was 39,120.

Notes

1 Brian M. Walker, *Parliamentary election results in Ireland, 1801–1922* (Dublin: Royal Irish Academy, 1992), p. 148. See Donal Hall, 'Violence and political factionalism and their effects in North Louth 1874–1943' (PhD thesis, 2010, NUI Maynooth) for a fuller discussion.
2 The National Archives, London (TNA), Colonial Office (CO) 904 Chief Inspector's Confidential Monthly Report (CICMR), Co. Louth, May 1916.
3 TNA, CO 904, CICMR, Feb. 1916.
4 Ibid.
5 *Dundalk Democrat*, 7 Feb.1914.
6 *Dundalk Democrat*, 28 Feb. 1914.
7 TNA, CO 904, CICMR, Co. Louth, Apr. and May 1914.
8 https://earlyirishcinema.wordpress.com/category/films/topicals/castlebellingham-feis-and-louth-volunteers-1914/.
9 *Dundalk Democrat*, 4 Jul. 1914.
10 *Dundalk Democrat*, 1 Aug. 1914.
11 Ibid.
12 *Dundalk Examiner*, 8 Aug. 1914.
13 *Dundalk Examiner*, 22 Aug. 1914.
14 The Military Archives, Cathal Brugha Barracks (MA), Bureau of Military History (BMH), Witness Statement (WS).353, 'Seamus McGuill'.
15 MA, BMH, WS.507, 'Joseph O'Higgins'.
16 *Dundalk Examiner*, 10 Oct. 1914.
17 *Dundalk Democrat*, 24 Oct. 1914.
18 MA, BMH, WS.695, 'Thomas McCrave'.
19 MA, BMH WS.238, 'Arthur Greene'.
20 *Dundalk Examiner*, 31 Oct. 1914.
21 TNA, CO 904, CICMR, Co. Louth, Feb. 1916, Mar. 1916.
22 MA, BMH, WS.238, 'Arthur Greene'.
23 MA, BMH, WS.161, 'Donal O'Hannigan'.
24 MA, BMH, WS.353, 'Seamus McGuill'.
25 TNA, CO 904, CICMR, Co. Louth, Sept. 1916.
26 MA, BMH, WS.494, 'Peter Kieran'.
27 TNA, CO 904, CICMR, Co. Louth, Jul. 1917.
28 TNA, CO 904, CICMR, Co. Louth, Sept. 1917.
29 MA, BMH, WS.507, 'Joseph O'Higgins'.
30 MA, BMH, WS.353, 'Seamus McGuill'.
31 TNA, CO 904, CICMR, Co. Louth, Jan. 1918, Jan. 1919.
32 MA, BMH, WS.353, 'Seamus McGuill'.
33 Roscommon (Feb. 1917), South Longford (May 1917), East Clare (May 1917) and Kilkenny City (August 1917).
34 TNA, CO 904, CICMR, Co. Louth, Nov. 1918.
35 The IPP held the South Down and South Armagh seats.
36 Tom Garvin, *1922, The birth of Irish democracy* (Dublin: Gill & Macmillan, 1996), p. 68.
37 Harold O'Sullivan, *A history of local government in the County of Louth: from the earliest times to the present day* (Dublin: IPA, 2000), pp. 52–4.
38 Ibid., p. 63.
39 MA, BMH, WS.1148, 'Patrick Casey'. In fact, according to BMH, WS.598, 'James Rogan', 'many' Dundalk volunteers took part in the Plaster ambush, which failed due to undisciplined firing contrary to instructions by a contingent of Armagh or Down IRA men.

40   MA, BMH, WS.353, 'Seamus McGuill'.

41   MA, BMH, WS.507, 'Joseph O'Higgins'.

42   University College Dublin Archives (UCDA), O'Malley papers, P19b/93, 'Aiken Memorandum'.

43   *Dáil Éireann debates*, vol. F, no. 21, 10 May 1921.

44   MA, BMH, WS.695, 'Thomas McCrave'; *Irish Times*, 11 Apr. 1921.

45   MA, BMH, WS.507, 'Joseph O'Higgins'; *Irish Times*, 24 Jun. 1921; *Irish Times*, 1 Jul. 1921.

46   *Irish Times*, 24 Jun. 1921, 1 Jul. 1921.

47   Michael Hopkinson, *The Irish War of Independence* (Dublin: Gill & Macmillan, 2002), p. 194.

48   S.J. Connolly (ed.), *The Oxford companion to Irish History* (Oxford: OUP, 2002), p. 16.

49   *Dáil Éireann debates*, vol. 3, col. 134, 22 Dec. 1921.

50   Ibid., 18 Mar. 1922.

51   Ibid.

52   Ibid., 8 Apr. 1922.

53   Ibid.

54   Tom Garvin, *The evolution of Irish Nationalist politics* (Dublin: Gill & Macmillan, 2005), p. 147.

55   UCDA, Mulcahy papers, p7a/175, Frank Aiken, 'Position of the 4th Northern Division from Jan. 1922 to 17 July 1922, 3 p.m.'

56   UCDA, Mulcahy papers, B7/B/59/117, 'Re the 124 Recruits returned to Dundalk', 10 Aug. 1922.

57   UCDA, Twomey papers, P69/35 (286), D(irector of) O(rganisation) to Chief of Staff (C/S), 22 Dec. 1922.

58   UCDA, Twomey papers, P69/35 (290), Aiken O/C Northern Command to C/S, 7 Jan. 1923.

59   UCDA, Twomey papers, P69/35 (256-9), HQ Northern Command to C/S, 13 Mar. 1923.

60   UCDA, Twomey papers, P69/35 (207-9), D/O to C/S, 21 Jul. 1923.

61   John M. Regan, *The Irish counter-revolution 1921–1936: Treatyite politics and settlement in independent Ireland* (Dublin: Gill & Macmillan, 1999), p. 146.

62   Ibid.

63   *Dundalk Democrat*, 18 Aug. 1923.

64   O'Sullivan, *A history of local government in the County of Louth*, pp. 116, 123.

65   Ibid.; Brian Feeney, *Sinn Féin: a hundred turbulent years* (Dublin: O'Brien Press, 2002), p. 158.

66   Richard Dunphy, *The making of Fianna Fáil power in Ireland 1923–1948* (Oxford: OUP, 2005), p. 65.

67   MA, BMH, WS.232, 'Thomas Hamill'.

68   UCDA Twomey papers, P69/35 (274) 'Report on action takin [sic] on operation & General Orders and instructions', O/C Dundalk to C/S, 1 Feb. 1923.

69   Tom Feeney, *Sean MacEntee, a political life* (Dublin: IAP, 2009), p. 35

70   Ibid. p. 46.

71   Getting to the heart of the history of Co. Louth during the troubled decade of 1912–23 has taken many years of research. I would like gratefully to acknowledge the continued assistance the staff of the National Archives Dublin, UCD Archives, Louth County Archives and the Public Records Office of Northern Ireland; my PhD supervisor and co-editor Dr Martin Maguire has kept me on track, as has Professor Terence Dooley, History Department, Maynooth University. I am also very grateful for insights on the officers and men of the 4th Northern Division of the IRA, and on the politics of the era, shared in many hours of conversation with Frank Aiken Jnr, Ardee and Dr Rory O'Hanlon, Carrickmacross.

2

Cumann na mBan in County Louth, 1914–1921

Ailbhe Rogers

The late nineteenth century in Ireland was characterised by an Irish cultural revival, beginning with the founding of the Gaelic Athletic Association (GAA) in 1884. Douglas Hyde founded the Gaelic League in 1893, becoming its first president along with University College Dublin (UCD) Professor Eoin MacNeill as its first secretary. Its primary objectives were the revival, preservation and development of Irish as the national language of Ireland. Unlike many of the nationalist and literary organisations and associations of the late nineteenth and early twentieth centuries, the Gaelic League accepted women as full members from the beginning. Even though men held the ultimate majority, women could also assume committee positions of authority.[1]

In July 1916, the Gaelic League began to appear on a list of political organisations compiled by Co. Louth inspector F.C. Ireland, for the monthly Inspector's Reports.[2] It seems that it was not until after the Easter Rising, of 1916 that the local Royal Irish Constabulary (RIC) in Co. Louth deemed the Gaelic League worthy enough to be included in the list as a significant political component of the Irish Volunteers. It can therefore be deduced that the RIC had very little knowledge, if any, before the Easter Rising of nationalist affairs being conducted under the auspices of the Gaelic League.

The RIC intelligence reports estimate that there was only one branch of the Gaelic League in Co. Louth and that it had a membership of one hundred. However, this figure is not very reliable, as until 1918 it remains precisely the same in the police reports for Co. Louth, year on year. According to the local newspapers, there was more than one branch of the Gaelic League in Co. Louth. The *Dundalk Democrat* and the *Dundalk Examiner* also reported on the events and activities of other branches in Drogheda, Dunleer, Ardee, Annagassan, Clogherhead and Castlebellingham. While the Dundalk branch may have been the most active, it may have been the only branch under continuous RIC surveillance at the time.

In the summer of 1915, the All-Ireland Gaelic League Festival or An tOireachtas was held in the town of Dundalk from 25 to 30 July. Two women who sat on the Executive Committee of the Oireachtas were Mrs Mary Whitworth (née. Clinton), or Máire Bean Uí Whitworth, as she was better known, and Miss Angela Mathews, or Aingilín Ní Mhata, in Irish.[3] Angela Mathews and her older sister, Margaret, ran a stationery and book shop on Clanbrassil Street in Dundalk and they lived on the premises with their widowed mother. Angela was very well known within Louth Gaelic League circles as she was Vice President of the Dundalk Gaelic League and was previously involved with the Ancient Order of Hibernians. She appears in the *Dundalk Democrat* and the *Dundalk Examiner* regularly, presiding at various Gaelic League meetings. An indication of how involved and how dedicated she and her family were to the Irish language movement is that the Mathews household returns for the 1911 National Census were filled out entirely in Irish.[4]

The 1915 Oireachtas was a complete success, with thousands of visitors flocking to Dundalk to take part in the different music, dancing, hurling and football competitions. Several prominent Volunteers, such as Piarais Beaslaí, The O'Rahilly and Seán MacDiarmada came under the local RIC radar as having attended the week-long festival.[5] In one of his speeches, Revd Father Lyons, who was president of Dundalk Gaelic League, advised that 'any man not in sympathy with nine-tenths of the people of the country should either give up his work in the Gaelic League or keep his opinions to himself'.[6] This was a warning to the Irish Volunteers who were slowly but surely bringing their influence into the very heart of the Gaelic League. The 1915 Oireachtas was particularly important because during the week Dr Douglas Hyde resigned his founding position as President of the Gaelic League for reasons of a political nature.

Many women were associated with the Volunteers from the beginning through their involvement with na Fianna Éireann, the Gaelic League, Sinn Féin or simply through their relationship with male members. Some women suggested organising a women's auxiliary segment of the Volunteers. Many informal meetings were held in Dublin at first to gauge interest, and to lay out aims and policy. One article that appeared in the

Irish Freedom in November 1913, written by a woman, encouraged women from all over Ireland to support the nationalist cause: 'There is nothing unwomanly in active patriotism. Nobody calls Jeanne d'Arc unwomanly. In the days when Ireland is free, no one will have anything but admiration for the women who contributed in however great or small a degree to the attainment of her freedom.'[7] Sympathetic women were encouraged to support the growing nationalist movement by learning the Irish language, by studying Irish history, by supporting native Irish industries and manufacturers and by taking part in anti-recruitment campaigns.

Meanwhile, the inaugural meeting of a women's auxiliary unit to the Irish Volunteers was held at 4 p.m. on Thursday, 2 April 1914, in Wynn's Hotel, Co. Dublin. The organisation was given the name 'The Women's Council', or in Irish, *Cumann na mBan*. In attendance at the meeting were Jennie Wyse-Power, Agnes O'Farrelly, Agnes MacNeill, Mary Colum, Louise Gavan-Duffy, Áine O'Rahilly, Elizabeth Somers, Margaret Dobbs, Elizabeth Bloxham and a handful of other women. Here was a mix of women who were involved in a wide range of nationalist activities and organisations in some way or another. Some were involved in the Irish language movement, some were members of the radical women's organisation *Inghinidhe na hÉireann*, while others were suffragettes. Most of the women listed above and those who were elected to the Executive Committee were married, middle-class women and ranged in age from their thirties to mid-fifties. O'Farrelly made the inaugural speech of the meeting. The most important part of her speech stressed the need for women to leave their political opinions behind when they entered the organisation: 'We here have women of various opinions in national life, but they are ready, we believe, to merge their divergent views in face of the common danger.'[8]

The Cumann na mBan Constitution which was drawn up stated that 'Cumann na mBan is an independent body of Irish women pledged to work for the Irish Republic by organising and training the women of Ireland to take their place by the side of those who are working for its recognition.'[9] The committee had its offices on Great Brunswick Street (now Pearse Street) in Dublin, but over time they shared offices with the Volunteers at 2 Dawson Street and 6 Harcourt Street. Activities included first aid training, intelligence work, scouting, carrying despatches, election work, the study of the Irish language and Irish history, the support of Irish manufacture, the carrying of arms and ammunition, signalling, assisting in the escape of prisoners, route marches, collecting for the

Defence of Ireland Fund and the commandeering of supplies.[10] As part of the Central Committee, Elizabeth Bloxham was appointed National Organiser. She spent most of the summer of 1914 travelling around the country helping to set up branches in the different counties.

The first branch of Cumann na mBan in Co. Louth was founded in Dundalk. From her memoirs, Deirdre Mathews, the niece of Angela Mathews, asserted that the inaugural meeting of the Dundalk branch took place in Angela's stationery shop in November 1915. However, according to the *Dundalk Examiner* and the *Irish Volunteer* newspapers, the branch wasn't founded until the first week in February 1916.[11] All Dundalk Volunteer witness statements agree that Angela Mathews was the de facto leader and organiser of Cumann na mBan in Dundalk.

It is possible that Angela Mathews may have called an informal secret meeting in November 1915. Only a select few women of keen nationalist outlook may have been invited to gauge interest. Once interest was established and contact made with Cumann na mBan headquarters in Dublin (the whole process may indeed have taken three months), the branch formation was advertised in local and nationalist newspapers. At the first meeting, around thirteen women were present and all save one went on to become members. A branch needed a minimum of fifteen members to affiliate with Cumann na mBan headquarters and by April 1916 the Dundalk branch had around twenty-five members.

From its inception in February 1916 until 1921, Cumann na mBan in Co. Louth managed completely to avoid attracting local RIC attention. Louth was one of only three counties which succeeded in doing this; the other two were Fermanagh and Monaghan.[12] For five years not one branch in Co. Louth showed up on the County Inspector political organisation lists. Perhaps the RIC did know about Cumann na mBan but they did not see a handful of women as any real threat to the safety of the realm and therefore did not deem it a worthy enough nationalist organisation in the county to include them in the monthly inspector reports. If they were not aware of the organisation's presence in the county, it would have been a source of considerable embarrassment for local RIC men. Deirdre Mathews explained how Dundalk Cumann na mBan managed to continue with its activities and evade police detection for so long. Very great care was taken in the admission of new members and many proposals were rejected. Quality rather than quantity was aimed at in membership. The Cumann activities were more or less carried out under the cloak of the Gaelic League without the general public or, more importantly, the authorities being very much the wiser.[13] No doubt successfully working for so long outside the constraints of the law would have provided the Dundalk women with a sense of amusement and enjoyment. So much so that one female member of the Dundalk Gaelic League wrote a satirical poem about Dundalk Cumann na mBan entitled 'A Police Lament'.[14]

Patrick Mathews, Deirdre's father, was editor and proprietor of the *Dundalk Examiner* newspaper with his editorial office situated in the family home on Clanbrassil Street. Traditionally, the *Examiner* was very sympathetic towards nationalist affairs. After Patrick's death in 1914, the newspaper's sympathies became even more pronounced when Dundalk Volunteer, Patrick Duffy, took over as editor. From February until the end of April 1916, the Dundalk Cumann na mBan had a weekly column in the *Examiner*. The RIC certainly knew that it was a nationalist newspaper and one of their duties was to report back to the District County Inspector on seditious material and literature in their respective counties. Yet, the newspaper does not appear on seditious literature lists until the War of Independence. So, the *Examiner* and the Mathews family should have been well under the notice of the authorities.

The first official meeting of Dundalk Cumann na mBan took place on 8 February 1916. It had been advertised the previous Saturday in the *Examiner* that anyone who wished to join had to apply in writing to the Secretary, St Leonards, Dundalk 'so as to enable their names to be put before the committee'.[15] Meetings were held on Tuesday and Wednesday evenings in the Gaelic League meeting rooms at St Leonards. Circulars were sent out to all branches by Cumann na mBan HQ with instructions as to what activities they should indulge in. The main activities as already outlined were first aid, drilling, signalling, rifle care and target practice, if at all possible. The members of Dundalk Cumann na mBan boldly approached Dr James J. Clarke of Jocelyn Street and asked if he would be willing to instruct them in first aid. For three years, not only did Dr Clarke teach the women the various first aid practices and how to make different types of bandages and dressings, he also did so without charging a fee and he supplied all the necessary first aid equipment. Cumann na mBan uniforms were optional and they really depended on whether a member could afford to have one made or if they had the skills to make one themselves.

Dundalk Cumann na mBan kept in close contact with the Dundalk Irish Volunteers. Some members had male relations in the Volunteers. Bridget and Mary McHugh were the sisters of Dundalk Volunteer, Paddy McHugh, while Annie McGuill's older brother, James McGuill, was also a Volunteer member. Sean MacEntee lectured the women on military subjects while another Volunteer, Frank Thornton, conducted drill and revolver practice with them. At this point, since the Irish Volunteers and Cumann na mBan in Dundalk were working under the auspices of the Gaelic League, it is very difficult to tell if concerts, raffles, flag days, lectures and céilithe were being organised in favour of the Gaelic League or in favour of the Volunteers' fundraising body, the Defence of Ireland Fund.

In early 1916, Paddy Hughes was briefed by the Military Council of the Irish Republican Brotherhood (IRB) on plans for a rising to take place on Easter Sunday. Hughes duly imparted the news to the other officers of the Volunteers: McHugh, MacEntee, Patrick Duffy and James McGuill. A lecture given in the O'Boyle Reilly Hall by Seán MacDiarmada, on the occasion of the Robert Emmet Commemoration almost six weeks before the Easter Rising, added to the increasing fervour. Deirdre Mathews recalls that at the last minute it was discovered that no water had been set out at the speaker's table. A carafe was sent up by Mrs Annie Mathews, Deirdre's mother, to solve the problem. After the Rising, Mrs Mathews would not allow the carafe to be put into daily use because she regarded it as an invaluable memento of a stirring patriot. It was carefully put away and never used again.[16] Two weeks after the lecture, MacDiarmada sent Donal O'Hannigan to Dundalk to take charge of the ill-trained Volunteers and to knock it into shape in time for Easter. With O'Hannigan's help the Volunteers began stepping out more into the open and engaging in weekly route marches, parades and manoeuvres while Cumann na mBan branches received instructions to begin making field dressings. There was a definite air of anticipation and excitement that something big was going to happen.

On the Wednesday of Holy Week, Angela Mathews took a trip to Dublin. Nobody knew who she was in contact with in the city but she returned home 'with an air of some definite excitement'.[17] Deirdre Mathews was apparently informed by Paddy Duffy, editor of the *Examiner*, on the plans for Easter Sunday and he asked her if it would be possible to get some field dressings made for Sunday. First aid classes had stopped for the holidays the week before Holy Week but Angela and Deirdre managed to procure Dr Clarke on Thursday evening to direct them on making the dressings. Linen, splints, gauze, bandages, cotton wool and other medical supplies and materials were all obtained and carried back home to Clanbrassil Street, hidden beneath coats and garments in case any suspicions should be raised. Angela and Dr Clarke were also very careful that all the materials purchased were obtained in small amounts from different chemist shops so as not to draw attention. Dr Clarke, Angela, Deirdre, her mother and her grandmother, who was then aged about eighty, spent the next three evenings feverishly making field dressings for the Volunteers: 'We were buoyed up to a high pitch of elation and we worked with a will. For we realised that of the new chapter of Irish history that was opening we would not be the thrilled readers only – but actual participants.'[18] While the four women worked away at the field dressings, the rest of Dundalk Cumann na mBan were not left idle. So as not to alarm the rest of the branch or to reveal the secret to too many people, Angela managed to find other jobs for all her workers without actually revealing to them the plans for a rising. Some worked on haversacks while others made coverings for the dressings. On Easter Saturday night, everything was packaged up and delivered to the John Boyle O'Reilly Hall, which was to be the starting point for the Volunteers the next day.

The mobilisation for Easter Sunday was carried out at 12 noon as around 100 Volunteers assembled at the Boyle O'Reilly Hall. There were very clear orders that Cumann na mBan were not to march out with the men. They were to stand by and give help wherever it was needed. Meanwhile, the leader of the Volunteers, Eoin MacNeill, was made aware of the impending Rising, of which he had been kept in the dark. He responded quickly by issuing countermanding orders and thereby cancelling all Volunteer manoeuvres for Easter Sunday. According to Deirdre Mathews, around lunchtime on Easter Sunday, Angela received a visit from a courier from Dublin on a motorbike with the countermanding orders written in the form of despatches addressed to both Paddy Hughes and Donal O'Hannigan. Upon finding that the Dundalk men had already marched out, the courier had been at a loss as to what to do next. He did not know anyone else in the town and it was of the upmost importance that the despatches should reach their destination. He suddenly remembered a person by the name of Whitworth of Blackrock whom he had met in Gaelic League circles. Bean Uí Whitworth was not directly involved with the Volunteer movement at the time but she was very friendly with Angela, with whom she put the courier in contact. Angela promised to deliver the important messages while the courier continued north with more countermanding orders.[19]

Angela Mathews knew of the importance of the despatch. But first the authenticity of the document had to be proven. Someone who was familiar with MacNeill's handwriting needed to be found so that the message could be verified. MacNeill was one of the founding members of the Gaelic League but he was also one of the founders of Coláiste Bhríde in Omeath on the Cooley Peninsula. Luckily, many of the Irish college's staff and associates lived in Dundalk so Angela wasted no time in tracking down one of them to authenticate the signature. Revd P. Macardle, who was a member of the staff of St Mary's College (The Marist), vouched for his signature.[20] At around 3 p.m. Angela delivered the news to Sean MacEntee and the gun-raiding party who were assembled at St Leonard's and were rehearsing their plan for later that evening. However, in his own book, entitled *Episode at Easter*, MacEntee says of this moment that 'a messenger brought me a despatch which had just been delivered to a Marist Father in Dundalk. I verified MacNeill's signature.'[21] In his witness statement, James McGuill remarks: 'The late Miss Angela Mathews Vice-President of Dundalk Gaelic League and also Cumann na mBan and the Rev. Peadar Macardle S.M., St. Mary's College College both confirmed MacNeill's signature as genuine and I had no doubt of its authenticity.'[22] In *Dundalk: a military history*, Harold O'Sullivan relays that, 'Miss Angela Mathews and Eugene Hughes brought MacNeill's countermand order to MacEntee.'[23]

After some time, MacEntee managed to secure two cars from the McGuills. Joe McGuill, Joe Berrill, MacEntee and Angela set off in the cars with Mathews only going as far as Hill Street to mobilise some of the Cumann na mBan members. However, not all Cumann na mBan members were mobilised during Easter week. The McHugh sisters and Nellie Gaynor were called upon but James McGuill says that his younger sister, Annie, wasn't mobilised.[24] Annie was only seventeen at the time and was perhaps perceived as being too young. According to Deirdre Mathews, the town of Dundalk was 'seething with rumours, excitement and general uncertainty' by nightfall on Easter Sunday.[25] The townspeople were used to seeing the Volunteers going on route marches but this one seemed different.

On Monday morning, Angela received another visit while working in her stationery shop but this time it was a young female caller. The woman was Julia Grenan and she was a member of the Inghinnidhe na hÉireann branch of Cumann na mBan in Dublin. Determined not to abandon the rebellion, the Military Council of the Volunteers sent out female despatch carriers around the country informing Volunteer units that the rising would now take place at 12 noon on Easter Monday instead. The messengers were mostly women as they could travel more freely and they were less likely to be searched than men. Julia Grenan was sent to alert the Monaghan and Louth Volunteers.[26] Paddy Duffy recalls that a despatch was brought by a member of Cumann na mBan from Pearse or somebody on his behalf for Paddy Hughes.[27] Angela Mathews agreed to deliver the Carrickmacross despatches as soon as possible so that Miss Grenan could return to Dublin. For the remainder of Easter Week, Julia and her friend, Elizabeth O'Farrell, attached themselves to James Connolly and the Irish Citizen Army and ended up working in the GPO in Dublin as despatch carriers alongside some of the Proclamation signatories and several other members of Cumann na mBan. By the end of the week, she was one of three women left in the GPO at the time of the surrender. She was arrested and imprisoned in Kilmainham Gaol until 9 May.

Meanwhile, in Dundalk, the members of Cumann na mBan were becoming increasingly concerned about the importance of somehow delivering Pearse's remobilisation orders. To add to their problems some of the Redmondite National Volunteers were drafted into the Home Defence Corps and were mobilised by the RIC to set up checkpoints in and around the town of Dundalk.[28] According to the rumours circulating around the town, the men had spent the night in Slane and were now on their way back to Dundalk via Dunleer and Ardee into what the women perceived as a trap. If they reached the town they would all surely be arrested. Angela Mathews decided that the only thing to be done was to set out on bicycle and hope to intercept them. She took another member, Nellie Clarke, with her because there were two roads by which the Volunteers could return to Dundalk from the south. The women did not take the despatches with them lest they fell into the wrong hands, for they feared that the police would be following the corps. Angela took the Blackrock detour while Nellie took the direct Dublin Road route. Both agreed to meet at the gates of Clermont Park. Miss Clarke, being on the shorter route, met the weary and footsore contingent a short distance from Fane Bridge.[29] In his witness statement, one of the men, Hugh Kearney, recalls: 'When we came to about four miles from Dundalk, a girl from the Dundalk Cumann na mBan – Miss Clarke – met us on a bicycle with a message that if we marched into Dundalk we were in danger of attack by Home Defence Forces in the town.'[30]

As Monday wore on, definite information began to seep through the town that the men were no longer on their way back. News came that vehicles had been commandeered at Castlebellingham and that the company were on their way to Dublin to take part in the fighting. On Tuesday morning, Angela and Deirdre Mathews set off on the train for Carrickmacross to deliver Miss Grenan's remaining despatches and a note from Patrick Duffy addressed to the Carrickmacross Volunteers. The women conveyed the papers to the commandant of Carrickmacross Cumann na mBan, who promised to transfer them on to the local Volunteer leader.[31]

Overall, the Rising was not well received by the people of Co. Louth and many local businesses condemned the actions of the Louth Volunteers. The *Dundalk Democrat* called the Rising 'an act of madness' while the *Drogheda Independent* newspaper described it as a 'miserable Rising'. Drogheda Corporation publicly condemned the 'deplorable occurrences in Dublin' and the parish priests of both Dundalk and St Mary's in Drogheda disapproved of the events that took place.[32] On 4 May there were mass arrests in the county, with around seventy men being arrested under the Defence of the Realm Act (1914).[33] No Louth women were arrested.

The arrests and deportations that followed left many prisoners' dependants in poverty with no income. Some of the bereaved female relations of those men who were executed or imprisoned, such as Kathleen Clarke, Áine Ceannt, Madge Daly, Margaret Pearse, Lil Colbert and Muriel McDonagh, came together and formed the Irish Volunteers Dependants' Fund (IVDF). Kathleen Clarke was given £3,000 by her husband Tom Clarke before the rebellion in case it was needed by the relatives. They went about distributing this money to the widows and families who needed it most. Around the same time the Irish National Aid Association (INAA) was set up and it adhered to similar aims and policies. Some of the women involved were Lily O'Brennan, Áine O'Rahilly, Louise Gavan-Duffy and Jennie Wyse-Power. Its main aim was to provide financial support for the families and dependants of the men who were executed, of those who fell in action, of those who were sentenced to penal servitude and of those others who suffered by reason of participation in the insurrection.

From 1916, the main focus of Cumann na mBan branches all over the country was fundraising for prisoner' dependents and the publication and distribution of propaganda. IVDF and INAA branches were set up in Dundalk and Drogheda. Unlike Cumann na mBan, the IVDF and the

INAA did not hide behind other organisations, they were a noticeable presence in the two main towns. This piqued the interest of local authorities and after a while it was discovered by the RIC that branches of the IVDF and the INAA were emerging in counties where Cumann na mBan had not established a noticeable presence.[34] This in turn had an effect on the membership of Cumann na mBan. Through fundraising and charitable activities, women were being introduced slowly but surely to nationalism through a new body.

There was a surge in new membership in the Dundalk ranks. Local branches organised public collections, church-gate collections, door-to-door collections, raffles, fairs, plays, flag days, céilithe, dances, concerts, lectures and Easter Mass anniversaries for the executed leaders. They also sent parcels of food, clothes and other comforts to the Irish prisoners in English gaols. Weekly subscriptions to the Dependants' Funds began to appear and over time organisations such as the Gaelic League, the Irish National Foresters, the Young Ireland League, the Ancient Order of Hibernians and the United Irish League began to support the fund financially, and representatives were sent to the distress fund committee meetings. This shows the change in attitude that was taking place, not just in the county, but all over Ireland with regard to the Rising, the executions and the deported Irish prisoners. Another indication of this turnaround is that the *Dundalk Democrat*, which had previously condemned the Rising and those who took part in it, was now advertising the Dependents' Fund in it pages.

Cumann na mBan's column in the *Dundalk Examiner* did not reappear in 1916 after the Rising and it is somewhat difficult to find any trace of them in the local newspapers. It is quite possible that the events at Easter frightened the women so much so that the organisation became even more elusive and secretive. However, by December 1916, a new society sprung up in Dundalk, the Cúchulainn Dance Club. According to the local RIC reports it was made up of around thirty men and thirty women who met quite regularly at the John Boyle O'Reilly Hall. It was suspected by the police that the Volunteers were using this as a cover to reorganising the corps.[35] In Drogheda, a Literary and Historical Society was formed in late December 1916/early January 1917 for the same purpose.[36] Over the years, many lectures were given in Dundalk by Mrs Pearse, Áine Ceannt, Fr Michael Flanagan, Countess Plunkett and Nancy Wyse-Power. In April 1918, Countess Markievicz gave a lecture on women and the cause for Irish freedom in the Town Hall in aid of the town's distress fund. The *Examiner* reported that, 'the Town Hall was crowded by an enthusiastic audience long before the lecture started. The Countess was greeted by loud cheering'.[37]

Nationalist leaflets, journals and pamphlets were also circulated by the women around the county.

This came to a head when all the stationery and newsagent shops in Dundalk were raided by the police on 6 September 1918.[38] It was reported that a large amount of Sinn Féin literature was seized and confiscated. It is quite likely that Angela Mathews' shop was one of those newsagents that were raided and searched. In the summer of 1917, large public receptions were organised for the returned prisoners from English gaols. The prisoners were met at the train station in Dundalk by throngs of people. They travelled by brake to Park Street where speeches were delivered by Messrs P. Hughes and MacEntee and a concert was held afterwards.[39] While all this was going on, Dundalk Cumann na mBan continued with its primary duties of training in the fields of first aid, drilling and re-establishing the arms fund. At the Cumann na mBan convention, held in 1917, the minutes showed that there were around 100 branches in the country. Within a year, at the next annual convention, it was announced that this had increased to over 600.[40] During this time, Louth gained new branches of Cumann na mBan in Blackrock, Cooley, Louth, Ardee and Drogheda.

By 1918, the Allies' situation in Europe was becoming precarious and conscription was on the cards for Ireland. However, the impending legislation was rejected by almost every nationalist organisation in Ireland, including the IRB, The Volunteers, Sinn Féin and Cumann na mBan. The Volunteers and Cumann na mBan were prepared to resort to violence to avoid conscription and began to prepare militarily in case of an invasion by British forces. The Volunteers in particular were preparing to 'take to the hills' and fight a guerrilla war against the Crown forces. An anti-conscription campaign was feverishly pursued by Sinn Féin, which was becoming more and more prominent amongst young Irish men. The women of Cumann na mBan in Dundalk also took part in the anti-conscription campaigns, attending demonstrations in Newry and Castleblaney. On 9 June 1918, Alice Stopford-Green organised a large public meeting to take place at City Hall in Dublin where the women of different political factions could express their opposition to conscription and sign a petition. This proved to be a template for Cumann na mBan branches all over the country and 9 June was named 'Women's Day'. At 5.30 p.m. on Women's Day, 1,200

Cooley women turned out. They carried bunches of flowers and walked in a procession from Grange School to Boher Church, a distance of about three miles. Upon arrival, they attended a prayer service.[41] The women of Dundalk attended devotions at St Patrick's before signing the pledge against conscription and afterwards undertook a pilgrimage to Ladywell 'under the auspices of Cumann na mBan'.[42]

After the Great War ended in 1918, a general election was called, with the franchise now extended to those women with property and who were over thirty years of age. Women were now a sizeable portion of the Irish electorate and it was in a political party's interest to secure the female vote: 'We appeal to the women voters to vote with Sinn Féin'.[43] Countess Markievicz, who had recently been elected President of Cumann na mBan and was imprisoned in Holloway Prison at the time, along with Winifred Carney of the Belfast branch, were the only female candidates in the election and Countess Markievicz became the first woman to be elected to the Westminster Parliament.

One of Sinn Féin's party policies was the act of nominating imprisoned Irish men and women as candidates for election. The Cumann na mBan in North Louth took on the responsibilities in connection with the South Armagh election. They engaged in selling emblems, badges and flags, transporting voters to polls, preparing meals for Volunteers and helpers at polling stations, raising money for campaigns, printing and selling Sinn Féin literature and canvassing. J.J. (Sceilig) O'Kelly was the Sinn Féin candidate for the election while Richard Hazleton was the Irish Parliamentary Party candidate in Louth. In the propaganda element of the election, heavy emphasis was placed on O'Kelly's wife and five children living off distress funds while he was imprisoned in England.

Dundalk became the base for the Sinn Féin election campaign and many famous speakers, including Éamon de Valera, took the podium in favour of O'Kelly in the town. According to the *Examiner* there were reports of altercations between Hazelton's women voters and O'Kelly's women supporters in Seatown, Dundalk: 'The disgusting displays of the Hazletonian Amazons gained many votes for Mr. O'Kelly'.[44] Sinn Féin went on to win 73 out of 135 seats and 46 of these were held by men still in prison.

Between 1917 and 1918, many Irish Republican Army (IRA) prisoners were sent to Dundalk Gaol under the Defence of the Realm Act and in 1918 as suspects in the 'German Plot'. Some of the more famous prisoners accommodated there were Austin Stack, Professor James O'Neill, Seán

Tracey, Terence MacSwiney and Diarmuid Lynch. In just a few weeks, the gaol was full with over ninety republican prisoners. Many of the men went on hunger strike as soon as they arrived, having been denied the title of political prisoner. Hunger strikes were a very controversial form of protest and were often utilised by the IRA in gaining certain privileges and rights. The subject was very topical in Ireland at the time because of the force-feeding and subsequent death of IRB man, Thomas Ashe, in Mountjoy Gaol on 25 September 1917. Ashe's funeral was used as a public demonstration for Sinn Féin, the Irish Volunteers and Cumann na mBan, with a crowd of 30,000 attending. Cumann na mBan in Dundalk received lists of all the prisoners incarcerated in Dundalk Gaol and they organised regular visits to all those who were not receiving visits from their own family and friends.[45] Deirdre Mathews explained that this was often a tedious and laborious job because lists had to be made daily of who was entitled to visits and these had to be cross-referenced with those who were expecting visits from home or family.[46] Cigarettes and other comforts were smuggled into the prisoners as well as despatches.

Many of the hunger strikers were ultimately released under the Prisoners (Temporary Discharge of Ill Health) Act of 1913 (also known as the 'Cat and Mouse Act'), but there was still a great amount of work involved for the Cumann na mBan members when men were released. They negotiated with prison authorities and the prison doctor over the issuing of medical reports, arranged local accommodation for large batches of prisoners upon their release, provided medical supervision and made special precautionary diets for those coming off hunger strike, and, finally, after a few weeks when the released inmates had sufficiently recovered, the Cumann na mBan made travel arrangements for their journey home. All the relatives who travelled from a distance to visit their loved ones in Dundalk Gaol were looked after by the Cumann na mBan women. When Terence MacSwiney was moved to Dundalk Gaol, his wife Muriel moved to Dundalk to be closer to him. She stayed with Miss Kiernan of Cumann na mBan who lived near the prison.[47] Mrs O'Neill, the wife of Professor James O'Neill, also took up residence in Dundalk while her husband was imprisoned. Cumann na mBan did what it could to relieve the wives' anxiety and distress by arranging outings and activities. This was especially important for Mrs MacSwiney, who was pregnant with her first child. Many of the prisoners were eternally grateful to the members of Dundalk Cumann na mBan and many sent thank you notes.[48]

In February 1918, the Executive Committee took measures to draw Cumann na mBan and the Irish Volunteer movements even closer together. In a circular that was sent out to each branch, officers in charge were ordered that 'for the purpose of military organisation and operations' each local branch was to answer to the local Irish Volunteer commander.[49] This order was to have repercussions for Dundalk Cumann na mBan and this is evident at the annual convention when Miss Mathews of Dundalk complained to the organiser, Alice Cashel, about the interference of a local Volunteer in the appointment of the branch's officers.[50] However, Eithne Coyle remarked: 'It was not a case of taking orders because we had our own executive and we made our own decisions but if there were any jobs or anything to be done – the men – they didn't order us, but they asked us to help – which we did'.[51]

In 1919, tensions within the country came to a head in the War of Independence against the British forces in the country. Throughout most of 1919, Dundalk Cumann na mBan had a regular column in the *Dundalk Examiner* which reported on their Dependants' Fund activities, concerts, céilithe, lectures, raffles and jumbles sales. A victory céilí, which was described as 'the social event of the week', was held in Dundalk Town Hall on 15 January 1919 to welcome the Sinn Féin election candidate, editor of the *Catholic Bulletin* and deportee J.J. O'Kelly, home from England where he had been confined since February 1917.[52] The article that appeared in the *Dundalk Examiner* paid special tribute to the members of Cumann na mBan who helped to organise refreshments on the night.[53]

On 20 January, Dundalk Cumann na mBan held a céilí, which had an attendance of around sixty members. In towns like Dundalk, the women very much added to the social momentum of the republican movement.[54] During the proceedings, two members who were recently married were presented with hand-painted black satin Dorothea bags with silk lining.[55] The following day was to be a momentous day in Irish history. The new Dáil Éireann, which had been elected by the people of Ireland, first met on 21 January 1919, and it was on the same day that two members of the RIC were ambushed and shot by the Irish Volunteers in Soloheadbeg, Co. Tipperary.

On 26 and 28 January, Dundalk Cumann na mBan organised masses for the dead or *Cuimhne na Marbh* for the Irish prisoners who died in English prisons.[56] The Irish Volunteers, or IRA as they were commonly known now, and Cumann na mBan were eagerly awaiting the return of Irish prisoners from English gaols after the mass arrests that were carried out in May 1918 as part of the supposed 'German Plot'. Around 150 were arrested altogether, including three women: Countess Markievicz, Kathleen Clarke and Maude Gonne MacBride. It was only in March 1919 that the British government eventually released all the Irish prisoners.

Three Co. Louth men were arrested as part of the German Plot in May 1918.[57] Two of these, P.J. Berrill and Peter Hughes, both returned to Dundalk via motor car on the evening of 8 March 1919, where they received a 'hearty welcome from the Volunteers, Cumann na mBan and others' who had all gathered on the Dublin Road to meet them.[58] The ex-prisoners exchanged the motor car for seats in a brake which formed part of a procession that marched through the town to Mr Hughes' shop on Park Street 'headed by the Emmet Band and consisting of the Volunteers, members of the National Clubs, the ladies of the Cumann na mBan, a Pipers' Band, torch bearers and flag carriers'.[59] The tri-colour was placed over the Town Hall at some stage during the day while along the route tar barrels blazed and windows had been decorated with candles and Irish flags. The large crowd that gathered in front of the Town Hall was addressed by a few leading members of the Volunteers and afterwards the two ex-prisoners, Peter Hughes and Joe Berrill, gave patriotic speeches, which encouraged people to join the national organisation and to speak the Gaelic language. The British army and RIC were also present at the event but there was no trouble other than some stone-throwing, which took place on Clanbrassil Street.

Fundraising for the local Dependants' Fund was a very important activity taken on by the members of Cumann na mBan and female relatives of deceased male nationalists. With many men imprisoned or on the run, fundraising became an essential propaganda tool in mobilising popular support at home and abroad. Cumann na mBan often made use of the image of a woman and child left at home, without any sort of income, to stir nationalist sympathy and emotion. Mrs Margaret Pearse, the mother of the executed Patrick and Willie Pearse, and Áine Ceannt, widow of executed leader Éamon Ceannt, both visited Dundalk on 24 April 1919 on the third anniversary of the 1916 Easter Rising. Their main reason for visiting was to assist the local branch of Cumann na mBan with the organisation of a concert in the Town Hall being held in aid of the Prisoners' Dependents' Fund. Angela Mathews presided over the event. Áine Ceannt in her speech spoke about the importance of the Gaelic language and she encouraged all nationally minded people to learn it, to speak it and to teach it to their children. Mrs Pearse was met with a huge amount of respect and her speech was emotionally felt by all on the day.[60] Hanna Sheehy-Skeffington, famous Irish suffragist and widow of the executed journalist, Francis Sheehy-Skeffington, and Min Ryan, member of Cumann na mBan and later wife of Richard Mulcahy, both made similar visits to Dundalk in November 1921 and gave lectures.[61]

Mrs Pearse made a second visit to Dundalk on 1 November 1923, this time accompanied by Countess Plunkett and Máire Comerford.[62] Deirdre Mathews asserts that these concerts and lectures were an important means of propaganda and Cumann na mBan women considered they did much to revive and maintain the national spirit.[63] However, Cumann na mBan did not receive support from all areas of Co. Louth as was evidenced when Dundalk Cumann na mBan were stoned in Carlingford by a group of young boys who were egged on by some of the locals, while returning from an excursion on 20 July.[64]

Because they were becoming so outwardly active and because they were coming out into the open more and more, Dundalk Cumann na mBan began attracting a lot of attention from the RIC. Women were known to distribute propaganda or (as it was called) 'seditious literature' on behalf of Sinn Féin and the IRA, and while women were rarely subject to searches in the street it did not stop their shops and business being searched by the local police force. Members Mary Mandeville, Annie Morgan and Angela Mathews all owned or worked in stationery and newsagent shops in the town and it seems likely that their shops were centres for purchasing and distributing Sinn Féin literature and national pamphlets such as *The Spark*, *Honesty*, and so on. Police raids were a common occurrence on the homes of known IRA members, but on the morning of 23 August, one police raid seemed intentionally aimed at the homes and businesses of known Dundalk Cumann na mBan members. The premises of Deirdre Mathews (*Examiner* office) Angela Mathews, Mary Mandeville, Mary McHugh, Margaret McDermott and Alice Murtagh were all raided, which yielded a quantity of Sinn Féin literature including some songbooks.[65] Angela Mathews' premises were again raided in September as part of mass raids that took place all over the county.

From the end of September to mid-December, the *Dundalk Examiner* was suppressed because of its publication of the Dáil Loan advertisement. It only managed to gain the right to publish again when Mrs Annie Mathews, the proprietor (Deirdre Mathews' mother), agreed to 'sell' the newspaper to a sympathetic man from Ardee and the official role of editor – manager was given to T. O'Hanlon of Phibsborough, Dublin, while Patrick Duffy of Dundalk IRA continued secretly to act in the position.[66] This suppression was to have a huge effect on the public relations department of Dundalk Cumann na mBan in 1920. It is very difficult to find any evidence of Cumann na mBan activity in the local newspapers during this period and one must turn to different sources to uncover what was going on during this time. There may have been a few reasons for the local branch becoming more secretive. Cumann na mBan, along with the Gaelic League, the IRA and Sinn Féin, was declared an illegal organisation by Lord French, the Lord Lieutenant of Ireland, in July 1919.[67] The closing of the *Dundalk Examiner* office at the end of 1919 for an extended period of time may have made Cuman na mBan more wary of reporting on its activities, and the raids on members' premises may have encouraged them to be more cautious as the authorities were now aware of their existence. Interestingly, the local branch of the Gaelic League also refrained from making appearances in the local newspapers.

Many IRA men were often 'on the run' and Cumann na mBan members frequently took it upon themselves to find safe houses to shelter 'wanted' men. They provided them with food, clothing and comforts such as cigarettes and tobacco. Women regularly acted as nurses for wounded spies, scouts and despatch carriers and were often responsible for the transporting, caring for and dumping of arms and ammunition during this period. Females were very rarely stopped and searched, and long dresses, skirts and petticoats, which were the fashion of the time, meant women could carry and hide arms and messages on their person. However, it is important to note that there appeared to be no possibility of women fighting alongside, men as they occasionally had during the Easter Rising, and women were becoming less and less involved in direct action, taking a more subordinate domestic role.[68]

On 20 June 1921, the *Dundalk Examiner* office was broken into and destroyed by a group of armed men with the result that the paper had no premises or equipment to produce, print or publish a newspaper from June until October. In his witness statement, given to the Bureau of Military History, the paper's editor – manager, Patrick Duffy, suggests the reason for the attack was because of the coverage the paper gave to a double shooting of two brothers that took place on 17 June.[69] John and Patrick Watters of Quay Street, Dundalk, were members of the local IRA.

They were both called out of their home in the middle of the night by a group of armed men. After leading the two brothers a short distance away, the party opened fire, killing the brothers instantly.

In the summer of 1921, the Co. Louth contingents of the IRA were ordered to burn all the coastguard stations along the coast because, like the big country estate houses, it was rumoured that they were occupied by the Black and Tans. Bridget O'Mullane was the organiser for the Executive of Cumann na mBan at the time and she was sent to Co. Louth to help co-ordinate the Cumann na mBan operation. The plan was carried out successfully and the coastguard stations at Blackrock, Clogherhead and Termonfeckin were burnt to the ground by the IRA with help, it seems, from local branches of Cumann na mBan. Bridget O'Mullane was herself present at the burning of Termonfeckin station but she says that they were 'surprised by the Black and Tans who arrived in their lorries just as the building was alight'.[70] In her panic and not knowing anyone in the vicinity, she took sanctuary in the presbytery of Termonfeckin Church until the danger passed.

While Dundalk was certainly the headquarters of Cumann na mBan in Co. Louth during the War of Independence, it is clear from the monthly County Inspector reports for Co. Louth and from the police raids that were carried out on the members' houses and businesses, that the RIC could no longer ignore the existence of Cumann na mBan in the county. Louth Cumann na mBan was first included on lists of political organisations in mid-1921. They give an estimate of six branches with a total membership of 264.[71] However, a membership affiliation fee notebook, dated November 1920 to October 1921, records at least fourteen branches of Cumann na mBan in Co. Louth.[72] Ann Matthews lists a total of twenty-one branches between July and November 1921.[73] Cal McCarthy writes: 'as soon as Cumann na mBan's formal organisation was driven underground in November 1919 police reports which were never very accurate to begin with, became almost entirely useless in attempting to analyse the numerical strength of the group.'[74]

A truce was called between the British and Irish sides in July 1921. In October, Michael Collins, Arthur Griffith, Robert Barton, Eamon Duggan and George Gavan Duffy went to London on behalf of Dáil Éireann as plenipotentiaries to negotiate a treaty. Meanwhile, the 1921 Cumann na mBan, with 702 branches now established, held its Annual Convention on 22–23 October.[75] Leinster sent 123 delegates and Louth sent seven of these: Miss Mara of Dundalk, Miss Collins of Termonfeckin, Lillis Ní Balb of Drogheda, Miss Harty of Churchtown, Miss Lynch of Ardee, Miss Morgan of Grangebellew and Brigid Ní hAoda of Dundalk.[76] Angela Mathews was one of three rural representatives of Leinster on the Executive Council for 1920–21, but of the forty-seven executive meetings that took place, she did not attend any.[77] However, this does not seem to hold any significance on her part because the rural attendance for each province was very poor in general. At the end of 1921, the IRA was organised into divisions and brigades in an effort to streamline and co-ordinate organisation. Cumann na mBan branches were absorbed into this divisional system. County Louth was separated into two divisions, with North Louth becoming part of the 4th Northern Division, which incorporated most of Co. Armagh and parts of Co. Down, while South Louth was absorbed into the 1st Eastern Division, which was made up of Co. Meath and Co. Kildare with parts of Co. Westmeath and Co. Cavan.

The Anglo-Irish Treaty was signed between the British and the Irish negotiators on 6 December 1921, and the resulting Dáil Eireann debates on the matter signalled that a Treaty split was imminent within the young Irish government. This split was reflected in the IRA, Sinn Féin and Cumann na mBan organisations. On 5 February 1922, a special convention of Cumann na mBan was called 'to reaffirm its allegiance to the Republic of Ireland'.[78] It was agreed by the Executive that they could not support the Articles of Agreement as laid out in the Treaty and therefore would not give any help to a candidate standing for the Free State elections. It was very clear from the outset that Cumann na mBan was identifying itself firmly with the anti-Treaty side. Each branch was given the choice to vote on the Treaty and the Louth branches that voted against it included Ardee, Ballapousta, Blackrock, Drogheda, Dundalk, Flurrybridge, Grangebellew, Heronstown and Annagassan.[79] On 11 February 1922, the Dundalk Cumann na mBan eventually broke its silence with the local newspapers to report on the Special Convention and the decision that was made.[80] Many of the branches that voted against the Treaty lost substantial membership for different reasons. Women who were pro-Treaty dropped out, some women who took a neutral stance and those women who were opposed to a civil war also left and distanced themselves from the organisation. According to Deirdre Mathews, when the Civil War broke out her aunt Angela refused to take sides and after six years as the founder and as President of Dundalk Cumann na mBan she stepped down. Mathews explains that some of the older members rejoined but many had lost heart due to the situation that was unfolding. Some women who distanced themselves became auxiliaries and were associated with it in many ways but did not rejoin as full members.[81] Deirdre Mathews was one of these women.

The year 1922 signalled a change in Dundalk Cumann na mBan. A new phase was brought about by the Civil War and while most branches that voted against the Treaty declined in membership, the Dundalk branch did not seem to suffer much at all: quite the contrary, it thrived. Miss Annie Keelan was elected President of the Dundalk branch in 1922 and she immediately went about reorganising it. Many of the younger members were radicalised, putting their lives at risk in developing a more active, extremist advocacy. They provided close support to IRA Active Service Units, and often clashed violently with Free State soldiers during raids for arms and seditious literature. They suffered for their revolutionary fervour with some of them experiencing instances of personal violence and intimidation, arrest and imprisonment.

As atrocities and attacks worsened and escalated throughout the country, the Provisional Government passed the Public Safety Bill of 1922, allowing the setting up of special military tribunals. These courts were empowered to impose life imprisonment and the death penalty on Irish citizens for a variety of offences. In all, about seventy-seven men were officially executed by the Free State for the part they played in 'irregular activities'. In January 1923, six IRA men were executed in Dundalk Gaol and one Louth man was executed in Portobello Barracks. The Free State never pursued the executions of republican women during the Civil War and some women began to believe that they had a certain amount of immunity, causing them to intensify their activities. However, women were not exempt from arrest and they did not escape penal servitude. During the Civil War, nine Louth women were arrested and interned in Mountjoy Prison, Kilmainham Gaol and the North Dublin Union.

After the Civil War, Cumann na mBan as an organisation went into decline and many became disheartened and discouraged by the traditional roles that were assigned to women by Archbishop McQuaid, Éamon de Valera and his Fianna Fáil government, especially those views expressed in Article 41.2 of the Irish Constitution of 1937. Angela Mathews died in 1928 and her niece Deirdre Mathews died in the early 1970s. There are no known surviving members of the old Cumann na mBan remaining in Co. Louth. It is interesting to see how the opinions of those women involved in the struggle for Irish independence have changed over time, or (in the case of Bridget Kelly) have not changed at all:

> It is my considered opinion that if and when the government changes, the whole matter of Cumann na mBan should be reopened with a view to ensuring that justice may at last be done and the part played by the Cumann in the War of Independence shall receive its proper recognition in the story of our country.[82]

> I will always hold onto my republican beliefs. We have fought a long battle and now we leave it to the present generation of youth to continue the fight and win back our six counties. What pleasure it would give to the remaining few to see our country united.[83]

> Although I supported the armed struggle in my day, the violence of the past thirty years in Northern Ireland has saddened me and I believe all the suffering and loss of life has not been worth it.[84]

NOTES

1 First, I would like to thank my Masters and current PhD supervisor, Professor Terence Dooley, for his dedication and guidance throughout my postgraduate career thus far. Thank you also to my mentor, Donal Hall, for all his input, insight and local knowledge. I am also indebted to the staff of Kilmainham Gaol Museum and Archives, UCD Archives, The National Library of Ireland, The National Archives of Ireland, The Military Archives and The Louth County Library and Archives. I am extremely grateful to all the descendants of Louth Cumann na mBan members I have met so far – thank you for sharing your family histories with me and I hope this chapter and future PhD thesis will do justice to the local women whose buried past has gone unnoticed for so long. Thanks especially to my family for their love and support: above all, my dad, Bryan Rogers.

2 The National Archives, London (TNA), Colonial Office (CO) 904/100, Confidential County Inspector's Monthly Report (CCIMR), Co. Louth, Jul. 1916.

3 *Dundalk Examiner*, 23 Jan. 1915.

4 National Archives Ireland (NAI), Census of Ireland 1911, '66 Clanbrassil Street, Dundalk town, County Louth'.

5 TNA, CO 904/97, CCIMR, Co. Louth, Jul. 1915.

6 TNA, CO 904/96, CCIMR, Co. Louth, Mar. 1915.

7 Margaret Ward, *In their own voice: women and Irish Nationalism* (Dublin: Attic Press, 1995), pp. 39–41.

8 Ibid., p. 42.

9 National Library of Ireland (NLI) MS 41,494/1, Ceannt-O'Brennan papers, Constitution of Cumann na mBan.

10 Ibid.
11 *Dundalk Examiner*, 5 Feb. 1916; *Irish Volunteer*, 19 Feb. 1916.
12 Cal McCarthy, *Cumann na mBan and the Irish Revolution* (Cork: Collins Press, 2007), p. 155.
13 University College Dublin Archives (UCDA), P106/1405, Sighle Humphreys papers, The Memoirs of Deirdre Little (née Mathews).
14 Ibid.
15 *Dundalk Examiner*, 5 Feb. 1916.
16 UCDA, P106/1405, Sighle Humphreys papers, The Memoirs of Deirdre Little.
17 Ibid.
18 Ibid.
19 Ibid.
20 Ibid.
21 Seán MacEntee, *Episode at Easter* (Dublin: Gill, 1966), p. 69.
22 Military Archives, Cathal Brugha Barracks Dublin (MA), Bureau of Military History (BMH) Witness Statement (WS) 353, 'James McGuill'.
23 Joseph Gavin and Harold O'Sullivan, *Dundalk: a military history with photographs and illustrations* (Dundalk: Dundalgan Press, 1987), p. 82.
24 MA, BMH WS.353, 'James McGuill'.
25 UCDA, P106/1405, Sighle Humphreys papers, The Memoirs of Deirdre Little.
26 Sinéad McCoole, *No ordinary women: Irish activists in the revolutionary Years 1900–23* (Dublin: O'Brien Press, 2003), p. 35.
27 MA, BMH, WS.237, 'Patrick Duffy'.
28 Donal Hall, *World War I and Nationalist Policies in County Louth, 1914–1920* (Cork: Four Courts Press, 2005), p. 23.
29 UCDA, P106/1405, Sighle Humphreys papers, The Memoirs of Deirdre Little.
30 MA, BMH, WS.260, 'Hugh Kearney'.
31 UCDA, P106/1405, Sighle Humphreys papers, The Memoirs of Deirdre Little.
32 Hall, *World War I*, p. 24.
33 Ibid., pp. 24–5.
34 McCarthy, *Cumann na mBan*, p. 75.
35 TNA, CO 904/101, CCIMR, Co. Louth, Dec. 1916.
36 *Dundalk Examiner*, 13 Jan. 1917.
37 *Dundalk Examiner*, 6 Apr. 1918.
38 *Dundalk Democrat*, 7 Sept. 1918.
39 *Dundalk Democrat*, 23 Jun. 1917.
40 NLI, MS 41, 494/1, Ceannt-O'Brennan papers, Cumann na mBan Annual Convention 1918.
41 *Dundalk Examiner*, 15 Jun. 1918.
42 *Dundalk Examiner*, 29 Jun. 1918.
43 Ward, *In their own voice*, p. 88.
44 *Dundalk Examiner*, 21 Dec. 1918.
45 NAI, BMH, WS.353, 'James McGuill'.
46 UCDA, P106/1405, Sighle Humphreys papers, The Memoirs of Deirdre Little.
47 MA, BMH, WS.637, 'Muriel MacSwiney'.
48 UCDA, P106/1405, Sighle Humphreys papers, The Memoirs of Deirdre Little.
49 Ann Matthews, *Renegades: Irish Republican Women: 1900–1922* (Cork: Mercier Press, 2010), p. 233.
50 NLI, MS 41,494/1, Ceannt-O'Brennan papers, Cumann na mBan Annual Convention Report 1918.

51 Michael Hopkinson, *The Irish War of Independence* (Dublin: Gill & Macmillan, 2002), p. 199.

52 *Dundalk Examiner*, 18 Jan. 1919.

53 Ibid.

54 Peter Hart, *The IRA and its enemies: violence and community in Cork 1916–1923* (Oxford: Clarendon Press, 1998), p. 235.

55 *Dundalk Examiner*, 25 Jan. 1919.

56 Ibid.

57 Matthews, *Renegades*, p. 216.

58 *Dundalk Democrat*, 15 Mar. 1919.

59 Ibid.

60 *Dundalk Examiner*, 26 Apr. 1919.

61 *Dundalk Examiner*, 3 Dec. 1921.

62 *Dundalk Examiner*, 3 Nov. 1923.

63 UCDA, P106/1405, Sighle Humphreys papers, The Memoirs of Deirdre Little.

64 *Dundalk Examiner*, 26 Jul. 1919.

65 *Irish Times*, 25 Aug. 1919.

66 MA, BMH, WS.237, 'Patrick Duffy'.

67 Matthews, *Renegades*, p. 246.

68 Hopkinson, *Irish War of Independence*, p. 199; Hart, *The IRA and its enemies*, p. 257.

69 MA, BMH, WS.237, 'Patrick Duffy'.

70 MA, BMH, WS.485, 'Bridget O'Mullane'.

71 McCarthy, *Cumann na mBan*, p. 155.

72 UCDA, P106/1132, Sighle Humphreys papers, Member affiliation address book.

73 Matthews, *Renegades*, p. 352.

74 McCarthy, *Cumann na mBan*, p. 161.

75 Ibid., p. 167.

76 UCDA P106/1131, Sighle Humphreys papers, List of Cumann na mBan members who were in attendance at the Cumann na Ban Annual Convention 1921.

77 NLI MS 41,494 /1, Ceannt-O'Brennan papers, Attendance of Cumann na mBan Executive Meetings, 1920–21.

78 NLI, MS 41,494 /1 Ceannt-O'Brennan papers, Cumann na mBan Special Convention to discuss the organisation's stance on the Anglo-Irish Treaty of 1921, 5 Feb. 1922.

79 MA, CBB, Captured papers Lot No. 51, 'The Louth branches of Cumann na mBan that voted against the Anglo-Irish Treaty of 1921'.

80 *Dundalk Examiner*, 11 Feb. 1922.

81 UCDA, P106/1405, Sighle Humphreys papers, The Memoirs of Deirdre Little.

82 Ibid.

83 The memoirs of Bridget Kelly, Grangebellew, Co. Louth, in private possession, 1970.

84 Interview conducted with Rose Hickey, Mountainstown, Dunleer, Co. Louth by Bryan Rogers, in private possession, 2001.

3

Labour in County Louth, 1912–1923

Martin Maguire

If the history of the Irish revolution 1912–23 is written as an armed struggle between the IRA and the Crown forces then Co. Louth, as one of the less active areas, would seem to be disengaged from the revolution. However, the strength of the national mobilisation in 1919–23 cannot be measured by IRA activity alone.[1] Labour militancy, whilst supportive of the abstract nationalism of the republican movement, mobilised the working class on concrete and specific grievances, which it was expected the republic would address.[2] In the course of the Irish revolution, labour resistance to the British state at local level in Co. Louth was organised in direct action, in non-violent strikes, embargoes and in civil disobedience.[3] When the working class organises itself as 'labour', the objective is to achieve better wages and working conditions. But militancy on wages is never about wages alone. It is also about a better and more secure future. This, as it seemed to some in Ireland in the years 1912–23, may be through revolutionary struggle to establish a completely new society, but for most workers it is usually through trade union mobilisation to confront capital or through political mobilisation to drive state action in support of the working class.

In Co. Louth between 1912 and 1923, working-class radicalism was more extensive than has been appreciated, with engagement in a range of labour struggles, calling upon an eclectic range of mobilisations. During the Great War, strike action compelled the state to intervene on behalf of labour to maintain industrial peace. In the period after the end of the war, as the nationalist revolution developed, labour fought hard to hold on to the gains made and to win new improvements. Various ideologies were drawn upon as required – 'Red Flag' Bolshevism, Sovietism, republicanism, syndicalism and agrarianism – but always in pursuit of the goal of securing a better life for the working class.

The first developments of the welfare state under Asquith's Liberal government, followed by the enormously complex task of mobilising society and economy for world war, aligned the British state with the social demands of the working class. The state became guarantor of sickness and unemployment benefits, old-age pensions, wage compensation for inflation, and regulation of workplace. The resurrection of the Irish Transport and General Workers Union (ITGWU) in 1917, after the crushing defeat of the Union by the combined forces of Martin Murphy-led employers in the Lockout of 1913, gave workers a powerful trade union organisation. The parliamentary Labour Party, formally created in 1912 but remaining aloof from activism for ten years, proved less useful to the working class. The emergence, after 1916, of the revolutionary Sinn Féin and its establishment of the republican counter-state of Dáil Éireann in 1919, created a new state force upon which labour could hope to exert pressure. Finally, the 1917 Russian Revolution inspired working-class militants with a new social model in the 'soviet' and also with the efficacy of the tactic of direct action.[4]

Dundalk and Drogheda developed initially as industrial and service centres for rural Co. Louth. Dundalk Distillery was established in 1799. The multi-storey tower windmill in the town was attuned to the extensive commercial market in cereal production across the county. Hoffmann's brick works, with a ten-chambered kiln, was built in the 1890s to service the expansion in house building. A water-driven spade mill in Ravensdale serviced the need for a variety of spade shapes for Irish agricultural production. However, it was the development of the railway that gave Louth 'industrial lift-off'. With the completion of the Boyne viaduct in 1853, Belfast and Dublin were linked by rail. The Great Northern Railway (GNR), established in 1875, amalgamated four separate enterprises: the Dublin and Drogheda Railway, the Dublin and the Belfast Junction Railway, the Ulster Railway and the Irish North Western Railway. With the creation of the GNR, Dundalk was selected as the site for the railway company workshop and engineering works.

In 1914, the works employed close to 1,000 skilled and well-paid tradesmen such as fitters, turners, boilermakers, blacksmiths and brass fitters. New housing was built close to the works to accommodate these workers. The railway, with its freight service, also enabled larger-scale production. In 1919, W. & H.M. Goulding established a chemical fertiliser factory in Drogheda. The railways also established the ports of Greenore, Dundalk and Drogheda for passenger and livestock trade. Local foundries, such as Shekletons and Manistys in Dundalk, and Grendons in Drogheda, that had been established in the 1820s and 1830s to service the local market, expanded in line with the growth of the railways. By 1914, Dundalk had, along with the railway works, two breweries, a distillery, Carrolls cigarette factory and May Street Linen Mills (both significant employers of women), three brickworks, and other manufacturing and industrial concerns. A large and complex working class of men and women, of various skills and trades, made Dundalk and Drogheda not unlike many British industrial towns.[5]

The 1911 census shows that Co. Louth had 3,642 agricultural labourers and 3,101 general industrial labourers, reminding us that the pay and benefits that attached to the skilled trades were very favourable compared with the condition of the mass of the unskilled rural and general labourers that constituted the working class of the rest of the county.[6] It also reminds us that labour in Ireland was still dominated by the rural economy and that it was agrarian rather than industrial unrest that traditionally fuelled militancy and political mobilisation. In January 1890, the agrarian radical and Fenian, Michael Davitt, formed the Irish Democratic Trade and Labour Federation to forward the demands of labour within the nationalist movement, hitherto dominated by the tenant farmers. Davitt's organisation aimed to organise town and agricultural labour as a single working class.[7] Out of this grew the Irish Land and Labour League that campaigned for housing, better wages and conditions for rural labourers.

In 1891, Davitt addressed the Drogheda Trades Council. The condition of the agricultural labourer, in Louth as elsewhere, was harsh; casualised under the hiring fair system, such labourers were subject to long hours and poor wages, of low social status and, as a live-in servant, vulnerable to the whim of the farmer.[8] Agricultural labourers looked to local authority direct labour schemes to tide them over periods of unemployment. The great advance for the agricultural labourer was achieved through political pressure by Parnell and later by Davitt and the Land and Labour Association, that led to the passing of the 1883 and 1906 Labourers (Ireland) Acts. These acts compelled the building of rural labourers' cottages by local authorities, thus giving agricultural labourers independence and security from eviction by the employing farmer class. In Co. Louth, over 1,500 rural labourer cottages were built.[9]

Trade unions, as the organisations of, for, and by the working class, began in the skilled trades and were confined to the craft and the locality. Local trade unions developed a rich culture of banners and ceremonies, expressing their local identity and craft pride.[10] These local trades councils maintained the craft tradition and represented a relatively secure and privileged sector of the working class that sought a non-confrontational relationship with capital. Drogheda Trades Councils, founded in 1887, was dominated by the local craft unions and sought to 'cultivate a spirit of harmony between employer and employee'.[11] The 1871 Trade Union Act gave legal status to labour organisations and encouraged the emergence of unions of a national rather than local character, with a head office, elected officers and a national executive governed by a formal rule book, with centralised funds and benefits. This 'new unionism' came into Ireland from Great Britain.[12] The British-based Amalgamated Society of Railway Servants (ASRS), forerunner of the National Union of Railwaymen (NUR), considered to be amongst the most radical sections of the Irish trade union movement, began to organise in Ireland in 1885 and by 1890 had branches in Dundalk and Drogheda.[13] The long-established, locally based, Drogheda Operative Painters Trade Union Society became the Drogheda branch of the Manchester-based Amalgamated Society of Operative House and Ship Painters and Decorators.[14]

A significant innovation of the new unions was the organisation of the unskilled labourers in transport. These workers on ships, docks and on the railways were highly casualised, often unemployed and badly paid. The most successful of the unions, initially, was the National Union of Dock Labourers (NUDL), founded in Glasgow in 1889 by Irish dock workers. One of the founders was Michael McKeown, a Newry man, who became the NUDL organiser in Ireland. By 1891, it had 2,000 members in Ireland and organised in fifteen ports, including Dundalk and Drogheda. The railway and shipping companies retaliated, breaking NUDL strikes in Dundalk and other ports in 1891. By 1905, it was a feeble union in Ireland, with a diminished base in Derry and Drogheda.[15]

In that same year, in a NUDL strike on Liverpool docks, it was recognised that a new powerful and inspiring leader had emerged in the figure of James Larkin. Dismissed by his employers, he was recruited by the NUDL's general secretary, James Sexton, as an organiser and was sent to Belfast in 1907 to revitalise the union there. Playing a key role in reorganising Co. Louth was James Fearon from Newry, secretary of the Newry and Dundalk branch of the NUDL. The NUDL was then carried into the Drogheda docks. Fearon used the weapon of sympathetic action in Newry and Warrenpoint in support of Belfast workers in the 1907 strike. Crushed in Newry, the NUDL branch in Dundalk was more successful, winning increases in wages, shorter hours and better conditions.[16] Larkin brought Belfast city to a halt in a general strike. Sidelined by Sexton, who quickly secured a weak settlement in Belfast, he was sent to organise in Waterford, Cork and then Dublin. His progress was marked by a series of strikes, which strained his relationship with the conservative and cautious Sexton, until in early December 1908 he was suspended as organiser of the NUDL. Larkins response revolutionised Irish trade unionism. On 28 December, at a meeting in the Trades Hall, Capel Street, Dublin of trade unionists and socialists, attended by Micheal Mckeown and Patrick Dobbins from Dundalk, the ITGWU was launched.

The ITGWU was a break with the established development of trade unionism in Ireland through the introduction and spread of British-based unions. This had helped foster a culture of cross-channel solidarity but Ireland was always marginal to British trade unionism. From its foundation in 1868, to 1918, the British Trades Union Congress (TUC) did not once consider a motion on the 'Irish question' that dominated parliamentary politics. The formation of an Irish Trade Union Congress in 1894 had been an attempt to address this problem but the reality was that Ireland would always be low on the agenda of British-based unions. The ITGWU was an avowedly Irish union with a strongly republican and socialist identity. It was also, as its name signalled, an industrial and not a sectional union, looking to organise the whole of the working class in a single 'One Big Union'. The ITGWU was also syndicalist in its ideology, emphasising industrial conflict as the truest form of class struggle. The working class discovered itself as a class in workplace struggle rather than in parliamentary struggle. The union should be a moral community of the whole working class united by a conviction that 'an injury to one is an injury to all'. The most powerful weapon available to the working class was the sympathetic strike that would expand industrial conflict in a widening battlefront. The basis of the union was the belief that worker solidarity was not simply a tactic but was a code of honour.[17]

The priority would be industrial struggle but the ITGWU rulebook also included a call for an Irish Labour Party to advance the political progress of the working class. The reality was that the greatest improvements in the condition of the working class were achieved through parliamentary action rather than strikes. Larkin well understood that state-imposed arbitration courts and laws governing improved working conditions were real and significant advances. The ITGWU rulebook looked for compulsory arbitration courts. The 1896 Conciliation Act encouraged voluntary industrial arbitration and the Board of Trade Conciliation Boards could be more effective, and less painful, in winning gains for workers than strikes.

The difficulty for Irish workers was that these measures were often simply not applied in Ireland. The National Insurance scheme, the centrepiece of the Asquith government's social reform programme, excited great interest amongst workers, and lectures explaining the 1912 scheme of insurance attracted large attendances in Dundalk and Drogheda.[18] Despite its popularity, the scheme was opposed by the *Irish Independent* newspaper, the Catholic hierarchy, the Irish medical profession and some of the Irish Parliamentary Party, leading to Ireland's inclusion in the unemployment benefits but exclusion from the medical benefits, with consequences for the Irish health service that are still evident today.

Fearon, McKeown and Dobbins immediately began a drive to recruit members for the ITGWU in Louth, mainly from the NUDL. Drogheda remained loyal to the NUDL, Dundalk No. 5 branch became one of the founding branches of the new union. This was an interesting reversal of the established pattern in which Dundalk looked to Belfast and Drogheda to Dublin. The ITGWU was announced in Dundalk as the 'Late Dockers' Union' and a handbill called on all unskilled workers on the railways, malt houses, breweries, distilleries, mills, stores and yards to 'join an Irish union'.[19] By Christmas 1911, McKeown claimed that 1,000 members had been recruited and to have organised in the breweries, the timber and coal merchants, and the brickworks in Dundalk. A comprehensive agreement on wages and conditions was negotiated with the McArdle Moore brewery.[20] Dundalk distillery also agreed on new wages and conditions, and labourers in the GNR won advances. Less successful was the attempt to organise the women in Carroll's cigarette factory. McKeown organised the women, bringing them out on strike in February 1912 in a demand for better conditions, but the strike was broken by Carroll's intransigence.[21]

Despite the strong opposition of the Drogheda NUDL delegates, the ITGWU was admitted to the ITUC annual meeting held in Dundalk in May 1910. This was the turning point for the ITGWU and for Irish labour as the traditional dominance of the craft and British-based unions was swept aside. On the motion of the ITGWU, the 1912 Congress agreed to the formation of an Irish Labour Party. The new title – Irish Trade Union Congress and Labour Party (ITUC&LP), or Congress-Party – reflected both the priority of the trade unions in the mobilisation of labour and the determination that labour would be a political force in a future Home Rule parliament.[22]

By the time of the 1913 Lockout the limits of sympathetic action were becoming evident as the leaders of capital mobilised against the new militancy. The NUR had suffered a severe defeat at the hands of William Goulding, Director of the GSWR, after taking sympathetic action in 1911. The British-based Shipping Federation organised ship owners in recruiting strike-breaking scabs to defeat the dock and transport trade unions.[23] In Dundalk port, an attempt to prevent the dismissal of a ship's mate by strike action was defeated. A strike for higher wages at Annagassan by workmen constructing a pier also failed, and a strike in a building yard in Drogheda led to the dismissal of the men and their instant replacement by willing strike breakers.[24]

The outbreak of foot-and-mouth disease also hit hard, severely disrupted farming, agricultural labour and transport, as cattle and pig exports were cut by half. Ironically, the Dublin 1913 Lockout led to a significant increase in work in Drogheda, Dundalk and Greenore ports as shipping was diverted away from Dublin to the Louth ports. P.T. Daly of the ITGWU visited Dundalk and Drogheda in November and tried to get the men to take sympathetic action. The men, having used the Dublin dispute to extract an increase in wages from the employer, refused to come out.[25] The 1913 Lockout revealed the difference within Irish nationalism on class and the social question. Generally, the republicans, cultural activists and advanced nationalists sided with the ITGWU, whilst the Catholic Church, the Irish Parliamentary Party and Arthur Griffith's Sinn Féin were hostile or silent.[26]

The 1913 Lockout in Dublin can be understood in the context of the 'Great Unrest' of 1911–14 in Great Britain, when trade disputes took on a national character, with large-scale mobilisation by both workers and industrial capital, eventually drawing the state into the developing class conflict. Whether the 'Great Unrest' held the possibility of a British social revolution is still debated, but what did happen was the emergence of an independent Labour Party in parliament, based on trade unions, and the beginning of the end for the Liberal Party.[27] The nineteenth-century two-party parliament of Conservatives and Liberals was being replaced by the twentieth-century Conservative- and Labour-dominated parliament. In Ireland, the period of the 'Great Unrest' saw not only large-scale industrial strife in Dublin and on the railways, but also the militarisation of Ulster Unionism in the Ulster Volunteer Force, Irish nationalism in the Irish Volunteers, Irish feminism in Cumann na mBan, and Irish labour in the Citizen Army. This period also saw, after the 1916 Rising, the beginnings of a national, if not a social, revolution.

The war that was confidently expected to be over 'by Christmas' was a severe disruption to the economy. Industry suffered the loss of labour due to the call-up and enlistment, whilst 'non-essential' trades suffered. Prices soared due to inflation whilst wages lagged far behind. This triggered waves of strikes. The government responded to labour unrest with increasing control over the economy and the workplace. The government, fearing the impact of strikes on war production, abandoned market forces in labour negotiation and, in the Munitions of War Act 1915, recognised collective bargaining on wages and conditions of employment and imposed an arbitration and conciliation scheme on employers. The 'war bonus' as a compensatory amount to offset inflation established a basic standard for periodic wage increases. State-appointed lawyers assessed the award, sweeping away the risk of industrial struggle.

Trade unions as a matter of course became the negotiators for labour. As a result, membership of trade unions soared. The war made the trade unions a powerful and well-organised force in Britain as the economic mobilisation for wartime production required their support, thus giving unprecedented bargaining strength to workers' claims. The linen works in Drogheda went onto 'short time'. A Trade Board for the Linen Industry was established to control the linen and cotton industry under the 1909 Trade Board Act, with the power to make obligatory orders on wages and conditions. The Belfast-based Textile Operatives Society of Ireland, organised by Mary Galway and representing the women workers in the mill, made huge progress in recruiting the women in the Drogheda mills.[28] Under the legislation the government made an order for a minimum wage for women workers as they began to move into industrial employment.[29]

In December 1916, after the British government refused to extend a compensatory 'war bonus' to Irish railways, the Irish local branches of the NUR, including Dundalk and Drogheda, threatened a national railway strike. The government in response took control of the entire Irish rail system and conceded the railway men the increase they demanded. The successful local action, taken in defiance of the British executive of the NUR, fuelled the demand for a local Irish railway workers' union.[30] In the Bourne Mills in Drogheda, the women in the weaving department struck for a higher war bonus and in Manisty's foundry in Dundalk, the moulders came out on strike because the foundry continued to employ a man who refused to join the union.[31]

Early in 1917, as agricultural labourers came out on strike in Louth and Meath, the Co. Louth Royal Irish Constabulary (RIC) District Inspector reported his unease at the rising level of industrial unrest, especially as he detected the growing influence of Sinn Féin in the labour organisations. In June 1917, the fitters, blacksmiths and turners at the GNR works in Dundalk struck in a demand for the same rate as Belfast. The company argued that Dundalk was traditionally paid the Dublin rate, then 48 shillings week, and not the Belfast rate of 55 shillings. The strike lasted six weeks and led to ninety-six of the men being brought to court and charged with 'taking part on a strike in connection with a difference as to the rate of wages affecting employment or in connection with munitions work'. With the high demand for their skills the men knew they could sit it out until, eventually, the Belfast rate was conceded and the strike ended.[32] The Louth County Council workmen, organised in local Labour Leagues at Lurgangreen, Dromiskin, Kilsaran and Stabannon, struck for an increase in wages and shorter hours.[33]

As the German U-boat war in the Atlantic threatened the convoys bringing food and armaments from across the British Empire and the United States into Britain, the security of the food supply became a critical issue. The inflation in food prices allied with food shortages and suspicion of profiteering raised social tensions. The Congress-Party annual conference in August 1917 approved a motion that food exports from Ireland be halted until a food census established the need and the available supply.[34] Sinn Féin, aided by the Irish Republican Army (IRA), led local land seizures, claiming that food exports threatened a new famine. Sinn Féin, working along with labour militants, established local food committees to prevent food exports. From February to March 1918, Drogheda Sinn Féin prohibited food exports from the port until a food census was completed. It seemed that Sinn Féin was being drawn into a social agitation led by labour and especially by the ITGWU. [35]

In response to the threat of a food shortage, the government imposed an unprecedented level of regulation on agriculture including compulsory tillage, guaranteed prices for grain, price controls on fertilisers and minimum wage orders. Under the Corn Production Act of April 1917, all occupiers of ten or more acres of arable land were required to cultivate 10 per cent more than they had in 1916. This order compelled the large graziers to set aside land for arable and either to employ extra labourers or let the land as conacre. This fuelled the demand for the breaking up of the grazier holdings.[36] In December 1917, Louth County Council 'called on the government to break up into economic holdings the lands in their possession and that we further request the government to insist on large graziers tilling a fair proportion of their lands'.[37] The implication was of course that only an independent national government could so act.

The outcome of these regulations was the creation, by the government, of the Agricultural Wages Board (AWB) to set wage rates. Made up of six representatives of the farmers, six representatives of the labourers and four government nominees, the AWB divided the whole of Great Britain and Ireland into regions and established a schedule of wage rates for each region. The ITGWU was hugely successful in recruiting the Irish agricultural labourers and in representing them on the AWB negotiations. Between its creation in September 1917 and its cessation in September 1921, the AWB for Ireland held forty-seven meetings and made nine orders fixing minimum wages and valuing benefits such as board and lodging. Louth and Meath formed one District Wages Committee. The 1,400 objections lodged by farmer representatives suggest that the agricultural labourer found the protection of the state a most powerful weapon in improving wages and conditions.[38]

By 1918, labour was showing its strength as mobilisation moved beyond wages and conditions to politics. The high point came in resistance to the threat of conscription in April 1918. Faced with Ludendorff's offensive on the Western Front, the British government extended the existing system of conscription in Britain to older men and formerly exempt groups of workers. Lloyd George also proposed to introduce conscription for the first time to Ireland. Objections to conscription were expressed by all shades of nationalist opinion but it was the labour movement that led effective resistance. On 23 April, a general strike, the first in Western Europe, was called and led by the Labour Congress-Party.[39] Work stopped on the railways, docks, factories and mills across

Co. Louth. In Drogheda, the anti-conscription strike was followed by a two-day strike by the building workers who refused to work with men who had not come out on strike on the day.[40] The conscription crisis was used by the ITGWU to establish itself in Drogheda where the NUDL was still dominant.

In June 1918, Thomas Foran and William O'Brien led a meeting in Drogheda to form a branch of the Union, both speakers emphasising the role that Labour would have to play in the event of conscription being enforced. William O'Brien also called on the executed James Connolly's (and now no longer Larkin's) idea of the 'one great National Union' to defend the country's interests and the welfare of the democracy. A new branch with 200 members was established and admitted to the Drogheda Trades' Council with Joseph Loughran as president, Tom Behan as secretary and Edward Mullen, Eamonn Rooney and Michael Connor as leading activists.[41] By November 1918, the Co. Louth RIC District Inspector was reporting with growing concern the confluence of labour and republican activism that fed the

> strong under-current of unrest among labourers partly owing to the cost of living but chiefly owing to political propaganda by Sinn Féin and the Irish Transport Union. Labour shows a tendency to organise and assert itself and Sinn Féin is fostering a spirit of unrest. Labour, particularly the mechanical and artisans is strongly Sinn Féin, efforts are being made to organize the farm labourers and this promises to meet with some success.[42]

Workers were striking at Drogheda Milling, the Boyne Spinning Mills and Usshers Mills, and the farm labourers were also on strike, all organised by the ITGWU. Strikes were now being used to force or accelerate arbitration and to draw the state in as conciliator between capital and labour. The IRA at this time also saw labour as a key part of the revolutionary struggle, advising its Volunteers to prepare for the pending general election by supporting 'every movement which makes for the building up of a free and prosperous Ireland: the political republican movement, the language movement, *the movement for the rights of the working class* [my emphasis] and the Irish industrial movement'.[43] In the eyes of republicans, the status of the ITGWU had been transformed by the 1916 Rising. Exhausted by the 1913 Lockout and the departure of

Larkin to the United States, it seemed to be beaten. The leading role in 1916 played by James Connolly and the Irish Citizen Army, the shelling of Liberty Hall and the internment of the leadership, placed the Union at the foundation of the Republic. The Union had now acquired an unassailable legitimacy within revolutionary and republican circles.[44]

The Union, dominated by William O'Brien, who saw the ITGWU as an industrial rather than a political organisation, concentrated on building a mass membership rather than a mass political consciousness as expressed in the Labour Party. In 1914, the ITGWU had 15,000 members. By 1919, it had 102,823 members and was the dominant union in Congress.[45] The Congress grew its affiliated membership from 100,000 in 1917 to 225,000 in 1920. The number of local Trade Councils had grown in the same period from seven to sixteen.

When the general election was called, the Labour Party-Congress decided to withdraw from the election and leave the field clear for Sinn Féin. The decision of the Party-Congress not to contest the general election in December 1918 has been a subject of debate ever since.[46] Although Labour did not contest the election, Thomas Johnson (leader of the Labour Party) and William O'Brien (of the ITGWU) did compose a radical 'Democratic Programme' for the revolutionary Dáil. But they then allowed Seán T. O'Kelly to purge it of its radicalism and present an anodyne version to the Dáil and the world.[47] Nor did the Party-Congress at any point recognise the revolutionary Dáil Éireann as the legitimate government of Ireland. The advantages of continuing to work within the apparently 'worker-friendly' British state were not to be abandoned, as working with the British Wages Board was almost the only way to secure wage increases. The tensions between Labour's industrial and political ambitions were clearly drawn.

However, the Irish Labour delegation to the Berne International Conference of the Socialist International in February 1919 pressed successfully for international support for 'Irish self-determination' whilst also voting with the more radical pro-Bolshevik faction of the International demand for the 'dictatorship of the proletariat' against the Social-Democratic opinion favouring parliamentary democracy.[48] Underestimating the popular appetite for change, radicalism within the Party-Congress would be confined to foreign policy whilst domestic policy would be cautious and conservative.[49] Across Europe, a revolutionary wave seemed to be triumphantly replicating the Russian Bolshevik's success in creating a new workers' society. As Ireland entered its national revolution, the working class was well versed in the syndicalist tactics of the sympathetic strike and also the general strike, but now also had a revolutionary model in the Russian 'Soviet'.[50]

In Britain, in the aftermath of the war, the government and employers immediately began an aggressive fight back against the trade unions. The Scottish TUC along with the Clyde Workers' Committee went on strike in April 1919 for a forty-hour week but was defeated by the arrest of the strike leaders and the deployment of police and troops in the docks. In 1920, unrest grew on the London docks and amongst the miners and railwaymen. However, the collapse of solidarity amongst the 'Triple Alliance' of transport, railway and mining unions on 'Black Friday', 15 April 1921, when only the miners came out on strike, cleared the way for the decontrol of the mines and railways and a full attack on wages. The government led the way with the 'Geddes Axe' reductions in civil service salaries followed by cuts in the education and housing budget. In Ireland, as the national revolution unfolded, the government was less confident in confronting labour and the trade unions were more successful in resisting cuts.

The first display of defiance made by labour in Co. Louth was on May Day 1919. The British army and the RIC in Drogheda anticipated that May Day would be a display of pro-Russian socialism and warned that it would be immediately proclaimed an illegal assembly if there was any display of the emblems of socialism. There would no 'Red Clydeside' in Drogheda! The Trades Council decided to abandon the procession but the ITGWU, led by Eamonn Rooney, went ahead. Rooney was the Union organiser for the agricultural labourers in Co. Meath. Headed by four bands, the procession passed through the town amidst a sea of red flags and trade union banners with the tricolour also being flown. Eamonn Rooney addressed the parade saying, in reference to the Wilsonian League of Nations, that a league of peoples and not of governments was wanted. He denounced the Trades Council and went on to say that the workers would never be intimidated by a few policemen and would never allow a policeman to tell them what colour of flag they could fly.[51]

In Dundalk, the GNR railwaymen stayed at work on the trains but the men in the locomotive workshops paraded, led by the Emmet Band, carrying red flags. The RIC did not interfere. The May Day climb-down was then used by the ITGWU, led by Eamonn Rooney, to purge the Trades Council, hitherto dominated by the craft unions. Michael McGowan of the British-based Postmen's Federation, the president of the Trades Council and Mayor of Drogheda, was voted down and a new council dominated by the transport union, 'men not afraid to carry the Red Flag', took control.[52] It is worth emphasising that it was the Red Flag and not the 'Sinn Féin' tricolour that dominated the parade, and Petrograd in 1917 was more significant than Dublin in 1916. McGowan was later a founder member of the Irish Post Office Workers' Union in 1922.

Rooney convinced the IRA Volunteers in Meath to engage with the cause of the agricultural labourers, despite the warning from headquarters to the Volunteers not to get involved in labour disputes. Rooney, using his NUR contacts, made the IRA aware that the British military, in response to a request from the Meath Farmers' Union, was bringing in extra soldiers to assist in breaking the strike. The IRA, anxious that an increased military presence might smother IRA activity, agreed to sabotage the rail line and succeeded in derailing the train. The agricultural labourers' strike was successfully settled in the aftermath of that operation.[53]

Labour, it seemed, was surging ahead as the Labour Party-Congress and ITGWU held their annual meetings in August 1919 in Drogheda. The address by the Lord Mayor, McGowan (the same that had been voted down by the Trades Council), at the welcoming civic reception confidently stated that 'the cry "Long Live the People" will resound above the Babel of capitalist interests'.[54] The Crown forces' response to the republican campaign was to launch an economic war, burning creameries and co-ops and destroying the rural economy. Prominent local members of Sinn Féin were targeted but, initially, labour activists were not.

In August 1920, the Dundalk Sinn Féin hall and the licensed premises of the Sinn Féin councillor, John McGuill, were sacked and looted.[55] In Co. Louth, however, ITGWU officials also came under attack from Crown forces. Charles F. Ridgeway, a Protestant radical republican from Belfast, was a prominent and effective organiser for the Union in the Louth–Monaghan area. A highly talented writer, under the pen-name Cefar, he wrote for the labour newspaper the Voice of Labour. He was detained by the RIC in Monaghan and threatened with being summarily shot as a renegade Protestant, a socialist and an ITGWU activist.[56] Gilbert Lynch, a Lancashire-born republican and trade unionist who had been in the GPO in 1916, was his fellow ITGWU organiser for Co. Louth.[57]

In Galway city, where he was branch secretary for the ITGWU, Lynch had been badly beaten up by the Black and Tans. The Union had moved him to Louth for his safety along with Denis Houston, who had escaped the attentions of the Auxiliaries. Lynch also acted as a judge in the local Sinn Féin courts. Clearly, the Black and Tans and the Auxiliaries now regarded trade union activists as members of the IRA. With the creation of the B-Special constabulary in November 1920, ahead of Partition, Union organising in Newry and Armagh became increasingly hazardous.[58]

The national strikes in support of the political prisoners, called by the ITGWU for 12 April 1920, were strongly supported in Co. Louth. The Dundalk power station staff came out, cutting off the light and power to the town. At the Dundalk railway works, columns of strikers moved through the yards and station, enforcing the strike. Paradoxically, this display of worker power culminated in a rally and recital of the Rosary in St Patrick's Church.[59] Alarmed at the growing mobility of the IRA units, in November 1919, the British army required all motor vehicle drivers to apply for a permit from the military authorities. The intent was to ensure only the loyal could have mobility. It led to a strike against the permits led by the ITGWU and the Irish Automobile Drivers & Mechanics Trade Union.[60] Mainly a Dublin strike, it was observed in Dundalk where the strikers held up traffic from Newry and Armagh and forced the drivers to return.[61] The Belfast boycott, in support of the Catholic workers expelled from the shipyards, was enforced in Dundalk and Drogheda, with the support of the Louth County Council.[62] On Dundalk docks the workers boycotted the firm of Wordie and Co., a Belfast-based company that distributed goods from the train station for loading onto ships and into Dundalk town, despite the Trades Council accepting the assurances that the company was a model employer of Catholics.[63]

The main political strike was by the NUR railwaymen in the 'Munitions of War' strike that lasted from June to December 1920. The original inspiration for the Munitions strike was the 'Hands Off Russia' campaign by the London dockers, who successfully led a workers' boycott of all munitions destined for the White Russian forces in Poland. The Irish members of the London-based NUR initiated a similar boycott of arms destined for Ireland, without London support. The strike began in May when the Dublin dockers refused to unload military supplies from a steamer.[64] The supplies were unloaded by the military and transferred to trains. NUR drivers then refused to work the train. The cause was taken up by the NUR Irish membership despite the opposition of the Union President J.H. Thomas, who now opposed the use of the strike weapon for political purposes.

The strike soon extended to refusing to drive trains that carried armed RIC or British army personnel. The railway companies then dismissed the crew although the men were technically not on strike as they agreed to operate all other traffic. By August, thousands of railwaymen had been dismissed. The authorities responded by putting pressure on both the railway workmen and the companies. Armed soldiers and RIC men were ordered to board trains up and down the country, leading the driver and crew to walk off, leaving the train stranded.[65] The companies were fined for failing to fulfil their public service obligations. Louth County Council strongly supported the railwaymen and pledged to support them. A 'Munitions Strike Fund' in Dundalk raised £240 in July. The government was determined to break the strike by shutting down the system if necessary. By September, the Dundalk–Enniskillen line was closed.

The strikers held out until the end of the year, mainly due to the full support of the general public, though some intimidation of strike-breakers did occur.[66] A feature of the strike was the rift that opened up between the railwaymen, north and south.[67] Despite the *Dundalk Examiner* urging a fight to the finish, the government strategy of throttling the whole network, thus isolating towns and stifling trade, worked and the strike ended in December.[68] The leadership of the strike remained with the trade union and though the IRA welcomed it, very little was done to assist. Strikes were never a part of the republican strategy. Through 1919, a wave of strikes across Co. Louth signalled the developing struggle on wages with industrial employers; in Cahill's printers and in the laundry in Drogheda, in Manisty's foundry and the distillery in Dundalk, and on the docks in both ports.[69]

The end of the Great War also transformed working conditions on the land as the state withdrew from managing the food economy. On the land, farmers began immediately to switch from tillage back to grassland, reducing the opportunity for rural employment. The abolition of the Agricultural Wages Board by the British government in October 1920 freed farmers to attack the agricultural labourers. The Irish Farmers' Union switched from resistance to government regulation to become an anti-Union strike-breaking force. At the same time, the withdrawal of the RIC from rural areas led to an increase in agrarian land seizures with local IRA units prominent in the initial seizures. The Dáil, anxious that the land question should not obscure the national question, decreed in July 1920 a cessation to all agrarian violence, saying, 'all our energies must be directed toward clearing out – not the occupier of this or that piece of land – but the foreign invader of our country'.[70]

The Dáil established a National Land Bank in direct response to the fear that the land agitation was diverting the mind of the people from the struggle for freedom by a class war.[71] The decree had limited effect in Co. Louth as a wealthy landowner, R.A. Gradwell, called on the Dáil for protection against land seizures. Protection was granted by the local IRA but then withdrawn when Gradwell refused to recognise the validity of the republican courts examining the agrarian claims.[72] In Dundalk, cattle were driven off the land of Mr Hearty, a grazier.[73] By the spring of 1921, the Labour Party-Congress was calling for the reintroduction of compulsory tillage by Dáil Éireann.

Trade unions now found themselves on the defensive and struggling to maintain the gains made under wartime conditions as employers pressed for pay cuts. New white-collar unions, such as the Irish Bank Officials' Association and the Irish Local Government Officers' Trade Union, emerged in the clerical sector and in local government.[74] In May 1920, a new Irish union for craft workers was launched, the Irish Engineering, Shipbuilding and Foundry Trades Union (IES&FTU), the forerunner to the Technical, Engineering and Electrical Union (TEEU) of today. This was an Irish Republican Brotherhood (IRB) -inspired Irish breakaway from the British Amalgamated Society of Engineers. This was an exclusively Irish union of craft workers that recruited with some success amongst the craft workers in Dundalk railway works.[75] Dáil Éireann, as a revolutionary counter state, had taken on the task of developing an arbitration and conciliation system for industrial workers. The expectations may have been that as a revolutionary government the Dáil would be on the side of labour. The limitations of the Dáil's social vision and the inherent conservatism of its members soon became apparent.

In the Dáil, de Valera dismissed the Democratic Programme as one that 'contemplated a situation somewhat different from that in which they actually found themselves', and so, 'while the foreigner occupied the country', labour must wait.[76] The Dáil decreed National Arbitration

Courts in June 1919 under Countess Markievicz's Ministry of Labour, notifying each Sinn Féin cumainn of the establishment of a National Conciliation Board for the settlement of industrial disputes.[77] After the local elections in January and June 1920, Sinn Féin and Labour dominated the local authorities across Ireland. These then declared allegiance to Dáil Éireann and refused to recognise the authority of the British Local Government Board. In Dundalk Urban District, Peter Toner, R. Minogue, James Coburn and Felix McGee were returned as Labour councillors. In Drogheda, the ITGWU members, Eamonn Rooney and Edward Mullen, who were prominent in the 'Red Flag' processions of May Day 1919, were returned to the Corporation as 'Workers' Republic' councillors, a deliberate echo of the title of James Connolly's newspaper *Workers' Republic*.

In the county council election in June 1920, two Trade and Labour candidates were successful as Sinn Féin swept to dominance.[78] Drogheda Borough Council, Dundalk Urban Council, Dundalk Rural Council and the Drogheda Board of Guardians all declared for Dáil Éireann.[79] Local authorities were key for labour organisation as they were sensitive to electoral pressure, as well being important in setting local wage rates for the unskilled and in providing work and easing unemployment. It was expected that these Sinn Féin and Labour-dominated local authorities would set a benchmark for wages and for normalising the Dáil conciliation and arbitration scheme. Dundalk Urban District Council had already agreed that claims from the council employees could only be made through a trade union.[80] Drogheda Urban District Council had preferred arbitration to confrontation and had generally referred wage claims to arbitration by the Industrial Department of the British Ministry of Labour.[81] The decision to refer to the Dáil Éireann conciliation board was therefore simply a relocation of the process, though it may have been expected the Dáil Éireann board would be more pro-labour. In fact, the Dáil Ministry of Labour arbitration board was largely inactive and the Ministry was mainly engaged in finding work for former policemen and for unemployed Volunteers.[82]

The July 1921 truce between the IRA and the Crown forces brought little relief to workers. The ITGWU had previously been in dispute with Wordie and Co. when the company tried to ignore the Belfast boycott. Wordie and Co. attempted to enforce the reduced Belfast rate on the Dundalk workers in the weeks after the truce was called. The

ITGWU called the men out on strike and arranged with local traders that the Union would ensure delivery of supplies. One local merchant, Patrick Moore, had a picket placed on his premises when he refused to work with the Union. Moore then called on family connections with the local IRA in an attempt to intimidate the pickets. The intimidation failed, but it signalled a worrying development.[83]

Labour began to demand shorter hours and higher wages in the local authorities. Before the First World War, road maintenance work had traditionally been put out to contract with the local farmers on a yearly basis, with details on the length of road and the quantity of stone required. The war economy created prosperity for the farmers and they lost interest in the roadworks. The local authorities then used direct labour for the work. The ITGWU organised the road workers and negotiated good rates. Drogheda Borough Council agreed to take a claim for a wage increase jointly lodged by the Dockers Union and the ITGWU to the Dáil Éireann conciliation board.[84] With the end of the war the farmers began to look for the restoration of the pre-war contract scheme.[85] By the end of 1921, as the slump hit, the ITGWU was urging Louth County Council to relieve distress by employing as many as possible on the direct-labour roadworks scheme.[86]

The Union had in fact already achieved its high point in Co. Louth in 1921. It had an estimated 3,689 members organised in eight branches: Ardee, Drogheda, Dundalk, Greenore, Kilsaran, Knockbridge, Louth and Ravensdale. The distribution of branches suggests that the Union organised most successfully amongst the agricultural labourers in the rural county, along with the unskilled labourers in Dundalk and Drogheda. These were workers who relied on the local authorities for occasional and casual employment on roadworks. In Drogheda, the ITGWU was to remain locked into a competitive struggle with the British-based NUDL, that later merged into the Amalgamated Transport and General Workers' Union (ATGWU). This competitive struggle did neither union any good.[87] The 'Red Flag' militants had a last mobilisation as the Irish Engineers and Industrial Union, seized control of Grendon's foundry in Drogheda in September 1921 and declared a 'soviet', but with no support and no strategy for spreading the action it soon fizzled out.[88]

A special meeting of Louth County Council on 2 January 1922 supported the Treaty with all the Labour councillors in agreement.[89] On 16 January 1922, Dublin Castle was handed over to the Provisional

Government, signalling the end of British rule. With the establishing of the Provisional Government the British administration began a hurried departure from Ireland, including the Ministry of Labour's arbitration scheme that was discontinued from 1 April. Though it took some time to be apparent the tide was turning against labour in the new independent Ireland. At a special conference in February 1922, the Party-Congress, the largest labour organisation in Ireland, acted as if the Treaty was a distraction to the central task of establishing the Workers' Republic. Speakers called for the seizure of the land, but for its working to be on a communal basis rather than fragmented small holdings. Gilbert Lynch, for the Dundalk ITGWU, outlined the difficulty that workers in Dundalk found themselves in now as it became a frontier town competing with lower wages and longer hours across the new border. Gilbert also spoke on the need for the Labour Party to contest all elections at parliamentary and local elections if it was going to achieve the Workers' Republic.[90] The Labour Party-Congress worked to prevent the descent into civil war over the Treaty. Asserting itself as a political force it called for a general strike 'against militarism' on 24 April 1922. This, the last general strike of the revolutionary period, was fully supported in Co. Louth.

Meanwhile, the retreat from the ground won in the years of struggle was unrelenting. In Drogheda, the Dáil arbitrator found for the corporation against the workers in its decision to reduce wages.[91] In February 1922, when the corporation workers rejected a further reduction in wages, the corporation, confident which side the Dáil would take, insisted the question of the reduction should go to arbitration.[92] The request from the Drogheda Trades Council for the corporation to set up an anti-profiteering committee was considered and rejected.[93] In Dundalk, the county council agreed to a direct-labour scheme at the suggestion of the ITGWU to relieve unemployment, but only if the men agreed a reduction in wages.[94] On the docks, the ITGWU was more successful in briefly holding back wages cuts, but by 1923 were in retreat there as well.[95] The Labour Party did spectacularly well in the June 1922 general election, suggestive of a continuing appetite for radial change within the working class, with seventeen of its eighteen candidates elected to the Dáil. In the Louth–Meath Constituency, Cathal O'Shannnon topped the poll, despite being identified as an atheistic pro-Bolshevik and a promoter of soviet-style direct action by the working class, receiving nearly 14,000 first preferences.[96]

The Civil War eased the pressure on wages but also made the Dáil irrelevant as state power moved to the military command of the National Army in Beggars Bush Barracks. As the Provisional Government refused to call the elected TDs to assemble, claiming it would too dangerous, the Labour Party-Congress threatened to resign en masse. The Third Dáil met eventually in early September to debate and approve the Free State Constitution. It was dissolved in August 1923. In the subsequent elections to the Fourth Dáil, Labour's vote collapsed. In the Louth three-seat constituency, Cathal O'Shannon came bottom of the poll. Labour, it would appear, was now identified as an ineffectual protest party rather than a party of radical change, and certainly not the party to win a Workers' Republic. On the land, the Special Infantry Corps of the National Army established specifically to tackle agrarian disorder and dismantle land seizures, ruthlessly suppressed the resurgence of agrarian class war that had emerged in the Civil War.[97] The employers, organised in the Dublin Employers' Emergency Committee, began a national mobilisation to attack the sympathetic action strike, the only effective weapon of labour.[98]

In October 1921, during the truce, the Socialist Party of Ireland (SPI) was taken over by Roddy Connolly and became the Communist Party of Ireland (CPI). Cathal O'Shannon was purged as a 'reformer'. The CPI attracted the political radicals within the ITGWU. The Comintern encouraged these radicals to move beyond the trade union-based tactics of syndicalism and develop a revolutionary political strategy. Within the Labour Party-Congress, the CPI members attempted to take the labour movement leftward and into the Moscow-led Communist International and away from the Social-Democatic Second International. In this attempt, Eamonn Rooney played a leading part. As the Congress executive pleaded that the disorganisation within the socialist parties of the world suggested non-affiliation to either International, Rooney challenged this 'specious neutrality' and urged labour to align with the Comintern.[99] Rooney, a Drogheda-based organiser in the ITGWU, was a member of the CPI and also a member of the Irish Communist Groups on the Comintern with the cover name 'Black'.[100] The communists anticipated that the Treaty would split the republican movement into left and right wings creating an opportunity to lead the left faction into a Bolshevik-style anti-imperialist revolution. For Eamonn Rooney, the ITGWU was the key organisation. It seemed possible to take the industrial militancy expressed in syndicalism and direct it toward a Bolshevik-style political vanguardism using the anti-Treaty IRA. When this failed, the return of Larkin on 30 April 1923 generated a brief false hope that he could once again resurrect the cause of labour.

With his ambitions focused on becoming the Irish representative in the Communist International, Larkin now proved as destructive a force as he had been creative in the formative years of the ITGWU. His Irish Worker League was damaging to the political left, organised in the CPI. His struggle to regain control of the ITGWU led to his suspension as General Secretary and then expulsion. Larkin launched a bitter attack on both the ITGWU leadership and the Party-Congress leading eventually to the formation of the breakaway Workers Union of Ireland (WUI). At the time when labour most needed to be united the split was catastrophic.[101] In Co. Louth, the WUI proved hugely damaging to the ITGWU as it organised as a 'Larkinite' union. M.P. Whittle, branch secretary in Dundalk, went over to the WUI bringing with him the Dundalk, Greenore, Carlingford and Knockbridge membership.[102] Denis Houston, ITGWU organiser since the foundation of the union, wrote to Liberty Hall detailing the collapse in branches. Kilsaran was down to twelve members and he was trying, with little success, to build up numbers through organising the men working on the roads and farms.[103]

The period 1912–23 created the most favourable conditions for labour militancy. The first developments of the British welfare state and the demands of the Great War aligned the state with the demands of the working class for higher wages and a better life. The Irish revolution created a republican counter state that also, as it seemed, was prepared to align with the working class. Internationally, the Russian Revolution and the wave of revolutionary movements across Europe created a model that inspired an increasingly radicalised labour. The resurgence of trade unionism, especially the ITGWU, gave an organisational base for direct action and the 'soviet' occupations. However, these were extraordinarily fortuitous and fleeting circumstances. The defence of wages and conditions, which forged unity across the working class of Co. Louth in the period 1912–23, was organised in the broadly democratic and egalitarian trade union movement. Connecting that sort of movement with the elitism of the national revolution, or the vanguardism of the communists, proved an impossible challenge.[104] With the end of the Great War, the state brought its power to bear on forcing down wages. Irish labour soon cooled on the attractions of the Bolshevik model. The Free State army was used to smash the remnants of the soviets.

Most telling of all, the republican revolutionaries with whom labour militants had made common cause proved to be very limited in their ambitions and revolutionary vision. In an early debate on industrial policy in the revolutionary Dáil, Minister for Industries Ernest Blythe asserted that the government of the republic 'would of course discourage the exploitation of Irish industries by foreign capitalists by every means in their power'. The implication, which was missed by the labour movement, was that republican government would not have any problem with exploitation by native capitalists.[105]

In 1912, it would have seemed probable that Co. Louth was about to experience industrial 'lift off' powered by its location midway between Belfast and Dublin. Dundalk, that had always looked toward Belfast, was already an important centre for railway engineering and was developing as a hub for the intersection of the Sligo–Greenore and Dublin–Belfast railways. Drogheda, that looked toward Dublin, was developing as an important port feeding into the railway network. Partition, by locating Dundalk and Drogheda at the periphery of newly independent Ireland, cut off this development, turning Louth from a central to a border county. The WUI declined but the ITGWU survived with strong organisation. The British-based ATGWU grew in both Drogheda and Dundalk, building on local loyalties to the older pre-partition NUDL. County Louth, with a rich working-class culture, a long tradition of trade unionism and a complex working class of the rural and urban, skilled and unskilled, was a relatively inactive area for the national revolution, yet proved an area of intense labour struggle.

But working-class militancy was primarily in defence of existing wages and conditions. As the post-war economic depression led to wage cuts and the erosion of conditions, partition cut the links with the wider labour movement in Belfast, and Dublin and localism prevailed. The difficulty of connecting labour militancy with the revolutionary nationalist objective of overthrowing the state could be overcome, as was shown in working-class support within Co. Louth for the general strikes against conscription, and in support of the prisoners on hunger strike as well as the 'Munitions of War' strike. The failure of labour to steer the national revolution or even to insert a social demand is striking. However, that failure does not mean it was not attempted.[106]

NOTES

1   Michael Hopkinson, *The Irish War of Independence* (Dublin: Gill & Macmillan, 2002), pp. 146–7.

2   Diarmaid Ferriter, *A nation and not a rabble: the Irish Revolution 1913–1923* (London: Profile Books, 2015), p. 7.

3   Natasha Claire Grayson, 'The quality of nationalism in Counties Cavan, Louth, and Meath during the Irish Revolution' (PhD thesis, 2007, Keele University) Claire Fitzpatrick, 'Nationalising the ideal: Labour and Nationalism in Ireland, 1909–1923', in Eugenio F. Biagini (ed.), *Citizenship and community liberals, radicals and collective identities in the British Isles, 1865–1931* (Cambridge: CUP, 1996), pp. 276–304.

4   Emmet O'Connor, *Syndicalism in Ireland 1917–1923* (Cork: Cork University Press, 1988), pp. xi–xix.

5   For the industrial development of Louth, see Colin Rynne, *Industrial Ireland 1750–1930* (Cork: Cork University Press, 2006); Harold O'Sullivan (ed.), *Irish historical towns atlas, No. 16: Dundalk* (Dublin: Royal Irish Academy, 2006); Richard Gerrard, *The mill: a history of Usher's linen mill, Greenhills, Drogheda and the people who worked there 1836–1993* (Drogheda: Anglo Printers, 2013); Maureen Wilson, 'The railways of Dundalk', *Tempest's Annual*, 1975–6; Jack McQuillan, *The railway town: the story of the Great Northern Railway Works and Dundalk* (Dundalk: Dun Dealgan Press, 1993); 'Manistys Dundalk Iron Works', *County Louth Archaeological and Historical Society Journal*, 23(3) 1995; Charlie Flynn, 'Dundalk: an oral history' (PhD thesis, 2000, NUI Maynooth).

6   Census of Ireland 1911, Co. Louth, Table XX, 'occupation of males'.

7   Laurence Marley, *Michael Davitt, freelance radical and frondeur* (Dublin: Four Courts Press, 2007), pp. 104–5.

8   Dan Bradley, *Farm labourers: Irish struggle 1900–1976* (Belfast: Athol Books, 1988), pp. 15–20.

9   Bradley, *Farm labourers*, Table 4(a), p. 22; Enda McKay, 'The housing of the rural labourers 1883–1916', *Saothar Journal of the Irish Labour History Society*, 17 (1992), pp. 27–38.

10 Frank Gallagher, 'Drogheda's early trade unions', in *Journal of the Old Drogheda Society*, 13 (2001), pp. 7–22; Moira Corcoran and Peter Durnin, *The Drogheda Banners: aspects of the history of Drogheda Number 5* (Drogheda: Old Drogheda Society, 2001).

11 Frank Gallagher, 'Founding of the Drogheda Council of Trade Unions – new research', *Journal of the Old Drogheda Society*, 18 (2011), pp. 61–70.

12 Francis Devine, *Organising history: a centenary of SIPTU, 1909–2009* (Dublin: Gill & Macmillan, 2009), pp. 1–2.

13 Conor McCabe, 'The Amalgamated Society of Railwaymen and the National Union of Railwaymen in Ireland 1911–1923' (PhD thesis, 2006, University of Ulster).

14 Charles Callan, 'The Painters of Drogheda and Co. Louth 1860–1920', *Journal of the Old Drogheda Society*, 13 (2001), pp. 149–66.

15 Laurence Marley, 'Michael McKeown', in Emmet O'Connor and John Cunningham (eds), *Studies in Irish radical leadership: lives on the left* (Manchester: MUP, 2016), pp. 71–84.

16 Bill McCamley, *The third James: James Fearon, 1874–1924. An unsung hero of our struggle, Studies in Irish Labour History 4* (Dublin: SIPTU and ILHS, 2000).

17 Emmet O'Connor, *Big Jim Larkin: hero or wrecker?* (Dublin: UCD Press, 2015), pp. 52–72.

18 The National Archives, London (TNA), Colonial Office (CO) 904, Chief Inspector's Confidential Monthly Report (CICMR), Co. Louth, 1 Jun. 1912.

19   Louth County Archives Services, PP240/6/2 'ITGWU Handbill'.

20   Louth County Archive Services, PP240/6/2 'ITGWU to McArdle Moore & Co.', 21 Sept. 1911.

21   Devine, *Organising history*, pp. 28–9.

22   The title of the organisation changed to reflect the shifting emphasis between political and industrial. In 1912, it was the Irish Trade Union Congress and Labour Party (called Congress-Party in this essay), then in 1918, the Irish Labour Party and Trade Union Congress (Party-Congress in this essay).

23   McCabe, 'The Amalgamated Society of Railwaymen and the National Union of Railwaymen in Ireland 1911–1923', pp. 16–54.

24   TNA, CO 904/86 CICMR, Co. Louth, 1 Mar. 1912, 1 Apr. 1913, 1 May 1913.

25   TNA CO 904/86 CICMR, Co. Louth, 1 Dec. 1913.

26   O'Connor, *Big Jim Larkin*, p. 144.

27   W.S. Adams, 'Lloyd George and the Labour Movement', *Past and Present*, 3 (1953), pp. 55–64.

28   William Mulligan, 'Forging a better world: socialists and international politics in the early twentieth century' in Paul Daly, Rónán O'Brien, Paul Rouse (eds), *Making the difference: socialists and international politics in the early twentieth century* (Cork: Cork University Press, 2012), pp. 54–66; Theresa Moriarty, 'Work, warfare and wages: industrial controls and Irish trade unionism in the First World War', in Adrain Gregory and Senia Paseta (eds), *Ireland and the Great War: 'A War to Unite Us All'* (Manchester: MUP, 2002), p. 79.

29   Louth County Archives Services, Dundalk Urban District Council minutes, DUDC/MB/1/3 'LGB letter ref women wages minimum', 11 Jul. 1916.

30   McCabe, 'The Irish railway unions, p. 64.

31   TNA, CO 904/86 CICMR, Co. Louth, Jul. 1918.

32   TNA, CO 904/ CICMR, Co. Louth, Mar., Apr., Jun. 1917; *Dundalk Democrat*, 1 and 23 Jun., 21 Jul. 1917.

33   Louth County Archives Services, Louth County Council minutes, LCC/MB/2/10, 'County Council Workmen', 19 Mar. 1917.

34   ILP & TUC, 23rd Annual Congress (Derry) 6–8 Aug. 1917, pp. 273–95.

35   John Borgonovo, '"A Soviet in Embryo": Cork's food crisis and the People's Food Committee 1917–18', *Saothar Journal of the Irish Labour History Society*, 34 (2009), pp. 21–38.

36   Dooley, 'Land and the people', in Alvin Jackson (ed.) *The Oxford handbook of modern Irish history* (Oxford: OUP, 2014), pp. 107–25.

37   Louth County Archives Services, LCC/MB/1/5, 'Motion on compulsory tillage', 6 Dec. 1917.

38   Agricultural Wages Board for Ireland (Corn Production Act, 1917), *Report on the Period September 1917 to September 1921.*

39   Arthur Mitchell, *Labour in Irish politics, 1890–1930: the Irish labour movement in an age of revolution* (Dublin: Irish University Press, 1974), pp. 87–8; Devine, *Organising history* pp. 117–18.

40   Moriarty, 'Work, warfare and wages', in Adrian Gregory and Senia Paseta (eds), *Ireland and the Great War*, pp. 73–93.

41   Frank Gallagher, 'Liberty Hall, Peter Street: the foundation of the ITGWU in Drogheda', *Old Drogheda Society*, 19 (2012), pp. 69–94.

42   TNA, CO 904/90, CICMR Co. Louth, Nov. 1918.

43   *An tÓglách*, vol. 1, no. 5, 30 Sept. 1918.

44   Niamh Puirséil, *The Labour Party 1922–73* (Dublin: UCD Press, 2007), p. 8.

45 Devine, *Organising history*, Appendix 7.
46 Mitchell, *Labour in Irish politics*, pp. 91–103.
47 Military Archives, Cathal Brugha Barracks (MA), Bureau of Military History (BMH), Witness Statement (WS). 1765, part 2, 'Seán T. O'Kelly'; Emmet O'Connor, 'Neither democratic nor a programme: the democratic programme of 1919', *Irish Historical Studies*, 40 (157) (2016), 92–109.
48 ILP & TUC, Report of the twenty-fifth annual meeting, Drogheda, Aug. 1919.
49 Emmet O'Connor, 'Hail Russia! Labour and the Bolshevik Revolution', *Saothar Journal of the Irish Labour History Society*, 42 (2017), forthcoming.
50 Emmet O'Connor, '"The Age of the Red Republic": The Irish Left and Nationalism 1909-36', *Saothar Journal of the Irish Labour History Society*, 30 (2005), pp. 73–82.
51 *Drogheda Independent*, 10 May 1919.
52 Frank Gallagher, 'May Day 1919 – Drogheda's Red Flag Revolt', *Journal of the Old Drogheda Society*, 21 (2014), pp. 119–34; *Irish Times*, 2 May 1919.
53 MA, BMH, WS.901, 'Seamus Finn'.
54 ILP & TUC, Report of the twenty-fifth annual meeting, Drogheda, 4–8 Aug. 1919.
55 *Irish Bulletin*, 2(82), 27 Aug. 1920.
56 ILP & TUC, Report of the twenty-eighth annual meeting, Dublin, Aug. 1922.
57 Aindrias Ó Cathasaigh (ed.), *The life and times of Gilbert Lynch, by Gilbert Lynch*, Studies in Irish Labour History, 13 (Dublin: Irish Labour History Society, 2011).
58 Ibid., pp. 39–41.
59 *Dundalk Democrat*, 17 Apr. 1920.
60 ILP&TUC, Report of the twenty-sixth annual meeting, Cork, Aug. 1920.
61 *Irish Times*, 18 Dec. 1919.
62 *Dundalk Democrat*, 31 Jul. 1920.
63 *Dundalk Democrat*, 11 Sept. 1920.
64 ILP & TUC, Report of the twenty-sixth annual report, Cork, Aug. 1920.
65 *Dundalk Democrat*, 31 Jul. 1920.
66 Charles Townshend, *The Republic: the fight for Irish Independence* (London: Allen Lane, 2013), pp. 144–8.
67 *Dundalk Democrat*, 3 Jul. 1920.
68 McCabe, 'Irish railway unions, chapter six'; Louth County Archives, LCC/MB/1/5, 'Munitions strike motion', 21 Jun. 1920.
69 TNA, CO 904/90, CICMR Co. Louth, May 1919–Aug., 1920.
70 *Irish Bulletin*, 2(56), 21 Jul. 1920.
71 Dooley, *Land for the people*, quoting Erskine Childers, 'The constructive work of Dáil Éireann (1921).
72 *Irish Bulletin*, 2(82), 27 Aug. 1920; Louth County Archives, LCC/MB/1/5, 'Motion by James McGuill', 21 Jun. 1920.
73 *Dundalk Democrat*, 19 Mar. 1921.
74 Martin Maguire, 'Civil service trade unionism in Ireland (part 1) 1801-1922', *Saothar Journal of the Irish Labour History Society*, 33 (2008), pp. 7–21; Maguire, 'Civil service trade unionism in Ireland (part 2) 1922-1990', *Saothar Journal of the Irish Labour History Society*, 34 (2010), pp. 41–60.
75 Padraig Yeates, *Irish craft workers in a time of revolution* (Dublin: TEEU, 2016).
76 Dáil Éireann, *Miontuairis an Chéad Dáil 1919–1921*, 11 Apr. 1919, p. 78.
77 MA, BMH WS.568 'Eilis Bean Uí Chonaill'; WS.979, 'Robert Barton'.
78 Harold O'Sullivan, *A history of local government in the County of Louth from the earliest times to the present time* (Dublin: IPA, 2000), pp. 50–70.

79 *Irish Bulletin*, 2(34), 18 and 29 Jun. 1920.

80 Louth County Archives Services, DUDC/MB/1/4, 'Motion on trade unions', 17 Jun. 1919.

81 Louth County Archives Services, Drogheda Minute Book, 21 Apr. 1919, 13 Feb., 2 Mar. 1920.

82 Arthur Mitchell, *Revolutionary government in Ireland Dáil Éireann 1919–22* (Dublin: Gill & Macmillan, 1995), pp. 161–2.

83 Ó Cathasaigh (ed.), *The life and times of Gilbert Lynch*, pp. 41–3.

84 Louth County Archives Services, Drogheda Minute Book, 2 Nov. 1920.

85 Cathasaigh *Gilbert Lynch*, pp. 43–4.

86 Louth County Archives Services, LCC/MB/1/6, 'Delegation of ITGWU', 15 Dec. 1921.

87 Francis Devine, 'The Irish Transport and General Workers' Union in Co Louth, 1909–1930', in *Journal of the Old Drogheda Society*, forthcoming.

88 Yeates, *Irish craft workers in a time of revolution*, p. 24.

89 Louth County Archives Services, LCC/MB/1/6, 'Special meeting on the Treaty, 2 January 1922'.

90 ILP & TUC, *Report on the twenty-eighth annual meeting, August 1922, Dublin and the Special Congress on election policy, Abbey Theatre, 21 Feb. 1922*.

91 Louth County Archives Services, Drogheda Minute Book, 2 Jan. 1922.

92 Louth County Archives Services, Drogheda Minute Book 7, 20 Feb. 1922.

93 Louth County Archives Services, Drogheda Minute Book 3, 10 Jan. 1922.

94 Louth County Archives Services, LCC/MB/1/6, 9 Mar. 1922, 'wages sub-committee'.

95 Devine, *Organising history*, p. 116.

96 Lawrence William White, 'Cathal O'Shannon', in James McGuire and James Quinn (ed.), *Dictionary of Irish Biography* (Cambridge: CUP, 2009).

97 Dooley, 'Land ford the people', p. 51, and Gavin M. Foster, *The Irish Civil War and Society: politics, class, and conflict* (Basingstoke: Palgrave Macmillan, 2015), pp. 117–41.

98 NLI, MS 15,679/5/8, Wm O'Brien Papers, 'Kelly, Dublin Employers Emergency Committee, Nov. 1924'.

99 Emmet O'Connor, *Reds and the Green: Ireland, Russia and the Communist Internationals 1919–43* (Dublin: UCD Press, 2004), p. 40.

100 Russian State Archive for Social and Political History (RGASPI), report on the work of the Irish Communist Groups 1921, 495/89/2-30. My thanks to Emmet O'Connor for a copy of this report.

101 Gerry Watts, 'The battle for Liberty Hall', *Saothar Journal of the Labour History Society*, 40 (2015), pp. 31–44.

102 NLI, MS 15,679/5/4 Wm O'Brien papers, 'Letter from Whittle ref WUI', 15 Jul. 1924.

103 NLI, MS 15,679/5/5 (1) Wm O'Brien papers, 'Kilsaran branch report', 17 Jul. 1924.

104 Brian Hanley, 'The IRA and Trade Unions, 1922–72', in Francis Devine, Fintan Lane and Niamh Puirséil (eds), *Essays in Irish labour history: a Festschrift for Elizabeth and John W. Boyle* (Dublin: Irish Academic Press, 2008), pp. 157–77.

105 *Dáil Éireann debates*, 18 Jun. 1919.

106 I would like to thank Lorraine McCann of the County Louth Archives, Eamon Thornton of the Old Drogheda Society and the staff of the National Library Ireland for their expert assistance. Also Padraig Yeates, Francis Devine, Emmet O'Connor, my co-editor Donal Hall, the DkIT Humanities students of the history module, 'Ireland in Revolution and Counter-Revolution' for their arguments and for helpful comments on earlier drafts, and my colleagues in the Department of Humanities at Dundalk Institute of Technology for their support.

4

Policing County Louth, 1912–1922

Brendan McAvinue

In April 1919, during a Dáil debate, Eoin MacNeill stated that, 'The police in Ireland are a force of traitors ... and perjurers.'[1] Similarly, Eamonn Broy, a former member of the Dublin Metropolitan Police (DMP) and future Garda Commissioner, later remarked that the Royal Irish Constabulary (RIC) had been 'oppressors to the end'.[2] Both MacNeill's and Broy's views of the RIC were perceptions of the force that are seemingly inconsistent with the position that the force held within society in general at the turn of the twentieth century. Indeed, Broy, in the same statement, surmised that 'by and large the members of the RIC were personally honest and decent [and] that it took some time and exhortation to convince people that [they] really were their enemies.'[3]

Following its inception in 1836 as the Irish Constabulary, the early force had certainly not endeared itself to the native Irish population with its participation in evictions and the suppression of rebellions, including the 1867 Fenian Rising which earned it the 'Royal' prefix from Queen Victoria. However, progressive developments in the late nineteenth and early twentieth centuries had allowed the police to be removed from situations where the enforcement of law was both confrontational and controversial. The various Land Acts of this period, resulting in the transfer of lands to tenants, reduced the power of landlords and greatly diminished agrarian tension. Employment through industrialisation and co-operatives, improved social structures and civil liberties alongside a cultural revival also combined towards a relative calmness within the country. Additionally, on the political front, militancy had taken a back seat to constitutional nationalism in the form of Home Rule, driven by John Redmond's Irish Parliamentary Party (IPP). As a result of these developments, by 1912 the RIC had, in the most part, assumed the role of a civil police force and the carrying of arms was generally unnecessary. Conor Brady describes how the RIC in the early twentieth century 'had mellowed so that in many ways it resembled more an English or Welsh constabulary'.[4] The RIC was, however, the very tangible face of British rule in Ireland and for this reason it was targeted, with increasing aggressiveness, by the republican movement.

In 1912, there were nineteen RIC barracks in Co. Louth, divided between Dundalk and Drogheda Districts. Anne Street in Dundalk was both the county headquarters and Dundalk District headquarters whilst Westgate Barracks in Drogheda was the Drogheda district headquarters. The seventeen sub-districts, each denoted by its barrack name, ensured a distribution of policemen across the county, with a minimum of a sergeant and three constables in any one place. Table 1 shows the distribution of barracks within each district in 1911, with barrack strength opposite. Of the 117 serving policemen in Louth, sixty-one were single and, under regulations, were billeted in their various barracks. Of the fifty-six married men, twenty-three were residing with their families in barracks, the remainder in rented 'lodgings' within their respective districts. Closely reflecting the demographics of the country, 80 per cent of the policemen in Louth were Catholic, the remainder being Church of Ireland, Presbyterian and Methodist.

Similarly, the barrack return forms for the 1911 National Census would indicate that over 80 per cent were from farming backgrounds, the remainder from occupations as diverse as shop assistants, clerks and teachers. Although Broy describes how members of the force were encouraged to mix with the people as part of an intelligence gathering policy it is also likely that, given their backgrounds, many of the men, particularly those with families, would have integrated naturally into their local communities, contributing both socially and economically to their environment.[5] In the combined districts of Ardee, Collon, Blackrock, Carlingford and Omeath, eighteen of the twenty-two policemen were married, with a total of forty-four children, some of whom were employed locally.

Every month, each RIC County Inspector (CI) submitted a report to the Inspector General (IG) in Dublin Castle, outlining the general situation and any notable incidents or activities within the county during the previous month. The originals of these reports are in the Colonial Office collection at the National Archives, Kew, in London. Copies of these reports, and of the consequent general reports compiled by the IG, are also available for viewing at the National Archives of Ireland and the National Library Ireland as the 'British in Ireland' microfilm collection.[6] With few exceptions, over the period 1912 to 1920, the CI for Louth described the county as being 'peaceable' or in a 'satisfactory condition', with the police being troubled by only minor offences and petty crime. At the Dundalk Quarter Sessions in March 1912, when Judge Green was presented with white gloves, symbolising that there were no criminal cases to be heard, he remarked that it was one of the most law-abiding counties in Ireland.[7]

Newspaper reports of the period indicate that the lower courts (Petty and Borough Sessions) in the county were dealing mainly with cases involving licensing offences, drunk and disorderly, cycling regulations and some minor riotous behaviour. In June 1912, when Ardee magistrates, concerned about a few unruly residents, suggested that the local police force should be increased to ten members, the *Dundalk Democrat* commented that an English town of comparable size would have only one or two policemen and suggested that 'it is time that sympathies for wrong-doing and wrong-doers was brought to an end'.[8] Court reports in local media for this period suggest that drunkenness, amongst both men and women, occupied a large part of police time. A letter to the *Dundalk Democrat* in February 1912 described how the writer had witnessed RIC men wheeling an inebriated woman homewards on a handcart and suggested that maybe the 'good Catholic publicans should be more careful about serving drink to people who have already had enough'.[9] Although, under police regulations, a riot was described as 'three persons or more in a state of quarrel', this was often loosely interpreted by both police and the judiciary.[10] At Dundalk Children's Court in July 1912, Constable Dwyer summoned eleven-year-old Michael Craig of Seatown for engaging in riotous behaviour by kicking a football in a public place, the defending solicitor describing it as 'the most abominable case in my experience'.[11] In January 1914, at Dundalk Borough Court, Constable Nicholls summoned Michael Grimes for riotous behaviour claiming when he (Constable Nicholls) greeted Grimes courteously, the defendant responded in an abusive manner.

Vagrancy and begging amongst adults and children also featured regularly in police work, with offending adults liable to up to three months in gaol whilst children who 'if not rescued from their surroundings, would grow up in vice, and add to the criminality of the country' faced committal to industrial school.[12] The police reports and media coverage indicated a relatively normal society for this period, with the IG reports being mainly concerned with agrarian unrest in the western counties and consequent use of resources to afford protection to landowners and grazers. There were, however, undercurrents of disaffection which, combined with certain events, led the country towards insurrection.

The 1913 series of labour strikes and the Dublin Lockout highlighted poor working conditions and pay, particularly for the unskilled, and the deplorable living conditions for the working classes. The reaction of the employers and the authorities to the strikes and lock-out, culminating in the events on 31 August 1913 when both the DMP and RIC baton-charged strikers and their supporters, led to the formation of the Irish Citizen Army (ICA), ostensibly to protect the strikers. Alongside this, the establishment of the anti-Home Rule movement, the Ulster Volunteer Force (UVF), provided a rare opportunity to unite nationalists under the umbrella of the Irish Volunteers, established in November 1913.[13] The 'Curragh Mutiny', in March 1914, further eroded constitutional nationalism as a number of army officers threatened to resign their commissions rather than proceed to Ulster to confront the growing threat from the UVF. In a report from the RIC Inspector General in May 1914, concern was expressed at the growth of the Irish Volunteers throughout the country with the comment that 'each county will soon have a trained army far outnumbering the police, and those who control the Volunteers will be in a position to dictate to what extent the law of the land may be carried into effect'.[14] In May 1914, the Louth CI reported that the Volunteers in the county had increased rapidly to 1,898 members, formed into companies of 80 to 100 each, and that drilling was being provided by ex-soldiers.

Nationally, in September 1914, the IG reported that Irish Volunteer membership was at 184,000 but that it lacked leadership and organisation and was ill-equipped in the use of an estimated 7,500 rifles at its disposal.[15] The same report stated that quarrels within the Irish Volunteers had led to the ousting of the Sinn Féin elements in both Dundalk and Drogheda and that the majority of the Volunteers in Louth, numbered at 4,862, were 'thoroughly pro-British in the current war'. It is notable that, even at this early stage, police reports commonly grouped the militant nationalists under the Sinn Féin banner despite the fact that that organisation was, by and large, pacifist. The split in Louth pre-empted a national split within the Irish Volunteers in September and October following Redmond's call to arms in support of the British war effort.

From this split evolved two distinct groupings; the pro-Redmond National Volunteers and the original but now smaller, but more militant and republican-minded, Irish Volunteers. The IG report for November 1914 expressed little concern about the National Volunteers, describing it as being disorganised, poorly armed and with no military training and that the Irish Volunteers, estimated at a national strength of 11,000 men, was mainly engaged in a campaign towards discouraging recruitment to the British forces.[16] Similarly, the Louth CI reported that 'it is remarkable what little interest is now taken in the National Volunteer Movement' and that 'nothing was heard of Sinn Féinism in the county'.[17] Weapons were being acquired by the Irish Volunteers and, in an indication of the level of police monitoring, the report also referred to a consignment of forty Lee-Metford rifles being delivered to Ardee, seventeen of which had been returned to Dublin, to be subsequently purchased by The O'Rahilly.

Police reports throughout 1915 indicated decreasing activity within the National Volunteers, with Louth membership falling to 3,400 by June, the same report making no mention of the Irish Volunteers. Close monitoring of political societies is evident, however, with the IG reporting that 'suspect P. Hughes' had attended O'Donovan Rossa's funeral and an Irish Volunteers General Council meeting in August and that suspects Patrick O'Malley from Galway and Darrell Figgis of Mayo had attended the Dundalk Feis in July.[18] The Louth CI described how persons with Sinn Féin ideas, 'mostly cranks and fanatics', were spreading disloyalty and deterring the mass of the people from openly declaring their convictions with regard to the war.[19] In January 1916, although the police reported that both the Drogheda and Dundalk branches of the Irish Volunteers were showing some activity in route marches and drilling, there is no indication of any concern about these activities, the report commenting that 'the Irish Volunteers have little influence in this county'.[20]

As late as March 1916, the police were more concerned with a cattle-driving incident on rented lands at Collon than with Irish Volunteer activities, merely mentioning that suspect John McDermott addressed a Dundalk meeting and that the membership had increased to 211, including about thirty boys, aged between twelve and fourteen years. Curiously, there is no mention in the reports of the arrival in the county of Donal O'Hannigan, sent in early March by Volunteer Headquarters to take command of, amongst others, the Louth Volunteers in preparation for the Easter Rising. Active preparations for the Rising had begun with the arrival of O'Hannigan who gauged the efficiency of the local Volunteers and advised them on manoeuvres.

Locally, and nationally, the mobilisation of the Volunteers was announced under the guise of route marches. However, the impending insurrection did not appear to be a well kept secret. Whilst some local men, like Patrick Hughes, were informed by headquarters, others either guessed or overheard of the plans. Drogheda man Joseph O'Higgins was informed by his brother at a Dublin concert on St Patrick's night whilst Edward Bailey overheard a conversation at the Dundalk drill hall.[21] The intensive drilling under Donal O'Hannigan, along with preparations being made, convinced both Thomas Hamill and Daniel Tuite that 'something serious was afoot'.[22] Sean MacEntee described how, at a well-filled drill hall on Holy Thursday night, 'exhilaration and excitement pervaded the room'.[23] In late March, *Volunteer Notes*, a column in the *Dundalk Examiner*, stated that funds were urgently required for 'a big undertaking … from which great things are to be expected'.[24]

Similarly, an editorial in the *Dundalk Democrat*, two days before the Rising, warned that the Irish Volunteers were contemplating an insurrection.[25] The consensus within the RIC, supported by reports from Special Branch infiltrators, seemed to be that the Volunteers were so disorganised and poorly armed that an uprising was unlikely.[26] The arrest of Roger Casement on Good Friday and the failure to land arms in Kerry would have added to the complacency both in the police and in the Dublin Castle administration. The attempted landing of weaponry provided evidence of 'hostile association', justifying the arrest of leading Sinn Féin members, but Dublin Castle officials saw no reason to put this into immediate effect.[27]

Unaware of Eoin MacNeill's orders countermanding the planned manoeuvres, approximately 120 Volunteers, led by Donal O'Hannigan, marched out of Dundalk at 10 a.m. on Easter Sunday, bound for the Hill of Tara in Co. Meath. The Drogheda Volunteers, having set out at a later time of 2 p.m., were overtaken by Dr William Bradley who delivered MacNeill's message. These men then dispersed. Marching towards Ardee, the Dundalk Volunteers were joined on bicycles by two RIC sergeants from Dundalk. The sergeants, Wymes and Connolly, had earlier been observing the Volunteers as they mobilised in Clanbrassil St, Dundalk, and, in what was normal practice, had then continued to monitor their movements. [28] At Ardee, Sergeants Wymes and Connolly and a number of local RIC men, all unarmed, did not interfere when the Volunteers, by means of a ruse, acquired a number of National Volunteer rifles at a house in the town.[29] Some miles short of Slane, O'Hannigan received MacNeill's orders, but, doubting the veracity of the message, dispatched some men, including Sean MacEntee, to Dublin to make contact with Padraig Pearse, the main body of the men continuing as far as Slane. According to O'Hannigan, about sixty RIC men from Co. Meath arrived into Slane and, following negotiations with the District Inspector (DI), the police agreed not to interfere with the Volunteers.[30] This large force of police would be consistent with events later in the week when a convoy of RIC travelled from Slane to Ashbourne for a disastrous engagement with Volunteers, during which eight RIC men were killed.

In the early hours of Easter Monday, having received no word from Dublin, O'Hannigan ordered the Volunteers to return towards Dundalk. With many of the Volunteers having already dispersed, O'Hannigan and approximately twenty-eight remaining men met up with Sean McEntee at Lurgangreen, a few miles outside Dundalk on Monday afternoon. Informed by McEntee of Pearse's orders to 'follow the original instructions', the Volunteers immediately placed the accompanying RIC men under arrest, commandeered several motor cars and proceeded to Castlebellingham to acquire provisions. A number of RIC men in Castlebellingham were also put under arrest, including Constable Charles McGee, who was relieved of some documents in his possession. Constable McGee was billeted at Gilbertstown Barracks, about five miles away, and was probably on routine duties, delivering documents, when he unwittingly came upon the scene. An army officer, Lieutenant Dunville was also put under arrest and, along with the other captives, was put standing alongside railings.

O'Hannigan gave orders to move out and as the commandeered vehicles moved off, a shot was fired. Lieutenant Dunville was badly wounded and Constable McGee was fatally injured. Volunteer Patrick

McHugh later described how he had fired at Lieutenant Dunville in the belief that Dunville was reaching for a weapon and that although Dunville remained standing Constable McGee fell to the ground.[31] From medical evidence presented at the subsequent inquest, it would appear that the same bullet had passed through Dunville and then struck McGee. Thirty years old, single and less than four years in the force, Constable McGee was the first of eleven RIC men to die violently during the 1916 Rising. A native of Inishbofin Island off the Donegal coast, he was later described by Sean MacEntee as 'a tall fine-looking fellow of rather a tougher spirit than his comrades'.[32]

Other than some individuals making their way to Dublin, the Louth Volunteers played no further active part in the Rising. However, in the weeks afterwards and with Martial Law declared, seventy-seven men were arrested in police and military operations in Louth. The Louth CI described how the county was 'in a state of great tension until the surrender of the rebels in Dublin' but that, owing to the effective measures adopted, no further outbreak took place.[33] The report also describes how the National Volunteers in both Drogheda and Dundalk assisted the police, the Dundalk branch actually putting its weapons at the disposal of the police. Four men: Sean MacEntee, Denis Leahy, Frank Martin and James Sally were subsequently court-martialled for Constable McGee's killing. All but Sally were convicted and sentenced to death, later commuted to various prison terms.

The assistance given to the police by the National Volunteers reflected the initial overall revulsion and condemnation in the immediate aftermath of the Rising. However, the executions of the rebellion leaders and the wholesale arrests and deporting of suspects drew a certain sympathy from the public, and in June, the RIC in Louth noted 'an increasing sympathy towards Sinn Féin'.[34] Renewed discussions on a Home Rule settlement continued to be of concern, and in July, police noted that the IPP's positioning was weakening in Louth, strengthening the position of the 'disloyal section'.[35] The gradual release of Louth prisoners during 1917 and in early 1918 led to close monitoring of their movements. In February 1917, police noted that a released prisoner, James Layng, was attempting to reorganise Sinn Féin in Drogheda and that regular meetings were held in a shop belonging to another released prisoner called Feely.[36] A similar report for July described how J. MacEntee, P. McMahon, J. Walsh and J. Murray addressed meetings in Clogherhead, Dunleer and Drogheda, the speeches being 'of a violent and disloyal nature'.[37] As more prisoners returned during 1917, the Volunteers also became more active, Volunteer Peter Kieran describing how route marches began around Dundalk in April and how, some days after a march to Louth village, nine of their men were arrested and received varying gaol sentences, 'leading to riotous clashes with the RIC'.[38]

In February 1917, Sinn Féin had begun to organise National Clubs and in July, the police reported that, over the previous six months, the number in Louth had risen to ten clubs with a membership of 700, also commenting that these clubs were spreading disloyalty, especially amongst the young men.[39] The support for Sinn Féin was not universal, however. When the organisation paraded in military order at a feis in Drogheda in July, the police had to intervene when the marchers were confronted by soldiers' wives.[40] Nationally, the collapse in support for John Redmond's IPP had boosted support for Sinn Féin, leading to a number of by-election victories in 1917. In October, a link between the traditionally pacifist Sinn Féin and the militant Irish Volunteers was firmly established with the election of Éamon de Valera to the Presidency of both organisations. Locally, the police estimated that the membership of the Irish Volunteers and National Clubs in Louth stood at 289 and 1,108 respectively by the beginning of 1918.[41]

In April 1918, with British forces on the Western Front under severe strain, a Military Service Bill was passed, giving power to extend conscription to Ireland. Amidst a storm of protest, from politicians, clergy and others, the membership of both the Irish Volunteers and Sinn Féin grew considerably, rising to 689 and 1,583 respectively in Louth by the end of the year.[42] In his report for May 1918, the IG also described how the country 'though prosperous and free from ordinary crime ... became ablaze with resentment' and how, at public meetings, people spoke of attacking barracks and shooting policemen and how strong efforts, including calls from church pulpits, were being made to induce the younger RIC men to resign rather than to enforce conscription.[43] The so-called 'German Plot', based on flimsy evidence pointing to collusion between Sinn Féin and the German Empire, led to arrests in May 1918 of approximately 150 Sinn Féin leaders, including Peter Hughes, P.J. Berrill and Philip Monahan in Louth. Seamus McGuill was arrested in June, his third arrest in seven months, but was acquitted and released the following month. On his return to Dundalk, he noticed a falling off in enthusiasm within the Volunteers, possibly due to the decreasing likelihood of conscription being introduced.[44]

In police reports throughout 1918, the Louth CI distinguished between the political activities and 'ordinary crime', reporting the county to be in a satisfactory condition with few indictable offences. Drunkenness was also reported to be in decline, due to the high price of alcohol caused by war rationing, excise increases and reduced opening hours of public houses. On the political front, the Louth police were mostly concerned about the anti-conscription activities of Sinn Féin and the spreading of disloyalty and disaffection by the organisation, also regularly noting the absence of drilling or route marching by Volunteers.

In a resounding victory for a party whose leaders were either interned or in prison, Sinn Féin won 73 of the 105 Irish seats in the General Election in December 1918, with Sinn Féin candidate, J.J. O'Kelly, taking the Louth seat in a close contest against IPP candidate, Richard Hazleton. In the run-up to the election, Fr O'Flanagan, acting President of Sinn Féin, addressed a crowd of 1,200 people in Drogheda, after which the crowd attempted to interrupt a nearby Hazleton meeting. Two days later, in an indication of the closer ties between the Volunteers and Sinn Féin, two companies of Volunteers, carrying hurleys, paraded and drilled close to the town hall in which Hazleton was holding a meeting. The police opinion was that the parade was a means of testing the water as to how far they would be allowed to go.[45]

The declaration of an Irish Republic and the establishment of Dáil Éireann, on 21 January 1919, coincided with the killing of two RIC men at Soloheadbeg in Co. Tipperary, an event generally recognised as the beginning of the War of Independence. Seamus Robinson, the commanding officer of the local Volunteers during that incident, later recalled that, in the period leading up to it, he had become disillusioned with the pacifism of Sinn Féin and that the killings were necessary to begin an open conflict.[46] In an address to Dáil Éireann the following April, Éamon de Valera moved a resolution declaring that members of the RIC be ostracised both publicly and socially. The ostracism of the RIC as part of a wider process of undermining the British administration extended beyond the mere boycotting of the force. Young single men and older men close to retirement were targeted and 'encouraged' to resign or retire, often with members of their families and even local priests being approached. As activities against the police intensified and became more aggressive, resignations and lack of recruitment seriously depleted the force, with over 1,300 leaving the force in the summer of 1920.[47] Seamus McGuill describes how, in Louth in 1920, there was 'an intense boycott of the RIC ordered' and that 'no Republican would speak or shake hands with them'.[48]

During 1919, the Volunteers in many parts of the country, and operating almost autonomously, concentrated on acquiring badly needed weaponry by raiding barracks and ambushing both military and police patrols, resulting in the deaths of eleven members of the RIC. In the late summer of 1919, the Volunteers were brought under the control of Dáil Éireann by swearing allegiance to the Dáil, thus forming the 'Army of the Republic of Ireland', otherwise known as the IRA. From early 1920, under increasing assault and under-resourced due to resignations and retirements, the beleaguered RIC began to abandon the more isolated barracks.

As early as August 1919, in a further process of undermining the administration, Dáil Éireann targeted the judicial system, beginning with the establishment of National Arbitration Courts, mainly to deal with property or agrarian disputes. In June 1920, the Dáil Courts were established, with Supreme, District and Petty Session (Parish Court) sittings, encompassing both criminal and civil proceedings. In August 1920, a Convention, chaired by Peter Hughes, Chairman of Dundalk Urban District Council, was held in Dundalk Town Hall to select arbiters for 'Republican Parish and District Courts' in Co. Louth. The *Dundalk Democrat*, in expressing some concern about 'midnight courts, masked judges and unknown destinations' stated that a 'prominent Sinn Féiner' had given assurance that the courts were entirely voluntary and that 'all are free to use the machinery of the established law'.[49]

The *Dundalk Democrat*'s concerns may have been valid; Conor Maguire, later to be Chief Justice, describes how the IRA enforced the boycotting of County Courts and Assizes by issuing warnings and by physically stopping litigants from attending.[50] Seamus McGuill and Peter Hughes were involved in establishing Dáil Courts in Co. Louth and in a collection of papers from the late Peter Hughes is a bundle of documents containing court listings, notes made and judgments handed down during a number of court sittings.[51] Although McGuill describes how the courts in Louth got a good reputation for 'fair and honest decisions', it does not seem to have had a good beginning.[52] In September 1920, the *Dundalk Democrat* reported that the 'zealous but inexperienced' judges were causing disaffection by the severity of penalties being imposed.[53] Those accused of offences or crimes would have been brought to court by members of the Irish Republican Police (IRP), a body set up in June and recruited mainly from within the ranks of the IRA. Although its main purpose was to provide protection for the Republican Courts and to ensure that decrees handed down were adhered to, it also engaged in 'ordinary' policing such as enforcing licensing regulations and investigating petty crime.

On a Sunday in July 1920, publicans in Blackrock, Co. Louth, were instructed by members of the IRP to close their premises by 10 p.m., with 'dreadful consequences for refusal'.[54] In Drogheda, Joseph O'Higgins describes how suspect criminals were arrested and, if found guilty, were detained in 'unknown destinations', and also how three young men were at one time held in the Sinn Féin Hall in Drogheda until deportation arrangements could be made.[55] In July 1920, three men, convicted of robbing an elderly woman, were bound together outside Reaghstown and Ardee churches on a Sunday morning, with a notice describing their offence hanging around the neck of one of the men.[56] The latter punishment was a policy adopted by IRA General Head Quarters (GHQ) in June 1920 in order to alleviate the strain on resources caused by holding convicted persons in remote imprisonment.[57] The retreat of the RIC had resulted in increased petty criminality throughout the country and undoubtedly the activities of the IRP would have been welcomed by many citizens. Seamus McGuill described how the IRP members were 'imbued with a high sense of duty and soon gained a great measure of respect'.[58]

Besides the Dáil Courts, the IRA also operated courts martial of persons suspected of being informants or otherwise associating with the 'enemy'. In February 1921, Henry Murray, a native of Carrickmacross and recently invalided from the British Army, was shot dead while walking in Chapel Street in Dundalk. Notices, displayed some days later at church doors, claimed that Murray had been 'tried as a spy, found guilty and convicted'.[59] Considering that he was apparently walking freely about town when he was shot, it must be assumed that he was tried and convicted *in absentia*.

In the early part of 1919, police in Louth believed Sinn Féin was remaining quiet, although organising and awaiting further developments and instructions. In February, following an arms raid on the home of the Earl of Arran at Ravensdale, in which a number of old ornamental guns were taken, the police were more concerned about the number of unlicensed shotguns discovered during follow-up searches.[60] The first casualty of that period in Co. Louth occurred on the night of 4 June 1919, when, following receipt of information of proposed 'Sinn Féin' raids, a joint police and military checkpoint was set up at New Inn, north of Dundalk.[61] When a motor car innocently drove through the unlit checkpoint the military opened fire, fatally wounding passenger Matthew Murphy. Following the inquest into Murphy's death, which found that the authorities had not taken sufficient precaution to protect members of the public, there was a hardening of attitudes towards the local military in Dundalk.[62] Later that month, police had to intervene in the town when, following the signing of the Treaty of Versailles, a number of drunken soldiers, waving Union flags, were violently attacked by a hostile crowd.[63]

In an embarrassing incident for the police, Volunteers raided a storage shed at Greenore Port on 1 August 1919 and stole nineteen rifles destined for the military in Dundalk, and the local RIC sergeant was subsequently reduced in rank for his failure properly to secure the weapons. The only other significant arms procurement by the IRA in Louth appears to have been the acquisition, through the Volunteer GHQ, of a number of grenades and the rifles which had been dumped by the Louth Volunteers in Co. Meath after the 1916 Rising.[64] For the latter part of 1919, Co. Louth remained relatively quiet, although the RIC conducted a number of raids on premises associated with Sinn Féin, Cumann na mBan and the Volunteers, particularly following the proscribing of these organisations and Dáil Éireann in September.

At the Dundalk Quarter Sessions in March 1920, Judge Green, on being presented with symbolic white gloves, remarked that 'The crimeless condition of the county spoke volumes, not only for the people, but for that splendid body of men in charge of the peace of the county'.[65] The judge may have been making a distinction between ordinary crime and militant offences considering that the previous month nine men were arrested in dawn raids in Dundalk and Greenore, all being released from Belfast Gaol within days. Also, early in March, the abandoned RIC barracks at Blackrock had been burned down. Within months, the barracks at Ballymascanlon, Louth Village, Omeath, Collon, Gilbertstown, Termonfeckin and Clogherhead were similarly destroyed, the attack on Louth Village also razing three adjoining houses.[66]

To augment the depleting RIC, Winston Churchill, then British Secretary for War, had authorised the establishment of the 'Special Reserves', the majority of whom were former British Army soldiers not long removed from trench warfare in Europe. Known as the 'Black and Tans' from the colour of their hybrid uniforms, the reserves began to arrive in Ireland in March 1920, followed, in May, by a separate reserve force, the Auxiliary Division of the RIC (ADRIC), recruited from former British Army officers and, known, colloquially, as the 'Auxiliaries'. Undisciplined and untrained in police matters, these counter-insurgency forces quickly gained themselves a reputation for engaging in acts of lawlessness, particularly in their participation in reprisal attacks on individuals and communities. Destruction of property was widespread, the most notorious being the sacking of Balbriggan in September 1920 and the burning of Cork three months later. Their atrocities also extended to the killing of civilians, usually suspected republicans, but also indiscriminate actions such as the Croke Park massacre of fourteen civilians in November 1920.

There are ample reports of the Black and Tans being in Co. Louth from mid-1920 on, where, as Reserve Constables, they would have been billeted with and under the control of the RIC. Research by Stephen O'Donnell indicates that the main force of Auxiliaries in the locality was based at Hope Castle in Castleblayney in Co. Monaghan, although there appears to have been a sub-unit, of possibly twenty-five men, based at Dundalk.[67] Since they were often collectively referred to as Black and Tans or 'Tans', particularly in witness statements, it is difficult to differentiate between the activities of the two reserve forces in Louth. The more nefarious activities of the police, viz. the premeditated murder of at least six civilians in the county, would almost certainly have been the work of the Auxiliaries rather than the Black and Tans, who, as Stephen O'Donnell discusses, were under the direct control of their RIC officers and would therefore have found it difficult to plan and carry out those actions.[68]

Hostilities by the IRA in Louth were very much restricted by a shortage of weapons and a lack of organisation. Drogheda Volunteer, Joseph O'Higgins, describes how aborted plans were made to raid the RIC barracks at Ardee and Dunleer, but he also states that, in general, there was a lack of enthusiasm and leadership for militancy.[69] Seamus McGuill recounted how Volunteers in the Dundalk area were insufficiently armed to carry out attacks on barracks, instead executing a small number of attacks on police patrols in order to acquire weaponry, and how subsequent plans to attack a number of barracks were thwarted by the evacuation of those buildings.[70] The first attacks by the IRA on the police in the county occurred in Dundalk on the night of 16 April 1920, when two RIC men were ambushed and disarmed by five IRA men at Seatown Place in Dundalk. Almost simultaneously, a three-man RIC patrol was ambushed at Bridge Street by approximately eight IRA men. During the ensuing struggle, Volunteer Thomas Mulholland, Quartermaster of the Dundalk IRA, was shot dead by the police. Following a funeral service at St Malachy's Dominican church in Dundalk, Mulholland's coffin, draped in a Republican flag, was removed to Castletown Cemetery with full military honours provided by members of the Volunteers and Cumann na mBan.[71]

Two months later, a similar scene, albeit with different trappings, was to take place at the same church with the funeral of RIC Sergeant Timothy Holland who was fatally injured during an IRA ambush at Cullyhanna in Co. Armagh. Following the funeral service, Sergeant Holland's Union flag-draped coffin, with military honours provided by members of the Royal Field Artillery, was taken by gun carriage to Dundalk train station and onwards to Belfast for interment.

In July 1920, the IG reported that Louth 'was not in a satisfactory state', particularly in the Dundalk area where the local police attributed a large number of 'outrages' to Sinn Féin, including the death of a man whilst attempting to steal a quantity of petrol from a slowly moving train and the tarring and feathering of a 'loyal' engine driver.[72] The latter incident was one of many similar cases of intimidation of railway workers who refused to participate in the transport workers' embargo on the movement of troops and munitions. Arms raids by the IRA on individual homes, for legally held weapons, were a regular occurrence, with such raids 'in practically every townland in north Louth' on a weekend in September 1920.[73] Robberies of businesses and individuals were commonplace, with an 'epidemic of robberies' in Drogheda towards the end of 1920, resulting in the arrests by the RIC of seven brothers, all ex-soldiers.[74]

At Drogheda Petty Sessions in March 1921, six serving soldiers based at Dunshaughlin were charged with the theft of goods from a drapery in Collon.[75] In Dundalk, in September 1920, a reserve constable, Terence Wheatly, employed as a driver with the RIC, died from a gunshot wound mysteriously received during what appears to be his involvement, with others, in the breaking and entering of a local shop. Police and military raids on private houses and business premises also became a frequent event, particularly in the north of the county, with many men taken into custody. Banks, county council offices and the homes of councillors in Drogheda and Dundalk were also targeted in attempts to locate council funds, which were being held in secret accounts to prevent the funds being appropriated by the authorities.[76]

On 22 August 1920, four RIC men, en route to crowd control duties at a local football match, were ambushed at Jocelyn Street in Dundalk, resulting in the death of Constable Thomas Brennan and serious injuries to two colleagues. Constable Brennan was later described by Volunteer Patrick Duffy as having been a 'helpful policeman'.[77] Whereas the Louth CI was of the opinion that the attack was carried out by outsiders to the town, Stephen O'Donnell describes how it was an impulsive and mishandled attempt by local IRA members to disarm the patrol.[78] Five days later, in a probable reaction to recent attacks on the Catholic population in Belfast, the Protestant-owned Craig's drapery shop in Clanbrassil Street was maliciously burned late at night, causing the deaths of three employees. Widely condemned and believed to have been the work of the IRA, a public meeting was held in Dundalk Town Hall to form a town guard to cooperate with the police and military against the IRA. Seamus McGuill, then Commander of the Dundalk IRA, forced his way onto the stage and vehemently denied the involvement of that organisation in the incident.[79]

Police reports for the latter part of 1920 suggested that, although Louth was not in a satisfactory state, Sinn Féin activities were being curtailed by police and military patrols, with many of the Sinn Féin leaders either in custody or on the run. The 'patrols' by security forces were not always directed at curtailment, however, as instanced by the terror inflicted on the people of Drogheda on the night of 19 October 1920 when a large number of reserve policemen conducted aggressive searches of premises, resulting in wholesale damage and the wounding by gunshot of a former RIC sergeant.[80] Police activities were to take a more sinister turn, however, with the murder of two young men in Ardee on the night of 30 November 1920. John O'Carroll and Patrick Tierney, both members of the IRA, were taken from their homes by a group of armed men and shot. Although Tierney's sister, many years later, described the perpetrators as 'drunken Black & Tans',[81] the killings were most likely carried out by Auxiliaries.

From early 1921, Louth was to feel the effects of greatly increased activity by the IRA, opportunistic criminals and security personnel. Robberies of individuals, traders, post offices and mail vans became quite common while, on instructions from GHQ, rate collectors were also targeted from April. The Belfast Boycott, introduced by Dáil decree in late 1920 in response to attacks on the Catholic population, also led to attacks on transport and traders, with goods either being destroyed or 'seized'. In response to the cutting of roads and communications around Drogheda it was 'quite a common sight to see [Black & Tans] go into shops and on the streets to commandeer men to clear the roads', with similar raids taking place in Ardee and Dundalk.[82] This activity was certainly condoned at a high level, the IG reporting in May that there was a good deal of road trenching and tree-felling in Louth but that 'the Sinn Féiners were made to make good the damage'.[83]

Drogheda was to suffer further at the hands of the reserve policemen based in nearby Gormanstown, with a looting spree on the night of 4 February 1921 followed, five days later, by the murder of two men, Sinn Féin councillor Thomas Halpin and John Moran, a member of the IRA. In a scene similar to that in Ardee the previous November, the men were taken from their homes late at night by a party of armed men and shot, Moran's wife describing the leader of the group as having an English accent.[84]

The IG's report for May stated that the police were generally successful in dealing with Sinn Féin activity, with about fifty Sinn Féin leaders in Louth in custody. However, ambushes were carried out on police patrols at Greenore in March and May 1921, in each case a policeman being injured, and shots were also exchanged with Black and Tan forces near Laytown and at Monasterboice in April 1921.[85] The RIC barracks at Ardee was put under fire on a number of occasions, as was a police outpost at Plaster, near Dundalk. On the night of 13 May, twenty-three-year-old John Magee was taken from his home in Cooley by two armed men, and murdered nearby. Mystery surrounds this killing, the Louth CI inferring that it may have been an IRA shooting, whilst a nephew of Magee's describes how the house was apparently surrounded by Black and Tans at the time.[86] Around midnight on 17 June 1921, the body of reserve constable William Campbell was discovered on the Newry Road in Dundalk. Campbell, who had been shot in the back and whose service revolver was missing, had earlier been observed by a colleague leaving town on a newly acquired bicycle.

Two hours after the discovery of Constable Campbell's body, two brothers, John and Patrick Watters, were taken from their home in Seatown, Dundalk, by a group of armed men and shot dead nearby. Considering that security forces would have been on high alert following Constable Campbell's killing, it would have been foolhardy for any IRA or criminal gang to be involved in the Watters killings. Combined with this, the fact that the killers departed the scene in the direction of Quay Street Barracks would indicate that it was a reprisal killing, almost certainly carried out by Auxiliaries.

Four days after the Watters killings, a Dundalk-based Black and Tan, Alex McDonald, disappeared without trace. Stephen O'Donnell raises the likelihood that he was abducted and killed by the IRA.[87] Further outrages reported by police for June 1921 included the burning of Ravensdale Park House, the Louth Archaeological Society's museum in Dundalk and coastguard stations at Baltray and Annagassan. A house and a shop were both burned at Greenore, the police reporting that the charred remains of a woman those found in the latter, whilst the *Dundalk Democrat* reported that the remains were that of one of the raiders.[88] Other incidents, among many, included the armed robbery of £500 at the Ulster Bank in Ardee and the derailing of a troop train at Avadoyle, north of Dundalk, resulting in the deaths of two soldiers and a train guard.

Following the calling of a truce on 11 July 1921, local Truce Liaison Officials were established in both the IRA and police. In an undated letter, J.E. Duggan, chief liaison officer for Dáil Éireann, describes how 'a most unprecedented outburst of brigandism swept the whole country ... Attacks upon British forces were of such frequent occurrence as to render Liaison work almost impossible.'[89] Louth appears to have had little or no 'brigandism' or attacks on police during the period of the truce, the Dundalk police actually appearing on the streets without firearms.[90] Local police reports expressed concerns, however, that, although generally the terms of the truce were being observed, the IRA was reorganising, with a training camp set up at Stonetown House at Dunleer.[91] The IRP and Republican Courts also became more active during this period, the RIC being somewhat circumspect in dealing with this issue. Aware of a man being held in custody at Stonetown House, awaiting deportation, the Louth CI recommended that no action be taken unless armed police and military intervention was allowed.[92] The collection of funds by the IRA was also noted, the CI commenting that the levies being imposed on the populace was provoking 'considerable hostile comment' even among nationalists.[93]

Following the ratification of the Anglo-Irish Treaty, in January 1922, and to replace the RIC who were to be disbanded under the terms of the Treaty, a Civic Guard was established by Dáil Éireann, with initial deployment beginning in late August. In the meantime, as the RIC gradually withdrew, maintenance of law and order was carried out by the National Army and the IRP, the latter setting up a local headquarters in Dundalk Town Hall in January 1922.[94] Republican courts also became more openly active, three bank robbers being convicted at Dundalk Courthouse in February.[95] As the country drifted towards civil war, the effectiveness of the IRP dwindled, with many of its members being recalled to IRA units, no doubt torn between pro- and anti-Treaty allegiances.

Despite the truce and the subsequent Treaty, the RIC in Louth was to suffer one final violent death, at Drogheda, on 30 April 1922, when Reserve Constable Benjamin Bentley, driving alone, was ambushed by anti-Treaty forces who were ensconced at Millmount. Late that night, Drogheda was terrorised by a large force of police reserves who caused widespread damage in the town centre. At this stage the reserves were demobilising and the disbandment of the RIC had already begun. As the police began to evacuate the Co. Louth Barracks in April 1922, the county was plagued by criminality, with a series of robberies on banks, businesses and goods trains and, sometimes questionable, 'Belfast Boycott' raids on traders. Concerned at the level of criminality, a public meeting was held in the Dundalk Town Hall in May where it was decided to form a temporary Civic Guard for North Louth.[96] Funded by voluntary subscriptions from the local populace, the force, recognised by distinctive red and white armbands, operated within an area from Narrow Water at Omeath to the Glyde River at Ardee.[97]

As the Civic Guard was deployed around the country from late August 1922, its members were targeted by anti-Treaty 'Irregular' forces in many parts of the country, with stations being destroyed and members of the force being stripped of their equipment and uniforms. However, the decision of Dáil Éireann that the Civic Guard would be an unarmed force was undoubtedly the reason why only one member died violently during this period. Despite the targeting by irregulars, the force seems to have been generally welcomed by the people and certainly in Co. Louth it does not appear to have suffered any aggression. Michael Morgan, a member of the first contingent of Civic Guards to arrive in Louth, in October 1922, described how they were welcomed and very well treated by the people of Drogheda when they took over the former RIC barracks at South Quay.[98] Perhaps in an indication of a 'new order', when Anne Street Barracks in Dundalk was taken over by the Civic Guard the following month, the sand bags placed in front of the building were immediately removed.[99]

Including the disappearance of Constable McDonald, the deaths of two members of the 'Old RIC', three reserve policemen and one civilian can be attributed to Republican Volunteers in Louth, whilst the deaths of nine, and possibly ten, civilians or active republicans can be put down to activities by the police or military. The level of violence experienced in Co. Louth was not as ferocious as in other areas, such as in the west and south of the country, but the violent deaths of sixteen people, the destruction of property and the outbreaks of criminality between 1916 and 1922 were certainly not mild incidents. The remilitarising of the RIC in 1920, by augmenting it with the Special Reserves and the Auxiliary Division, badly tainted the force and contributed to the violent targeting of its members.

Although to a certain extent under siege and in need of reinforcement, it is doubtful if the members of the RIC in general welcomed the arrival of the Reserves. In December 1920, when Seamus McGuill was arrested by Black and Tans at a house in Dundalk, DI Gallagher intervened and personally took him into his protective custody, later telling him that 'you have no idea how hard it is to control these savages'.[100] Whilst many RIC men resigned during that turbulent period, most members remained within the force for many different reasons, ranging from purely domestic or financial, to an ingrained belief that they were a police force charged with the task of maintaining law and order. Many would have had nationalist leanings, but would have believed in the IPP principle that the objectives should only be achieved by political means.

Following disbandment, the former members of the RIC dispersed, many retiring under special pension arrangements or emigrating with financial assistance from the British Government. Others joined the Royal Ulster Constabulary or other colonial police forces, and a small number were enlisted into the Civic Guard. The demise of the RIC resulted in a new dawn of policing in Ireland and within not much more than a decade, under difficult and sometimes dangerous conditions, the Civic Guard, or An Garda Síochána, managed to establish itself as a fair and competent, unarmed, civil police force.[101]

Table 1. Co. Louth Barracks with barrack strength

Dundalk Anne Street HQ:14	Drogheda Westgate:14
Dundalk Quay Street: 8	Drogheda South Quay: 12
Dundalk Bridge Street: 8	Ardee: 6
Carlingford: 4	Dunleer:4
Castlebellingham: 5	Collon: 5
Ballymascanlon: 4	Clogherhead: 5
Louth: 4	Reaghstown: 4
Omeath: 4	Tallanstown: 4
Greenore: 4	Gilbertstown: 4
Blackrock: 4	

Source: National Archives Ireland, Census of Ireland 1911 returns.

NOTES

1   Tim Pat Coogan, *De Valera: long fellow, long shadow* (London: Hutchinson, 1993), p. 133.
2   Military Archives (MA), Bureau of Military History (BMH) Witness Statement (WS) 1285, 'Eamonn Broy'.
3   Ibid.
4   *Irish Times*, 24 Aug. 2012.
5   MA, BMH, WS.1280, 'Eamon Broy'.
6   The National Archives, London (TNA) Colonial Office (CO) 904, Chief Inspector's Confidential Monthly Report (CICMR), Co. Louth.
7   *Dundalk Democrat*, 23 Mar. 1912.
8   *Dundalk Democrat*, 29 Jun. 1912.
9   *Dundalk Democrat*, 24 Feb. 1912.
10 *Standing rules and regulations of the RIC* (Dublin 1911), rule 1745.
11 *Dundalk Democrat*, 20 Jul. 1912.
12 *Standing Rules and Regulations of the RIC* (Dublin 1911), rule 297.
13 Bulmer Hobson, 'Foundation and growth of the Irish volunteers, 1913–1914', in F.X. Martin (ed.), *The Irish volunteers 1913–1915: recollections and documents* (Dublin: James Duffy & Co., 1963; republished Merrion Press, 2013), pp. 19–26.
14 TNA, CO 904, CICMR, Co. Louth, May 1914.
15 Ibid., Sept. 1914.
16 Ibid., Nov. 1914.
17 Ibid.
18 Ibid., Jul. 1915.
19 Ibid., Aug. 1915.
20 Ibid., Jan.1916.
21 MA, BMH, WS.507, 'Joseph O'Higgins'; WS.233, 'Edward Bailey'.
22 MA, BMH, WS.232, 'Thomas Hamill'.

23   MA. BMH, WS.1052, 'Sean McEntee'.

24   *Dundalk Examiner*, 25 Mar. 1916.

25   *Dundalk Democrat*, 22 Apr. 1916.

26   Diarmaid Ferriter, *A Nation and not a rabble: the Irish Revolution, 1913–23* (London: Profile Books, 2015), pp. 153–4.

27   Dorothy Macardle, *The Irish Republic* (Dublin: The Irish Press, 1951), p. 162.

28   MA, BMH, WS.353, 'Seamus McGuill'.

29   MA, BMH, WS.161, 'Donal O'Hannigan'.

30   Ibid.

31   MA, BMH, WS.677, 'Patrick McHugh'.

32   MA, BMH, WS.1052, 'Sean McEntee'.

33   TNA, CO 904, CICMR, Co. Louth, Apr. 1916.

34   Ibid., Jun. 1916.

35   Ibid., Jul. 1916.

36   Ibid., Feb.1917.

37   Ibid., Jul. 1917.

38   MA, BMH, WS.494, 'Peter Kieran'.

39   TNA, CO 904, CICMR, Co. Louth, Jul. 1917.

40   Ibid.

41   Ibid., Jan. 1918

42   Ibid., Dec. 1918.

43   Ibid., May 1918

44   MA, BMH, WS.353, 'Seamus McGuill'.

45   TNA, CO 904, CICMR, Co. Louth, Nov. 1918.

46   MA, BMH, WS.1721, 'Seamus Robinson'.

47   Ferriter, *A nation not a rabble*, p. 193.

48   MA, BMH, WS.353, 'Seamus McGuill'.

49   *Dundalk Democrat*, 14 Aug. 1920.

50   MA, BMH, WS.708, 'Conor A. Maguire'.

51   Peter Hughes papers, in private hands.

52   MA, BMH, WS.353, 'Seamus McGuill'.

53   *Dundalk Democrat*, 25 Sept. 1920, as cited in Kevin McMahon (ed.), *A time of trouble: a chronology of the Anglo-Irish and Civil Wars in Armagh, South Down and North Louth 1919–1923 as compiled by Éamonn Ó Huallacháin* (FeedARead.com, 2014) (hereafter *A time of trouble*), p. 160.

54   *Dundalk Democrat*, 10 Jul. 1920.

55   MA, BMH, WS.507, 'Joseph O'Higgins'.

56   *Dundalk Democrat*, 4 July 1920; *A time of trouble*, p. 100.

57   Charles Townshend, *The Republic; the fight for Irish independence 1918–1923* (London: Allen Lane, 2013), p. 133.

58   MA, BMH, WS.353, 'Seamus McGuill'.

59   Stephen O'Donnell, *The Royal Irish Constabulary and the Black and Tans in County Louth 1919–1922* (O'Donnell: 2004), p. 110.

60   *Newry Reporter*, 8 Feb. 1919; *A time of trouble*, p. 10.

61   TNA, CO 904, CICMR, Jun. 1919.

62   O'Donnell, *The Royal Irish Constabulary and the Black and Tans*, p. 83.

63   *Dundalk Democrat*, 5 Jul. 1919.

64   MA, BMH, WS.353, 'Seamus McGuill'.

65   *Newry Reporter*, 27 Mar. 1920; *A time of trouble*, p. 61.

66 *Dundalk Democrat*, 5 Jun. 1920; *A time of trouble*, p. 84.
67 O'Donnell, *The Royal Irish Constabulary and the Black and Tans*, pp. 46–50.
68 Ibid., pp. 161–4.
69 MA, BMH, WS.507, 'Joseph O'Higgins'.
70 MA, BMH, WS.353, 'Seamus McGuill'.
71 *Dundalk Democrat*, 24 Apr. 1920; *A time of trouble*, p. 74.
72 TNA, CO 904, CICMR, Co. Louth, Jul. 1920.
73 O'Donnell, *The Royal Irish Constabulary and the Black and Tans*, p. 143.
74 *Dundalk Democrat*, 8 Jan. 1921; *A time of trouble*, p. 221.
75 *Dundalk Democrat*, 12 Mar. 1921; *A time of trouble*, p. 254.
76 MA, BMH, WS.353, 'Seamus McGuill'.
77 MA, BMH, WS.237, 'Patrick Duffy'.
78 O'Donnell, *The Royal Irish Constabulary and the Black and Tans*, p. 92.
79 MA, BMH, WS.353, 'Seamus McGuill'.
80 O'Donnell, *The Royal Irish Constabulary and the Black and Tans*, p. 119.
81 Ibid., p. 115.
82 MA, BMH, WS.507, 'Joseph O'Higgins'.
83 TNA, CO 904, CICMR, May 1921.
84 O'Donnell, *The Royal Irish Constabulary and the Black and Tans*, p. 122.
85 MA, BMH, WS.507, 'Joseph O'Higgins'.
86 O'Donnell, *The Royal Irish Constabulary and the Black and Tans*, p. 129.
87 Ibid., p. 174.
88 TNA, CO 904, CICMR, Co. Louth, Jun. 1921; *Dundalk Democrat*, 25 Jun. 1921; *A time of trouble*, p. 336.
89 MA, truce liaison and evacuation papers, LE/B/4-11.
90 *Dundalk Democrat*, 16 Jul. 1921; *A time of trouble*, p. 354.
91 TNA, CO 904, CICMR (Secret & Crime Report), Co. Louth, Sept. 1921.
92 Ibid., 25 Sept. 1921.
93 Ibid., 10 Oct. 1921.
94 *Dundalk Democrat*, 21 Jan. 1922; *A time of trouble*, p. 396.
95 *Dundalk Democrat*, 11 Feb. 1922.
96 *Dundalk Democrat*, 6 May 1922.
97 *Dundalk Democrat*, 13 May 1922; *A time of trouble*, p. 449.
98 *Journal of Old Drogheda Society*, 1977.
99 *Dundalk Democrat*, 4 Nov. 1922; *A time of trouble*, p. 557.
100 MA, BMH, WS.353, 'Seamus McGuill'.
101 I wish to acknowledge the assistance offered by the staff of the Military Archives, Dublin, the National Archives of Ireland, UCD Archives, the National Library of Ireland, Louth County Library and Louth County Archives. Thanks also to Pat O'Donoghue for giving me access to his collection of police memorabilia and to Lucy Hughes for allowing me to peruse the papers of the late Peter Hughes.

5

'Playing the Rebel': Propaganda and Amateur Dramatics in County Louth, 1902–1916

Fiona Fearon

The Cultural Revival and the development of a new kind of Irish drama has rightly been the focus of much research over the last century. However, the focus has been almost entirely on how this has manifested itself in the large cities, Dublin in particular, but occasionally Belfast, Cork or Galway. What is less clearly articulated is how the struggle for a nationalist cultural and political identity was played out in the towns and villages of Ireland, away from the major metropolis. This essay will explore the cultural life of Dundalk in the years approaching the 1916 Rising, as the various cultural and political organisations sought to ignite visions of a future independent Ireland, based on popular representations of Ireland's rebellious past. Dundalk between 1901 and 1911 had a population of just over 13,000 people, making it among the largest towns in Ireland during the era. By comparison, Galway city had a population of 13,255 in 1911 and Kilkenny city had 10,514 people.[1] Clearly, Dundalk's location on the eastern seaboard, almost equidistant between Dublin and Belfast, at the centre of both rail and shipping networks and therefore a hub of industry and commerce, as well as a military base, had a great deal to do with its population size. This location also meant that touring theatre and musical companies that typically played on an axis between Belfast, Dublin and Cork would regularly stop off in Dundalk.[2] After the refurbishment of the Town Hall Theatre in 1901 to accommodate a proper stage and audience seating, not only did the number of local amateur performances increase, but a regular diet of London comedies, farces and musicals were served to the discerning population of Dundalk.[3]

That population was not content with being just an audience, and it becomes clear, looking at the local papers from the early twentieth century, that there was a vibrant amateur theatre community at the time, which was beginning to see the potential for performance in bringing together young men and women to discuss and enact ideas of nationalism. Between 1900 and 1916, the Catholic Young Men's Society (CYMS), the Young Ireland Society (YIS) and Sinn Féin in Dundalk performed both popular melodramas and revival dramas, which, despite their possible lack of artistic merit, supported a growing nationalist culture in the town of Dundalk. There were also productions in Irish, new plays written by local playwrights, and visits from Cumann na nGaedheal and Patrick Pearse's boy performers from St Enda's school. In playing the rebel, they imagined and embodied the performance of a revolution that was to come.

Dundalk, as a garrison town, had a significant military presence. Alongside the patriotic melodramas and Cultural Revival nationalistic performances you also had members of the British Army stationed in Dundalk producing their own plays and entertainment. In 1904 alone, there were amateur performances of *The Colleen Bawn*, Boucicault's melodrama, by the CYMS, a new version of *Robert Emmett* by Cumann na nGaedheal under the auspices of the YIS, and a charity performance of *The Manoeuvres of Jane* by a company of officers and their wives organised by Lady Louth.[4] It seems clear that playing and performing were important to both sides in the future production that would be the Rising of 1916. Although Yeats' and Lady Gregory's play, *Kathleen ni Houlihan*, definitely made an appearance in Dundalk, it was more likely that the soldiers of the Rising and War of Independence had their imaginations fuelled by melodramas like *The Shaughraun, Lord Edward or '98* and *Robert Emmet*.

Christopher Morash describes the theatrical context of Ireland in the late nineteenth century as 'a crowded room'.[5] Where early historians and propagandists for the Irish National Theatre Society conceived of themselves as bringing light to the ignorant darkness of Irish theatre, the reality was much more complex. Any survey of Dublin in 1900 would see a city saturated with multiple theatres and music halls, some of them seating up to 3,000 people. These were commercial theatres providing popular entertainment for working-class Dubliners, as well as the middle classes, and their fare was not without a strong element of nationalist sentiment.[6] Irish-born playwright, Dion Boucicault, created a number of popular nationalistic melodramas, *The Colleen Bawn, Arrah-na-Pogue* and *The Shaughraun,* which skilfully balanced a sentimental patriotic feeling with successful entertainment. As Mary Trotter explains, 'heroes were nationalists, villains were traitors, heroines loved heroes while being stalked by villains', and through it all strode a comic character actor with a thick brogue who would 'laugh and fight and endure for Ireland'.[7]

By the 1890s, Boucicault's plays were revived on an almost annual basis in Dublin at either the Theatre Royal or the Queen's Royal Theatre.[8] In fact, the Queen's, under the management of the English entrepreneur, J.W. Whitbread, became known from 1883 as 'The House of Irish Drama'.[9] As the centenary of the 1798 rebellion approached, there was a surge of interest in patriotic dramas with a strong helping of sentiment. Whitbread produced Boucicault plays, as well as works like Hubert O' Grady's *The Famine, The Insurgents* and *For the Land She Loved,* and his own creations *Robert Emmet* and *Wolfe Tone.*[10] At the Queen's, audiences were encouraged to sing along with popular nationalist songs, as well as enjoy the spectacle of Irish landscapes like Kerry and Mayo that many of the urban working-class Dublin audience might never have seen. Plays like *Robert Emmet, Wolf Tone, Lord Edward Fitzgerald or '98* and *Sarsfield* not only combined clever peasant comic characters in the mode of Conn the Shaughraun, but presented the great orators and heroes of nineteenth-century nationalist Ireland.

There was an element of 'preaching' to audiences in Dublin, London and New York on the conditions in Ireland but also a depiction of the 'nationalist project as one that united social classes, one that in fact required the cooperation of brave peasant and Anglo-Irish gentry alike'.[11] Perhaps it was this combination of nationalism and social reform that appealed so much to popular audiences, and made these plays the most frequent choices for amateur productions in Dundalk in the era before the Rising.

Although popular with the general Irish audience at home and abroad, the standard fare of the Queen's was the target of much criticism from the nationalist and Celtic Revival intelligentsia. Lady Gregory and Yeats rejected the easy sentimentality and comic buffoonery of the 'Stage Irishman' in their Manifesto for the Irish Literary Theatre in 1898, as they sought to establish ownership of the right to define Irish national identity.[12] The Fay brothers, William and Frank, criticised the shallowness of this popular form both in their frequent editorials in the *United Irishman* as well as in their own attempts to create a new style of indigenous theatre with the Irish National Dramatic Society.[13] The political and ideological battle to define Irishness through drama was not just the preserve of artists and writers, but could be seen in the activities of many nationalist organisations. There is evidence that the Gaelic League, Inghinidhe na hÉireann and the boys from St Enda's School, all engaged in the performance of dramas and tableaux on folk and mythic themes as national identity was imagined and reimagined before the Rising.[14]

Away from the salons and theatres of Dublin, Alice Milligan's were perhaps the most popular of these amateur entertainments. Milligan was appointed travelling lecturer for the Gaelic League in 1904, and her dramatic presentations, 'part tableau, part magic-lantern show, part didactic narration',[15] were important in drawing audiences and participants into the world of politics as well as the dynamic world of performance in early twentieth-century Ireland. Her productions were associated not only with the Gaelic League but with Maud Gonne's Inghinidhe na hÉireann. Although Lady Gregory dismissed her efforts as 'tawdry', she successfully disseminated her populist nationalistic message to a wide audience. More importantly she also provided a model for 'do-it-yourself Irish drama in undemanding but widely read journals such as *Ireland's Own* and the *Irish Weekly Freeman*'.[16] It is not clear whether Milligan ever visited Dundalk, but certainly the Dundalk YIS were inspired by the visit of the Cumann na nGaedheal Dramatic Company in 1904, a company she may have had contact with through her many associations within the nationalist amateur drama movements in Dublin.

The drama class of the Dundalk YIS premiered their own productions of Abbey plays *The Eloquent Dempsey* and *Kathleen ni Houlihan* in 1908, but were soon followed by amateur companies producing similar plays in Reaghstown, Dunleer and Carrickmacross. These productions required an immense commitment from both performers and producers, as they took on learning lines, making costumes and building sets outside their normal working lives. Amateur performances in the early twentieth century had all the same drawbacks and advantages of amateur theatre today, but what seems clear is that whatever the quality of the productions, there were both performers and an audience willing to support these amateur exploits. As Foster says, 'they found each other'.[17]

The pattern of populist melodrama appreciated by the many, and artistic, mythic or modernist nationalist drama appreciated by the few, is largely repeated in the amateur and professional performances in Dundalk between 1900 and 1916. The CYMS regularly ran into criticism from the local Redmonite paper, the *Dundalk Democrat*, for presenting popular melodramas, while the YIS and other amateur groups who performed Revival-inspired productions were generally celebrated. The *Dundalk Democrat* promoted both the Irish language and Irish culture in all its forms, but also records the 'crowded room' of popular entertainment in Dundalk, from visiting melodramas, farces and musical comedies, to day trips to pantomimes in Dublin and even the first experiences of modern technology, moving images, phonographs and the first cinema.[18] Dundalk was not an isolated cultural wasteland, but a microcosm of the capital in miniature. It is interesting that the cultural activities of Sinn Féin in 1909 did not focus on nationalist mythic drama or even Irish language drama, but on a contemporary adaptation of those patriotic sentimental melodramas so hated by the nationalist elites.

Performance venues in Dundalk varied from church halls, club rooms and gymnasiums to the newly refurbished Town Hall theatre. The Town Hall was constructed as a corn exchange in the early 1860s, and was used for many years as a fairly multi-purpose space with a temporary stage for performances constructed with 'planks and barrels'.[19] After it reopened in January 1902, it had a fixed extended stage, a proscenium arch, fireproof curtain with an image of Narrow Water, Carlingford Loch and Flagstaff on it, as well as 160 leather armchairs closest to the stage, scarlet plush seats in the balcony and wooden benches at the back of the stalls for the cheap seats.[20] There was another venue for performances in the Assembly Rooms above the Market House, demolished in 1968, where Baden Powell, founder of the Scouting Movement, took part in an amateur performance of a one act farce, *Box and Cox*, by and for the officers based in Dundalk.[21]

Other venues included the gymnasium at the back of the CYMS club rooms where the first performances of their drama group were held in 1901, and the hall of the newly finished St Malachy's Dominican Priory National School, referred to locally as 'the Friary', completed in 1900. Concerts and entertainments of both classical music and Irish traditional songs took place not only in the Town Hall but in various churches and schools around the area. Within the first few months of 1900 both the Dundalk YIS and the CYMS advertised meetings and dances in their club rooms or halls, which included songs and recitations, as well as 'phonograph selections'.[22] In the same few months at the start of 1900 there were concerts advertised in St Vincent's School and St Mary's College, Dundalk; Kilcurry New Church; Mullabawn [sic]; Castleblaney National Forrester's Dramatic Club; and the Boy's School, Ardee.[23]

There was a strong nationalist element to many of these presentations, apart from the obvious Annual St Patrick's Concert held in the Town Hall.[24] A review of a concert at Grange, Carlingford, in May 1900, which included songs like *The Irish Emigrant* and 'other ballads of patriotic feeling or of the pure and simple sentiment of the Irish heart', provoked the *Democrat* columnist to criticise other non-Irish style entertainments, 'and why should the organisers of other entertainments of the kind seek their material amongst the inane and maudlin and tuneless rubbish that some of us over here affect to like because it is "English – quite English you know"'.[25]

The opening of the refurbished Town Hall in 1902 with the increase of both visiting professional productions and more frequent and ambitious amateur productions, prompted the *Democrat* to run two columns in October under the title 'The Modern Stage'. Principal among their concerns were that 'some of the very modern forms of entertainment that are promised to us are not as clean-minded people on this side of the water will care to attend'. The columnist complained that although these things might be acceptable in London, 'whence morals have long since departed', and are tolerated in Dublin, 'the provincial mind is, thank Heaven, cleaner, and its critical faculties acuter than are those of the Dublin public'.[26]

The particular object of the *Democrat's* ire was the professional visit of a musical comedy called *The Belle of New York*, which played to packed houses in the Town Hall despite the protestation of not only the local paper, but D.P. Moran's *The Leader*. The play had been a huge success in New York and London in 1897–98, running for nearly 700 performances in London, but was clearly exactly the type of modern drama at odds with a pure vision of Catholic Ireland, favoured by a certain type of nationalist.[27] The *Democrat* was resigned to the fact that much of the audience were 'soldiers and their friends', but was disgusted that many were the curious 'respectable people of the town', 'some of the

Catholic *elite*' and 'country people in their evening dress'. He is entirely scathing of the play, a melodrama based on a reprobate American youth who decided to have an adventure with a sixteen-year-old French maid in the Chinese quarter of New York the night before his wedding to a 'high-kicker from the music halls'. He then falls in love with the 'Belle', a Salvation Army missionary in this den of vice, who is miraculously found to be a lost heiress at the conclusion of the play. The *Democrat* columnist is particularly upset by the effect such a production might have on the 'giggling empty-headed Miss who thinks the Gaelic Movement "such rot"', and fears the effect of both 'the Gay Parisienne' maid and the Belle herself, who are both 'poor specimens of womanhood for our daughters to copy'. [28]

There were many such professional productions that visited Dundalk in the pre-Rising years and although there were some Queen's type melodramas, the majority of productions were West End farces and comedies, with the occasional Shakespearean play to provide an element of culture. In 1902, two Irish-based impresarios, Lena Lewis and Kennedy Miller, both brought Irish melodramas to Dundalk with titles like *The Rebel's Wife – A Tale of the Rebellion of '98*, *The Insurgent Chief*, *Michael Dwyer* and *Lord Edward or '98*.[29] However, more typical fare was brought by the British theatre producer, W. Payne Seddon, who, in 1904 alone, brought six productions to the Town Hall, from April to November, including comedies like *Are you a Mason?*, *A Message from Mars* and *A Chinese Honeymoon*.[30]

The choice of play seemed to be entirely dependent on availability and viability of the touring companies who were engaged on a circuitous route from Belfast to Cork or Wexford, via Dublin.[31] *A Message from Mars* was advertised as having been performed 700 times at the Avenue Theatre, London, while *The New Clown*, also performed in 1904, was advertised as having been recently shown at the Gaiety, Dublin, and the Theatre Royal, Belfast.[32] These advertisements suggest that Payne Seddon was aware that his audience in Dundalk were interested in successful productions from both Dublin and London. Although a small town, Dundalk was close enough to Dublin, that regular special trains would be organised in January each year to bring Dundalk residents to the pantomimes in the Gaiety and the Theatre Royal.[33]

It is also clear from the 'About Town' sections, and editorials like the 'Modern Stage' discussion of 1902, and reprinted excerpts from *The Leader* and other nationalistic journals, that the *Democrat* saw the Dundalk audience as cosmopolitan, educated and discerning. In 1907, there were four visiting productions of Shakespeare plays, and in February 1908, Payne Seddon brought productions of *Hamlet* and *Romeo and Juliet*.[34] At a benefit performance in May 1908 to celebrate fifteen years of visiting Dundalk, Payne Seddon complemented his audience: 'In Dundalk he found the people could laugh at a farce and occasionally enjoy the jingle of musical comedy; but even the man in the street, who occupies the back seats, commonly known as the region of the gods, can appreciate in its turn a really good play.'[35]

That Payne Seddon could keep returning to Dundalk, and run touring versions of West End productions for two or three nights four to six times a year, suggests that there was a significant proportion of the population who were happy to pay to see these plays. Audiences also flocked to see amateur performances in the Town Hall, perhaps because they knew the performers, but also because productions were entertaining or even controversial. The most successful productions in terms of achieving audience capacity in the Town Hall seem to have been the run of melodramas performed by the drama class of the Dundalk CYMS, which premiered its first full-scale production in 1901. Their premiere production was *The Shaughraun* by Dion Boucicault, first performed at their 200-seat gymnasium at the end of March 1901. On 9 April, Easter Tuesday that year, they reproduced their performance in the Town Hall with 'beautifully illuminated tableaux and mechanical effects'.[36]

The columnist for the *Democrat* was supportive, if not enthusiastic: 'The piece was very well presented, the acting being very good in some parts, and the staging was first rate'.[37] The lack of success of some of the acting may have been because the CYMS did not consider it appropriate for young women to spend their evenings 'in an exclusively male club, especially when they would be called upon, without even a chaperon, to rehearse a loving embrace, or even a kiss'. This prudishness meant that all the female romantic leads were played by 'beardless youth' until 1904.[38]

The company was more successful in the casting of its comic lead, Conn, the Shaughraun, played by Hugh McDermott, who became a leading member of the company. Boucicault's play premiered in New York in 1874, and although set during the Fenian insurrection of 1866, contains 'young lovers, a priest, an English gentleman' and the archetypal 'Stage Irishman' in Conn, 'the soul of every fair, the life of every funeral, the first fiddle at all weddings and patterns.'[39] The production was so popular that it was revived the following year as a benefit production for the 'Christian Schools, Dundalk'.[40] Many came to see the production again, however the *Democrat* considered the choice of play lacked merit. The antagonist of the play is Kinchela, an evil double-crossing squireen who is aided by the police agent, Harvey Duff. In addition, one of the two heroes is a sympathetic portrayal of an English character, Captain Molineux, who falls in love with an Irish heiress who has fallen on hard times.

The problem for the columnist of the *Democrat* was that although he saw the value in the dramatic class as a 'very pleasant and useful recreation', he objected to the poor quality of the play choices by the CYMS. He described Irish drama as in a 'transitional stage', with no good-quality plays as yet produced by the Gaelic movement and the old melodramas seeming not only unfashionable but too British and in poor taste.[41]

Their 1902 production of Whitbread's melodrama, *A True Son of Erin*, provoked the *Democrat* columnist vigorously to criticise the author for his 'strong melodrama' and an unnecessary amount of 'slewsthering' or love-making, as well as taking the heroes from the Irish landlord class and the British Navy. Considering that all the female parts were played by boys, the columnist's anxiety about the how 'Irish girls love without loss of modesty' seems misplaced. He accepted that Whitbread's work was 'a laudable attempt' but felt it was unrealistic, and bemoaned the lack of a true Irish drama that looked at the 'deep tragedy of Irish life':

> It is saying much for him that he has contrived to make his plays much less offensive than many; but when – oh when? – will an Irishman worthy of the part arise to give us, after centuries of Mickey Frees, plays showing us Irish life as it is, bringing out the nobilities that underlie our national character, not the idiosyncrasies that be on the surface.[42]

By 1908, the CYMS had to accept their melodramas were beginning to seem outdated. Not only had they produced all of Boucicault's major Irish plays, *The Shaughraun*, *Colleen Bawn* and *Arrah-na-Pogue*, they had also produced many by Whitbread and Hubert O'Grady. The most notorious was probably O'Grady's *The Fenian*, produced in 1903, which did not even merit a review from the *Democrat*, but instead prompted a reprint of comment made in the *United Irishman*. The production was criticised for having 'all the worst faults of this class of drama'. Although from the title you would expect a nationalist theme to emerge, the *United Irishman* describes it as a 'common place love story' the hero of which is a young lieutenant in the British Army. Worst of all, the 'Irish characters are made to appear stupid, low and vulgar, while the English personages are well-nigh perfect'.[43]

The poor choice of play was seen as symptomatic of a lack of patriotism and nationalistic fervour in the CYMS in which the Irish class and hurling club had both seemed to die out through lack of interest. This attack was followed up the next week by a reprint from *The Leader* in which not only was the play described as 'a glorification of a British military officer' but the members of the CYMS were described as 'West British', and accused of tearing up copies of *The Leader* in their reading room.[44] The *Democrat* pointed out that this information must have come from a member and there is the suggestion that internally the CYMS was undergoing a breakdown in the group between those who saw it as a social club and those who saw it as a proto-political organisation.[45]

Many of those dissenting voices may have taken up membership of other social and political organisations by 1908, as the *Democrat* has a number of pages in each weekly edition devoted to notices and reports from meetings of local branches of the Ancient Order of Hibernians, the United Irish League, the Irish National Foresters and Sinn Féin. Perhaps because of this and a shift in the temperament of the time, the CYMS drama class, which still included many of the original members like Hugh McDermott, P.J. Murphy and P.J. Watters, decided to produce *O'Donnell's Cross* by Lottie MacManus in 1908. McManus's play seems to have been first produced at the Rotunda, Dublin, in 1907, and is associated with the National Players Society, a nationalist organisation that combined Edward Martyn, members of the Gaelic League, and Cumann na nGaedheal.[46] The *Democrat* was pleased with the choice of play by the CYMS, describing it as a 'play of a different character' that represented 'a higher aim than its predecessors'.[47]

O'Donnell's Cross is a reworking of the popular melodrama *Sarsfield* by Whitbread, although from the *Democrat's* description it is difficult to tell the difference. The O'Donnell's Cross of the title is a diamond crucifix that is entrusted to Lady Sarsfield by a young officer during the Siege of

Limerick. The cross is lost and then rescued by a young Irish woman, Eithne Ni Brien, and returned in time to save the reputation of Iveagh, the hero of the piece. The *Democrat* concludes that the play ends in the usual way 'with the preliminaries for a marriage'. Peace had obviously been restored between the columnist of the *Democrat* and the CYMS as he complemented each member of the company individually and concluded, 'Altogether the production reflected the greatest credit upon the members of this Club, who with each succeeding production prove themselves more and more entitled to commendation and support.'[48]

O'Donnell's Cross may have been associated with many of the organisations of the Cultural Revival, but it was still essentially a melodrama that ended with marriage after intrigue and comedy. The CYMS would continue with its populist dramas until the 1920s when it became more noted for 'Savoy operas'.[49] However, it failed to engage in serious intellectually or politically motivated drama. The criticisms of the organisation in 1903 seemed to be symptomatic of a strong conservative element. For a more radical engagement with the artistic exploits of the Revival, Dundalk needed to turn to the YIS.

The YIS may have engaged in drama classes for some time before their premiere productions in 1908, but they were a much more politically and artistically minded group than the CYMS. In 1904, they invited Cumann na nGaedheal to perform two plays as part of their St Patrick's Day celebrations. Cumann na nGaedheal brought a new version of *Robert Emmet* by Henry Connell Mangan that had only premiered in 1903 at the Samhain Festival to celebrate Emmet's centenary. This was quite a different play from the 'burlesque under the same name written by a certain English comedian'.[50] Both Whitbread and Boucicault had produced versions of the life story of Robert Emmet, which were highly wrought, melodramatic and inaccurate.[51] The Mangan version had none of this artifice, and the columnist of the *Democrat* could not speak highly enough of this version of Emmet's life story:

One sees faithfully reflected the high and noble aims of the young patriot, the really well-matured wisdom of plans that a rash world has called foolhardy; the steadfast loyalty and self-sacrifice of Anne Devlin, Dwyer, and a very few conspirators; the cowardice and falseness of too many, the hideous web of treachery woven by England's watchdogs in the Castle.[52]

The production itself was aided by a fine performance from Abbey actors Dudley Digges and Maire Quinn in the lead roles of Robert Emmet and Sarah Curran, and was altogether described as a fine amateur production, 'vastly superior in artistic comprehension to many professionals we have known'. The evening was completed by a short bilingual comedy by Douglas Hyde called *Bursting the Bubble* in which a group of university professors who mock the Irish language are cursed to speak only Irish when the Lord Lieutenant visits their college in Dublin. After the drama of *Robert Emmet* this seems to have been a very welcome relief, provoking 'roars of laughter'.

This visit, organised by the YIS, was obviously inspirational as four years later they produced their own productions of similar Revival plays. The *Democrat* not only ran advertisements for the YIS premiere production in the two weeks running up to their opening night on St Patrick's night, 17 March 1908, but devoted a full page-length column to a review of their two offerings, *Kathleen ni Houlihan* and *The Eloquent Dempsey*. The Town Hall was full and they were not disappointed, 'even experienced actors could hardly have done better', according to the *Democrat*. *Kathleen ni Houlihan* was considered an 'ambitious effort' and 'one which might try the capacities of seasoned actors'. In fact, the *Democrat* columnist was very impressed with this first public effort from the YIS, particularly the performance of Miss Matthews in the role of Kathleen. The lead role in William Boyle's *The Eloquent Dempsey* was taken by P. O'Connell, who 'astonished even his intimate friends by the fervour and enthusiasm with which he threw himself into the part'.

The second play was a comedy, but equally challenging theatrically in that Dempsey is required to give 'half a dozen lengthy and ornate speeches' in his attempt to avoid committing to either side in his manoeuvres between the Home Rulers and Unionists in small town Ireland. The 'audience dispersed in a state of high good humour' and it seemed that the *Democrat* felt they had found a new popular theatre group who produced true Irish drama.[53] There is little suggestion that there was any political motivation in this presentation, from either the performers or the audience. Although Boyle's play was relatively modern, only having premiered at the Abbey in 1906, *Kathleen ni Houlihan* had been in circulation both as a performance and in print since 1902. Boyle's play is essentially a representation, in comic form, of problems of modern contemporaneous Irish life, whereas Yeats and Lady Gregory's play has a good deal in common with the patriotic associations of a Queen's melodrama as a young man is called to join the rebellion of 1798. Unlike a Queen's melodrama, however, there is no comedy, no happy ending with marriage, and the only solution to the hero's problem on offer is self-sacrifice and death in the service of Ireland. Although the reaction of the audience to this was not really described as the *Democrat* focused on the positive feeling left by the second comedy, the columnist's concentration on the skill of the performance suggests that the play was at least impressive from a theatrical perspective.

As with the CYMS, the YIS drama class only made one presentation a year, and chose to perform on St Patrick's Day in a deliberate attempt to provide an Irish themed celebration for the evening. Over the following years, plays from both the Abbey catalogue and that of the Ulster Literary Theatre were presented, and represented by the YIS. In March 1909, Rutherford Mayne's interesting play analysing the response of the Northern Protestant community to the arts was the opening play. It had premiered in 1906 at the Examination Hall of Queen's University Belfast, performed by the Ulster Literary Theatre, and was then published in 1907 in Dublin. The play's central problem was whether the Co. Down-based protagonist, Robbie John, should give up his gift for music to settle down to work and marriage. Having destroyed his own violin at the behest of his father, he is offered temptation when he inherits a violin from a tramp he befriends. His fiancée supports him in following his dream but his father disowns him and drives him from the home. This drama was contrasted with Lady Gregory's comedy *Hyacinth Halvey*, originally produced at the Abbey in 1906.[54]

The following year, 1910, the YIS presented four one-act plays over a matinee and evening performance, two previous presentations and two new plays. *The Eloquent Dempsey* was the matinee performance, and the evening performance ended with a representation of *Kathleen ni Houlihan*. The evening performance opened with Synge's tragedy, *Riders to the Sea*, followed by another Lady Gregory comedy, *The Jackdaw*. Again, the *Democrat* refers to how the Town Hall was 'packed to the doors' and goes into considerable detail naming each cast member and their qualities of performance. However, the columnist did not seem to be greatly impressed by either tragedy, and reserved his briefest comments for these two plays. He only listed the cast of *Kathleen ni*

Houlihan saying their parts were 'well taken', but since it had already been reviewed in 1908, he did not feel the need to repeat himself. He might have said more about *Riders to the Sea*, as it was a new production for the company, but all the columnist could say was that 'while it gives scope for very good acting, is not a piece which appeals in any sense to an audience'.

By comparison, both comedies got up to half a column of description, suggesting that although the *Democrat* could write extensively on the value of the Irish language and the cultural Revival, it still preferred its Irish culture to be comic rather than tragic.[55] As an amateur group who were largely involved in drama for enjoyment, it is hardly surprising that in the following years they focused on similar comedies from the Abbey school of playwrights like William Boyle's *The Mineral Workers*. The group's drama activities seemed to fade away by the 1920s, probably choosing to focus on the strength of their Gaelic football club.[56]

Prior to 1916, however, the YIS Dramatic Class quickly became one of many associated with the villages and towns of north Louth. In January 1909, Reaghstown Temperance Solidarity Dramatic Class performed *The Eloquent Dempsey* and another comedy by Lady Gregory, *Spreading the News*.[57] In April 1910, the Dunleer Dramatic Class were more ambitious, performing a patriotic melodrama by Ira Allen called *Father Murphy, or the Hero of Tullow*.[58] In January 1911, the Farney Players in Carrickmacross were more inclined towards Revival plays, producing a comedy by Lady Gregory called *The Workhouse Ward* and a four-act drama by Count Markievicz called *The Memory of the Dead*. This play again recounted the story of 1798, as it dealt with 'Ireland after the French invasion, and presented in vivid colour the story of failure, ruin and gloom, with tragedy surmounting all.' The *Democrat* was impressed that this Polish Count had captured the tragedy of the situation and had not resorted to the humour of most Irish playwrights: 'It was a triumph for our amateurs that with such material in hand they not only made the piece interesting, but succeeded in giving that lump in the throat arising from a sympathetic feeling between the auditorium and the stage'.[59]

The wide variety of groups performing in Dundalk and the surrounding areas shows that there was clearly a great excitement and feeling of engagement with the process of creating plays. Paige Reynolds describes the 'craze for drama supported by the volume and variety of theatrical activity in Dublin and across the country', and there is certainly wide evidence of this in Dundalk.[60] And nowhere can the symbiotic relationship between performance and politics be seen more clearly than in the plays presented by the Sinn Féin drama class in 1909. Sinn Féin struggled as a political force in Dundalk in the early years of the century, as it competed with the strong Redmonite feelings in the town, and the numerous diverse political and social organisations.[61]

Apart from the dramatic attempts to defend the Catholic community of Rostrevor from attacks by the Orange Order during the July marching seasons from 1903 on, the president of Sinn Féin in Dundalk, Paddy Hughes, was most noted by his followers for his enthusiasm for lectures and plays.[62] Hugh Kearney explained that Hughes' idea was for Sinn Féin to organise 'plenty of lectures, plays and concerts in which the policy of physical force was stressed as a means of obtaining our freedom from English rule'.

According to Hughes, such entertainment attracted large audiences even though most of those present 'had no use for Sinn Féin as a serious political weapon'. Kearney complained that their performances were not rewarded with the increase in recruits they felt their efforts deserved, but he argued that the performances did 'create an interest among the people in a general way' that later helped to swell the ranks of the Irish Volunteers.[63] Although the witness statements refer to productions of two plays, *Lord Edward Fitzgerald* and *Robert Emmet*, the only production that seemed to be reviewed by the *Democrat* was Mangan's version of the Emmet story performed by the dramatic class of the Sinn Fein Society in the Town Hall on 20 April 1909. However, this was not the first public performance of this production, as the *Democrat* recorded that 'the class had already produced the latter piece in their own hall'.

The Sinn Féin Dramatic Class were hugely ambitious, performing two three-act dramas on the same night, *Robert Emmet* and *The Patriot Priest*. There is no author listed for this second play, and very little detail given of the production, except to complain that one of the actors overdid his part 'as to more faintly resemble that almost extinct monstrosity, the stage Irishman'. Dundalk had already seen Mangan's version of *Robert Emmet* performed by the semi-professional players of Cumann na nGaedheal in 1904, so the *Democrat* was conscious that this was 'an ambitious piece for any company to tackle, doubly so for amateurs'. However, the Sinn Féin actors seem to have produced a creditable performance, with Joseph Berrill being described as particularly good in the role of Emmet. The major criticism of the presentation was that the evening was too long and that the class had made a 'major error of judgement' in doing two full-length plays on the one evening. This did not seem to deter the 'very large audience' in attendance, so perhaps Hughes was not boasting in his suggestions that these entertainments were popular.[64]

He was also incorrect in suggesting that there were no recruits for the organisation through these productions, as at least two members of the cast for these plays in 1909 appear on a list of those involved with the Irish Volunteers in 1916. Joseph Berrill, who played Emmet, James Jennings who appeared as Billy Byrne in *The Patriot Priest*, and possibly Pat McHugh, who may be the 'Mr MacHugh' who played a minor role in *Robert Emmett*, all appear on the list. There is also a Maria Jennings on the cast list, who might have been a relative of James Jennings, as well as Michael and Gilbert Coburn who could have been related to Frank Coburn who is listed as one of the Volunteers.[65] The lack of secondary reports of these Sinn Féin productions beyond this appearance in 1909 may be because the Dramatic Class chose to keep their performances for the internal audience at their own hall, or that the class declined very soon after this performance as the Sinn Féin members became more involved in political activity. James McGuill's witness statement is the only one to refer to both *Robert Emmet* and *Lord Edward Fitzgerald*, although there is no other evidence that Sinn Féin produced the second play.

It is interesting to note, however, that less than two months before the Sinn Féin production of *Robert Emmet*, the CYMS produced Whitbread's version of *Lord Edward, or '98*. Perhaps McGuill had confused the groups who produced these plays in his memory, and if not as performers, then certainly as audience, there was probably considerable crossover between the amateur groups performing in Dundalk.

There is one final group of performers in Dundalk who were perhaps growing in awareness of nationalism during this time, and this was the children of the Friary schools. Below the controversial review of *A True Son of Erin* in 1902, the *Democrat* took note of a new play by Shemus O'Toole called *The King of West Britain* to be produced by the Oriel Amateur Dramatic Company. The columnist was obviously familiar with this upcoming production in writing his review of *A True Son of Erin* as this new production seemed to attempt to fulfil his desires for a new Irish drama. Although the children of the Friary schools presented the production, it merited a full column on the 'About Town' page both on opening in February and when it was revived in May 1902. It seems that the true author of this allegorical piece was Father Ambrose Coleman, a priest from the Friary who was clearly a convert to the Celtic Revival.

In the programme distributed at the second performance of the play in May he complained that the conventional fare of popular Irish drama, 'highly-wrought and blood-curdling melodramatic productions, with comic parts well-seasoned with vulgarity' were 'unsuited to the aspirations of our people'. He suggested that audiences were now looking for 'something that will elevate and refine the mind, rather than for what evokes storms of shallow laughter while it reduces us all to one common level of vulgarity'.[66] However, he tried to suggest the aspirations of the play were not political, 'The play is an attempt to put into dramatic form the National ideals, and is in no sense political. The burthen of it all is the cultivation of the National language, National music and customs – the formation in a word of a self-conscious and self-respecting Irish-Ireland.'[67]

The play seems to have been a poetic musical mythic fantasy with large sections in Irish, performed by forty schoolgirls. The play had three acts. In the first, 'The Coming of the Stranger', the King and Queen of Oriel are shown falling under the influence of English 'ways and manners'. In the second act, 'The Great Enchantment', the King and Queen are enchanted and fall asleep allowing their places to be taken by John Bull and Eliza Jane Hopkins, a 'denationalized person'. The King's son, Donagh, is forced to change his name to Alfred, and the country falls under the spell of worshipping all things English. Maura, the Irish nurse, is the only dissident voice who deplores the 'terrible abasement of her country'.

In the third act, 'The Great Awakening', the true king's second son, Colm, who was stolen by the fairies as a baby, is returned as an adult who can only speak Irish. The fairies represent authentic Irishness, they speak only Irish and perform traditional Irish songs and dances. They have given Colm a charm to wake his parents, and when he does so the country also awakes to see what they have been sleepwalking through. They banish John Bull and his partner, and the play concludes with 'a magnificent chorus of "Awake, ye men of Erin," led by the faithful Maura'.[68]

When first performed in February, the house was a little disappointing, and the *Democrat* felt it necessary to go into a detailed explanation of the plot. However, when the play was presented again in

May the matinee and evening performances were both crowded and the audience was 'sympathetic and at times quite wildly enthusiastic'. [69] The *Democrat* columnist was obviously a supporter, and he described the ovation Coleman received at the end of the play when he stepped in front of the curtain, so his audience at least appreciated his efforts. One must be mindful though that any audience for a children's performance is liable to be partial as it will contain family, so it would have been interesting to see reactions to an adult performance of the same play. However, Coleman's troupe of child performers were not unique at the time, as can be seen by Pearse's plays for St Enda's School in Dublin. In fact, the boys from St Enda's visited Castlebellingham in June 1911 to perform *The Pageant of the Boy Deeds of Cuchulainn*, and were anticipated with such excitement that the *Democrat* printed two articles with detailed descriptions of the pageant in the weeks before the performance.[70]

Coleman's play does not seem to have been revived after 1902, and the Oriel Amateur Dramatic Company may have continued to give performances in their own hall in the Friary school, but the *Democrat* does not seem to have reported on these efforts. However, the little girls who performed in this nationalist allegory in 1902 would have been aged between nineteen and twenty-five at the time of the Rising, as would the audience of schoolchildren brought in to watch the drama for the matinee in May 1902. The concluding lines of Coleman's play, spoken by Maura, might well have had some significance for them:

> Learn that the country is not dead; the seeds
> Scattered by hands like mine, will germinate
> And sprout in barren soil, on naked rocks,
> Spreading an emerald carpet o'er the land.
> What seemeth dead is not dead but asleep,
> And though the nation in deep slumber lie,
> 'Twill wake again.[71]

Coleman may not have been a poet in the same class as Yeats, but he certainly created a play that might stand with the efforts of Pearse and Markievicz to create an authentic nationalist or national drama.

Dundalk was perhaps an unusual small town at the beginning of the twentieth century in having such a significant number and diversity of theatrical performances. This research has not been able to cover all the efforts of the different groups, both professional and amateur, who performed in the Town Hall, never mind the smaller venues around the town that were not even covered in the local papers. That so much of the work produced by the amateur groups should focus on ideas of playing the rebel is quite striking. Robert Emmett and the history of 1798 seems to be a recurring motif, whether in melodramas or Revival plays.

The intense scrutiny and discussion of the need for a national drama as well as language, music and culture, which is frequently a topic of the *Dundalk Democrat,* is also an important theme to emerge from this analysis. The regular voice of the *Democrat* is concerned that the people of the town should learn Irish, practise Irish sports and cultural activities, and that their minds should not be corrupted by immoral English or American imports, as well as stale anti-nationalist representations of 'Stage Irishmen'. That the plays most closely associated with the 'Stage Irishmen' should be the standard fare for both amateur and many professional groups performing in Dundalk shows another interesting theme to emerge: the battle between the popular and the artistic vision of Ireland. Yeats and Lady Gregory, among others, would have the same arguments about whether new Irish drama should be mythic, poetic and esoteric, or popular and realistic as well as national.

What does seem clear from the frequent mention of the significant audiences for these productions, is that the people in Dundalk were regular theatregoers. It may have been only the select few who engaged in performing in the plays, but there must have been a wide variety of classes represented in the audience of all these plays. Whether it was soldiers and townspeople at *The Belle of New York* or children at *The King of West Britain*, audiences seemed to represent all classes and all political allegiances.

The dominance of plays celebrating and commemorating nationalist heroes and condemning the impoverishment of Irish life lived under colonisation may not have directly prompted anyone to join the Rising in 1916. But, as Yeats famous poem 'The Man and the Echo' suggested, it is not difficult to see how Joseph Berrill playing Robert Emmet might have felt his role in the Irish Volunteers in 1916 was legitimated. There is also a correlation to be made between Fr Coleman's play and Yeats' own thoughts. When Coleman suggested that 'the seeds scattered by hands like mine, will germinate and sprout in barren soil', he could not know that fourteen years later 'The Great Awakening' would finally come. We have no record of whether Coleman was in Dundalk at the time of the Rising, but many of his audience certainly were, and maybe they had been inspired to take part by watching his play, just as Yeats reflected on the effects of his own play *Kathleen ni Houlihan*.[72]

NOTES

1   W.E. Vaughan and A.J. Fitzpatrick, *Irish historical statistics: population 1821–1971* (Dublin: Royal Irish Academy, 1978), pp. 29–31.

2   Christopher Morash, *A history of Irish theatre: 1601–2000* (Cambridge: CUP, 2002), pp. 104–5.

3   About Town, 'Mr Payne Seddon's Benefit', *Dundalk Democrat*, 2 May 1908; *Dundalk Democrat* 16 Apr. 1904, 27 Aug. 1904, 3 Sept. 1904, 1 Oct. 1904, 29 Oct. 1904, 26 Nov. 1904. See also Joan Fitzpatrick Dean, *Riot and great anger: stage censorship in twentieth-century Ireland* (Madison: University of Wisconsin Press, 2004), p. 104.

4   *Dundalk Democrat*, 23 Jan. 1904, 12 Mar. 1904, 30 Apr.1904.

5   Morash, *History of Irish theatre*, p. 117.

6   See Paige Reynolds, *modernism, drama, and the Audience for Irish spectacle* (Cambridge: CUP, 2007), p. 23.

7   Mary Trotter, *Ireland's nationalist theatres* (Syracuse, NY: Syracuse University Press, 2001), p. 41.

8   Stephen Watt, 'Late nineteenth-century Irish theatre before the Abbey – and beyond', in Shaun Richards (ed.), *The Cambridge companion to twentieth century Irish drama* (Cambridge: CUP, 2004), p. 20.

9   Morash, *History of Irish theatre*, p. 109; Trotter, *Ireland's Nationalist Theatres*, p. 40.

10   Ibid.; Watt, 'Irish Theatre before the Abbey', pp. 21–30.

11   Ibid., p. 28.

12   Morash, *History of Irish theatre'*, p. 116.

13   See Roy Foster, *Vivid faces: the revolutionary generation in Ireland 1890–1923* (London: Allen Lane, 2014), p. 83; Trotter, *Ireland's nationalist theatres*, pp. 57–8.

14   Ibid., p. xiii.

15   Foster, *Vivid faces*, p. 87.

16   Ibid.

17   Ibid., p. 80.

18   Padraic Ua Dubhthaigh, *The Book of Dundalk* (Dundalk, 1946), p. 120. See also Advert for 'Edison's Animated Picture – Life and Scenes in Dundalk', *Dundalk Democrat*, 15 Feb. 1902.

19   Arthur Curran, 'Drama in Dundalk', *Tempest's Annual*, 1959, p. 28.

20   About Town, *Dundalk Democrat*, 11 Jan. 1902.

21   Curran, 'Drama in Dundalk', p. 27.

22   About Town, *Dundalk Democrat*, 10 Feb. 1900; see also About Town, *Dundalk Democrat*, 24 Feb. 1900.

23   *Dundalk Democrat*, 6 Jan.1900, 17 Feb. 1900, 24 Feb. 1900, 10 Mar. 1900, 21 Apr. 1900, 28 Apr. 1900.

24   *Dundalk Democrat*, 10 Mar. 1900.

25   *Dundalk Democrat*, 26 May 1900.

26   About Town, 'The modern stage', *Dundalk Democrat*, 4 Oct. 1900. See also advert for the Ben Greet Company, 'The Great American Play', *Dundalk Democrat*, 24/25 Sept. 1900.

27   *The Belle of New York* was advertised at the Gaiety Theatre, Dublin, 12 Dec. 1899, at Theatre Royal, Dublin, 24 Aug.–3 Sept. 1898 and 12–16 Aug. 1900: For these dates, see *Irish Times*.

28   About Town, 'The modern stage II: "The Belle of New York", *Dundalk Democrat*, 11 Oct. 1900.

29   Advertisements in *Dundalk Democrat*, 19 Apr., 26 Apr. 1902.

30   *Dundalk Democrat* 16 Apr., 1 Oct., 26 Nov. 1904.

31   About Town, 'Mr Payne Seddon's Benefit', *Dundalk Democrat*, 2 May 1908. See also Fitzpatrick Dean, *Riot and great anger*, p. 104.

32   Advertisements in *Dundalk Democrat*, 3 Sept. 1904 and 1 Oct. 1904.

33   Advertisements for special trains on the front page of the *Dundalk Democrat*, 6 Jan. 1900, 5 Jan. 1901.

34   About Town, *Dundalk Democrat*, 29 Feb. 1908, 2 May 1908.

35   W. Payne Seddon, quoted by the *Dundalk Democrat*, 2 May 1908.

36   Advertisement in *Dundalk Democrat*, 6 Apr. 1901.

37   About Town, *Dundalk Democrat*, 30 Mar. 1901.

38   Arthur Curran, 'Drama in Dundalk', *Tempest's Annual*, 1959, p. 27.

39   Richard Fawkes, *Dion Boucicault: a biography* (London: Quartet Books, 1979), p. 194. See also character list in Andrew Parkin's introduction to *Selected Plays of Dion Boucicault* (Gerrards Cross: Colin Smythe, 1987), p. 258.

40   Advertisement in *Dundalk Democrat*, 5 Apr. 1902.

41   'A True Son of Erin', Review, *Dundalk Democrat*, 8 Feb. 1902.

42   Ibid.

43   Review of *The Fenian*, United Irishman, reprinted in About Town *Dundalk Democrat*, 7 Mar. 1903.

44   Quote from *The Leader*, reprinted in About Town *Dundalk Democrat*, 14 Mar. 1903.

45   See About Town *Dundalk Democrat*, 14 Mar. 1903.

46   Trotter, *Ireland's nationalist theatres* p. 129; Nelson O'Ceallaigh Ritschel, *Productions of the Irish theatre movement, 1899–1916: a checklist* (Westport, CT: Greenwood Press, 2001), p. 37; Eileen Kearney and Charlotte J. Headrick, *Irish women dramatists 1908–2001* (Syracuse, NY: Syracuse University Press, 2014), p. 5.

47   About Town, *Dundalk Democrat*, 15 Feb. 1908.

48   'Catholic Young Men's Society Dramatic Entertainment', 22 Feb. 1908.

49   Arthur Curran, 'Drama in Dundalk', *Tempest's Annual*, 1959, p. 32.

50   About Town, *Dundalk Democrat*, 12 Mar. 1904.

51   See, for example, *Robert Emmet*, Act 4, 'Last Tableau', in *Selected Plays of Dion Boucicault*, p. 397, in which Emmet is shot in the Yard at Kilmainham Gaol, and then a figure of Ireland appears like Mary, Mother of Jesus, to create a pietà-like tableau.

52   'Irish Plays in The Town Hall', *Dundalk Democrat*, 19 Mar. 1904.

53   '"The Eloquent Dempsey", dramatic performance by Dundalk Young Ireland Society', *Dundalk Democrat*, 21 Mar. 1908.

54   'The Turn of the Road', *Dundalk Democrat*, 20 Mar. 1909, p. 4. See also http://www.irishplayography.com/play.aspx?playid=1353 (accessed 24 Jun. 2016).

55   'Young Ireland Dramatic Class Production of Four Plays', *Dundalk Democrat*, 19 Mar. 1910, p. 4.

56   Arthur Curran, 'Drama in Dundalk', *Tempest's Annual*, 1959, p. 32.

57   *Dundalk Democrat*, 6 Feb. 1909.

58   *Dundalk Democrat*, 2 Apr. 1910.

59   'The Farney Players, Production of "The Memory of The Dead" and "The Work House Ward"', *Dundalk Democrat*, 21 Jan. 1911, p. 3.

60   Reynolds, *Modernism, drama, and the audience for Irish spectacle*, p. 21.
61   Bureau of Military History (BMH), Witness Statements (WS) 494, 'Peter Kieran'; WS.353, 'James McGuill'; WS.677, 'Hugh Kearney'; WS.644 'Patrick McHugh'.
62   See, for example, *Dundalk Democrat*, 4 Jul. 1903, 18 Jul. 1903; BMH WS.494, 'Peter Kieran' WS.353, 'James McGuill'.
63   BMH, WS.677, 'Hugh Kearney'.
64   'Robert Emmet', *Dundalk Democrat*, 24 Apr. 1909, p. 4.
65   List of Volunteers, Victor Whitmarsh, *Old Dundalk* (1988), pp. 80–2.
66   Father Coleman, quoted by Arthur Curran, 'Drama in Dundalk', *Tempest's Annual*, 1959, p. 29. See 'The King of West Britain', *Dundalk Democrat*, 17 May 1902.
67   'The King of West Britain', *Dundalk Democrat*, 17 May 1902.
68   'The King of West Britain', *Dundalk Democrat*, 15 Feb. 1902.
69   'The King of West Britain', *Dundalk Democrat*, 17 May 1902.
70   See 'The Cuchulainn Pageant', *Dundalk Democrat*, 28 May 1910, p. 4 and 'The Boy Deeds of Cuchulainn', *Dundalk Democrat*, 11 Jun. 1910, p. 4.
71   'The King of West Britain', *Dundalk Democrat*, 17 May 1902.
72   I wish to acknowledge with thanks the assistance of Lorraine McCann at the Louth County Archive, Alan Hand and the staff of the reference section of the Louth County Library, Dundalk, and my colleague in the Department of Humanities, Dundalk IT, Dr Martin Maguire, for setting me off on the trail of drama in Dundalk at the time of the Rising.

6

The Railways of County Louth, 1912–1923

Peter Rigney

In 1913, the Irish Railway system was at its largest. Two companies operated in Louth, the Great Northern Railway (GNR) and the Dundalk Newry and Greenore Railway (DNGR), a subsidiary of the London and North Western Railway. Louth's railway map was in the shape of a reversed number four, with the vertical bar the Dublin Belfast main line being crossed at Dundalk by the line from Enniskillen to Greenore, the final part being the line from Greenore to Newry (see map on p. vii). When four companies amalgamated to form the GNR in 1871, they chose Dundalk as a central location for their new workshops. In winter 1910, there were seven departures northwards from Dundalk to Belfast at approximately two-hourly intervals from 07.17 to 22.11, with a similar service pattern towards Dublin.

For passengers travelling from London to Belfast an overnight was involved. The options were to leave Euston at 20.45, travel to Holyhead and board a through train from Kingstown at 05.37, arriving in Belfast at 08.40. The more discerning traveller might get a longer sleep on the boat from Holyhead to Greenore, from which the Greenore boat express would take them to Belfast, arriving at 07.45. There were four trains a day between Dundalk and Greenore and four between Dundalk and Enniskillen with an additional service to Carrickmacross and back. By 1925, the Greenore boat train had disappeared and the number of mainline Belfast–Dublin trains had reduced to five – but with a new service from Dublin to Dundalk at 17.30. The service westwards to Enniskillen remained unchanged.

In 1914, railways had a virtual monopoly of land transport. Railway company shares were a blue-chip stock, and the GNR returned a dividend of 5 per cent in 1913. The Irish railway companies had avoided the labour militancy that had affected their British counterparts, having seen off a strike by their workers in September 1911. In addition to the political changes the period 1913 to 1923 witnessed two revolutionary changes for the railway system – the development of road transport and the development of collective bargaining structures. This latter development is beyond the scope of this essay as it was a national concern.

The outbreak of war in August 1914 saw the mobilisation of army reservists, who were employed by the railways in large numbers. This was followed by a rush to enlist by civilians. The GNR decided that the terms applied to those enlisting at the outbreak of the Great War should be the same as those that applied to the men who had served in the Boer war. Their jobs were kept open for them and an allowance was paid by the company to dependants. Many of those who went to war in 1914 were reservists, recalled to the army from their railway jobs. From 1915, the emphasis was on encouraging workers to enlist and employers to facilitate enlistment. In contrast to the Great Southern and Western Railway (GSWR), which refused to allow army recruiting staff to approach their blue-collar workforce, the GNR adopted a positive attitude to recruitment. In December 1914, the GNR board decided to 'allow every volunteer to go … who could possibly be spared even at the sacrifice of some degree of efficiency'.[1] At the same meeting it was decided to stop paying the income tax of new recruits to its white-collar staff, and to cap the level of payment for existing staff at 1915 levels. This reflected increased taxes to pay for the war.

The war also meant a significant increase in traffic, which required more staff, and 114 young men were recruited as locomotive cleaners in the period August 1914 to November 1918.[2] Of the 665 Great Northern railway staff who served, 253 index cards survive in the GNR staff records. This company served an area where recruitment rates were politically contentious. The pattern of enlistment is compared with the geographic distribution of employment using locomotive crew numbers as a proxy for total employment. While Dundalk had a rate of enlistment consistent with its size, the only significant positive divergence is Belfast. Willingness to volunteer declined west of the Bann as can be seen from the figures from Enniskillen and Derry[3] (see Table 1: Recruitment rates on the GNR, 1914–1918).

The most likely GNR categories to enlist were those occupied by the younger age cohort such as porters, engine cleaners and clerks, who together constituted 56 per cent of the total. Apprentices also enlisted but they might have been less likely to get permission. Twelve per cent of the GNR workforce enlisted, compared with enlistment rates of between 8 per cent and 9 per cent for the other three railway companies serving Dublin.[4] In the post-war period, the GNR, like the other Irish railway companies, re-employed those of its workers who had joined up, if necessary providing them with light work. In addition, the companies strove to give jobs to returning ex-soldiers who had no previous connection with railway. The GNR recruited clerks by open competitive exam, but between 1918 and 1921 held a number of competitions for clerks which were confined to relatives of existing employees and ex-soldiers.[5]

In December 1916, the Irish railway companies were subjected to government takeover in the face of a strike threat by locomotive drivers on the GSWR. Their British counterparts had been taken over in August 1914. In the face of war, a railway strike could not be countenanced. This meant that revenue was guaranteed by the government. It also meant that the government had a key role in policy-making in areas such as wages and industrial relations. This in turn meant that the agreement for an eight-hour day, concluded in Britain in 1919, was extended by the government to the Irish railways over the heads of the boards or the management of the Irish companies. With the unions anxious to retain the gains made under government control, there was uncertainty as to what would happen when control was handed back to the companies.

In May 1920, railway workers and dockers commenced a campaign of civil disobedience, refusing to handle armed troops or munitions. This campaign was called the munitions strike – slightly misleading as most railway workers remained in work. Normally when a driver or train guard refused a train they were dismissed. This process led to the closure of much of the railway system in the south and west. On the GNR things took a different turn. The first refusals took place on Friday, 25 June, and were followed by the suspension of the men concerned. On 30 June, the Dublin branch officers of the Associated Society of Locomotive Engineers and Firemen (ASLEF) met the GNR locomotive engineer and 'asked if there was any possibility of transferring all munitions train work to men from the Northern division'. They stated that 'They had seen Mr Johnson [Irish Trade Union Congress secretary] who said that he could do nothing and that Sinn Féin would go to any length to stop the Great Northern'.[6]

The munitions strike failed to achieve the success on the GNR which it achieved on the other railway companies. The GNR, whose centre of gravity was in Ulster, had a different political reality than that which prevailed in Dublin, and in the south and the west. Some GNR staff were committed but many were hostile and others reluctant. A certain amount of intimidation had to be applied to secure the stoppage. An example of intimidation may be found in the Bureau of Military History witness statement of Michael Sheerin.[7] Sheerin was a Derry city based volunteer and describes the kidnapping of a locomotive driver on his way to work.

The GNR responded to the munitions strike in September by closing the line from Dundalk to Enniskillen and the Carrickmacross, Cootehill and Bundoran branches with effect from 20 September. This meant that towns like Enniskillen and Cavan had a rail route open to Belfast but that the westward route to Dundalk or Greenore ports was closed. The *Ulster Gazette* reported that a number of traders were considering the purchase of lorries to fill the gap in goods transport services.[8] The line remained closed until January 1921.

From the point of view of unionist railwaymen, breaking the munitions strike had both a political and a financial attraction. Extra hours worked or extra trains run were frequently done on overtime. In addition, locomotive staff moved up from cleaner to driver to fireman in accordance with a system which mixed seniority with the number of turns of duty (313) worked. The strike also altered the disciplinary culture. In July 1920, driver Hagan of Belfast 'was informed that he was much to blame in the working of the 15.05 goods ex Dublin and only that he had shown himself as a man willing to stand by the company he would have been fined'.[9]

In November, faced with the possible closure of the entire railway system, the Irish Labour Party and Trade Union Congress (ILP & TUC) held a special congress at which it was decided to call off the strike. Catholic locomotive crew in Belfast did not support the munitions embargo – a point made by a loyalist delegation of workers when discussing the expulsion of maintenance staff from Adelaide depot. Catholic drivers and firemen had not been targeted 'as these men … By driving their trains and carrying out government duty had … proven sufficiently that they are loyal'.[10]

The reinstatement of men on the GNR went more slowly than on the other companies. While most staff were reinstated at the end of the strike, a file was opened entitled 'refusal to work traffic men NOT to be reinstated in the company's service'.[11] Those on the list were those who had refused on principle (as opposed to personal danger) and those who had signed an undertaking never to strike again at the conclusion of the 1911 strike. There were thirty-seven drivers and twenty-nine firemen dismissed on the GNR due to the munitions strike.[12] The Dundalk names on that list were a fireman, a foreman and two signalmen. These men were not re-employed until March 1922, compared to with their colleagues who were reinstated on 6 January 1921. The reinstatement issue on the GNR was described as 'delicate' by the general secretary of ASLEF, and for drivers and firemen it was only achieved after the company received a letter from the union recording that each of their branches approved of the reinstatement.[13] This reversed a position taken on November 1920 when 111 'loyal enginemen of the Belfast district' signed a petition threatening a stoppage if any reinstatement so took place.[14] A deputation of the signatories met the GNR board on 25 January and was told that the railways were under government control and the government would have its own views on reinstatement, but that in any event the company could not undertake 'to reject anything like all of the men who were out'.[15]

The munitions strike witnessed one significant turning point. On 14 August 1920, an attempt was made to burn two military lorries which had been marooned in Dundalk station for six weeks while en route from Dublin to Carrickfergus. What was significant was not the attack itself – it was typical of many raids – but that lorries would be sent by rail from Dublin to Carrickfergus. Just over a year later, on 25 November 1921, the general manager of the GNR prepared a memo outlining the effect of road competition on the rail business. He stated:

In the case of goods train traffic no less than 200 motor vehicles were plying daily and tapping our tonnage … to the extent of 70,000 tons per annum … the receipts on which would amount to 1.5% dividend on the ordinary stock. The motor competition in the passenger traffic was also considerable: Char a bancs and other vehicles (were) running at scheduled times daily between Dublin and stations 40 miles distant and between Belfast and stations 25 miles distant.[16]

The war provided men trained to drive and maintain vehicles and army surplus trucks came on sale shortly after the war's end. This can be seen in Derry at the north-western end of the GNR, where the corporation were developing a bus network as early as 1920.[17] In Dundalk, Halpenny's bus service was founded in 1919 when Joe Halpenny returned from serving with the British army in the Middle East.[18] Parts of Ireland, such as the territory west of Dundalk, were early learners in coping without rail transport due to the munitions strike closure and the closures during the civil war.

In late August 1920, a campaign was mounted by Belfast loyalists to expel Catholics (and some Protestants who held socialist views) from the workplace. The GNR, due owing to its dispersed nature, had the options of moving staff either northwards or southwards depending on the vicissitudes of the political situation. A GNR file survives detailing the campaign in the locomotive depot and wagon works at Adelaide in south Belfast. Dundalk works provided a place where expelled staff could be employed until things quietened down, but the resource was not limitless. The Midland railway asked whether two of its clerks, displaced from Belfast, could be accommodated in Dundalk – a request which was declined.[19] In October 1920, 67 of the 269 were 'displaced' and 45 had returned to duty. On 21 September, eleven men had been transferred to Dundalk. This situation was on a strictly temporary basis as any permanent vacancies arising in Dundalk were reserved for apprentices coming out of their time.[20] The last manifestation of the expulsion was on 7 December when it was noted that 'fitter Mc Guinness may be given a month's employment at Dundalk works after which he will have to present himself for duty in Belfast shops again'.[21]

In retaliation for the Belfast expulsions, the Dáil proposed a boycott of goods originating from Belfast. This had no effect on the shipbuilding and engineering industries from which most of the workers were expelled. The boycott was a prime example both of the law of unintended consequences and of the danger of policy initiatives undertaken 'in order to be seen to be doing something'. It failed to have workers reinstated in the jobs they had been driven from in the engineering and shipbuilding industries, while causing the layoff of workers, many of them Catholic, in Belfast-based distribution companies.[22] The implementation of the boycott involved raiding trains by stopping them on the line or by raiding stations. In this context, the Louth–Armagh border had no relevance other than for local authority rates or for Gaelic Athletic Association (GAA) purposes before 1922. The section between Dundalk and Adavoyle was a hot spot for train raids, but we do not know which were in Louth and which were in Armagh. However, for the year 1921, where figures are available, the section between Drogheda and the current Newry station accounted for 10 per cent of the route mileage of the GNR but for 21 per cent of incidents and 25 per cent of the cost of such incidents.[23] The term 'incident' covers everything from the breaking open of trackside tool huts and theft of tools (the most common one) to spectacular derailments. The most notable pre-truce incident was the derailing of the troop train near Adavoyle.

Although the ending of the boycott was not an explicit part of the truce, things quietened down with no significant incidents recorded between August 1921 and January 1922. However, raiding recommenced as political uncertainty grew. The *Railway Gazette* reported that on 24 March 1922, twelve armed men held up a goods train at Adavoyle. On 3 April, the *Railway Gazette* informed their readers that 'An Irish contemporary gives an account of further raids on trains on the GNR system.' (The same issue reported that The Canadian Pacific Railway had submitted proposals to the British Government for the settlement of ex-RIC officers and men in Canada.) On 11 April, a parliamentary question was put down asking was the government aware that trains arriving at Dundalk and other places were being searched for goods from Northern Ireland, which were being removed and destroyed. Winston Churchill replied that the Provisional Government was aware but that they were confronted with many difficulties.[24]

Dundalk was the single biggest rail conduit of north–south traffic (the others being Clones and Enniskillen). Train-raiding incidents seem to have been centred on the Newry to Dundalk and the Monaghan to Richill sections. Train raiding helped foster the image of the anti-Treaty sides as bandits and wreckers, which the Provisional Government sought to promote. The *Irish News* reported on a meeting of the South Monaghan Comhairle Cheantair of Sinn Fein, which condemned the unofficial raids on trains which were being carried out.[25]

On 19 June 1922, Peter Murray, a GNR electrician (and Catholic war veteran) working temporarily in Newry, was taken from the station and shot dead. On the following day, shots were fired into a number of houses in Demesne Terrace, Dundalk. Two things mark out Demesne terrace – one is its proximity to the countryside, and the other is the occupation of its inhabitants. They were traffic workers – guards, signalmen and the like and so were involved in keeping the railway running during the munitions strike. Other company houses in Brook Street and Ardee Terrace had the same religious mix as Demesne Terrace but were generally occupied by trades such as fitters and boilermakers. Of the ten houses in Demesne terrace, five were vacated in 1922, according to the company rent books.

Where names can be traced to the 1911 census it is clear that all those transferred were Protestants. Signalman Moorhead was transferred to Scarva, guard Compton to Belfast, guard Johnston to Omagh, guard McAlester to Enniskillen and station foreman Robinson to Belfast. Number 1 Demesne Terrace had already been the subject of an arson attack in February 1922. Its occupant was John Harvey, a signalman, who started work with the company in 1919, making it probable that he had been a soldier.[26] While part of the motivation for the Demesne Terrace attacks was undoubtedly sectarian, the fact that the shootings were aimed exclusively at traffic staff would indicate another motive, probably linked to the messy and protracted end to the munitions strike on the GNR.

It is also important to remember that there was a vacuum in policing between the disbandment of the RIC in 1922 and the establishment of a Garda Siochána in 1923. An attempt was made by an ad hoc committee to establish a North Louth police force. The GNR was asked for a subscription, which was agreed subject to the outcome of certain enquiries, but in the event no payment was made.[27] Attacks on the railway system intensified during the course of the Civil War in all areas of the country. As the war dragged on, the focus of the Anti-Treaty side was to show that the Free State government was not in control. The severity of the attacks on the railways can be seen as a substitute for rather than as an adjunct to a military strategy. We can see the same thing in rural India where the railway system was and remains a prime target for Naxalite Maoist guerrillas. Railways are a manifestation of the state, and attacking them undermines the legitimacy of the state.

The Civil War in Louth had two phases. The first, early phase was around August 1922, when Aiken was forced to take the anti-Treaty side. In this period, Aiken's men took both Dundalk and Drogheda for a brief period, before being dislodged by Dan Hogan (who prior to his military career had been a clerk on the GNR). There then followed a guerrilla phase, when the main focus of the anti-Treaty effort was to make the Free State ungovernable. From a railway perspective, this culminated in the destruction of the Ballymascanlon viaduct on the Dundalk, Newry and

Greenore Railway, and in the derailment and burning of an express train at Castlebellingham on 29 December 1922. On 4 January 1923, a goods train was derailed and set on fire between Dundalk and Iniskeen. Driver Rourke was awarded a bonus of £2 (about a week's wages) for uncoupling burning wagons from the derailed train – thus stopping the fire from spreading.[28] Despite these spectacular actions, Aiken was a relatively inactive commander. In September 1922, Ernie O'Malley reported to anti-Treaty headquarters that Aiken, 'seems to be pressed in against the Border between Free State and Specials and his policy is seemingly to allow things to quieten down in the North Louth area so that he can resume offensive operation when things are quiet'.[29]

The scale of attacks on the GNR was less than on the railways of the south and west. The number of derailments recorded in the engineer's file index averaged 160 between 1919 and 1924. In 1922, it was 190, an increase of 18 per cent (see Table 2: Incidents in Co. Louth recorded in GNR divisional engineer's correspondence index, 1922). However, the main contributory factor in this increase was not the civil war but the introduction of the new 'D class' locomotives whose weight made them derailment prone, to the extent that they were barred from the Monaghan to Clones line and from crossing the Boyne viaduct.[30] Just as in the Boycott period, the bulk of the attacks were in Louth. A memorandum prepared by the GNR in December 1922 stated that 9.32 per cent of the system mileage lay within Louth but that it accounted for 67.5 per cent of incidents. In a letter to Dick Mulcahy, the Army Commander, W.T. Cosgrave wrote that Bagwell, the GNR manager, had observed to him that 'People had got more or less accustomed to outrages in the South and West of Ireland but when they occur up towards the North they reflect more discredit on us than if they happened down south ... His company was thinking of stopping all passenger trains in the dark, but they had decided that the better course is to carry on'.[31]

Armoured trains were put into service in autumn 1922 on the Dublin based railways, and together with Lancia armoured cars, fitted with rail wheels, were deployed throughout the south and west. Up to recently it had been thought that armoured trains were not deployed on the GNR until early 1923 where a locomotive and two wagons were armed in Dundalk at a cost of £750.[32] However, GNR accounts reveal an expenditure of £52 in October 1922 in respect of the provision of pilot drivers for GSWR armoured train no. 1 working over the GNR system.

Given that drivers were paid between £2 and £2 10s a week at the time this represents a significant amount of operation.[33] However, the physical effects of the Civil War disruption were soon repaired, with contracts for the reconstruction of bridges going to tender in early 1923. The amount of agreed claims from the British government for pre-truce damage was £6,666. In comparison, the amount claimed from the Saorstát government for Civil War damages was £40,200, of which an advance of £10,000 had been paid by the end of 1923.[34]

The Treaty and the drift to civil war was not the only thing happening in the 1921 to 1922 period. The railways were handed back to their shareholders on 1 August 1921. This caused the issue of wages and conditions to come to the fore. The companies refused to countenance the continuation of the eight-hour day agreement which had been imposed on them in 1919. The companies met the unions in London in August 1921 and made it clear that they would impose a new set of working rules at an early date upon the cessation of control. The unions for their part made it clear that any such arrangement would be met with strike action. This problem was handed over to the two governments then in the course of being established. The salient point is that after a series of crises, and a rejected arbitration award, the matter came to a head in mid-1922, just as the civil war was commencing. The Free State government made it clear that they would not contemplate a strike.

The number of GNR staff involved in the events of 1916 to 1921 is difficult to gauge. One or two Dundalk staff took part in the rising and were dismissed. The board meeting of 16 December 1921 authorised the locomotive engineer to re-employ six men from Dundalk who had been interned.[35] In June 1923, the board decided to 'pay clerk M.J. Keenan who was arrested in May 1916 and who returned in February 1922 on the basis of continuous service'. This reflects the agreement negotiated by Joe McGrath, Minister for Labour of the Provisional Government, with the railway companies for the reinstatement of those who were out in 1916. There is no reference to this in any railway company archive, and our knowledge of it comes from military service pension applications.

The conventional view of 1921 to 1923 focuses on partition and the widening splits that led to a civil war. There was a parallel process going on in the railway system. The British railway system was transformed with sixty or so companies reduced to four in 1921 by a process of amalgamation. This was undertaken to get to grips with the weak financial state of the British companies. If the argument for amalgamation was based on financial weakness it applied more strongly in Ireland. As things turned out all lines lying wholly in the Free State were merged in 1924 to form the Great Southern Railway, and the GNR was left on its own. However, in the early part of 1922, a proposal was floated to merge the GNR with the Midland Great Western Railway. This would have resulted in a company stretching from Clifden to Derry and from Dublin to Belfast. The exploratory talks got nowhere but their existence warns us against history as an inevitable process leading from the past to the present. If such a company had been formed, it would have had two workshops – one in Dublin and one in Dundalk. It is possible that some of Dundalk's capacity would have been shifted northwards for political reasons.

The revolutionary decade wrought many changes for the railway system in Louth. For the GNR, its workshops while still at a midway point on the system were now on the frontier. The DNGR lost one of its raisons d'être – the provision of the shortest sea crossing from Belfast to London. The interruption caused by civil war damage was followed by the erection of the land frontier in 1923, and the Belfast to Greenore boat train never resumed. This, together with the closure of the Castleblaney to Keady line a short fourteen years after it opened, was one of the few manifestations of partition on railway working.

The year 1923 witnessed the end of the Civil War and the building of the infrastructure required by the new frontier. The *Railway Gazette*, 23 March 1923, noted that the GNR crossed the frontier at seventeen points. The economic effects of partition were less marked. In the proceedings of the Irish Railway wages board from 1924 to 1927 the railway companies spoke at length about their economic problems. However, the GNR never once mentioned the border but frequently mentioned road competition and the wages and conditions of their workers. In their evidence to the transport tribunal given in 1939, the GNR stated that the major disruption of traffic was caused by the economic war in 1932 rather than the institution of the land frontier in 1923. The revolutionary decade had brought about revolutionary change for Irish railways and their workers. While the highly visible destruction of trains at Adavoyle or Castlebellingham, and structures such as at Ballymascanlon, were no longer visible, by 1924 the institutional changes were highly visible.

Perhaps the most revolutionary change in the period between 1913 and 1923 was the emergence of road transport as a serious competitor.

This was to a great extent driven by developments in motor vehicle technology during the war. It proved particularly difficult for railway companies, which had enjoyed a virtual monopoly on land transport for the eight or so decades of their existence. Combined with this was the effect of war on government attitudes to the possibility of railway strikes and to trade unions. The Provisional Government acted in the spring of 1922 in precisely the same manner as the British war cabinet did in 1916; a rail strike could not be countenanced and the demands of the railway unions had to be met, if necessary by forcing the companies to concede. These issues remained unresolved and were fought out again in a long and bitter strike of 1933. *Ach sin scéal eile.*

Table 1. Recruitment rates on the GNR, 1914–1918

Location	Soldiers (%)	Loco crew (%)	divergence (%)
Belfast	30.8	26.0	+4.8
Dublin	13.4	11.5	+1.9
Dundalk	14.2	14.2	+0.0
Portadown Lurgan	7.5	12.0	−4.5
Newry	5.1	4.0	+1.1
Enniskillen	3.5	6.0	−2.5
Derry	1.9	6.0	−4.1
Clones	3.0	6.6	−3.6

Table 2. Incidents in Co. Louth recorded in GNR divisional engineer's correspondence index, 1922

Dundalk

Goods trains held up Adavoyle section Tool huts broken into	15/03/1922
Wagons raided goods burned	16/04/1922
Goods trains held up	08/04/1922
Goods train 12.50 p.m. to Enniskillen	06/04/1922
10.00 a.m. held up at Inniskeen	18/04/1922
Goods train 8.30 a.m. to clones raided	04/05/1922
Barrack street goods trains raided at	31/03/1922
Four wagons of goods burned at	03/04/1922

Table 2. *Continued.*

Damage to station premises by shooting 5.40 p.m. ex Portadown 6.10 p.m. ex Adelaide raided	03/05/1922
Barrack Street sawmill raiders in possession of	
Telephone smashed by Irregulars	14/08/1922
5.30 a.m. goods raided at Mountpleasant	19/09/1922
Trees cut down stones placed between rails	23/10/1922
East cabin protection of signalman	
Iniskeen attempt to wreck empty per way train	03/12/1922
Tool huts broken into MP 56 also MP 51	12/12/1922
Telegraph wires cut MP 56	12/12/1922
Iniskeen section removal of fishplates	16/12/1922
Down mail stopped	19/12/1922

Drogheda

Kellystown section rail removed	
Wagons searched at	31/03/1922
Goods train held up MP 36.5	04/04/1922
Goods train held up MP 39.5	06/04/1922
Goods burned at MP 35.5	05/04/1922
Two goods trains raided at	06/04/1922
Goods trains held up	08/04/1922
5.40 p.m. ex Portadown held up	19/04/1922
All trains raided at	21/04/1922
5.40 p.m. ex Portadown held up	20/04/1922
Two goods trains raided at	26/04/1922
Laytown Bridge blown up	05/07/1922
Tool huts broken into	
Damage to line 36.25	02/07/1922
Engine derailed	04/07/1922
Engine shed Irregulars in	01/07/1922
Damage to property by Irregulars	02/07/1922
Bridge 94 blown up Kellystown	

Table 2. *Continued.*

Protection of signalmen	
Telegraph wires cut Laytown section	13/09/1922
Telegraph wires cut Dunleer section	15/09/1922
230 up passenger searched	22/04/1922
Station damaged by rifle fire	11/10/1922
Telegraph wires cut	23/11/1922
Tool huts broken into	14/12/1922
Cooking accommodation for military	
Telegraph wires cut Duleek section	21/12/1922
Castlebellingham	
Goods train held up	5/4/1922
Parcels office broken into	14/4/1922
Tools stolen at	14/8/1922
Raid on signal cabin	19/8/1922
Tool hut mp 47.25 broken open	13/12/1922
Tool hut mp 48 broken open	13/12/1922
Tool hut mp 51.5 broken open	19/12/1922
Dundalk Down limited mail stopped	19/12/1922
Malicious derailment of limited mail	19/12/1922
Signal cabin maliciously burned down	31/12/1922

NOTES

1   Irish Railway Record Society Archive (hereinafter IRRS), Heuston Station Dublin, Great Northern Railway (GNR) loco dept. Minute Book 6, 14 Dec. 1914.
2   IRRS, GNR locomotive staff seniority list 1928.
3   The term Derry was the name in common usage. There is a petition to the GNR board from the loyal enginemen of Derry in file LE/20/2225.
4   *Railway Gazette*, 28 Sept. 1919.
5   IRRS, GNR clerkship exam register.
6   IRRS, GNR locomotive engineer file LE 20/2225, minutes of meeting.
7   Military Archives Cathal Brugha Barracks (MA), Bureau of Military History (BMH), Witness Statement (WS)803, 'Michael Sheerin'.
8   Des Fitzgerald, 'The GNR and the IRA' (undated typescript), p. 43.

9   IRRS, GNR enginemen's record book, p. 28.

10   IRRS, GNR LE 20/2972, copy of minute, 'Meeting of GNR workers' undated.

11   IRRS, GNR LE 20/2225F.

12   IRRS, GNR LE 20/2225C Glover to Dennis, 2 Mar. 1923.

13   IRRS, GNR LE 20/2225C, Greene to Glover, 20 Feb. 1920, Squance to Glover, 26 Feb. 1920.

14   IRRS, GNR LE 20/2225 E.

15   IRRS, GNR Board, 25 Jan. 1921.

16   IRRS, GNR GM 790/6.

17   MA, BMH WS.1004, 'Dan Kelly'.

18   *Dundalk Argus*, 18 Aug. 2005.

19   IRRS, GNR LE 2972. The file detailing the Midland Railway side of the correspondence does not seem to have survived although other files from the period were transferred to PRONI by the Ulster Transport Authority.

20   IRRS, GNR LE 2972, Glover to fitter Murray, 10 Sept. 1920.

21   IRRS, GNR LE 2972.

22   A.F. Parkinson. *Belfast's unholy war* (Dublin: Four Courts Press, 2004), pp. 73–82.

23   IRRS, GNR personal ledger, p. 408.

24   *Hansard Debates* [Commons], 11 April 1922, vol. 153, cols 205–7.

25   Fitzgerald, *The GNR*, p. 102.

26   IRRS, GNR General Manager's file index register, year 1922; IRRS archives, also tenancy ledger and staff record cards.

27   IRRS, GNR Board minutes, 23 May 1922; GNR personal ledger 9; covering 1919 to 1923.

28   IRRS, GNR enginemen's record book, p. 82.

29   Anne Dolan and Cormac O'Malley (eds), *'No surrender here!': the Civil War papers of Ernie O'Malley, 1922-1924* (Dublin: The Lilliput Press, 2007), p. 93.

30   IRRS, GNR Board minutes, 26 Jun. 1923.

31   Cosgrave to Mulcahy, 21 Dec. 1922, copy in the author's possession.

32   IRRS, GNR Board minutes, 20 Feb. 1923.

33   IRRS, GNR Board minutes, 20 Feb.1923.

34   IRRS, GNR personal ledger 9, Jan.–Mar. 1923, p. 412.

35   See P. Rigney, 'The rising and railway workers', *Saothar Journal of the Irish Labour History Society*, 41 (2016), pp. 186–7 for a general treatment of this issue, and for Joe McGrath negotiation. Other references in this paragraph come from the GNR board minutes in CIÉ, Heuston Station.

7

The Big House in County Louth, 1912–1923

Jean Young

Soon the magnificent building was a mass of seething flames [which] roared like a furnace throughout the night and lit up the country for miles around.

The 1923 burning of Clermont Park.[1]

The story of the decline of the Big House in Ireland spans a period from the middle of the nineteenth century through the twentieth, arguably continuing to the present day.[2] Within this timespan, the decade corresponding to Ireland's revolutionary period was one in which a number of events in close succession effected a significant change across the country in the role and status of the Big House and in the lives of the associated families.[3] The alienation of many landed estates in the years following the Wyndham Land Act, the impact of the Great War on the Big House families, and the attacks on Big Houses during Ireland's War of Independence and Civil War resulted in the destruction and abandonment of some houses. Clermont Park, whose destruction was so dramatically reported, was one such house.

This essay explores the impact of these events on the Big Houses of Co. Louth. While the burning of Big Houses is a particular focus, the ongoing land transfers and the role of Co. Louth's Big House families during the Great War are also examined. Sources used include contemporary newspaper records together with government records and documentation arising from the numerous claims made in the aftermath of the turbulent early 1920s. A more personal insight into events of the period is provided by the diaries of Miss Vera Bellingham, a member of one of Louth's most prominent landowning families.[4]

In embarking on this study, it is necessary first to identify the houses and families of interest. As in Terence Dooley's much wider-ranging exploration, the Big House is defined here as a large country house, typically set in a private demesne, which was the primary country residence of a landholder with estates of at least 500 acres, which included land rented to tenants.[5] Houses of interest are therefore those meeting these criteria and located in Louth (see the map on p. vii); the families of interest are those owning and occupying the houses thus identified. Land ownership data published in Ireland in 1878 is used to compile the list of houses shown in Table 1. This date provides a convenient reference point as it marks the end of a period of relative prosperity for landlords and their tenants and falls immediately before the agricultural depression of the late 1870s and the ensuing Land Wars. By the start of Ireland's revolutionary period some of these houses had passed from the original families and much of the tenanted land sold. Nevertheless, the houses were still viewed largely as the homes and legacy of the landlord class. Readers should note that the acreage criterion does exclude some mansions such as Killineer House and Mount Pleasant (now Mount Oliver). The residence criterion similarly excludes some major landlords such as the Earl of Roden, by this date primarily resident at Tollymore Park in Co. Down, and the Smith-Barry family, who never had a Louth seat.

In 1912, the editor of the third edition of *Burke's Landed Gentry of Ireland* wrote in the preface that 'one is now confronted with the problem whether there still remains a Landed Gentry at all in that country, so great has been the compulsory alienation of land in Ireland during the last decade'.[6] He was of course referring to the sale of land by landlords to tenants under the Wyndham Act of 1903 and the subsequent Land Act of 1909.

While earlier Land Acts had provided some mechanisms to facilitate the transfer of land to tenants, it was only after the 1903 Act that widespread land sales occurred. The success of the Wyndham Act was partly due to the incentives it offered to both landowners and purchasers. Tenants were guaranteed that the annual repayments on the purchase price advanced would be less than their annual rentals. Landowners were attracted by the fact that payments made under the 1903 Act would be cash, rather than stocks as in earlier land acts.[7] An additional incentive for vendors was a 12 per cent bonus on the sale price of the land sold. For many landlords, particularly those who were heavily indebted with little hope that rental income would meet those debts, the land sales allowed them to clear debts and make investments which would hopefully thereafter provide funds to maintain their family homes.

Despite initial editorial opinion expressed in the *Dundalk Democrat* that the Wyndham Act had been 'received without any great enthusiasm on the part of either landlords or tenants' and that the bill appeared 'to be in the interest of the landlords only', tenants on estates across Louth were soon negotiating purchases under the Act.[8] Among the first of the Louth landlords to sell under the Wyndham Act was Blayney Reynell Townley Balfour of Townley Hall.[9] In 1878, the Balfour estates had included 3,173 acres in Louth.[10] The 1908 records for advances made under the Wyndham Act show that some 2,500 acres in Louth were sold to tenants.[11] The 856-acre Townley Hall demesne was also resold under the Wyndham Act to its owner.[12] This resale of the demesne to the owner was yet another incentive for landowners as the owner was advanced the price for the demesne lands, £14,000 in the Townley Hall case, together with the 12 per cent bonus and thereafter made annual repayments on the purchase advance.[13]

Details of advances finalised in 1909 show that most of the Collon estate of Viscount Massereene and Ferrard was sold with over 5,000 acres transferred to tenants.[14] The 951-acre Oriel Temple demesne was also resold to the Viscount with an advance of £8,500.[15] Much of the Bellingham estate also changed hands. The sale of 2,886 acres to Sir Alan Henry Bellingham's Louth tenants was completed by 1912.[16]

The 20,369-acre Louth estate owned by Thomas Fortescue, Lord Clermont, in 1878 passed to his brother Chichester Fortescue, Lord Carlingford, after Clermont's death in 1887. Lord Carlingford's death in 1898 ended the male line of their branch of the family. Lord Carlingford's Ardee estate of 1,452 acres passed to his nephew Francis Fortescue Urquhart, an Oxford academic who was quick to divest himself of his inheritance under the Wyndham Act.[17] The much larger entailed estate inherited by Lord Carlingford from his brother was fragmented. Clermont Park and the Clermont estate lands passed to the Stephenstown branch of the Fortescue family, Ravensdale Park and lands on the Carlingford peninsula passed to the Viscount de Vesci.[18] Most of the land was sold soon afterwards. The sale of approximately 5,500 acres of the de Vesci

Irish Volunteers, Co. Louth, 1922 (courtesy of IrishVolunteers.org).

Group of Irish Volunteers and Cumann na mBan, Dundalk, 1921. Mary McHugh, middle front (courtesy of Barbara McCourt).

1911

TAKE THIS

AND TELL YOUR FRIENDS THERE IS GOING TO BE A

Meeting Outside the Railway Works

At 5.30 p.m.,

On Thursday, 7th January,

FOR THE PURPOSE OF

Organising the Unskilled Workers

Employed on the Railway.

All Labourers Employed in Malt-Houses, Breweries, Distilleries, Mills, Stores and Yards in Dundalk and District are Eligible for Membership in a section of the

Irish Transport Workers' Union

(Late Dockers' Union).

Mr. P. J. Dobbins is Appointed Organiser for Dundalk

Entrance to this Section, 1s 3d ; Weekly Subscription, 3d.

Further information can be had from the Organiser at 22, Quay Street.

Arise, you sufferers, who are only getting a Pittance to Keep a Home.

Mr. P. J. DOBBINS will address the above Meeting.

Workers, Join an Irish Trades Union.

JAMES LARKIN, *General Sec and Organiser.*

J. ROE, DEMOCRAT OFFICE, DUNDALK.

ITGWU flyer, 1911 (courtesy of Louth County Archives).

RIC departing Quay Street Barracks, Dundalk, Co. Louth, 29 March 1922. Sgt Taylor first from left and Constable James Morrissey third from left (courtesy of the Morrissey family).

Armoured train, GNR works, Dundalk, Co. Louth, 1923 (courtesy of Railway Record Society Archive).

Derailment, GNR works, Co. Louth, 1922 (courtesy of Railway Record Society Archive).

Ravensdale House, Co. Louth, burned 18 June 1921.

Braganstown House, Co. Louth (courtesy of *Tempest's Annual*, 1918).

RIC District Inspector Carberry, 1912 (courtesy of John McCullen).

William McQuillan and Margaret Kelly, 1897 (courtesy of John McCullen).

Angela Mathews, Cumann na mBan, c.1916 (courtesy of Joseph Gavin & Harold O'Sullivan, *Dundalk: A Military History*).

Millmount, Drogheda, Co. Louth, after bombardment, July 1922 (courtesy of Old Drogheda Society).

Charles Gyles, 1914 (courtesy of Maud Keery).

Grave of Charles Gyles, St Patrick's cemetery, Dundalk, Co. Louth (courtesy of Don Johnston).

Irish Volunteer memorial, Ardee, Co. Louth (courtesy of Séamus Bellew).

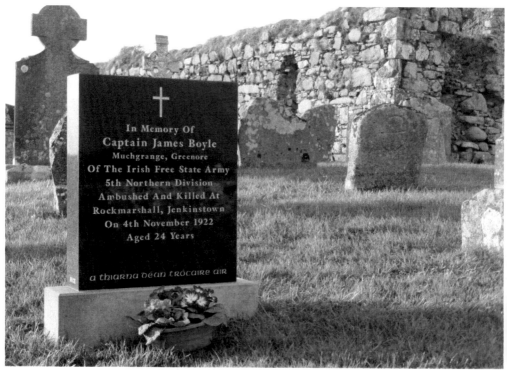

Civil War grave of James Boyle, Kilwirra, Co. Louth (courtesy of Don Johnston).

inheritance was completed by 1907.[19] Major Matthew Fortescue of Stephenstown House, who had inherited heavy debts from his father, sold the Clermont estate in 1908, with advances paid for almost 9,000 acres in February 1913.[20]

Negotiations for the sale of Lord Rathdonnell's estate had been underway since 1903, the sale of the Drumcar estate was finalised by 1913.[21] In 1878, John McClintock, Lord Rathdonnell, was one of the largest landowners resident in Louth, owning over 13,000 acres across Ireland, which included his 3,188-acre Drumcar estate. His nephew Thomas McClintock-Bunbury inherited the estate and title in 1879. Almost 2,500 acres were sold to tenants by 1913 for a total purchase price of £46,604, with the advances made mostly in 3.25 per cent annuities.[22] A year later, the resale of the 600-acre Drumcar House demesne to the owner for £16,000 advanced in 3.5 per cent annuities was also completed.[23]

Further land sales occurred across the county. The 609-acre Smarmore Castle demesne was resold to its owner, George Taaffe, by 1913 for a purchase price of £13,331; the advance was made with a cash payment of £2,345 with the balance in 3.25 per cent annuities.[24] The remaining land owned by Taaffe in Louth, 769 acres, had already been sold to tenants and other purchasers.[25] The 307-acre Rathescar demesne was also sold to the owner, A.J. Dawson Henry, for a purchase price of £5,280 with the full price advanced in 1915 in 3.25 per cent annuities.[26] Edmond O'Conor of Charleville, who inherited the entailed estates of Mathew O'Reilly-Dease in 1887, had sold 880 acres of his Louth estate to tenants by 1916.[27] The returns of advances for 1918 show advances to tenants for sales of 1,568 acres of Lord Louth's land in the county.[28] Advances for purchases of 2,256 acres of the Ballymascanlon estate were also recorded the same year; the estate by this time had been inherited by sisters Katherine Plunket, Gertrude Plunket and Lady Mary Elizabeth Forster from their maternal uncle Frederick John Foster.[29]

Not all land sales of this period were effected under the Wyndham Act. The Rokeby Hall estate was sold by Mrs Maud Montgomery née Robinson who inherited after the death of her uncle in 1910. Maud, who was the first wife of Richard Johnston Montgomery of Beaulieu House, sold the tenanted farms under the Wyndham Act but opted to sell the demesne and adjoining farmlands by public auction in 1912.[30] This decision was controversial. Maud wrote in a letter that she had been asked by Joseph Nolan, the nationalist MP for South Louth, 'for the "sake of avoiding trouble" to withdraw the Auction and to place the property in the hands of the Land Commissioners to have the lands divided up amongst the neighbours and labourers!!!' [31] While Maud attributed Nolan's concerns to a small number of local agitators, she considered the incident to be a precursor 'as to what will happen when things have come to such a pass before Home Rule is assured' as 'even demesne lands may not be Auctioned though put up in small lots.'[32] The auction proceeded and a large attendance with brisk bidding for the thirteen lots was noted. Rokeby Hall was sold to businessman, John Harmon Clinton.[33]

As can be seen from the examples above, land sales in the years following the Wyndham Act resulted in a significant transfer of land, and in some cases the Big Houses themselves, from the landholding families of the nineteenth century to their tenants and other purchasers. For many former landlords, this process alleviated immediate financial difficulties, but it also served to isolate further those who remained to farm the lands still in their possession. Although the editor of *Burke's Landed Gentry of Ireland* described the replacement of a 'landed gentry' by a new 'landless plutocracy', in reality the political and social power once wielded by the landowning occupants of the Big Houses had already been greatly diminished and the establishment of the Irish Free State would largely end it.[34]

But against the backdrop of financial difficulties and ongoing land sales, the outbreak of war in 1914 would temporarily provide a different focus. For many of the Big House families, military service had long been a tradition, and both men and women were quick to become involved in the war effort both at home and abroad. The Co. Louth branch of the British Red Cross Society was inaugurated at a meeting in December 1914 in Castlebellingham with Lady Bellingham as president.[35] Under the auspices of this organisation, groups of women and some men across the county worked in a number of depots throughout the war on a diverse range of activities, including bandage-making, egg collecting, wood-working and running the Louth Red Cross Hospital in Dundalk, which opened in 1917.[36] Ladies from the Big Houses involved in the management and daily work of the groups included Lady Bellew, Mrs Fortescue, Mrs Balfour, Mrs Montgomery, Mrs Guinness and Mrs Bellingham.

Amongst the more unusual of the various Red Cross activities was the sphagnum dressing depot at Milestown House in Castlebellingham, which was run by Mrs Woolsey-Butler and her daughter Mrs Cecilia Barrow.[37] Sphagnum moss was collected from bogs and mountains in Louth and neighbouring counties and then cleaned and sewn into dressing pads of different sizes, which were shipped to hospitals for use in treating the wounded. The ladies of the Big Houses were also largely responsible for the establishment of the Co. Louth fund to purchase a motor ambulance for the front.[38]

In 1919, the group's committee made a presentation to Lelgarde Bellingham in recognition of her 'whole-hearted and arduous labours in the cause of the Red Cross.'[39] Her husband, Sir Alan Henry Bellingham, usually known as Sir Henry, was also involved in establishing a branch of the National War Relief fund.[40] Mrs Maude O'Conor, wife of Edmond O'Conor of Charleville House and a great-niece of Daniel O'Connell, was created an officer of the Order of the British Empire (OBE) in 1918 for her services with the Leinster Regiment Central Advisory Committee.[41] This organisation was responsible for the 'supply of comforts to the fighting men of the Leinster Regiment' and was recorded as having despatched 126,785 gifts to combatant troops and 1,752,000 cigarettes.[42]

Not all volunteer work was conducted at home. Vera Bellingham, a niece of Sir Henry Bellingham who lived with her widowed mother and sister at Dunany House on the Bellingham estate, travelled to France in 1916 to work as a volunteer in Rouen. However, her departure from Ireland was unexpectedly delayed. She arrived in Dublin on Saturday, 22 April with her mother to spend a few days at the Kilworth Hotel in Kildare Street before travelling onwards.[43] Two days later, while walking in St Stephen's Green on Easter Monday, they were surprised to be told by a man armed with a rifle that they should leave 'for their own safety'.[44] Throughout the day, the unexpected closure of public buildings and train stations caused them some bewilderment. By evening, news of shootings and the death of an officer made it clear that something serious was occurring; Vera wrote 'that wretched Countess Markievitz [sic] is said to be at the head of it'.[45]

The imposition of martial law forced Vera to remain in Dublin until 3 May, spending a week at the Kilworth Hotel before moving to the Hibernian in Dawson Street. She fearlessly ventured into the streets each day and wrote detailed accounts of the many sights and sounds in the city. On 27 April, she described columns of smoke over Sackville Street and shouting and cheering, which could be heard after every crash. After attending Sunday service in St Ann's in Dawson Street on 30 April, she commented that there was no music and only a short address. The parson wisely skipped a sermon but instead asked the congregation to sing *God Save the King*, which they 'did with a will'.[46] Vera finally reached Kingstown on 3 May, where, after lengthy security checks, she embarked to travel onwards. On her departure, she wrote: 'It is odd to think I have been through an exciting episode of history, sometimes during the last week I felt it must have been a queer dream. What effect it will have on our unhappy country goodness knows, it is heart rending for any one who really loves their country'.[47]

On arriving in Rouen, Vera spent three months working in one of the clubs providing meals and accommodation for military personnel and other war workers in the city. Rouen was a major logistical base for the British forces with numerous hospitals in operation treating wounded soldiers. In Vera's descriptions of life in Rouen her intrepid personality is evident. She thought the occasional sounds of distant gunfire quite exciting and seemed regretful that she was not closer to the action at the front.[48]

Another young lady from Louth had a very different experience of wartime France. Miss Aline Henry spent four years in the German-occupied town of Saint-Mihiel; her story was widely reported when a war correspondent was surprised by an Irish accent after American and French troops liberated the town on 13 September 1918 during the Battle of Saint-Mihiel.[49] Aline, eldest daughter of John Henry of Toberdoney and a granddaughter of Francis William Henry of Richardstown Castle, travelled to Saint-Mihiel in June 1914, aged twenty, to visit her aunt whose husband was a French army major; she was trapped when the town was occupied shortly after the outbreak of the war.[50] Reports described Aline's imprisonment as a suspected spy for three weeks after the occupation and the difficulties in getting food, clothes or any news during the four-year period.[51] In a letter written while in France, Aline wrote of unvarying daily activities with no news and nothing interesting to read. She looked forward to music, dances and all kinds of sport in Ireland after the war.[52] The newspaper report from Saint-Mihiel in 1918 concluded with Aline's statement that all she wished for was 'to go back to dear old Ireland and England and see my mother and father once more'.[53] Sadly, that homecoming would have been bittersweet as her mother had passed away the previous year.[54]

But, of course, for many who travelled to France and other battle zones there was no homecoming and the families of the Louth Big Houses were included amongst those who lost sons, husbands and brothers. On 4 March 1915, Captain Roger Bellingham, the younger son of Sir Henry Bellingham, died at the front, aged thirty. At the outbreak of the war he had been serving as Aide-de-Camp (ADC) to the Lord Lieutenant but had resigned that position to return to active service.[55] Sir Henry's eldest son Edward also served and was awarded the Distinguished Service Order (DSO) and achieved the rank of Brigadier-General. In 1918, he was captured during the German spring offensive and spent six months as a prisoner of war in Germany.[56]

Major William Fortescue Garstin, only son of John Ribton Garstin of Braganstown, was killed in action in August 1915.[57] *Tempest's Annual* noted that his death left his father 'the only male member of the name of this branch of a family seated for over two and a half centuries in the County Louth'.[58] When John Ribton Garstin's own death followed two years later, his obituary included the observation that the knowledge that his name and line would not continue at Braganstown had been a great blow.[59]

Major William Eastwood, son of Major Francis Eastwood of Castletown Castle, was killed in action in Gallipoli in August 1915.[60] His brother Captain Francis E. Eastwood also served and was reported wounded in 1915.[61] Rifleman Cecil Chester-Walsh, son of Richard Walsh and Ismay Walsh née Chester of Williamstown House, died in August 1917.[62] His brother James Henry Chester-Walsh served with the Royal Flying Corps.[63] Lieutenant Hugh Turner Macan of the Middlesex Regiment, a son of Arthur Macan of Drumcashel House and Mary Louisa Bellingham, died in action in France in March 1918 at the age of thirty-one.[64] His sister Sybil Norah Macan died in 1920, aged forty-two, from illness contracted while nursing at Salonika during the war with Queen Alexandra's Imperial Military Nursing Service.[65]

Other Louth casualties included Captain Thomas William Filgate, Lieutenant W.H. Ruxton and Lieutenant Humphrey O'Brien Thornhill (Woolsey family).[66] There were additional casualties within the extended families of the Louth houses. Richard Courtenay Bellew, a nephew of Lord Bellew of Barmeath Castle, died aged nineteen in August 1917 from wounds received in action.[67] Willoughby Tichborne Montgomery, a nephew of Richard Montgomery of Beaulieu House, was killed in action in July 1918 at the age of eighteen while serving with the Canadian Mounted Rifles.[68] Others who served included Edmond O'Conor of Charleville, formerly a captain with the 6th Royal Irish Rifles, who volunteered as a Red Cross ambulance driver in France.[69] All three of his sons were in active service. Captain Richard Daniel O'Conor of the Leinster Regiment spent some time as a prisoner of war in Germany.[70] Richard's brother Edmond served with the Royal Navy.[71] The youngest son, Evelyn John O'Conor, served with an infantry regiment before transferring to the Tank Corps.[72]

Captain Owen Charles Guinness, son of Colonel Charles Guinness of Clermont Park, was created an OBE in 1919 for his wartime service with the Worcestershire Regiment.[73] Thomas Leopold McClintock-Bunbury, son and heir to Lord Rathdonnell, served in East Africa and Italy and was awarded the Croce di Guerra.[74] George Leopold Bryan (formerly Bellew), Lord Bellew, served with the Territorial Force.[75] His nephew and eventual successor to the barony, Edward Henry Bellew, served as a captain in the RAF and was created a Member of the Order of the British Empire (MBE) in 1919; Edward's brother Bryan Bertram Bellew, the future 6th baron, was awarded a Military Cross (MC) in 1916 while serving with the South Irish Horse.[76] Algernon Skeffington, Viscount Massereene and Ferrard, by this date resident in Antrim Castle rather than his Oriel Temple seat, served with the North Irish Horse throughout the war.[77] Arthur Gore, Earl of Arran and owner of Ravensdale Park, served with the Horse Guards.[78]

Otway Randall Plunkett, Lord Louth's eldest son, served with the Canadian Forces.[79] George Charles Pentland, only son of George Pentland of Blackhall, served as an officer with the 10th Battery Machine Gun Corps.[80] Sir Augustus Vere Foster of Glyde Court served with the Norfolk Yeomanry.[81] Richard Alexander Bailie Henry (later Filgate) of Rathnestin and Lisrenny served as a captain with the North Irish Horse.[82] Walter Henry of Richardstown Castle also served.[83] Captain George Taaffe of Smarmore Castle joined the Royal West Kent Regiment in 1914 as a reservist.[84] His eldest son, George Randal Joseph Taaffe, served with the same regiment.[85]

Charles Myles O'Reilly, younger brother and heir presumptive of William Joseph O'Reilly of Knock Abbey, served as a major and later lieutenant-colonel during the war.[86] Although he survived, his wife Sybil was a casualty of the war. Major and Mrs O'Reilly were passengers on SS *Persia* when the ship was torpedoed and sunk in the Mediterranean by a German U-boat on 31 December 1915. Major O'Reilly survived after thirty hours on an open boat but his wife drowned.[87] One further death might be in part attributed to the war. Matthew Charles Edward Fortescue, owner of Stephenstown House and a retired major with the 6th Battalion Royal Irish Rifles, volunteered for active service but died suddenly of heart failure at Stephenstown on 24 August 1914, reputedly on receipt of his call-up telegram.[88]

While the men lost from the Big Houses were a small fraction of the hundreds of Louth men who also served and did not return, the losses did leave a noticeable absence in the social circle of these families.[89] This loss was mirrored in the wider social circle of aristocratic and landed families across Ireland and Great Britain. In January 1918, Vera's younger sister, Alice Marian (May) Bellingham, married Royal Navy Commander Hugh Turnour England; their first child Marian Joy was born in December 1918.[90] At the close of 1918, Vera wrote of the happiness these events had brought to the family, but added that she wished she could be as happy as her sister, commented, 'I never seem to meet a man to speak to these times'.[91]

In February 1919, Vera was asked to go to France as a YMCA volunteer to help in the camps run by that organisation for military and other personnel.[92] She spent five months in France, working in camps in Étaples and elsewhere, eventually returning to Dunany in September. In writing about the readjustment to post-war life, she commented that 'it seems quite strange now to go into tennis at Castle Bellingham instead of going to the Bandaging'.[93] But the final entry in her 1916–19 diary foreshadowed what was to come when she wrote, 'several police have been murdered the last few months and the county seems much more un-settled now than it was during the war, there have been robberies and hold-ups in many places. The war has left an aftermath of discontent it seems to me'.[94]

The peace which followed the Great War was short lived in Ireland as the fight for independence erupted. For the families of the Big Houses the following years were traumatic. Dooley has described Ireland's revolutionary period as one in which landlords suffered 'outrage and intimidation on a scale the like of which their class had not experienced in living memory'.[95] This included the burning of almost 300 Big Houses.[96] Reasons for the burnings varied; many were ostensibly for military reasons while others can be attributed wholly or partly to agrarian agitation and land distribution issues.[97] In Louth, Ravensdale

Park, which had long been the principal seat of the Fortescue family, was burned in the final weeks of the War of Independence. After passing to the de Vesci family in 1898, Ravensdale Park was sold several years later to Sir Daniel Dixon, then Lord Mayor of Belfast and later an Ulster Unionist MP.[98] Following Dixon's death in 1907, Ravensdale was sold in 1910 to Arthur Jocelyn Charles Gore, 6th Earl of Arran.[99] Ravensdale Park was raided for arms in February 1919; the Earl of Arran was not present at the time.[100]

In September 1919, Arran sold the property to Thomas Archer, a Dublin-based timber merchant, for £15,000.[101] Archer's reasons for purchasing the property are unclear. Despite a later claim that he had intended to reside in the mansion with his family, it seems more likely this was a speculative purchase given the potential to sell timber and smaller holdings.[102] In February 1920, the mansion on 2,000 acres was advertised for auction.[103] At the auction in May 1920, bidding reached 21,000 guineas (£22,050) before the property was withdrawn.[104] Archer's withdrawal of the property following a bid significantly in excess of his original purchase price suggests a financial motivation for the sale rather than fear prompted by the ongoing unrest.

A year later, in the early hours of the morning of 18 June 1921, the unoccupied mansion was burned and completely destroyed by a group of armed men.[105] The Ravensdale courthouse was burned the same night.[106] On 29 June 1921, a claim for £75,350 was reported for the burning of the mansion and its contents.[107] Later records show Archer's final claim was for £91,000.[108] The Shaw Commission records of that claim noted Archer's purchase price of £15,000 in 1919 and the rejected auction bid of £22,050 in 1920; the latter figure was accepted as the value but deductions made in respect of land and timber already sold reduced Archer's award to £14,000.[109]

Archer also made numerous post-truce claims for later damage to ancillary buildings, loss of timber and damage to fencing, a bridge and garden features.[110] The claim documentation shows that while some damage resulted from occupation by Irregulars, much of the damage was due to looting of timber and building materials by the local population. The Clerk of the Peace in October 1922 reported 'the place was practically derelict and everybody from across the border came and helped themselves to gates etc., etc. Archer did simply nothing but served claims under the Malicious Injuries Acts'.[111]

Contemporary reports examined do not suggest an explanation for the burning of Ravensdale. The presumed reason is that it was to prevent its use as a barracks and the burning of the Ravensdale courthouse the same night seems to support a political or military motive. There had also been a failed attempt to burn Castletown Castle, the Eastwood residence, the previous night.[112] Its association with the Earl of Arran may have made it a target. Arran was a prominent Southern Unionist and Castle Gore, the family seat on his principal estates in Mayo, was burned a year later on 3 September 1922.[113] And the possibility of agrarian motives cannot be discounted as the history of landlord–tenant relationships on the estate in the Fortescue era was at times turbulent: even the short period of Sir Daniel Dixon's ownership was not without tension.[114]

Within weeks of the fire, the Anglo–Irish truce came into effect and during this period a number of Big Houses across the country were commandeered as Irish Republican Army (IRA) training camps.[115] One such house was Stone House in Mullary. Stone House was owned by Sir Vere Foster of Glyde Court and had been the original seat of that family before the building of Glyde Court. In 1921, it was unoccupied and therefore ideally suited for IRA purposes. Police reports for September 1921 noted that a man calling himself Commandant Sullivan had asked the Foster land-agent for permission to use the house but was unwilling to wait while the owner was contacted.[116] On 5 September, thirty men commandeered the house and by 8 September about 100 men were in occupation.[117] Reports describe daily drilling in the grounds with the occupants' numbers augmented in the evenings by local men.[118] The house was also used as a court and jail.

September police reports noted that a local labourer, Thomas Moonan, had been kidnapped by Sinn Féiners and that his whereabouts were unknown.[119] Moonan later made a statement to officials in Liverpool, describing how he had been kidnapped on 22 September 1921 and taken to Stone House where he was detained for eight days.[120] He was tried in a court convened in the house and convicted to seven years' transportation for burning a rick of hay, a crime of which he claimed to be innocent. He was taken to Drogheda, put on a boat to Liverpool and warned he would be shot if he returned.

Use of Stone House as a training camp reportedly continued beyond the signing of the treaty and into the Civil War. Other houses were also impacted in the following months.

During the first year of the war, numerous disturbances involving Louth Big Houses were reported and extensive detail is available from the many claims subsequently filed. Incidents involving the commandeering of cars and raids for arms and other supplies were common. Both Rathescar House and Smarmore Castle were briefly occupied in July 1922, presumably as a result of military activity in the area during and following the battle for Millmount in Drogheda. On 4 July 1922, Rathescar was occupied by armed Irregulars who left the following evening, taking with them some jewellery, £2 15s. in cash and other items.[121] A few days later, Smarmore Castle was occupied by Irregulars. Troops surrounded the castle on 8 July and the men surrendered.[122] George Taaffe later claimed for damage to the building and loss of rifles, clothing and a bicycle pump.[123] On 5 December 1922, sawmills employing twenty men at Rokeby Hall were completely destroyed in a fire, together with the machinery and some timber.[124] John Clinton's claim documents provide no reason but in later years his daughter stated that he believed the fire had been a reprisal for selling horses to the British military.[125] At least one family left Louth in 1922. In a claim for a car commandeered from his home in April 1922, George Henry Pentland of Blackhall wrote that 'I had to leave Ireland in 1922 & took little but my clothes with me'.[126] The Pentlands never returned; the contents of the house were auctioned in 1924 and the property was sold in 1926.[127]

But the incidents impacting the Big Houses in 1922 paled in comparison to what followed in early 1923. In January 1923, the executions of six men by the Free State government in Dundalk triggered a wave of house burnings in Louth over a five-week period. Of the six large houses burned in Louth in what would later be described as a 'barbarous mania of incendiarism', three were Big Houses associated with large landed estates.[128]

Three men were executed on 13 January 1923 and a further three on 22 January.[129] On the night of Monday, 29 January 1923, Milestown House in Castlebellingham was completely destroyed by fire.[130] Milestown was the home of Major Ronald Barrow, his wife Cecilia, their four young sons and Cecilia's widowed mother, Mrs Alice Woolsey-Butler. Milestown was part of the former Woolsey estate; Mrs Woolsey-Butler was a niece of the 1878 owner William Woolsey. Newspaper reports describe the arrival of about ten young men aged about seventeen, all unmasked and armed, at 11.30 p.m.[131] The family and servants were ordered out, petrol was sprinkled through all the rooms and the house set on fire. The men waited to ensure the house was fully ablaze before leaving, preventing attempts to rescue furniture from the house.

Once the men departed, the staff and local men from the village managed to save some furniture from the burning house, including the billiard room chimneypiece, which was removed with crowbars.[132] As the telegraph lines to Dundalk had been cut prior to the burning, Free State troops did not arrive until four in the morning.[133] Reports of the incident all observed that Major Barrow was an Englishman, and it is generally thought that he was targeted as a British army officer. However, the Irish Farmers Union, of which he was a prominent member, said Barrow was told during the attack that the fire was a reprisal for the failure of the Union to condemn the recent executions.[134] Vera Bellingham, who visited the house after learning of the fire, provided the following description:

> I drove off and found the shell of the building remaining, several people standing about who told me the Irregulars about 9 came at 11.30 demanding admission. Ronald threw up a window and asked what they wanted & was told they had come to burn the house down as a reprisal for the executions in Dundalk. Ronald said he had nothing to say to that & they replied that he belonged to the Farmers Union which as a body had not denounced the executions.[135]

Vera had earlier described attending a dramatic performance at Milestown two or three days before the fire which had been 'got up for the Farmers Union'.[136] The timing might support the contention that the attack was a reprisal against that organisation, although Barrow's nationality and military career presumably also played a role in making Milestown a target.

Although the Barrows remained at Milestown, another Big House was abandoned as a result of the fire. The Crescent in Castlebellingham, also part of the former Woolsey estate, was occupied by a different branch of that family. Charles John Thornhill was the manager of the Castlebellingham Brewery and lived in the Crescent with his wife, Helen, and their fourteen-year-old daughter, Eleanor.[137] Several days after the Milestown House fire, Vera visited the Crescent to see Mrs Thornhill, only to find the house 'dismantled', Mrs Thornhill, her elder daughter from a previous marriage and Eleanor 'gone for good', and the furniture being shipped to Liverpool.[138] Vera wrote that she thought Mrs Thornhill had never recovered from an earlier raid and the Milestown burning had 'finished her', and commented 'so that makes another family gone from Ireland'.[139] Vera described how, on the night of the fire, the family 'sat up all night imaging every horror. It all got on their nerves so much they could not sleep not even Eleanor'.[140] Thornhill resigned from the brewery. The family's governess told Vera she thought the family might go to New Zealand where Mrs Thornhill's son had a good appointment.[141] Several months later, the closure of the Castlebellingham brewery with a loss of many local jobs was announced. While it was reported that 'Customs regulations were mainly responsible for this decision', it seems likely the sudden departure of the Thornhills was also a contributing factor.[142]

Four days after the Milestown fire, Clermont Park suffered the same fate. This house, about four miles from Milestown, was originally part of the Fortescue estates. Colonel Charles Davis Guinness occupied the property as a tenant of the Land Commission from January 1908 and purchased the house and 138 acres from the Land Commission in 1915 for an annuity of £85 0s. 6d.[143] On 2 February 1923, some twelve men armed with rifles and shotguns arrived at about 11.15 p.m. and ordered the Colonel, his wife and their staff to leave, allowing them a short time to collect some valuables.[144] Petrol was sprinkled through the house and the building set alight. The *Northern Whig* reported that 'Soon the magnificent building was a mass of seething flames, which, being fanned by a strong wind, roared like a furnace throughout the night and lit up the country for miles around'.[145]

Colonel Guinness was a prominent unionist, a British Army officer and had been High Sheriff of Louth in 1918.[146] All these factors made him a potential target. Following the attack, he described the raiders as very friendly and civil and also stated 'I don't think these men had anything against me, personally. It is all just a part of the campaign that is ruining poor old Ireland.'[147] In a 1927 claim to the British government's Irish Grants Committee, he wrote that he had been burnt out as an act of reprisal along with other unionists because he was an army officer, a county representative of the Irish Unionist Alliance, a declared unionist and a loyalist.[148] But it is also conceivable that land issues might have played some part. In 1906, it had been suggested that the untenanted Clermont Park property be sold to the Land Commission for division amongst the evicted tenants of Louth. Following sometimes heated negotiations, much of the demesne was allocated to evicted tenants in 1908 with advances made at the same date as that to Colonel Guinness.[149]

Three days after the fire, Vera Bellingham wrote, 'Needless to say they [the Guinnesses] are leaving the country and vans have come to remove what was saved which is going to England'. Colonel and Mrs Guinness later described how they 'had to wander all over Europe and England for 2 and a half years living in hotels' before returning to live in Co. Dublin.[150] In April 1923, Clermont Park was advertised for sale; later records suggest it failed to sell at that time.[151] Mrs Guinness suffered significant health problems following the attack, the timing of the fire was in all likelihood particularly difficult for the Guinnesses as it followed shortly after the death of their eldest son.[152]

On 3 February 1923, twenty-four hours after the Clermont fire, Ballygassan House near Annagassan, home of the sub-sheriff John J. Russell, was also burnt.[153] The men responsible were reported as being young, unmasked, and strangers to the area. An enquiry by Russell as to whether his membership of the Church of Ireland was the reason for the attack was met with the reply that they 'cared nothing for religion'.[154] In a letter two days later notifying the Ministry of Home Affairs of the burning, Russell wrote that 'the reason alledged [sic] is, as a reprisal for shooting of the irregulars and when I pointed out that I had nothing to do with that, they said I was a government official and sympathizer'.[155] Russell, his wife, two daughters and servants were given only ten minutes to leave the property and lost most of their possessions as a result. Vera noted that 'rumour has it that poor Mr R could not even get his false teeth'.[156]

Ballygassan was a two-storey house on a farm owned by Russell who had resided there from 1881.[157] Although not a 'Big House', this attack on a government official within four miles of Dunany House was worrying for the Bellinghams. Vera wrote that 'this destruction is getting horribly close and Mother [is] very perturbed'.[158]

Over the following days, Vera wrote further about their concerns. She described taking down pictures in the drawing and dining rooms and putting good china away for safety, her clothes were collected 'in bundles ready to throw out of the window in case of emergency'.[159] On the day of the Louth Hunt Ball, due to be held at Beaulieu House, she wondered who would attend, commenting 'It seems hardly the time for dancing while these burnings are going on, rather like "Nero fiddeling [sic]" etc'.[160] But she also acknowledged that both hunting and dancing had continued in England throughout the Great War. Although Vera apparently decided against attending that year, the *Freeman's Journal* reported the Ball had been a 'great success' with dancing 'kept up until nearly daylight'.[161] But on the same page of the *Freeman's Journal* was an article describing the destruction of yet another Louth house.[162]

On Sunday, 11 February, Annaskeagh House, near Dundalk and the residence of Mr A.N. Sheridan, his wife and their three small daughters, was destroyed by a mine detonated in the drawing room.[163] The family and staff were given only minutes to leave after six or seven armed men arrived at 10.30 p.m.; the children were carried out in blankets. Sheridan was told the attack had been ordered because he was a government official. Augustine Nicholas Sheridan was a local solicitor and had been clerk of the peace since 1908.[164] Sheridan, whose wife was English, was also a Catholic; the attack occurred shortly after the departure of two local parish priests who had spent the evening with Sheridan. The house, while not a Big House in the landed estates sense, was described as a modern and well-appointed mansion.[165] In reporting the incident, the *Dundalk Democrat* referenced Milestown and Clermont and claimed that several Louth families had left the country and others were making preparations to leave. The Sheridan family sailed to France from Liverpool on 22 February 1923.[166]

On the night of 17 February 1923, Cavananore House, located a few miles from the borders with Armagh and Monaghan and the property of Senator Bernard O'Rourke and his brother Patrick from Inniskeen, was destroyed by fire.[167] The house was unoccupied at the time; flames were seen by neighbours at about 2 a.m. The O'Rourkes had purchased the house and 152-acre farm several years earlier from the Jackson family, extensive renovations had just been completed and Patrick O'Rourke planned to move in the following week.[168] This house, described as 'one of the finest residences in the county' is best classed as a large farmhouse: it was never the seat of a major landed family.[169] It had been a focus of military activity for several years. An earlier attempt to burn it was due to rumours that it would be occupied by the Black and Tans; the house was also used as an IRA camp after the Truce.[170]

Three days earlier, an attempt to blow up Senator O'Rourke's home in Inniskeen had been abandoned when raiders learnt that Mrs

O'Rourke was unwell.[171] The raiders instead continued to the nearby home of O'Rourke's sister and brother-in-law, which they tried to blow up but the explosive failed to detonate.[172] The unoccupied Cavananore a few miles away was presumably an easier target and it seems reasonable to attribute its destruction to the ongoing campaign targeting Free State senators.

Following a two-week lull, Knock Abbey became the final casualty in the series of burnings. On the night of 2 March 1923, armed men arrived and told the occupants they had orders to burn all the Big Houses in the county.[173] The owner, William O'Reilly, and his brother and sister-in-law were given a few minutes to remove personal belongings while four men sprinkled the house with petrol.[174] The house was set afire as soon as the O'Reillys left the building. A passer-by, seeing the flames, alerted Free State troops in Ardee who arrived at Knock Abbey before the raiders had left. A gun battle ensued between the troops and raiders hidden in the shrubbery as lookouts; two men were arrested and it was reported that one raider ran into the burning building and was never seen again. The fire destroyed much of the building, including a private chapel within the house.

It is possible that the Catholic faith of the O'Reilly family made the house a target. Oral tradition within another prominent local Catholic landowning family, the Bellews of Barmeath, says there were rumours an order had been issued to burn a Catholic household to counter accusations of sectarianism in earlier attacks.[175] But rumours during the earlier Castlebellingham area attacks that Knock Abbey 'had been similarly dealt with' suggest that the burning of Knock Abbey might have been considered much earlier.[176]

If orders were issued to burn a Catholic Big House, there were several potential targets in addition to Knock Abbey and Barmeath Castle. Other Catholic families included the Taaffes of Smarmore Castle, Lord Louth's family at Louth Hall, the O'Conors at Charleville, and the Chester families of Williamstown House and Carstown House. Bellingham Castle was also a Catholic household. Sir Henry Bellingham had converted to Catholicism in 1873, serving as privy chamberlain to three Popes and publicly working in support of the Church.[177] Sir Henry died in 1921 and was succeeded by his son Edward, who was appointed as the last lord lieutenant of Louth; Edward was also nominated, although not appointed, to the Free State Senate in December 1922.[178] But despite these associations and the proximity of the Milestown and Clermont burnings, the family's history as Catholics and their support for Home Rule and various Gaelic organisations appear to have prevented any attempt to target Bellingham Castle.[179]

The burning of Knock Abbey did, however, shake whatever sense of security Sir Edward might have felt as a result of his Catholic faith. Vera wrote that her cousin and his wife seemed 'rather "rattled"' since the burning of Knock Abbey'. She believed the fact that the O'Reillys were Catholic had made Edward and Elizabeth 'extra nervous' and as a result had taken down several pictures and put away china and silver for safekeeping.[180] Another house apparently protected, in this case by the owner's cooperation with the IRA, was Stephenstown House where Mrs Fortescue allowed local IRA men to use the grounds as a hideout. Following reports that the IRA planned to burn all the Big Houses in the area, she asked one to intervene and as a result an order was reputedly issued to spare Stephenstown.[181]

While there were no more Big House burnings in Louth after the Knock Abbey fire, the families remained concerned for some time. A large van full of paintings and the best furniture was shipped from Dunany House for safekeeping on 23 March 1923. Vera noted that many other families had done the same.[182] Her comments also suggest that people continued to leave. After attending a hunt in March and finding she knew very few of those present, she wrote, 'it is sad the way the country is getting depleted, there will be hardly anyone left to talk to'.[183]

Of the four Big Houses burnt in Louth, two were not rebuilt. Thomas Archer and Colonel Guinness were awarded compensation for Ravensdale Park and Clermont Park. Archer was initially awarded £14,000 by the Shaw Commission with additional lesser awards made for post-truce claims.[184] Guinness was awarded £2,600 with a partial reinstatement condition requiring that he build on or near the site of the burned house.[185] It is unlikely that either award would have fully funded rebuilding works; the majority of awards for claims made for Big Houses were insufficient to pay for rebuilding.[186] Both men applied to redirect award money to building development in Dublin and despite opposition from Louth County Council both requests were allowed.[187] Archer built three houses in Upper Kenilworth Park in Rathmines; Guinness built three bungalows at Censure in Howth. The Land Commission purchased the Ravensdale property from Archer in 1924. The stone from the ruins was subsequently sold for £250 to build a new church at Glassdrummond.[188] The Clermont property was eventually bought by local farmers; part of the house was repaired but later became derelict.[189] Recent aerial map imagery shows the building partly derelict and partly completely ruinous.[190]

Cecilia Barrow was awarded £11,750 following the destruction of Milestown, subject to a reinstatement condition of £8,500.[191] Milestown House was rebuilt over several years during which time the Barrow family resided in a hastily renovated steward's house in the yard.[192] Cecilia later applied to the Irish Grants Committee for a further £10,572 and was awarded a further £5,000.[193] Knock Abbey was also restored. William O'Reilly made an application for £35,000 to cover the damage to the building and the loss of contents.[194] He was subsequently awarded £3,100 for the contents and £6,250 for rebuilding, with a reinstatement condition applied to the rebuilding costs.[195]

In the discussion of house burning in Co. Louth, one other house merits mention. Corbollis House, near Tallanstown, was the home of Luke Alexander Lee-Norman in 1878. On his death in 1918, the house and estate passed to his son Alexander Henry Lee-Norman.[196] Oral history in Louth includes the dramatic story of the Civil War burning of Corbollis House after a government official was seen in the area and locals concluded the house was to be commandeered.[197] Lee-Norman was a deputy lieutenant for Louth and a justice of the peace; he was also appointed high sheriff for 1922 and by default still held that position at the start of 1923.[198] Given the burning of the sub-sheriff's home at Ballygassan, Corbollis House could conceivably have been a target.

In the course of researching this work, no documentary evidence of this event has been located. Sources identified show that Alex Lee-Norman and his wife Alys were resident during that period; Vera Bellingham wrote of rumours in February 1923 that the family were leaving but then wrote that they had simply sent away two van loads of furniture for safe-keeping.[199] An earlier legal notice showed that some or all of the tenanted lands were in the process of being sold at the time of Luke Lee-Norman's death.[200] In March 1923, Vera recorded a conversation with Alex Lee-Norman in which he told her that 'he could see no future for this country at present'. He sold Corbollis House and its 381-acre demesne the same month to Michael McGuinness of Summerhill near Dundalk.[201] A purchase price of £15,000 was reported although the memorial for the conveyance records £13,250; either figure suggests a house in good condition.[202]

There is no evidence of any urgency to leave on the part of the Lee-Normans after the sale – an advertisement for a parlour maid at Corbollis in August 1923 stated that applicants should be willing to move to England in the autumn.[203] In September, the family left Corbollis; Vera visited Alys there before their departure and was given 'a lot of flowers for the border'.[204] Given the extensive reporting for other fires and the claims documentation generated as a result, the apparent lack of such records for Corbollis suggests there was no major fire. While it is possible some minor incident was exaggerated over time, it is nevertheless curious that the story of the civil war destruction of the house should exist at all. Further investigation is required.

The eventual fate of Corbollis House was less dramatic, although it was a fate shared by many other houses across the country in the middle decades of the twentieth century.[205] Michael McGuinness died in 1936 and the property passed to his brother John, a Dundalk-based builder.[206] In 1944, Corbollis was advertised for sale with suggestions that the mansion might be used by a religious order or institution or modified to create a smaller dwelling or demolished to provide 'excellent and very extensive materials for re-building'.[207] The house failed to sell and John McGuinness eventually demolished the house himself. An auction on the site of building materials was conducted in 1946. Lots included seventy door frames and mahogany doors, seven tons of sheet lead, 400 rafters, staircases and four enamel baths.[208] Tea and refreshments were served![209]

While the preceding is by no means a complete account of the Big Houses and the families during the revolutionary period, it does show that events in Louth mirrored those across the country. The widespread sale of estates and land distribution meant that by the end of this period most of the houses were no longer the focal point of landed estates. War losses were responsible for some diminishment of the social circle of the families. And while only two houses were irretrievably lost, the departure of families such as the Pentlands, the Thornhills and the Lee-Normans further reduced that social circle. The era of landlordism was largely at an end and for the families who remained in Ireland, their future in the new Free State would be in a very different world.[210]

Table 1. Big Houses of Co. Louth in 1878 occupied by owners of 500+ acres

House	Owner in 1878	Total acreage owned in Ireland	Acreage owned in Louth
Oriel Temple	Viscount Massereene and Ferrard	21,024	7,193
Barmeath Castle	Lord Bellew	5,314	5,109
Drumcar House	Lord Rathdonnell	13,265	3,188
Louth Hall	Lord Louth	3,760	3,578
Ravensdale Park Clermont Park	Lord Clermont	21,127	20,369
Red House	Lord Carlingford	2,138	1,452
Bellingham Castle Dunany House	Sir Alan Edward Bellingham	15,996	4,186
Glyde Court Stone House	Sir Cavendish Hervey Foster	2,769	2,769
Rokeby Hall	Sir John Stephen Robinson	2,941	2,941
Ardee House	William Ruxton	2,262	2,262
Ballymascanlon House	Frederick John Foster	4,154	4,154
Beaulieu House	Richard Thomas Montgomery	1,364	1,364
Bellurgan House	Edward Tipping	1,245	1,245
Blackhall	George Henry Pentland	1,159	700
Braganstown House	John Ribton Garstin	930	928
Carstown House	Miss Henrietta Chester	2,412	1,978
Castletown Castle	Mrs Louisa Eastwood	877	0
Castletown House	John Murphy	3,110	2,799
Charleville House	Mathew O'Reilly-Dease	6,488	1,894
Corbollis House	Luke Alexander Lee-Norman	2,155	1,185
Drumcashel House	Richard Macan	2,191	2,009
Falmore Hall	Mrs Charlotte Bigger	1,351	77
Fane Valley	Percy Fitzgerald	1,938	1,938
Knock Abbey	Myles William O'Reilly	4,561	473
Lisrenny House	William de Salis Filgate	883	883
Milestown House The Crescent	William Woolsey	812	812

Table 1. *Continued.*

Monasterboice House	Hon. Mrs Anne E. Dunlop	3,265	1,214
Newtown House, Drogheda	Francis Donagh	1,207	906
Newtown House, Termonfeckin	Ralph Smyth	1,513	549
Piperstown House	Henry St George Smith	755	755
Rath House	Rev William Brabazon	1,155	1,155
Rathescar House	Reps of Alexander Henry	1,531	793
Richardstown Castle	John Henry	505	505
Smarmore Castle	John Taaffe	5,186	1,277
Stephenstown House	John Charles William Fortescue	5,262	5,262
Townley Hall	Blayney Townley Balfour	6,936	3,137
Williamstown House	Finlay Chester	2,166	1,186

Source: U.H. Hussey de Burgh, *The landowners of Ireland: an alphabetical list of the owners of estates of 500 acres or £500 valuation and upwards in Ireland* (Dublin, 1878); *Return of owners of land of one acre and upwards in counties, cities and towns in Ireland*, p. 61 [C. 1492], HC 1876, lxxx.

NOTES

1   *Northern Whig*, 5 Feb. 1923.
2   Terence Dooley, *The decline of the Big House in Ireland: a study of the Irish landed families, 1860–1960* (Dublin: Wolfhound Press, 2001).
3   Ibid.; W.E. Vaughan, *Landlords and tenants in mid-Victorian Ireland* (Oxford: OUP, 1994), pp. 227–8.
4   Vera Susan Bellingham (1880–1966), daughter of Revd William Claypon Bellingham and Susan Caroline Power; Charles Mosley (ed.), *Burke's peerage and baronetage* (107th edn., London, 2003), p. 338.
5   Dooley, *The decline of the Big House in Ireland*, p. 10.
6   Bernard Burke, *A genealogical and heraldic history of the landed gentry of Ireland* (3rd edn., London, 1912), p. iii.
7   The later 1909 Land Act reintroduced the use of stock for payment of advances.
8   *Dundalk Democrat*, 28 Mar. 1903; *Dundalk Democrat*, 17 Oct. 1903; *Dundalk Democrat*, 7 Nov. 1903.
9   *Dundalk Examiner and Louth Advertiser*, 28 Jan. 1905.
10   U.H. Hussey de Burgh, *The landowners of Ireland: an alphabetical list of the owners of estates of 500 acres or £500 valuation and upwards in Ireland* (Dublin, 1878), p. 18.
11   *Return of Advances for May 1908*, p. 239 [Cd. 4453], HC 1909, lxxxiii; *Return of Advances for June 1908*, pp. 309–12 [Cd. 4463], HC 1909, lxxxiii.
12   *Return of Advances for October 1908*, p. 496 [Cd. 4601], HC 1909, lxxxiii.
13   Dooley, *The decline of the Big House in Ireland*, p. 118.

14   *Return of Advances for January 1909*, pp. 6–8 [Cd. 5059], HC 1910, lxxvi; *Return of Advances for March 1909*, p. 106 [Cd. 5178], HC 1910, lxxvi.

15   *Return of Advances for April 1909*, p. 214 [Cd. 5195], HC 1910, lxxvi.

16   *Return of Advances for July 1912*, pp 552–3 [Cd. 6812], HC 1913, liii.

17   *Return of Advances for February 1907*, pp. 49–50 [Cd. 3921], HC 1908, xc.

18   Pádraig Ó Néill, 'The Fortescues of County Louth', *CLAHJ*, 24(1) (1997), p. 18.

19   *Return of Advances for June 1907*, pp. 279–89 [Cd. 4113], HC 1908, xc.

20   Ó Néill, 'The Fortescues of County Louth', p. 18; Noel Sharkey, *The Parish of Haggardstown and Blackrock: A history* (Dundalk, 2003), pp. 20–2; *Return of Advances for February 1913*, pp. 150–3 [Cd. 7143], HC 1914, lxvi; ibid., pp. 196–9.

21   *Dundalk Democrat*, 7 Nov. 1903.

22   *Return of Advances for February 1913*, p. 203 [Cd.7143], HC 1914, lxvi; *Return of Advances for May 1913*, pp. 448–9 [Cd. 7231], HC 1914, lxvi.

23   *Return of Advances for June 1914*, p. 392 [Cd. 7762], HC 1914–16, liii.

24   *Return of Advances for December 1913*, p. 751 [Cd. 7577], HC 1914, lxvi.

25   *Return of Advances for February 1911*, pp. 167–8 [Cd. 6137], HC 1912–13, lxx.

26   *Return of Advances for April and May 1915*, p. 247 [Cd. 8164], HC 1914–16, liii.

27   O'Reilly-Dease's will directed that his personal estate, with the exception of a few bequests, should be used to help extinguish the National Debt; *Freeman's Journal*, 5 Nov. 1887; Burke, *Landed gentry of Ireland*, p. 525; *Return of Advances for January, February and March 1916*, pp. 16–17 [Cd. 8753], HC 1917–18, xxv.

28   *Return of Advances for January and February 1918*, pp. 76–8 [Cd. 582], HC 1920, xi.

29   *Return of Advances for March and April 1918*, pp. 137–8 [Cd. 767], HC 1920, xi.

30   *Return of Advances for March 1915*, p. 131, [Cd. 8159], HC 1914–16, liii; *Dundalk Examiner*, 6 Jan. 1912.

31   The Rainey-Robinson Family Chronicle, 1986 (Armagh Public Library, P001873160).

32   Ibid.

33   *Dublin Daily Express*, 28 Feb. 1912.

34   Burke, *Landed gentry of Ireland*, p. iii.

35   *Tempest's Annual*, 1919, pp. 27–34; Donal Hall, 'The Bellingham family of Castlebellingham, Co. Louth, 1914–24', in Terence Dooley and Christopher Ridgway (eds), *The Country House and the Great War* (Dublin: Four Courts Press, 2016), p. 107.

36   *Tempest's Annual*, 1919, pp. 27–34.

37   Ibid., pp 33–4; Sean Boyle, *Looking forward, looking back: stories, memories and musings* (Dundalk: Liam Flynn Printing, 2004), pp. 85–7.

38   *Irish Times*, 3 Dec. 1914; www.jbhall.freeservers.com/1915_ambulance_fund.htm (18 Sept. 2016).

39   *Dundalk Herald*, 2 Aug. 1919.

40   Hall, 'The Bellingham family', p. 107.

41   Basil Morgan O'Connell, *O'Connell family tracts No. 2* (Dublin, 1947), p. 14; *Freeman's Journal*, 10 Jun. 1918.

42   *National scheme of co-ordination of voluntary effort resulting from the formation of the D.G.V.O. Department, Appendices iii and iv* (London: HMSO, 1920), p. 34.

43   Diary of Vera Bellingham, 1916–19 (Private collection, Dunany House), hereafter Bellingham diary 1916–19.

44   Ibid.

45   Ibid.

46   Ibid.

47   Ibid.

48 Ibid.
49 *The Times*, 16 Sept. 1918.
50 Ibid.
51 Ibid.
52 Aline Henry, undated letter or draft letter from Saint-Mihiel, apparently unsent, 1914–18 (Private collection, Filgate family).
53 *The Times*, 16 Sept. 1918.
54 Pádraig Faulkner and Noel Ross, 'Gravestone inscriptions in Dunleer', *CLAHJ*, 22(4) (1992), p. 449.
55 Donal Hall, *The unreturned army: County Louth dead in the Great War, 1914–1918* (Dundalk: County Louth Archaeological and Historical Society, 2005), pp. 37–8.
56 Hall, *The Bellingham family*, p. 107; *Larne Times*, 20 Apr. 1918.
57 Hall, *The unreturned army*, pp 88–9.
58 Ibid., p. 89; *Tempest's Annual*, 1916, p. 2.
59 James B. Leslie, 'In memoriam: John Ribton Garstin, D.L., F.S.A.', *CLAJ*, 4(2) (1917), pp. 125–8.
60 Hall, *The unreturned army*, p. 78.
61 Ibid.
62 Ibid., p. 202.
63 2nd Lieut. James Henry Chester-Walsh, Royal Flying Corps, 1914 (NA, WO 339/20313); Air Ministry: Chester-Walsh, James Henry, 1918 (NA, AIR 76/527/180).
64 Séamus Bellew, 'Inscriptions and heraldry from St Michael's Church, Charlestown, County Louth', *CLAHJ*, 27(4) (2012), pp. 611–25.
65 Ibid.
66 Hall, *The unreturned army*, pp. 83, 186–7, 197–8.
67 Mosley, *Burke's peerage and baronetage*, p. 335.
68 Hall, *The unreturned army*, p. 155.
69 Donal Hall, '1914–1918, The returned army: County Louth Servicemen in the Great War', www.jbhall.freeservers.com, consulted 10 Sept. 2016.
70 O'Connell, *O'Connell family tracts No. 2*, p. 14.
71 Ibid.
72 Ibid.; E. J. O'Conor service records, www.forces-war-records.co.uk, accessed 12 Sept. 2016.
73 www.worcestershireregiment.com, accessed 10 Sept. 2016.
74 Mosley, *Burke's peerage and baronetage*, p. 3280; www.turtlebunbury.com, accessed 20 Sep. 2016.
75 Mosley, *Burke's peerage and baronetage*, p. 335.
76 Ibid.
77 www.northirishhorse.com.au, accessed 10 Sept. 2016.
78 Hall, 'The returned army'.
79 Mosley, *Burke's peerage and baronetage*, p. 2411.
80 www.termonfeckinhistory.ie, accessed 14 Sept. 2016; Hall, 'The returned army'.
81 Hall, 'The returned army'.
82 www.northirishhorse.com.au, accessed 10 Sept. 2016.
83 Hall, 'The returned army'.
84 Ibid.; *The Tablet*, 16 Jun. 1923.
85 G.R.J. Taaffe service records, accessed www.forces-war-records.co.uk, accessed 12 Sept. 2016.

86 Hugh Montgomery-Massingberd, *Burke's Irish family records* (London: Burke's Peerage, 1976), p. 931.
87 Ibid.; *The Tablet*, 15 Jan. 1916.
88 *Irish Times*, 26 Aug. 1914; Ó Néill, 'The Fortescues of County Louth', p. 18.
89 Hall, *The unreturned army*.
90 *Freeman's Journal*, 8 Jan. 1918; Bellingham diary 1916–19.
91 Bellingham diary 1916–19.
92 Ibid.
93 Ibid.
94 Ibid.
95 Dooley, *The decline of the Big House in Ireland*, p. 171.
96 Ibid., pp 171–207.
97 Ibid.; Ciarán Reilly, 'The burning of country houses in Co Offaly during the revolutionary period, 1920–3' in Terence Dooley and Christopher Ridgway (eds), *The Irish Country House: its past, present and future* (Dublin: Four Courts Press, 2011).
98 *Dundalk Democrat*, 3 Jan. 1903.
99 Indenture – sale of Ravensdale from Dixon family to Earl of Arran, 1 Jan. 1910 (Registry of Deeds, 1910.16.16).
100 *Irish Times*, 5 Feb. 1919; Kevin McMahon, 'The time of the trouble 1919–21: Armagh, South Down and North Louth, Part 1', *Seanchas Ardmhacha*, 25(1) (1992), pp. 224–5.
101 Post-truce claims, Archer, Ravensdale Park, 1922 (NAI, FIN/COMP/2/15/452); Conveyance – Arran to Archer, 7 Feb. 1920 (Registry of Deeds, 1920.20.273).
102 Post-truce claims, Archer, Ravensdale Park, 1922 (NAI, FIN/COMP/2/15/452).
103 *Freeman's Journal*, 28 Feb. 1920.
104 *Freeman's Journal*, 7 May 1920.
105 *Irish Times*, 20 Jun. 1921.
106 Ibid.
107 *Freeman's Journal*, 29 Jun. 1921.
108 Post-truce claims, Archer, Ravensdale Park, 1922 (NAI, FIN/COMP/2/15/452).
109 Ibid.
110 Ibid.
111 Ibid.
112 Eamonn O Huallachain (ed.), *The Time of the Trouble: A chronology of the Anglo-Irish and Civil Wars in South Armagh, South Down and North Louth 1919–1923 Compiled by Kevin McMahon* (no place of publication: FeedARead.com, 2014), p. 328.
113 *Freeman's Journal*, 5 Sept. 1922.
114 Don Johnston, 'Post-famine landlords of the Flurry Valley', *CLAHJ*, 27(3) (2011), pp. 410–19.
115 Dooley, *The decline of the Big House in Ireland*, pp. 186–7.
116 Police reports, 1921 (NA, CO/904/154).
117 Ibid.
118 Ibid.
119 Police reports, 1921 (NA, CO/904/116).
120 Police reports, 1921 (NA, CO/904/154).
121 Post-truce claims, Henry, Rathescar House, 1923 (NAI, FIN/COMP/2/15/388).
122 O Huallachain, *The Time of the Trouble*, p. 505.
123 Post-truce claims, Taaffe, Smarmore Castle, 1923 (NAI, FIN/COMP/2/15/372).
124 *Larne Times*, 16 Dec. 1922.

125 Post-truce claims, Clinton, Rokeby Hall, 1923 (NAI, FIN/COMP/2/15/237); thanks to Bryan Rogers for details of his conversation with Miss Ann (Nancy) Clinton.
126 Post-truce claims, Pentland, Blackhall, 1923 (NAI, FIN/COMP/2/15/76).
127 *Irish Independent*, 24 Sept. 1924; Conveyance – Pentland to Thunder, 25 Jun. 1926 (Registry of Deeds, 1926.27.45).
128 Seosamh Ó Dolain, 'Knock Abbey', *CLAJ*, 5(3) (1923), p. 179.
129 McMahon and O Huallachain, *The time of the Trouble*, pp. 571–2.
130 *Freeman's Journal*, 31 Jan. 1923.
131 Ibid.; *Dundalk Democrat*, 3 Mar. 1923.
132 Diary of Vera Bellingham, 1923–28 (Private collection, Dunany House), hereafter Bellingham diary 1923–8.
133 *Irish Times*, 31 Jan. 1923.
134 *Irish Independent*, 3 Feb. 1923; *Derry Journal*, 5 Feb. 1923.
135 Bellingham diary 1923–8.
136 Ibid.
137 Charles John Thornhill was a grandson of Margaret Woolsey, daughter of John Woolsey and Janet Jameson.
138 Bellingham diary 1923–8.
139 Ibid.
140 Ibid.
141 Helen Thornhill, née McCulloch, was Australian by birth. Her son from her first marriage was Victor Eagar.
142 *Dundalk Democrat*, 28 Apr. 1923.
143 *Dundalk Examiner and Louth Advertiser*, 22 Jan. 1910; *Return of Advances for April and May 1915*, p. 265, [Cd. 8164], HC 1914–16, liii; Post-truce claims, Guinness, Clermont Park, 1923 (NAI, FIN/COMP/2/15/439).
144 Post-truce claims, Guinness, Clermont Park, 1923 (NAI, FIN/COMP/2/15/439); *Northern Whig*, 5 Feb. 1923.
145 *Northern Whig*, 5 Feb. 1923.
146 Ibid.
147 *Freeman's Journal*, 5 Feb. 1923.
148 Irish Grants Committee – Col. C.D. Guinness, 1928 (NA, CO 762/104/14).
149 *Dundalk Democrat*, 21 Jul. 1906; *Dundalk Examiner*, 19 Jan. 1907; Sharkey, *The Parish of Haggardstown and Blackrock*, p. 22; *Return of Advances for April and May 1915*, pp 265–6, [Cd. 8164], HC 1914–16, liii.
150 Irish Grants Committee – Col. C.D. Guinness, 1928 (NA, CO 762/104/14).
151 *Dundalk Democrat*, 21 Apr. 1923.
152 Irish Grants Committee – Hon. Mrs L.M.A. Guinness, 1928–29 (NA, CO 762/104/15); Hugh Spencer Guinness died at sea 20 Sept. 1922.
153 *Irish Times*, 10 Feb. 1923; *Dundalk Democrat*, 10 Mar. 1923.
154 *Dundalk Democrat*, 10 Mar. 1923.
155 J.J. Russell to the Ministry for Home Affairs, Dublin, 5 Feb. 1923 (NAI, FIN/COMP/2/15/493).
156 Bellingham diary 1923–8.
157 *Dundalk Democrat*, 10 Mar. 1923.
158 Bellingham diary 1923–8.
159 Ibid.
160 Ibid.
161 *Freeman's Journal*, 13 Feb. 1923.

162 Ibid.
163 *Dundalk Democrat*, 17 Feb. 1923.
164 *Dundalk Examiner*, 12 Sept. 1908.
165 *Dundalk Democrat*, 17 Feb. 1923.
166 Orcoma passenger manifest departing Liverpool, 22 Feb. 1923, www.ancestry.com, accessed 1 Sept. 2016.
167 *Dundalk Democrat*, 24 Feb. 1923.
168 Conveyance – Jackson to O'Rourke, 29 Mar. 1920 (Registry of Deeds, 1920.36.162); *Dundalk Democrat*, 24 Feb. 1923.
169 *Dundalk Democrat*, 24 Feb. 1923; Jackson family – Cavananore timeline 1641–1915, www.thesilverbowl.com, accessed 2 Sept. 2016.
170 *Dundalk Democrat*, 24 Feb. 1923; Witness statement: Thomas Luckie, 22 Apr. 1952 (Military Archives, BMH WS/672).
171 *Larne Times*, 24 Feb. 1923.
172 Ibid.
173 *Irish Times*, 5 Mar. 1923; *Dundalk Democrat*, 10 Mar. 1923.
174 *Dundalk Democrat*, 10 Mar. 1923.
175 Thanks to the Bellew family for this information.
176 *Dundalk Democrat*, 10 Mar. 1923.
177 Hall, *The Bellingham family*, p. 102.
178 Ibid., p. 109.
179 Hall, *The Bellingham family*.
180 Bellingham diary 1923–8.
181 Ó Néill, 'The Fortescues of County Louth', pp 18–19; Pádraig Ó Néill, *History of Knockbridge* (1994), p. 385.
182 Bellingham diary 1923–8.
183 Ibid.
184 Post-truce claims, Archer, Ravensdale Park, 1922 (NAI, FIN/COMP/2/15/452).
185 Post-truce claims, Guinness, Clermont Park, 1923 (NAI, FIN/COMP/2/15/439).
186 Dooley, *The decline of the Big House in Ireland*, pp. 197–207.
187 Post-truce claims, Archer, Ravensdale Park, 1922 (NAI, FIN/COMP/2/15/452); Post-truce claims, Guinness, Clermont Park, 1923 (NAI, FIN/COMP/2/15/439).
188 Johnston, 'Post-famine landlords of the Flurry Valley', p. 420.
189 Sharkey, *The Parish of Haggardstown and Blackrock*, p. 28.
190 Satellite imagery at www.google.ie/maps, accessed 1 Sept. 2016.
191 Post-truce claims, Barrow, Milestown, 1923 (NAI, FIN/COMP/2/15/575).
192 Ibid.
193 Irish Grants Committee – Cecilia Frances Barrow, 1926–29 (NA, CO 762/79/1).
194 Post-truce claims, O'Reilly, Knock Abbey, 1923 (NAI, FIN/COMP/2/15/225).
195 Ibid.
196 *Belfast Newsletter*, 6 Sept. 1918.
197 Thanks to Bryan Rogers and Micheál McKeown for this information.
198 *Irish Times*, 22 Jan. 1923.
199 Bellingham diary 1923–8.
200 *Meath Chronicle*, 3 Jul. 1920.
201 Bellingham diary 1923–28; *Irish Independent*, 21 Mar. 1923.
202 Conveyance – Lee-Norman to McGuinness, 21 Jun. 1923 (Registry of Deeds, 1923.33.2).
203 *Irish Times*, 23 Aug. 1923.
204 Bellingham diary 1923–8.

205 Dooley, *The decline of the Big House in Ireland*, pp. 142–3.
206 *Irish Press*, 1 May 1936.
207 *Irish Press*, 25 Nov. 1944.
208 *Irish Press*, 19 Apr. 1946.
209 Ibid.
210 My thanks to those who have generously shared family papers and research, and to those who have assisted with advice, suggestions and answering queries. In particular, I would like to thank Dr Donal Hall and the Workman family of Dunany House. Thanks also to Bryan Rogers, Caroline Purcell, Alan Hand, Séamus Bellew, Micheál McKeown, Lord and Lady Bellew, Patrick and Patricia Barrow, Deirdre Naughton, Professor Terence Dooley and Dr Ciarán Reilly.

8

William McQuillan of Drogheda: An Unlikely Rebel

John McCullen

From the point of view of a small boy in 1951, two significant things happened in Drogheda that year. They were, first, the erection and illumination of the 'Holy Year Cross' atop the tower at Millmount, in ruins since bombardment by the National Army at the outbreak of the Civil War in 1922, and second, I went on my first holiday away from home, for three nights. My mother was a Dolan from Brookville House, a large and rambling place in its own ornamental gardens, which John Dolan had purchased out of liquidation, with a market garden and farm of about thirty statute acres. His wife was Mary Jane McQuillan, and here they lived with a family of twelve children. At the time of my holiday, two sisters of my mother and a blind brother occupied the house. One of the sisters ran the declining market garden, and the second was on vacation from a teaching job in Northern Ireland. Uncle Patrick had spent decades in Australia, as a sales representative, and returned home in 1949, with failing sight. Granny Mary Jane had died in 1934, and the decor of the house had remained respectful ever since, especially the Japanese wallpaper in the sitting room that cost one guinea a yard for Patrick Casey in 1853.

On one of the days I wandered around the large sitting room with a splendid bay window. Dark Victorian gentlemen looked down on me from their framed pictures on the walls. One was identified to me as my grand-uncle John, who was a doctor in Dundalk but had died during the great flu epidemic in 1919. The second was identified to me as Uncle William McQuillan – a 'black sheep' of the family. It was to be many years of research before I established how 'Uncle Willie' had blotted his copybook. Willie McQuillan came from a family of twelve that included two priests, a doctor and five significant businessmen – three in Drogheda, one in Navan and one in Australia. One surviving sister, Mary Jane, had married John Dolan who was elected Mayor of Drogheda in 1905. Willie was a distinguished athlete and gymnast and was a member of the Drogheda rowing club.

Willie married Margaret Kelly in 1897, whose father was a prosperous sack manufacturer, with business in Dublin and Drogheda, and was known as 'Kelly the Sack'. With the passing of time, Willie took over the running of the Kelly business. Margaret and Willie had a family of ten children, six girls and four boys, and lived in 26 Fair Street, Drogheda. An indication of the increasing popularity of the gaelicisation of the population is the fact that the McQuillans, Willie, Peter and Al changed their surnames from 'Mc' to 'Mac' between the census of 1901 and that of 1911. A family group photograph taken at Brookville in 1912 shows Willie, second from right, in the back row, with the smile of a satisfied gentleman, at the age of forty-one, with Margaret and nine of their children.

The *Drogheda Independent* and the *Drogheda Argus* were the major sources of world news for the local population, frequently making informed commentary on political and economic questions at home and abroad. On 5 January 1901, the *Drogheda Independent* reported that the freedom of the town of Drogheda was granted to President Kruger of Transvaal and the Orange Free State. During the debate on the matter, Mr Gorman said: 'This resolution should appeal to all men who were fighting for their freedom … the strongest Government (Britain) in the World had been held at bay by a handful of farmers.'[1] When Paul Kruger died, the *Argus* lead writer commented, 'Kruger was a man of keen insight, and was the first to read bad news in the fact that gold was discovered in South Africa, because the British were on its borders and he recognised with unerring instinct, their lust for gold, which would soon cause trouble; a loss to the world of a great man'.[2]

In November 1904, the freedom of the town was conferred on John Redmond MP, and amongst those in attendance were John Dolan, another uncle, Thomas V. (T.V.) McQuillan, and Patrick McCullen, my paternal grandfather.[3]

Willie's brother, T.V. McQuillan, was elected to Drogheda Corporation in 1908 and was a candidate for the position of mayor in 1914 but was defeated thirteen to nine by Councillor Callaghan, the sitting mayor.[4] Another of Willie's brothers, Alphonsus (Al) McQuillan, who spent a considerable part of his time in amateur theatre, was also elected to the Corporation in 1914. Willie himself concentrated on his business, physical fitness and his growing family. There was a tragic loss for their sister Mary Jane and John Dolan when their two eldest daughters Rosaleen (sixteen) and May (eighteen) died on 8 and 13 June 1914. The first death occurred at home and the second in Verviers, Belgium, where May had been sent in hopes of a recovery from tuberculosis.

Two general elections in 1910 left the Liberal Party under Herbert Asquith requiring the support of Redmond's Irish Parliamentary Party. Home Rule had become inevitable, and the Ulster Unionist Council, seeing the way legislation and politics were progressing, tendered for a shipment of 20,000 rifles and a million rounds of ammunition from Germany in November 1910.[5] Sir Edward Carson addressed 50,000 men in Belfast on 23 September 1911, saying 'the morning Home Rule passes, ourselves will become responsible for the government of the Protestant Province of Ulster'.[6]

Asquith introduced the Home Rule Bill in the House of Commons on 11 April 1912. By January 1913, the Ulster Volunteer Force (UVF) had been formed to use 'all means' to stop Home Rule.[7] A report in the *Drogheda Independent* of 21 June 1913, headlined 'Drogheda Sensation', reported on an attempt to run guns through Drogheda port on board SS *Colleen Bawn*. Four cases of arms consigned to addresses in Ulster were seized, each case contained sixty rifles of an old Italian make, dated 1888, plus an older variety of bayonet, but with no ammunition. District Inspector Carberry and several customs officers boarded the ship, which had come from Liverpool, and removed the arms to the Customs House.[8] In direct response to the UVF, a public meeting was held in Dublin on 25 November 1913, presided over by Professor Eoin MacNeill, an occasional teacher at the Irish College in Omeath, leading to the establishment of the Irish Volunteers. A large rally on 5 May 1914, addressed by Professor MacNeill and Tom Kettle, Dr Bradley and Peter Clinton, President of Ancient Order of Hibernians (AOH), led to the formation of the Drogheda Corps of the Irish Volunteers. Both T.V. and Al McQuillan were prominent in their attendance.[9] Three other names are noted for the first time that will feature later. These were L. Walsh and the Hon. Secretary Joseph Carr and Vice-President Joseph Finnegan. Two weeks later the *Argus* reported the first meeting of the 'Permanent Committee', with T.V. listed as a vice-president with Dr Bradley.[10]

The landing at Larne of 24,000 rifles and five million rounds of ammunition by the UVF took place on 25 April 1914 with no official interference. Smaller-scale operations by the Irish Volunteers took place at Howth and Kilcoole in July and August 1914, totalling 1,500 guns. The official reaction was different, as the military attempted to intercept the Volunteers returning from Howth. Four civilian deaths ensued at Bachelors Walk, Dublin, due to a panicked response by the army. The message got abroad that Orange and Green were being treated differently, and this triggered a flood of funds to the Irish Volunteers from home and abroad.

While T.V. and Al McQuillan, apparently, were involved with the Irish Volunteers, Willie was keeping himself removed. This was perhaps due to his experiences of the previous year when, owing to the Dublin labour dispute and lock-out, Willie McQuillan, whose business was in Dublin, found it necessary to arm himself with an automatic pistol for his own protection.[11] Victory for the employers came in January 1914, but left a legacy of bitterness, mistrust and rage behind, and sent poverty-stricken emigrants from Dublin who would not forget nor forgive.

By July 1914, the government was caught in a bind between the threat from Ulster Unionists and the legitimate and long-held expectations of the Nationalists. To avert a probable civil war, King George V called a conference at Buckingham Palace in July 1914, seeking a compromise. The conference failed but within days everything changed with the outbreak of the Great War as the British government pledged to defend Belgium against German aggression.

By early 1916, 210,000 Irishmen had joined the British Army, with various motives of money, adventure and patriotic fervour. Both Sir Edward Carson and John Redmond gave enthusiastic support to the recruiting drive. Despite the outbreak of the war, Nationalists were certain that Home Rule was imminent. T.V. McQuillan withdrew from the Drogheda mayoral contest in January 1915 to allow the unanimous election of Alderman Luke Elcock as a stalwart worker for Home Rule. In a speech of congratulation to the new mayor, McQuillan said he 'trusted that before the year had passed, he would have the honour of attending at the opening of their native Parliament in College Green'.[12] The expectation was for a short war in Europe and the dream of Home Rule fulfilled.

On 17 March 1915, Lance Corporal William Kenny VC, whose parents lived in Drogheda, was feted as part of the recruiting campaign for the army. T.V. McQuillan seconded the motion to grant the freedom of the borough to Kenny, and the presence of two other McQuillans, Al and James J. (who was a rate collector), was noted.[13]

At the Mayoral Banquet on New Year's Night 1916, hosted by Mayor Luke J. Elcock, various toasts were made. In seconding 'Ireland a Nation', T.V. McQuillan complimented the Mayor on his toast of the King, which could only be made because Home Rule had been passed and said 'England owes a deep debt of gratitude to John Redmond, who had transformed Ireland from being the darkest spot on the Empire, to its brightest'. When the seventh of twelve toasts came, it was seconded by Al McQuillan JP, who stated:

> In spite of the War, the prosperity of the town was exceptionally good. The farmers around were getting good prices for their produce, and owing to the wonderful contribution of Drogheda to the Allies, the separation allowances were bringing a great deal of dead money into local circulation. Drogheda was getting on fairly ... the world had been depending on Germany for dyes and this now showed a great lack of technical training on our part.

Between the toasts ten gentlemen rendered songs, including Peter Dolan, John McGolrick and Denis Reddin, and the proceedings terminated with the singing of 'A Nation Once Again' by T.V. McQuillan.[14]

At the beginning of 1916, some members of the Drogheda Irish Volunteers came to Willie and asked could they rent an old egg store in Fair Street from him to equip it as a gymnasium and also to drill there.[15] As a former gymnast himself, Willie was keen that his sons have some gymnastic training, and said, 'Very well. I won't let it to you but I will give it to you, and a subscription to put up poles and rings, which you see used in these somersaults.[16] His two sons, Peter and Laurence (Lennie), then became members of the Irish Volunteers. Shortly afterwards, RIC Sergeant Sharpe called on Willie and said 'You have let your store to the Sinn Féiners', to which McQuillan replied, 'I have done nothing of the kind. In my opinion they are not Sinn Féiners and would have nothing to do with Sinn Féin, who in my opinion, are in the pay of Dublin Castle. These men are in favour of the Parliamentary Movement, not opposed to it!'[17] The sergeant accepted this and departed. Joe Carr, assistant in the Town Clerk's office in Drogheda, was the man who rented the store, and about twenty Volunteers used it to drill and practise shooting at targets.

The narrative of the story then moves on to Sunday, 23 April 1916, when a number of men from Drogheda marched via Mell to the Obelisk to meet up with volunteers from further afield, en route to Dublin to join the uprising. Leading them was Philip Monahan, the local Sinn Féin president and science teacher in the Christian Brothers School (CBS), cycling to Slane for the planned rendezvous with the Dundalk men.[18] Others named were Michael Harkin, reporter with the *Drogheda Advertiser*; William McQuillan, Fair Street, businessman; Joe Carr, assistant town clerk, Michael Keenan, railway clerk, Fintan Lawler, projectionist, Frank Bateson, shop assistant; Joseph Finnegan, publican; Laurence J. Walsh, shopkeeper; Thomas Halpin, Stockwell Lane; William Branigan, plumber; Thomas and Gerard Malone, butchers in West Street; William Monaghan, James Street; and Jim O'Mara of Shop Street.

Dr William Bradley arrived later in the day by car, with a messenger carrying the countermanding order from Professor Eoin MacNeill. The presence of those sixteen men who met at Mell on Easter Sunday p.m. 1916, was confirmed in a speech at a Rotary Club dinner in August 1953 by Alderman L. J. Walsh TD (Teachta Dála – member of Dáil Éireann), who listed these aforementioned with some detail as to their local connections. The *Drogheda Independent* report describes his speech as 'one of the most interesting statements of a historical nature made in Drogheda for several years'.[19] Another person who mobilised was Tom Burke, a very fine athlete and footballer, who had a rendezvous arranged with an armed man at Kilmoon. Burke waited for four days to no avail, before he walked home.[20]

Most of the group walked back to Drogheda. On Monday, Philip Monahan went to the races at Fairyhouse, convinced that a rising would now be 'absolute folly'.[21] William Branigan headed off to Dublin on foot, to join in with the GPO garrison where the Rising was actually going ahead from 12 p.m.[22] William McQuillan went back to Fair Street. Various reports came about some events in Dublin, but he discounted them.[23] On Tuesday, 25 April, Willie took a car and travelled with his brother Vincent, a Vincentian priest, to Dublin to check his shop and a large number of horses in stables, which required feeding. Leaving the car and the priest at Drumcondra, he walked to a crowded O'Connell Street and down the Quays to Chancery Street and his shop premises, where he gave instructions to his staff. As the gunfire was intensifying, he went to Moran's Hotel and spent the night there.[24]

On Wednesday, Willie obtained a pass from the military to make journeys without hindrance, but only got as far as the North Circular Road, where a landlady, with a Drogheda connection, had a lodging house.[25] Public transport was disrupted and Willie seems to have been unable to return home by train until the following Monday. The rebels surrendered on Saturday, 29 April 1916 and, in the words of Tim Pat Coogan, 'The Rising had killed and severely wounded some 1,350 people. The centre of Dublin was gutted. Approximately 61,000 square yards of buildings were destroyed. Damage was estimated at £2.5 million in the values of the day. On top of this, one third of the city's population had to be given public relief'.[26]

The Drogheda Nursing Association's annual concert was scheduled for Tuesday, 25 April 1916 at the Whitworth Hall. Owing to the

hitch in the railway arrangements caused by the disturbances that broke out in Dublin, a number of eminent artists were unable to appear. However, local artistes stepped in to the breach, proving the merit of Drogheda talent. Mr. Peter Dolan, with a fine baritone voice sang 'The Diver' and later 'Out on the Deep'. Miss Ismay McKeever brought out all the senses in a selection 'Dolce Far Niente', for which she was encored, while the accompaniments were faultlessly played by Miss McGough, ARCM.[27]

Returning from Dublin, on Monday, 1 May 1916, Willie went about his normal business in Drogheda. On Wednesday, 3 May, he was woken in the middle of the night by the loud knocking of a party of police, about ten in number. He was taken from his wife and family, his pistol confiscated, and he was marched to Millmount barracks. Willie was ushered into a room holding twenty-one other prisoners from Dunleer and Drogheda and given a blanket, where he remained locked up overnight. He was given no explanation for his arrest nor was he interrogated.[28] On the following day, Thursday, 4 May, the prisoners were handcuffed in pairs and marched through the streets of Drogheda to the railway station, a distance of about one mile. En route, soldiers' wives and relatives abused them. [29] Photographs of the prisoners were taken at Drogheda station, some of which appeared in British Newspapers. Thursday night and Friday night were spent in Dundalk Gaol, in separate cells. In the meantime, eight of the rebel leaders in Dublin were court-martialled and shot on the 3, 4 and 5 May 1916.

The Dublin fighting was covered in the *Drogheda Independent*, published on 6 May 1916 under the headline 'Disturbances in Dublin'. Before publication, there was a board meeting of the newspaper at which the editorial line to be taken by the newspaper on the fighting was discussed. The minute book records:

> Attendance – Peter McNamara (Chairman), David Sheridan, Michael Casey (Editor).

> Mr. McNamara said that they should follow the policy of the '*The Argus*' and make no editorial comment, because of the local Sinn Féin members. Mr. Casey objected to this, on the grounds of ethos and the Nationalist standards of the paper. Eventually it was agreed to follow the line of the Editor, which was to denounce this 'wicked and insane' revolution, to use the words in which John Redmond had described it. Mr. Sheridan said that the '*Argus*' was looked on as a 'contemptible rag', while the *Drogheda Independent* was a newspaper of principle.[30]

On Saturday, 6 May, handcuffed again under the direction of District Inspector Carberry, they were transported by rail to Amiens Street station, Dublin, and marched in torrential rain to Richmond Barracks, a circuitous route of about three miles. Without food or drink, they were locked in a room of twenty people.[31] On the following day, a bucket of tea arrived at 10 a.m., with no means of drinking it. Eventually a tobacco tin was found and used as a drinking cup for each ration. No sanitary arrangements were provided. The whole group were still soaking wet from the rain.[32] Meanwhile, at home in Drogheda, the McQuillan family were outraged and their solicitor, Mr Tallan, was dispatched to Dublin. After some feverish enquiries, he tracked down his client and was horrified to find Willie in filthy conditions. According to District Inspector (DI) Carberry, he (Carberry) went to a great deal of trouble and pains to get McQuillan released, as a favour to Mr Tallan, whom he claimed had 'gone security' for Willie.[33] Willie was released on the afternoon of Monday, 8 May, after six days' incarceration. Four leaders of the rebels were executed on that morning in Dublin and during the week, three more were shot.

Martial law was imposed in Ireland and operated ruthlessly.[34] In all, 3,430 men and 79 women were arrested, severe sentences of long penal servitude were imposed and eventually 75 death sentences were passed, though then commuted to penal servitude. The Drogheda prisoners were deported to England and Wales and kept locked up for periods of weeks to months. Joe Carr, who had been handcuffed to Willie, was taken back from England on 10 May and released following a vigorous campaign by the Corporation. Tom Burke, Michael Finnegan, Tom Halpin and Larry Walsh were eventually released at Christmas 1916.[35]

The events of Easter Week and thereafter caused revulsion among the McQuillans. Both of Willie's brothers, Al and T.V., and his brother-in-law, John Dolan, were followers of Redmond and did not approve of the Rising. A generation of political energy had been spent in attempts to gain Home Rule and the reaction of Mr Collins of Shop Street would have been typical, 'Oh, the Blackguards, now we will never get Home Rule!'[36] When the Meath County Surveyor, James Quigley, was arrested, in the same week as the Drogheda men, he was accused of being in the vicinity of Rath on the date of the Battle of Ashbourne, and as 'having shaken hands with Thomas Ashe, the leader of the insurgents'. At his trial in June, a large number of witnesses spoke on his behalf, including Peter McQuillan, a brother of Willie's and Treasurer of the Redmondite Irish National Volunteers (INV) in Navan, who stated that 'Navan INV were against the principles of Sinn Féinism'. At the end of a two-day trial, Quigley, chairman of the Volunteer committee, was found not guilty of all charges.[37] Encouraged by his family, Willie decided to take legal advice to sue District Inspector Joseph Carberry of the RIC for damages in connection with his arrest. The claim was for £50 and the civil bill set out that 'the defendant did assault and beat plaintiff on the 5th May 1916'.

This case was heard on Friday, 4 January 1917, at Drogheda Quarter Sessions before Judge Green.[38] Mr T.M. Healy, KC, MP, later Governor General of the Irish Free State, instructed by Mr P. Tallan, solicitor, appeared for the plaintiff and Mr Cusack, BL, instructed by Mr Gartlan, crown solicitor, appeared for the defendant. It was a news item of considerable interest, added to by the appearance of Mr Healy, a very well-known Nationalist MP famed for his eloquence. The *Drogheda Independent*, of which John Dolan, Willie McQuillan's brother-in-law, was a founding shareholder, produced a special issue of a single large page.[39]

Seven full columns reported the day's hearing and Mr Healy's eloquence managed to fill four of them. Despite the deaths, imprisonments and injuries of the previous Easter there was 'laughter in court' on at least eighteen occasions. Mr Healy was used to playing to the gallery, humouring the judge, and throwing innuendo and red herrings in the direction of the defendant. In summary, he took the court through the week with Willie, objected vehemently to the handcuffing and the photography at the station, queried the lack of questioning, identified Carberry as the prime mover, and compared Willie to St Paul, a Roman citizen, with the rights of a free man, 'subjected to contumely, outrage and hardship'. Having spoken at length, Mr Healy requested small but sufficient damages as would show the disapproval of the law.

Mr Cusack for the defendant made two major points: 'The claim is outside the statutory period of six months, having been lodged on 15 December, and the actions of Mr Carberry were justified by the Defence of the Realm Act.'[40] The Judge remarked that the question at issue was as to whether there was 'excess after arrest'. Three witnesses were called, all backing McQuillan's case. They were Michael Harkin, Frank Bateson and Joe Carr. The defendant, DI Joseph A. Carberry, was called. He said that he had been eleven and a half years in Drogheda District as DI, did not know Mr McQuillan, and had never spoken to him in his life. Denying all the charges, he claimed that he had been instrumental in getting Mr McQuillan out, and did it as a favour to Mr Tallan. Under questioning from T.M. Healy, Carberry passed all responsibility over to the military, denied the evidence of the three witnesses and said of Bateson, 'I got him out of prison, owing to the influence of his Parish Priest.'

In essence, the only case against Willie McQuillan was that he let a store to a party of Irish Volunteers for training. In conclusion, Mr Healy again rebutted and belittled the evidence of the DI and emphasised that the case was for the vindication of the liberty of the subject and asked for nominal damages. Judge Green required time to examine the authorities quoted, saying he would give his opinion at the conclusion of his circuit. On the following Saturday, he again referred to the case explaining how difficult a decision was, and announced that he would leave it stand until the next sessions for judgment.

In the *Drogheda Independent* of 24 March 1917, a half column reported on the judge's decision in the case of *McQuillan* v. *Carberry*. After much verbal agonising, Judge Green stated that the action was taken outside the six-month window of opportunity, and also that DI Carberry fairly claimed protection under the Defence of the Realm Act 1913, on the basis that he was doing his public duty. Bearing these issues in mind, he was dismissing the case.[41]

In the fashion of local newspaper reporting, and the juxtaposition of the serious and the facetious, much more column space is devoted alongside Judge Green's judgements to the comedy of *HMS Pinafore*, by the Navan Musical Society, where the 'Sisters, Cousins and Aunts' feature names like Kitty Carberry, Bridie Plunket, May Burke, Eily Colbert, Lilly Lawler and Chrissie Collins.[42]

Hoping to leave his 1916 history behind him, Willie returned to his busy life, with Margaret and ten children in Fair Street, his business in Dublin at Kelly's of Chancery Street and family summers spent in Laytown at St Anne's on the sea front, which he had purchased for £820 in 1913, along with another house, St Mary's, which cost him £650.[43]

Referring back to my mother's reticence to discuss the 'black sheep', she did once tell me that she would pass the residence of DI Carberry at Beechgrove House on her way home to Brookville from school. One day, Carberry's daughter was standing on the front gate and, making a face at my mother, stuck out her tongue and said 'You are only a publican's daughter!' In fairness to both schoolgirls, Dolly Dolan, my mother, hardly ever criticised anyone and Josephine Connolly, née Carberry, became a most generous donor to many charitable causes in later life, particularly the Community Services Centre.

While the War of Independence in Louth did not reach the intensity of some other counties, a number of notable events occurred in the Drogheda area. In April 1918, an anti-conscription mass meeting was held on the Mall in Drogheda, addressed by the Mayor W.T. Skeffington JP; Monsignor Segrave PP, St Peter's; Reverend Denis Flynn, PP, St Mary's; Philip Monahan, President of Sinn Féin; Alderman Elcock; Fr Richard McCullen, Meath Catechist.[44] In June, a Drogheda Sinn Féin concert in Whitworth Hall was proclaimed, by order of DI Carberry. An impromptu céilí was then held in the Mayoralty House.[45] On 9 June 1918, the Women's Day of 'No Conscription' headed by Mrs Elcock, 2,000 women gathered to sign the pledge at the Mall. The groups included Cumann na mBan, women's confraternities, Foresters and Hibernians. They marched to St Peter's, sang 'Faith of Our Fathers' and attended Benediction.[46]

On 14 December 1918, a general election was held which resulted in an overwhelming victory for Sinn Féin who won seventy-three seats, whilst the Irish Party won six and Unionists twenty-six.[47] In January

1919, the seventy-three Sinn Féin MPs established Dáil Éireann.[48] On 20 September 1919, by order of the Chief Secretary in Dublin Castle, the Dáil was suppressed as a 'dangerous association'.[49] Sinn Fein's pre-eminence was further reflected in the results of the Drogheda Corporation Elections held in January 1920. The twenty-four seats were divided as follows: Sinn Féin – thirteen, Chamber of Commerce – five, Nationalists – three (J.J. Callan, T.V. McQuillan, Luke Elcock), Worker's Republic – two, Labour – one.[50]

The new Mayor was elected on 31 January 1920. He was Alderman Philip Monahan, president of Sinn Féin, who had languished in prison four years previously.[51] With this election came the end of the political road for John Dolan, aged eighty-five, and Al McQuillan. The struggle for independence was proceeding on a political front and on a military front. Members of the Irish Volunteer Police Force policed Laytown and Bellewstown Race meetings in the summer of 1920[52] and Volunteer Courts were set up to deal with ordinary crime.[53] At Grangebellew on 10 July, a man found guilty of stealing £10 from a woman was ordered to be paraded after the principal mass in Dunleer on the following Sunday, with a placard of his crime hung around his neck.[54] The first official Sinn Féin Drogheda court was held on 14 August 1920 before Mr Peter Hughes, when Patrick Connor, Priest's Lane, was summonsed for selling milk deprived of 36 per cent of its fats. Witnesses Mrs Connor and her daughter Julia said the milk was 'the pride of the town', but the chairman fined him 2s 6d.[55]

Five Drogheda magistrates, including Al McQuillan, resigned in protest at the arrest and maltreatment of the Lord Mayor of Cork, Terence McSwiney.[56] Public order was breaking down and on 25 September, the sacking of Balbriggan by Black and Tans followed the killing of a Royal Irish Constabulary man.[57] Two local Balbriggan men, named Jim Lawless and John Gibbons, were murdered, forty houses were burned and wrecked and a warning issued to Drogheda by the Black and Tans:

Drogheda, Beware!

If in the town of Drogheda or its vicinity, a policeman is shot, take notice that for each member of the force killed or wounded, five of the leading Sinn Féiners will be shot without trial. It is not coercion. It is an eye for an eye. We are not drink-maddened savages, as we have been described in the Dublin 'rags'. We are not out for loot. We are inoffensive to women, we are as humane as other Christians, but we have restrained ourselves too long. Stop the shooting of police or we will lay low every house which smells Sinn Féin! Remember Balbriggan!

By order, 'The Black and Tans'.[58]

Shortly after this a series of indiscriminate raids occurred in Drogheda. Denis Reddan TC was arrested and shot in the leg.[59] Duffners Jewellers in Shop Street was raided and valuables worth £300 to £400 were taken.[60] The Boyne Cinema in Fair Street had the admission money taken and Maguire's licensed premises on the Back Strand was rifled. Two young men, Seán O'Carroll and Patrick Tierney, were kidnapped and murdered by Crown Forces in Ardee, on 30 November 1920.[61] Nine weeks later, in a similar incident, John Moran and Tom Halpin were shot at the Marsh Road, Drogheda, on 9 February 1921.[62]

The Treaty of December 1921 established the Irish Free State of twenty-six counties, with the six northern counties forming Northern Ireland retaining the choice of remaining in the United Kingdom. A narrow majority of sixty-four votes to fifty-seven of the Dáil accepted the Treaty.[63] A general election on 16 June 1922 resulted in a clear majority for the Treaty; Sinn Féin (pro) – fifty-eight; Sinn Féin (anti) – thirty-six; Labour – seventeen; Farmers – seven; Independent – ten.[64] On 28 June, civil war broke out, with the shelling of anti-Treaty forces in the Four Courts in Dublin.[65] One of those guns was used later to shell Millmount Barracks in Drogheda, occupied by 'Anti-Treaty' Irregulars.[66] The gun was sited at the Linen Hall beside the Dominican Church and shell-cases were kept by Fr Joe McQuillan OP as souvenirs. In lining up the aim, the initial shells fell in a field in Beamore, two miles to the South East. Fr Joe's card to my mother Dolly, with the 'rock' on one side and 'censor IRA' on the other tells the history of the time, dated 9 September 1922. This was the worst period of all, as brothers killed brothers. The old Nationalist, John Nolan, died in July of 1922.

The eleven months of the Civil War claimed the lives of Arthur Griffith, Michael Collins, Cathal Brugha, Erskine Childers, Liam Mellows, Rory O'Connor, Richard Barrett and Joe McKelvey. Among others were James Flanagan at Gormanston on 29 May 1922 and Liam Leech at Pitcher's Steps on 29 June 1922.[67] The total cost was 927 dead, including 77 executed by the government, £30 million in destruction and a debt of £17 million.[68] Back in 26 Fair Street, Willie McQuillan's family was growing up and his two eldest sons were in their early twenties, when an incident occurred which changed the life of the McQuillan family forever. This account was given to me by Nora, the sixth child of ten, in 1983.

> The boys, Peter and Lenny, came home one night after having been away for some days. Father, 'The Mac', as we called him, opened the front door. They explained that they had been 'on manoeuvres' in the South. Some kind of altercation happened and 'The Mac' fell over. Getting up, he told them to leave and stay away. My mother went to prevent this, and in the ensuing argument, Father shouted, 'If he won't leave, then I will!' In November 1924 he packed and set out for Australia. I was on the stairs and watched the whole thing.

The reason that Willie chose Australia was that his younger brother Charlie was living there. Folklore suggested that Charlie had drunk too much one night as a youth and when he returned home, his older brothers – seven of them – had a whip-round, collected five pounds and told him to 'leave'. He went to New South Wales in 1903 and eventually opened a pub and the Imperial Hotel in Armidale where he prospered and became a millionaire. As a result, his nephews Patrick, Peter and John Nolan all followed him to Australia in the 1920s with hopes of similar success.

Willie's wife, Margaret, kept her family together, but in 1923 her eldest daughter Queenie died. Margaret left Drogheda and moved to a house in 95 North Circular Road in Dublin. Her son, Peter, had joined the Capuchin Order and was now called Fr Jerome. In May 1926, Peter Dolan and his widowed mother Mary Jane set sail for Australia, a six-week trip one way. Peter was emigrating and his mother was attempting to persuade her brother Willie to return to his wife and family. She was not successful and before she was due to return in July, Margaret died at the age of fifty-six, on 21 February 1927. Willie was still in Australia. Once more, I will refer to the story as told in 1983 by their daughter, Nora, Sister Gerard DC. Nora recalled:

> It was terrible. We were all brought into a court. The Judge ruled that the family members aged under 21 must be sent to live with their father in Australia, since he was now their sole legal guardian. I was 19 at the time, and when documents were signed for Ita,

Vincent, Sheila and Doreen to go, the Judge called me up to the bench and said that he was aware that I had entered the Religious Community of the French Sisters of Charity, so he would make Reverend Mother responsible for my welfare and I need not go to New South Wales.[69]

Later she wrote to me: 'They went off in the boat and we got a photograph from Armidale showing them with "The Mac". It was a terrible start for the girls. Vincent joined the Capuchins and came back to Cork as a novice in 1933. He became Fr Albeus and spent a lifetime in South Africa.'[70]

It was only then I understood exactly who was the strange man in the brown robe and sandals, who would come on the train to Drogheda, walk the two miles to visit my mother in Beamore, make Rosary beads all the time, stay for an hour, and then insist on walking off again. When he retired to Dublin in the late 1980s, I met him several times in Church Street Friary. Sheila married a Michael Jeffrey in Australia, but she also returned to Ireland and lived at Sandyford with her son Michael, who became a doctor.

Shortly after I met Sister Gerard in 1983, she asked could she come and stay with us on the farm for two nights because she had been searching for a family since her own had broken up. 'Of course,' I said. Until her death in the early 1990s, she wrote regularly to me and from the forty letters I have been able to fill in the gaps in the story of her father Willie and his scattered family. Having found a family after sixty years, she came yearly until unable to travel, due to infirmity, and asked me to travel to Liverpool for her funeral 'so that she would have "family" there'. When the time came, I did. She had outlived her nine brothers and sisters. Willie remained in Australia until the 1930s, when he returned and lived as a semi-recluse in an apartment in Dun Laoghaire. Noel McQuillan, a son of Al's, recalled visiting his uncle in the 1940s; 'I wondered what to bring him, because he was known to be a bit moody. Then I got a great idea and purchased a copy of the *Irish Times*. Willie took it from me and rolling it into a ball, fired it out the door, shouting "Get rid of that English rag!" I was not too anxious to visit him again.'[71]

Willie collapsed and died on Dún Laoghaire Pier, on a June day in 1945, and is buried with his wife and daughter Queenie, in St Peter's Cemetery in Drogheda. The balance of probability and historical evidence points towards the fact that Willie McQuillan was not a rebel in 1916.

However, his generous donation in 1916 of the use of the old egg store in Fair Street to the Irish Volunteers, was sufficient to mark him out for his arrest, his consequent improbable case against DI Carberry for assault, calling on the use of one of the most famous barristers and politicians in the land to plead his case, is unique. The strains of the politics of the time proved too much for his family and his estrangement from them and the dismemberment of that family was the sad outcome.[72]

NOTES

1 *Drogheda Independent*, 5 Jan. 1901.
2 *Drogheda Argus*, 16 Jul. 1904.
3 *Drogheda Argus*, 19 Nov. 1904.
4 *Drogheda Argus*, 24 Jan. 1914.
5 Jonathan Bardon, *A history of Ireland in 250 episodes* (Dublin: Gill & Macmillan, 2008), p. 433.
6 Ibid., p. 432.
7 Ibid., p. 435.
8 *Drogheda Independent*, 21 Jun. 1913.
9 *Drogheda Independent*, 9 May 1914.
10 *Drogheda Argus*, 23 May 1914.
11 *Drogheda Argus*, 6 Sept.1913.
12 *Drogheda Independent*, 30 Jan. 1915.
13 *Drogheda Independent*, 20 Mar. 1915.
14 *Drogheda Independent*, 8 Jan.1916.
15 *Drogheda Independent* (Special Edition), 8 Jan. 1917.
16 Ibid.
17 Ibid.
18 Aodh Quinlivan, *Philip Monahan, a man apart: the life and times of Ireland's first Local Authority Manager* (Dublin: IPA, 2006), p. 10.
19 John McCullen, 'Events of Easter 1916 in Drogheda', *Journal of Old Drogheda Society*, 8 (1992), p. 116.
20 Joe Coyle, *Athletics in Drogheda* (Tafford, 2003), p. 48.
21 Quinlivan, *Philip Monahan*, p. 10.
22 McCullen, 'Events of Easter 1916' 1992, p. 121.
23 *Drogheda Independent* (Special Edition), 8 Jan. 1917.
24 Ibid.
25 Ibid.
26 Tim Pat Coogan, *1916, The Easter Rising* (London: Cassell, 2001), p. 135.
27 *Drogheda Argus*, 29 Apr. 1916.
28 *Drogheda Independent* (Special Edition), 8 Jan. 1917.
29 Ibid.
30 *Old Drogheda Society, Drogheda Independent Board Minutes Book 1916.*
31 *Drogheda Independent Special Edition*, 8 Jan. 1917.
32 Ibid.
33 Ibid.
34 Bardon, *History of Ireland*, p. 449.

35 McCullen, 'Events of Easter 1916', p. 122.
36 Ibid.
37 Oliver Coogan, *Politics and War in Meath 1922–23* (Navan: Meath County Council, 1983), p. 61.
38 *Drogheda Independent* (Special Edition), 8 Jan. 1917
39 Ibid.
40 All subsequent quotes: *Drogheda Independent* (Special Edition), 8 Jan. 1917.
41 *Drogheda Independent*, 24 Mar. 1917.
42 Ibid.
43 John McCullen, *The Call of St Mary's* (Drogheda: J. McCullen, 1984), p. 46.
44 *Drogheda Independent*, 20 Apr.1918.
45 *Drogheda Independent*, 8 Jun. 1918.
46 *Drogheda Argus*, 15 Jun. 1918.
47 Bardon, *history of Ireland*, p. 456.
48 Ibid.
49 *Drogheda Independent*, 20 Sept.1919.
50 Ibid., 24 Jan. 1920.
51 Ibid., 31 Jan. 1920.
52 Ibid., 31 Jul. 1920.
53 Ibid., 17 Jul. 1920.
54 Ibid.
55 Ibid., 14 Aug. 1910.
56 Ibid., 11 Sept. 1920.
57 Ibid., 25 Sept. 1920.
58 Ibid., 2 Oct. 1920.
59 Ibid., 20 Nov. 1920.
60 Ibid.
61 *Drogheda Argus*, 4 Dec.1920.
62 James Garry, 'The streets and lanes of Drogheda', *Journal of the Old Drogheda* (1996), p. 49.
63 Bardon *history of Ireland*, p. 471.
64 Ibid., p. 474.
65 Ibid., p 457.
66 Oral interview with my father in 1966.
67 James Garry, 'The streets and lanes of Drogheda', p. 49.
68 S. J. Connolly (ed.), *Oxford companion to Irish History*, 2nd edn. (Oxford: Clarendon Press, 2002), 'Irish Civil War', p. 277; Michael Hopkinson, *Green against green: the Irish Civil War* (Dublin: Gill & Macmillan, 1998), p. 273.
69 Author's collection.
70 Ibid.
71 Interview with the late Noel McQuillan, 1991.
72 I am grateful to the people who inspired and assisted in the writing of this article, particularly Sr Gerard McQuillan RIP, who provided the key to the mystery; Seamus Dolan, who provided extra pieces of the jigsaw puzzle; Moira McQuillan (née McLysaght) for assistance; Donal Hall for guidance and suggestions; local historians Brendan Matthews, Noel Ross, Seán Collins, Seamus Bellew and Audrey Smith for the sourcing of extra material and the various descendants of those arrested in 1916, who were very willing to share the history of their families; Dermot McCullen for advice on layout and other complicated technical matters, and my wife Ann and family for constant positive support.

9

In the Shadow of Altnaveigh: Political Upheaval and Sectarian Violence in County Louth, 1920–1922

Conor McNamara

This essay examines the dynamics of revolutionary violence in Co. Louth during the War of Independence and, in particular, the intersection between political violence and sectarian and communal violence.

The trajectory of the independence struggle in Louth cannot be analysed without reference to the evolution of the Volunteer campaign in south Armagh and Co. Down. The founding of the northern state and the establishment of the Ulster Special Constabulary (or 'Specials' as they were commonly referred to) in October 1920 created a situation where Volunteer units on the northern side of the border used the north Louth countryside, and Dundalk, in particular, as a base for their operations to disrupt the foundation of the northern state.[1]

Faced with a dispersed, but significant population of Protestant unionists in south Armagh, the Volunteers' campaign evolved considerably from late 1920 with both the Specials and the Volunteers drawn into an escalating cycle of communal violence culminating in a series of sectarian killings throughout 1922.[2] This was not a new development, however, and the War of Independence in the south Armagh/north Louth district was characterised by significant and escalating levels of sectarian violence.

The context and background to the massacre of six Protestants by the 4th Northern Division of the Irish Volunteers under Frank Aiken at Altnaveigh, Co. Down on 17 June 1922 has been convincingly analysed by Robert Lynch.[3] The purpose of this essay is to provide an account of the Independence struggle in Louth in the period before the killings. It is the intersection between communal conflict and political violence that remains at the heart of debates surrounding the legitimacy of the Independence struggle in Ireland and any account of the period must engage with the inherently local dynamics of revolutionary violence. The degree of popular approval among the nationalist community for the armed struggle in Louth should not be exaggerated and support for the Volunteers was limited throughout the period. The Volunteers in Louth, Monaghan and Armagh faced concerted opposition from 'respectable nationalist opinion', specifically, supporters of the Irish Parliamentary Party, members of the Ancient Order of Hibernians, sections of the mercantile community and both the Catholic bishops and the ordinary clergy. As police intelligence reports for Louth demonstrate, both the Volunteers and Sinn Féin were relatively well organised across the county; nonetheless, the authorities did not fear any immediate threat to their authority. From August 1920, however, the Royal Irish Constabulary (RIC) began to show alarm at the activities of the Volunteers, particularly in Dundalk, which became the epicentre of the republican campaign.

There were seventeen police stations in Co. Louth before the Volunteer campaign commenced in earnest in 1920, under the command of County Inspector F.C.W. Ireland (subsequently replaced by County Inspector Oulton), who operated with two District Inspectors under their command. Three police stations in Dundalk were under the command of District Inspector Henry Nelligan: Anne Street, Bridge Street and Quay Street; with District Inspector Meredith J. Egan stationed in Drogheda.[4] The total strength of the force in the county was reflective of the limited threat the republican movement was perceived to represent and in September 1920, the regular police constituted just ninety-eight rank and file constables (see Table 1: Membership of nationalist organisations, Co. Louth, Jan. 1920/Jan. 1921).

The *Dundalk Democrat*, which reported on events in Monaghan, south Armagh and north Louth, was a vocal critic of the republican movement throughout the period and gave prominent coverage to the Catholic hierarchy's condemnation of the republican campaign. While the Bishops across Ireland were consistent in their condemnation of violence, attitudes of the younger clergy varied. Fr James McKeone of Dundalk emerged as a particularly trenchant opponent of local republicans and he echoed Archbishop Logue's disapproval of the republican campaign in July 1921: 'I don't know what Dundalk is coming to or how it will end. It must have a rare supply of desperate rascals and robbers. I am deliberating whether I should not be up on Sunday and put the whole place under excommunication.'[5]

In June 1920, the RIC County Inspector reported approvingly to his superiors in Dublin Castle that there were twenty-three 'National Clubs' in Louth.[6] The reference to the growth of the National Clubs is intriguing, as the energies of the old Parliamentary Party increasingly found expression in these social clubs, rather than in the moribund National Volunteers or United Irish League. These clubs served a social function (often focused around the 'respectable' and mercantile elite), while keeping the organisation of the National Party in a state of readiness in advance of elections. The growth of the National Clubs shows that while Sinn Féin's electoral gains may have been at the expense of the Parliamentary Party, the latter body could still mobilise support and had not completely gone away.

The Volunteer campaign in Louth was consistently condemned as criminal in the local press and, in January 1921, the *Dundalk Democrat* claimed, '1920 will figure as one of the blackest years in modern Irish history. Its story is unrelieved by a gleam of brightness or any ray of hope. It is a record of blind violence and savage reprisal, of reckless recourse to methods of despair, of inhuman butchery and wanton destruction.'[7]

The paper consistently condemned the actions of the Volunteers and, subsequently, the Special Constabulary, in equal measure. Following the shooting of RIC Sergeant Holland at Cullyhanna in June 1920, the paper noted that the policeman received a 'most impressive funeral' at the Dominican Church in Dundalk.[8] The paper was particularly emphatic in its condemnation of the Volunteers after the shooting of RIC Constable Brennan in the town in August 1920, condemning 'the bloody death of this simple-hearted Irishman … a wrong has been done that there can be no undoing.'[9]

The residual strength of conservative nationalist opinion, buttressed by the local Ancient Order of Hibernians, which was traditionally strong along the border, was apparent in local politics. In the elections to the rural district councils held in June 1920, Sinn Féin won a clear majority of eighteen out of twenty-eight seats in the county. Republican success masked a strong showing by their nationalist rivals, however, when contrasted with elsewhere in the country. The division between republicans and nationalists was a persistent source of friction in Monaghan and Armagh at this time and contributed to the shootings of three Monaghan Hibernians by the Volunteers of the 5th Northern Division under the command of Eoin O'Duffy in November 1920 and March and April 1921.[10]

The fact that not all nationalist districts in Armagh or Louth supported the Volunteers' campaign infuriated many republicans. Volunteer Patrick Casey bitterly recalled that in the Ballyholland district of south Armagh, 'they [local nationalists] were a poor grovelling lot and it would have served them right if they had tasted some of the Black and Tan atrocity menu.'[11] Casey highlighted the prominence of working-class communities, small farmers and labourers as the base from which the republican campaign drew strength. The houses where they sought shelter 'were almost 100% the houses of the working class people; the middle and upper classes were too fond of the old money bags and usually only facilitated us when they had no option'.[12]

RIC men from the nationalist tradition were often as enthusiastic as their Protestant colleagues in their campaign against the Volunteers. Patrick Casey recalled that in Newry, 'this time we had merited the close scrutiny of the RIC and amongst the most aggressive of that body were Head Constable Kearney, Sergeants Little and Henry, all good Catholic Irishmen ... Moryah!'[13] Catholic RIC men were regarded as particularly valid targets, as Casey recalled, 'Towards the end of November 1920, it was decided to ease the enemy pressure by eliminating Head Constable Kearney and, accordingly, on a Sunday evening in November 1920 he got what he richly deserved.'[14]

During the War of Independence in Louth, the RIC and Crown Forces were successful in preventing the Volunteers from launching a wide-scale series of attacks on the police and military. Despite occasional lethal operations by the Volunteers, Dundalk remained the only district where the Volunteers were able to carry out a concerted series of attacks that led directly to loss of life among the Crown Forces. These attacks generally took the form of the shooting of isolated policemen by Volunteers, dressed in civilian clothes, travelling in small groups on foot and under the cover of darkness. Large-scale attacks involving relatively significant numbers of Volunteers, such as the ambush by republicans on the police at Plaster on 17 April 1921, were rare.

At the beginning of 1920, the RIC informed Dublin Castle that Louth was 'in a fairly quiet condition', despite 'Sinn Féin being strong and well-regulated but for the last seven months the members have kept quiet and nothing unusual has been observed regarding their movements except the establishment of an IRB [Irish Republican Brotherhood] branch in Dundalk'.[15]

The first republican casualty occurred on 16 April with the killing of Volunteer Thomas Mulholland, aged twenty-eight, a labourer and native of Belrobin, Barronstown.[16] Mulholland was shot by police on Bridge Street when the RIC claimed their patrol was attacked by armed men; however, local people disputed their account of events.[17] Mulholland had been interned following the 1916 Rising and his funeral was attended by thousands of local people. The inquest into the killing found that he 'died from shock and haemorrhage following wounds caused by a bullet fired from a revolver by Sergeant Joseph Bustard ... with the intention to kill, and we also find that there was no justification for the shooting'.[18] The killing increased sympathy for the republican movement but did not lead to an upsurge in attacks on the Crown Forces.

Following the arrival of the Black and Tans in July of 1920, the dynamics of the republican campaign across Ireland escalated with increasingly lethal attacks by the Irish Republican Army (IRA) met with brutal reprisals on the civilian population and republicans alike. Louth was largely spared the widespread violence witnessed in places such as Tipperary, Dublin and Clare, however, and there were no reprisals on the scale of the burning of Tuam and Cork City or the killing of large numbers of civilians.

The killing of Volunteer Mulholland was avenged on 22 August, however, when Constable Brennan was shot dead and two RIC and a civilian seriously wounded in a gun battle on Jocelyn Street.[19] The attack drew fierce local criticism, with the *Democrat* lamenting, 'Poor, big and inoffensive constable Brennan, stationed at Omeath for years past and only recently brought to Dundalk – a man who did his duty, but no more, and had given no man offence or ground for hostility'.[20] Fortunately for the local community, the Crown Forces were restrained in the aftermath of the attack and there was no reprisal.

Killings were occasionally blamed on republicans in which they took no part and it is not always possible to be emphatic regarding responsibility. Terence Wheatley, a motor vehicle driver for the military, was shot in Dundalk on 16 September and subsequently died in Louth infirmary. He was an ex-soldier and a native of Dublin and claimed he was held up in the Market Square and shot. From evidence produced at his inquest, however, it is possible that he was killed as a result of a row with some drinking companions.[21] A letter from the Volunteers threatening Wheatley was produced at his inquest but this was believed to have been written by Wheatley himself, who was also in possession of a number of stolen items when shot.[22]

Shootings continued intermittently after the arrival of the Black and Tans and the Crown Forces struck at republicans in November in a pattern that was reflected across the country. Patrick Tierney, a labourer, and John O'Carroll, an Irish teacher, were taken from their homes by uniformed men and shot dead at Ardee on 30 November. Both men were reported to be members of Sinn Féin and were killed a short distance from their homes in the early hours of the morning.[23] Two other homes were visited by the killers but no one was home. The County Inspector of the RIC reported to Dublin Castle that the men were killed by 'persons unknown' and 'it is alleged locally that the perpetrators were uniformed men but there is no evidence forthcoming to their identity'.[24]

By the end of 1920, the Volunteers across Ireland were emerging as a smaller, younger and more committed force. In Louth, the police reported that republicans were 'ready for action at short notice'; however, the growing capacity for violence was tempered by the arrest of leading republicans, with the authorities noting, 'its members have not shown great activity during the month due probably to the fact that many of its members are interned or on the run.'[25] The police may have had an informer close to the Louth Volunteers, evidenced by the authorities' ability to arrest republicans in advance of ambushes. In January 1921, the RIC Inspector reported:

Sinn Féin arrangements were made to ambush the police going to Dundalk Post Office but information on the proposed attack was received on the 7th. Four of the men who had been told to take part in it were arrested and interned. Sixty rounds of .303 rifle ammunition were found by the police and seized in a store in a yard from which the attack was to have taken place. A number of IRA local leaders have been interned or are on the run.[26]

Arrests continued to cripple the organisation and on 23 January 1921, twenty-four Volunteers were arrested near Drogheda.[27]

As the year progressed the military continued to foil ambushes and in March the County Inspector reported that 'police received quite a number of anonymous letters warning them of intended Sinn Féin ambushes but the police always turned out with the military assistance to meet the attacks and they never matured.'[28] He subsequently claimed to 'have had letters (anonymous) from young men in the movement begging me to have certain organisers arrested.'[29] During the same month, the police reported that forty of 'the county's most prominent men in the Sinn Féin movement' were interned.[30] In May, the County Inspector reported to Dublin Castle, 'the Drogheda police obtained information which led to the capture of a large quantity of arms, ammunition at Baymore on 23rd. On the whole the police have been successful in dealing with Sinn Féin activity during the month.'[31]

Drogheda was not immune from violence and the Crown Forces killed Alderman Thomas Halpin and John Moran of Magdalene Street, Drogheda, on 9 February. Both men were taken from their homes during the night by men dressed in civilian clothes and shot dead.[32] The RIC Inspector, as had become standard practice, provided fictitious circumstances for the killings: 'The former were Sinn Féiners of some prominence but there is reason to believe they were suspected by others in the organisation of having refused to carry out orders given by the IRA.'[33]

Republican violence did not cease, however, and the killing of ex-soldier, Henry Murray, in Dundalk on 25 February, reflected a hardening approach to suspected informers.[34] Murray was thirty-five, unmarried and a native of Carrickmacross, Co. Monaghan. He worked as a shop assistant in the town before joining the military and was working as a photographer.[35]

The south Armagh Volunteers under Patrick Rankin of Newry and Frank Aiken of Camlough were particularly active in the new year. In January alone, the RIC were attacked by the Volunteers at Carrickbraken, Camlough, Crossmaglen, Armagh City and again in Aiken's home district of Camlough. The attack at Armagh resulted in the death of Sergeant J.T. Kemp, with a B Special and civilian postman killed at Crossmaglen.[36] In retaliation for the attacks, a republican, John Doran, was taken from his home at Keegal, Camlough, on 10 January and shot dead. A reporter noted, 'there is a great sense of insecurity in the neighbourhood and scarcely a person is to be seen about after dark.'[37] The body of William Canning, a farmer's son, was found on the railway line near Newry in early January.[38]

In the midst of the Volunteers' campaign, the establishment of the Belfast boycott in the summer of 1920 provided a means through which the wider nationalist community could demonstrate their disgust at outbreak of anti-Catholic violence in Belfast, Lisburn and elsewhere in the north-east. With Protestants prominently represented among the mercantile elite in many border regions, however, republicans were often forced to enforce the boycott by intimidating Protestant businesses that were unwilling to cease trading with their co-religionists.[39]

The Great Northern Railway became a recurring target for the campaign in Dundalk. In July 1920, an engine driver, Michael McGee, was stopped on his way to work by republicans who stripped him and tarred the upper portion of his body. He had been an engine driver for twenty years and refused to stop driving troop trains.[40] In August, another driver, Owen McKeon, was shot in the leg in the vicinity of the station after being led from his cabin by armed men.[41] Frequent raids were subsequently made on the train throughout the period with Belfast goods removed and burned.

The local community was initially ambiguous about the boycott and the *Dundalk Democrat* noted at the commencement of the campaign: 'There is no doubt that a boycott of Belfast business interests could be made very effective in bringing home to Belfast merchants, and those depending on their trading, the opinion of nationalist Ireland. It is not so clear that it would have the effect of getting the unjustly dispossessed Catholic workers of Belfast back to their jobs.'[42] As the scale of violence in the north-east escalated, the paper concluded that some form of protest was imperative, noting that nationalist victims of unionist violence were 'Catholics and have an unanswerable claim on the bounty and generosity of Catholics everywhere.'[43]

The boycott had only commenced when it brought tragedy to the Protestant community with the burning to death of three Protestant dressmakers in Dundalk on 27 August. The fire was believed to have been started by prominent local individuals, the identity of whom was widely known. The premises of the Ulster Bank, Thomas Craig's department store and McGorisk's grocery and wine merchants store were destroyed. The inferno spread quickly, with the adjoining post office saved by the military and police while Melville's drapery store failed to ignite.[44] With the exception of the McGorisks, all premises targeted in the attack were the property of Protestants. Thirteen employees were sleeping above Craig's dressmakers when it was set alight, with ten managing to escape. Three Protestant women: Georgina Rice, a dressmaker aged twenty-four from Ardee; Elizabeth Wilson, aged thirty-six from Ballynure, Antrim; and Alexandrea Alderdyce, a draper's assistant, aged fifteen, of Drogheda, perished.[45]

A public meeting of the local Protestant community was held on 31 August to discuss the atrocity. One speaker summed up the tone of the meeting declaring, 'while they did not approve of the treatment their Catholic friends in the North were receiving, neither did they approve of the indiscriminate shooting of policemen.' Likewise, while anti-Catholic violence was denounced by Canon Hamilton as, 'unchristian', and for which, 'there could be no justification', such actions were the result, 'of the most tremendous provocation.'[46] Following the meeting, a fund was set up, which subsequently subscribed £2,000 to an 'Expelled Workers Fund'.

At a subsequent meeting of nationalists, the clerk of Dundalk Urban Council, A.N. Sheridan, claimed, 'In Dundalk, 94 per cent of the population was Catholic yet all the princely establishments were owned by Protestants. Did that not prove that they in Dundalk were not intolerant'. Sheridan went on to criticise Canon Hamilton's earlier claim of 'severe provocation': 'If the Canon read the newspapers for the last fifty years, or even for the last few months, he would find these outbreaks always commenced on 12th July.'[47]

Following the atrocity, a public meeting was convened by the chairman of the Urban Council, Peter Hughes, with armed police and representatives of all shades of political opinion attending. Prominent republican, James McGuill, representing the Dundalk Volunteers, 'assured those that did not agree with him in religion or politics that he abhorred the outrage which had occurred and asked them not to regard it as a reprisal for anything that had happened to him personally or in Belfast.' McGuill claimed, 'he had been approached by a section of men in the town with a list of houses they intended to burn', but threatened the men with a gun and told them that if anything of that kind occurred he would 'deal drastically with them'.[48]

The *Dundalk Democrat* was unambiguous in its condemnation of the atrocity:

Those responsible will assuredly have to pay, either here or hereafter. There are ugly rumours afloat of even worse things to come, in certain eventualities ... let there be an end. Let us remember our obligations as Irishmen and Christians. Let us, in God's name have no more bloodshed ... But these are the acts of revolutionaries, desperate men avowedly disregarding all laws, avowedly seeking to wreck by violence the fabric of all established government. The reprisals are the acts of men who are the servants of the government whose duty it is not to avenge outrages but to prevent them and to bring perpetrators to justice.[49]

Notwithstanding local revulsion at the killings, witnesses were not forthcoming and attacks on members of the Protestant community continued. On 25 September, John McNello, a native of Co. Monaghan, was shot in the legs by a group of armed men who were demanding the keys to his premises.[50] William Barrett was attacked in a botched shooting on the night of 23 December and the RIC concluded, 'it is feared he might be murdered or kidnapped. He is a unionist and the raiders wanted money for arms which he refused to give.'[51] Some £300 worth of jewellery and £200 worth of whiskey were stolen by raiders from premises in January 1921.[52] Such robberies were not all a result of the intimidation of Protestant traders, however, and in March 1921, six soldiers were arrested by police in Drogheda in connection with robbery in the town.[53]

The formation of the 4th Northern Division in March 1921, under the command of Frank Aiken, came as part of a national reorganisation of the Volunteers and transformed the structure of the Volunteers in north Louth. The new brigade consisted of north Louth, south and west Down, parts of Tyrone and Antrim, and all Co. Armagh. Aiken had gained the respect of the Volunteers in Armagh through the organisation of a series of daring and lethal attacks, which he personally organised and led. One senior officer recalled, 'At any time the membership of the division hardly exceeded 1,000 members, although in the period following the truce to the outbreak of the Civil War it is likely that this number was substantially increased.'[54]

Frank Aiken (1898–1983) was a native of Carrickbracken, Camlough, south Armagh. He was the youngest of seven children of prominent local nationalist politician, strong farmer and builder, James Aiken.[55] Captain of the Camlough Volunteers at just fifteen, Aiken was among the most competent and ruthless leaders the revolution was to produce.[56] Selected as vice commandant of the Newry brigade under Paddy Rankin in 1920, he replaced the much older Rankin as commander of the 4th Northern Division from March 1921 onwards.[57] The formation of the new division brought north Louth into the remit of a leadership that viewed the Special Constabulary as a particular target due to their targeting of the Catholic community, as one officer later wrote:

> The creation of this force [B Specials] and the sectarian outrages which followed spread widespread alarm in the six county area resulting in thousands of the nationalist population moving as refugees to the south. Inevitably Dundalk was the recipient of many of these displaced persons. Unfortunately, as the sectarian outrages spread throughout the six counties they inevitably spread to the border districts with tit for tat attacks being made on Protestants. Eventually these troubles had crossed the border to Dundalk by 1921.[58]

The 4th Division was an uneasy alliance of disparate rural districts attuned to the profound localism of republican activism. Some Armagh officers took a dim view of the North Louth Brigade and Patrick Casey, OC, of Newry, recalled that in relation to an attack on the RIC at Plaster in April 1921:

> It is significant to note that although this operation took place near Dundalk, few men from that town took part. I know of none. It is also true to say that, taking them by and large, the men of north Louth took little if any part in the fight for Independence. It was necessary to take men from all parts of Armagh and Down to do the work that should have been done by the Dundalk men.[59]

From 1921, Volunteers from across the new frontier in Co. Down and Co. Armagh increasingly sought refuge over the border and established camps in north Louth. Volunteer John Grant from Co. Down noted:

> The idea behind those camps was to safeguard the men from our Six Counties area from capture by the Crown Forces there; to provide

the men in camp with an intensive course of military training and to use the camp as a base for sending men into Northern Ireland to protect our civil population or to attack the British forces there.[60]

Republican attacks were concentrated in the catholic districts of south Armagh and in the Newry district. Volunteer Edward Boyle recalled, 'While republicans exercised considerable control in nationalist districts, in areas while large Protestant populations, social control was not possible.'[61] Aiken's most daring operation was launched to mark the opening of the new northern parliament at Stormont by King George V on 24 June. The Volunteers managed to derail a train carrying soldiers and cavalry of the 10th Hussars to the Curragh Camp at Adavoyle, near Newry, killing a guard and four soldiers.[62] The explosion destroyed a number of carriages and killed numerous horses, with the Crown Forces subsequently killing a local civilian, Patrick McAteer.[63]

The killing of republicans by the Crown Forces continued in Louth despite the Volunteers being reinforced and reorganised. In the second week of May, John J. McGee, railway clerk, was taken from his bed by masked men near Greenore and shot dead. The police offered an unconvincing explanation, claiming the 'motive was not very clear but a few days before he had made a statement to the police as to his movements which did not agree with that of another Sinn Féiner who was suspected of having taken part in an ambush of police in the locality.'[64]

The final months of the War of Independence saw an escalation of attacks by the recently formed 4th division based in Dundalk. Constable William Campbell, a native of Glasgow, was shot dead on the night of 17 June while cycling on the Newry Road in Dundalk.[65] His killing was in retaliation for the killing John Watters, aged twenty-three, and Patrick Watters, aged nineteen, who were taken from their beds and shot dead by Crown Forces in the early hours of Sunday morning.[66] The premises of the Dundalk Democrat, which had opposed the Volunteers, was raided and destroyed by the military during the same month. Meanwhile, violence connected with the Belfast boycott continued and masked men raided Carson's Auctioneers in May, burning £200 worth of Belfast tweed.[67] Parcels of the Belfast Telegraph newspaper were taken from the train and burned during the same week.[68]

The final week of the War of Independence saw a series of atrocities on Catholics in south Armagh committed, it was widely believed, by the Specials. The significance of these atrocities on the subsequent direction of the Volunteer campaign cannot be underestimated. On 6 June 1921, Hugh O'Hanlon, aged thirty-five, of Camlough, was shot dead by masked men who took him from his home. On the same night, James Smyth of Keggal, aged forty-five, was taken from home by men claiming to be police and shot dead.[69] Both victims were farmers and members of the Ancient Order of Hibernians. One week later, on 23 June, John Cosgrave, also from Camlough, was taken from his home by masked men and shot dead. The County Inspector of the RIC for Armagh attempted to divert responsibility for the attacks and claimed the killings were the result of an internal feud among the Catholic community in the locality.[70]

Attacks on the Catholic community in the Bessbrook district escalated in the days leading up to the Truce. On 6 July 1921, Peter Quinn, aged thirty-eight, a quarry worker; John Reilly, aged twenty-four, a schoolteacher; his brother, Thomas Reilly, aged twenty-one, a farmer; and Peter McGinnity, aged twenty, a farmer's son, were taken from their homes and shot dead by masked men. Ironically, John and Thomas Reilly's father was an ex-sergeant in the RIC.[71]

The ending of hostilities in the War of Independence came as a shock to many Volunteer leaders, as Frank Aiken later recalled, 'the truce came as a great surprise to us and we did not think it would last long'.[72] Aiken was under no illusion, however, that for the five northern divisions, the truce was merely an intermission and, 'whether there would be peace or war in the twenty-six counties there was bound to be fighting in the north and it was our duty to be prepared for it'.[73] The truce was welcomed by ordinary Volunteers, however, as an opportunity for rest and recuperation, not always with Aiken's approval:

The burst of enthusiasm after the truce began to slow after two or three months and after that its prolongation was bad for army units which were not well disciplined and hardworking; both officers and men in such units were inclined to have a good time and do no work. In our division we had to dismiss two officers for getting drunk in the late autumn.[74]

The Anglo-Irish Treaty in December 1921 was a turning point for the 4th Northern Division and, as Robert Lynch has observed, Aiken was to implement a 'distinctively active form of neutrality', impeding the establishment of the northern state through attacks launched from Dundalk, while refusing to support either side of the emerging divide in the Volunteers.[75] A memorandum on the situation written by an officer of the 4th Division reveals the complexities of the situation:

> The situation confronting the 4th Northern Division at this time was a complex one: while the officers of the Division overwhelmingly rejected the Treaty, the continued support of the Dublin government was a necessity in order to provide some form of defence for the nationalist community in the six counties. While Aiken's position was one of neutrality, there were some within his division who supported the extremist anti-treaty side, notably Brigadier-General [Patrick] McKenna and the two North Louth Battalions … a divide became apparent between these contingents located in the Ann Street and Bridge Street Barracks, and the contingents located at the military barracks.[76]

With his own forces divided over the Treaty, Aiken was primarily concerned in the early months of 1922 with keeping his division together and avoiding internecine bloodshed. To complicate matters, the first six months of 1922 saw the arrival in Dundalk of significant amounts of arms from the southern divisions as part of a wider attempt to forge unity in the army through a focus on equipping the northern divisions for an offensive against the new northern state. With arms travelling north to Dundalk, men and equipment were travelling south from Armagh and Down, as Volunteer Thomas Luckie recalled: 'About April 1922 about thirty of the Crosmaglen Company moved into County Louth to a place named Cavanore where we took over a large farmhouse and started an armed camp.'[77] Newry Volunteer Edward Fullerton remembered: 'The material we transported included rifles, ammunition, revolvers, hand grenades, etc. We were engaged on this work each day for a whole week … I know that a constant traffic in IRA men and IRA material crossed the [Carlingford] Lough whenever conditions favoured crossing.'[78]

The military departed Dundalk in the early months of 1922. The King's Own Yorkshire Light Infantry Regiment stationed at Dundalk Grammar School departed in January, followed by the evacuation of the RIC Barracks in Ann Street and Bridge Street, with the military handing over the barracks to Aiken on 13 April 1922. Following the evacuation, Aiken moved his headquarters from Newry to the barracks, while the north Louth battalions took occupation of the Ann Street and Bridge Street barracks. Further encampments were established in the north Louth countryside at Dungooley (Kilcurry) and Ravensdale.

Aiken and other northern commanders had no incentive to support the National Army in their campaign against the emerging anti-Treaty IRA, if they could not guarantee them full support in their campaign against the northern state. Aiken was not prepared to support the anti-Treaty IRA either, in what he anticipated being a hopeless and divisive campaign against their former comrades, which was ultimately distracting both wings of the Volunteers from supporting the northern divisions. Aiken later recalled his decision to keep his division neutral:

On that day, July 14th, I ordered all arms and war material in the Division to be concealed, and that if we finally broke with GHQ, all military posts and camps were to be evacuated, the Divisional organisation to be kept intact along Volunteer lines until, an ordered state of government obtaining in the South, we could attack the North, with a chance of getting a united Ireland, which was always the immediate job to us as Northerners.[79]

The Volunteers' so-called 'Northern Offensive' of May 1922 was designed to destabilise the northern state and unify the Volunteers through joint support for their northern comrades. The Ulster Council was established in February 1922, bringing together both sides of the emerging split in the Volunteers. Located in Clones, and controlled by Eoin O'Duffy, Frank Aiken and Michael Collins, the council was formed to co-ordinate, arm and direct the northern divisions. The failure of the northern offensive in March 1922 highlighted the limitations of the northern divisions and the limited support for their situation among the wider Volunteer movement.[80] The offensive saw the killing of six Crown Forces in west Ulster before the badly stretched northern units were forced to concede they had not the support, membership nor co-ordination to launch a wide-scale offensive. On both fronts, it was a failure, and Aiken, anticipating the collapse of the action, ensured the 4th Northern Division took no part. Volunteer Pat Casey recalled, 'That finished the fight for

Ulster, and so, gradually, eyes were turned to the conflict already raising its ugly head in the south.'[81]

Between June 1920 and June 1922 over 400 people, mostly Catholics, were killed in sectarian violence in Belfast, with killings also taking place in south Down, east Tyrone, Derry city and south Armagh.[82] Volunteer John Grant recalled:

A feeling of apprehension and fear of reprisals by Crown Forces in the North existed amongst our civilian population in south Armagh districts. This feeling prompted large numbers of the male population residing within four to five miles of the Border to cross into Co. Louth each night for safety and a sleep.[83]

For these nationalist communities, most of whom did not have active Volunteer companies, the emerging split in the Volunteers was effectively abandoning them to their fate in the face of an onslaught of loyalist violence. Aiken was determined to pursue his own strategy to defend his community; however, it was not a strategy that would have been acceptable to either of the emerging Volunteer headquarters. The brutality of the Special Constabulary was to be met in kind, demonstrating to the Protestant community their vulnerability in south Armagh. Volunteer John Grant recalled one element of Aiken's emerging strategy to combat the activities of the Specials by targeting prominent unionists:

Plans envisaged the capture of a number of prominent Unionists in each district in Northern Ireland within our Divisional area, and also the sending of columns of well armed men into districts where it was a military feasibility to do so. It was hoped by sending our columns into certain areas that we would improve the morale of our own civilians and make the Unionist civilians (if any Unionists could then be classed as civilians) realise that even in their own districts they were not immune from punishment for the misdeeds of their relatives serving in the B Specials.

About the last Saturday night in May orders were issued to capture a large number of prominent Unionists as outlined above. I got orders at Dungooley Camp to arrest four men, Jim Murdock, a man named Patterson, Richard Stokes and William Smyth. We captured three of them, William Smyth being away from home when we called. Many others were captured from Mid and North Armagh, Newry and South Down. All those Unionists were taken into the Military Barracks in Dundalk and informed there that they were being held as hostages for the good conduct of the other Unionists in their several districts.[84]

The kidnapping of prominent unionists by Aiken's men in south Armagh was not unique. The 5th Northern Division kidnapped over forty Protestants, mainly Orangemen, B Specials and unionist officials, along the border in Derry, Tyrone and Fermanagh on 7 February 1922.[85] The hostages were taken in retaliation for the arrest of Dan Hogan O/C of the 5th Northern Division and other republicans. Specials were also killed in reprisals by the same division at Clones, Co. Monaghan, on 11 February and at Rolsea, Co. Fermanagh on 21 March 1922. The atrocity at Roslea targeted the homes of Protestant members of the B Specials, with fourteen houses burned and three Protestants, two of whom were B Specials, killed.[86] Four B Specials were shot at the train station in Clones in March in the so-called 'Clones Affray', as they were waiting to proceed to Fermanagh.[87]

In light of atrocities carried out by the B Specials in south Armagh, an attack on the Protestant community by Aiken's men was ultimately, unsurprising. On 17 June 1922, about twenty Volunteers left Dundalk Barracks and travelled across the border to the Newry hinterland. The killings took place in the town lands of Lisdrumliska and Altnaveigh, a mile west of Newry town. Two Catholics, Thomas Cawley of Whitecross and Patrick Cregan of Bessbrook, had been killed and their bodies found at Lislea Road, in the same district, three days earlier. Six Protestants were shot dead in the massacre, many others severely injured and over a dozen properties burned out. The dead consisted of John Heaslip, aged fifty, a farmer, and his son Robert, aged seventeen, of Lisdrumliska; James Lockhart, a farmer's son, aged twenty-three from Lisdrumliska; Joseph Gray, aged twenty, from Lisdrumliska; Thomas Crozier, aged sixty-seven, a pensioner farmer; and his wife Elizabeth, of Altnaveigh. The homes of the Gray, Lockhart, Little, Crozier, Heaslip and McCullough families were burned.[88]

Tensions remained high in Dundalk and, at the end of June 1922, a meeting of the town's Protestants was held in response to threatening notices that were pinned around the town. It is unclear what was contained in the notices but they appear to have been critical of the Protestant community in light of the ongoing violence against Catholics in the North. The meeting passed a resolution:

> That this meeting of the principal Protestants of Dundalk, assembled in view of the notices posted in Dundalk, desires to confirm the resolutions already carried out at a previous public meeting of the Dundalk Protestants by which all outrages on Roman Catholic Irishmen in the North of Ireland and reprisals were expressed to be abhorrent to the Protestant community in Dundalk.[89]

Five Protestant families, all of whom worked on the Great Northern Railway, fled their homes in the town in June 1922. All the families involved resided in Demesne Terrace and, of the ten homes on the street that were owned by the Railway, six were attacked, of which five were Protestant. The attacks were carried out by bands of armed men who fired into the homes during the night. The families of Alex Moorehead, George McAlester, Thomas Johnston, William Compton, and Station foreman Robinson all fled the town.[90] During the same month, two Volunteers from Dundalk Barracks, in violation of the truce, shot dead magistrate James Woulfe Flanagan, leaving Newry Cathedral after mass on 3 June 1922.[91] The killing increased the already heightened tension in Armagh, with all five bridges over the Newry canal closed and local roads manned by the Special Constabulary for two weeks.

Partition and the Civil War had profound effects for Co. Louth. As Robert Lynch noted: 'Aiken was pitted against every counter revolutionary force in Ireland, from the notorious Auxiliaries to the Ulster Special Constabulary and the Free State Army to the armed nationalist grouping, the Hibernians.'[92]

Aiken was to be exhaustive in his efforts to prevent the outbreak of the Civil War. Failing to do so, he managed at least to keep his own division together. The outbreak of the Civil War posed a major dilemma and 'that which they had most feared had happened and consequently the possibility of presenting a united front against the six county administration was at an end.'[93]

Events during the Civil War were to consolidate Aiken's reputation and the breakout of over 100 men from Dundalk Gaol on 27 July and the retaking of the town from Monaghan units of the National Army under Dan Hogan on 14 August were arguably the most efficient operations carried out by republicans during the entire period.[94]

Events at Altnaveigh, however, cast a shadow over the reputation of Aiken and his men. The killings took place in the context of escalating sectarian tension and the killing of Catholics with impunity by the Special Constabulary in the south Armagh countryside. The massacre reflected the Catholic community's fear and powerlessness in the new northern state and was intended to bring home to the Protestant community their own vulnerability in light of the actions of the Specials. The message from Altnaveigh was clear: if the Specials were going to kill Catholics in south Armagh, their community would face equally vicious retribution.

The notion of such a thing as a 'clean war' during the War of Independence is naive, or worse, and denies the fundamental realities of Irish society during this period. While it was convenient to generations of political adherents of either side of the Civil War divide, as well as the unionist community, to perpetuate notions that their side fought a clean war, it ignores the suffering of both Protestant and Catholics communities at the hands of armed groups.

Sectarian killings did not begin or end at Altnaveigh, however; as events in Dundalk during the War of Independence demonstrate, the Belfast boycott legitimised popular resentment against the Protestant population. While there is a grim inevitability regarding the rise in sectarian sentiment, events in Dundalk cannot be understood without reference to the atrocities committed against the Catholic community in Belfast, Lisburn, Banbridge and elsewhere in the north east. Ultimately, given the fear and loathing within both communities in Louth and Armagh, the atrocities committed by both sides, while brutal, were unsurprising. To highlight such events is not to seek to sully the achievements of the revolution or bring the reputation of an entire body of Volunteers into disrepute. The majority of Volunteers in Louth, Armagh and elsewhere, played no role whatsoever in such events and deplored the killing of civilians. An authentic account of the period, however, necessitates the restoration to the historical narrative of the deep loss suffered, and inflicted, by both communities and the inevitability of ethnic conflict in a divided society in a time of war.

Table 1. Membership of nationalist organisations, Co. Louth,
Jan. 1920/Jan. 1921

Organisation	Branches Jan. 1920	Members Jan. 1920	Branches Jan. 1921	Members Jan. 1921
United Irish League	25	2,226	24	2,345
National Volunteers	23	2,177	23	2,062
Irish Volunteers	2	1,000	2	1,070
Sinn Féin Club			23	1,992
Cumann na mBan			6	264
ITGWU			4	1,354
Ancient Order of Hibernians (BoE)	23	2,008	22	2,066
Ancient Order of Hibernians (AA)	3	548	3	540
Gaelic League	3	200	4	424
National Club	23	1,969		
Irish Republican Brotherhood	1	60	1	140

Source: TNA, CO 904, CICMR, Co. Louth, Jan. 1920–Jan. 1921.

NOTES

1   The new constabulary comprised A, B and C Specials consisting of full-time, part-time and unpaid volunteers, respectively. A and C Constabulary were disbanded in 1926. The B Specials remained notorious for their sectarianism until disbandment in 1970.
2   Pearse Lawlor, *The Outrages, 1920–1922: the IRA and the Ulster Special Constabulary in the border campaign* (Cork: Mercier Press, 2011).
3   Robert Lynch, 'Explaining the Altnaveigh massacre', *Éire-Ireland*, 45 (2010), pp. 184–210.
4   County Directory, Louth, *Thom's Directory*, 1921, p. 1,263.
5   *Irish Independent*, 31 July 1921, p. 5.
6   TNA, CO 904, CICMR, Co Louth, June 1920.
7   *Dundalk Democrat*, 1 Jan. 1921.
8   *Dundalk Democrat*, 12 Jun. 1920.
9   *Dundalk Democrat*, 28 Aug. 1920.
10 Fearghal McGarry, *Eoin O'Duffy: a self-made hero* (Oxford: OUP, 2005), pp. 62–73.
11 Bureau of Military History, Witness Statement, 1,148, 'Patrick J. Casey', p. 17.
12 Ibid., pp. 11–12.
13 Ibid., p. 5.
14 Ibid., p. 6.
15 TNA, CO 904, CICMR, Co. Louth, Feb. 1920.
16 *Irish Independent*, 17 Apr. 1920, p. 4; 19 Apr. 1920, p. 5; 26 Apr. 1920, p. 5.
17 *Irish Times*, 19 Apr. 1920, p. 5.
18 *Irish Times*, 8 May 1920, p. 4.
19 *Irish Independent*, 23 Aug. 1920, p. 5; *Irish Times*, 23 Aug. 1920, p. 6.

20   *Dundalk Democrat*, 28 Aug. 1920.
21   *Irish Times*, 20 Sept. 1920, p. 5.
22   *Irish Times*, 25 Sept. 1920, p. 8.
23   *Freeman's Journal*, 1 Dec. 1920, p. 5.
24   TNA, CO 904, CICMR, Co. Louth, Nov. 1920.
25   TNA, CO 904, CICMR, Co. Louth, Dec. 1920.
26   TNA, CO 904, CICMR, Co. Louth, Jan. 1921.
27   Ibid.
28   TNA, CO 904, CICMR, Mar. 1921.
29   Ibid.
30   TNA, CO 904, CICMR, Mar. 1921.
31   TNA, CO 904, CICMR, May 1921.
32   *Freemans' Journal*, 10 Feb. 1921, p. 5.
33   TNA, CO 904, CICMR, Feb. 1921.
34   *Irish Times*, 26 Feb. 1921, p. 5.
35   *Irish Independent*, 26 Feb. 1921, p. 5.
36   TNA, CO 904, CICMR, Armagh, Jan. 1921.
37   *Freeman's Journal*, 12 Jan. 1921, p. 3.
38   *Freeman's Journal*, 1 Jan. 1921, p. 6.
39   For a study of the boycott in Co. Monaghan, see Terence Dooley, 'From the Belfast Boycott to the Boundary Commission: fears and hopes in County Monaghan, 1920–1926', *Clogher Record: Journal of the Clogher Historical Society*, 15(1) (1994), pp. 90–106.
40   *Irish Times*, 20 Jul. 1920, p. 5.
41   *Irish Times*, 21 Aug. 1920, p. 3.
42   *Dundalk Democrat*, 7 Aug. 1920, p. 4.
43   *Dundalk Democrat*, 28 Aug. 1920, p. 4.
44   *Irish Times*, 4 Sept. 1920, p. 2.
45   *Irish Times*, 30 Aug. 1920, p. 6.
46   *Irish Independent*, 1 Sept. 1920, p. 7.
47   *Irish Independent*, 6 Sept. 1920, p. 7.
48   *Irish Times*, 20 July 1920, p. 5.
49   *Dundalk Democrat*, 2 Oct. 1920.
50   *Irish Times*, 19 Jan. 1921, p. 6.
51   TNA, CO 904, CICMR, Louth, Dec. 1920.
52   TNA, CO 904, CICMR, Louth, Jan. 1921.
53   TNA, CO 904, CICMR, Louth, Mar. 1921.
54   Typescript article, 'The commencement of the Civil War in Dundalk', p. 2, P104/1,300 (Frank Aiken Papers), UCDA.
55   Ronan Fanning, 'Aiken, Francis (Thomas)', *Dictionary of Irish biography*.
56   For details of Aiken's early military career, see Eoin Magennis, 'Frank Aiken: Family, early life and the revolutionary period, 1898–1921', in Bryce Evans and Stephen Kelly (eds), *Frank Aiken, nationalist and internationalist* (Dublin, 2014), pp. 59–80.
57   Matthew Lewis, *Frank Aiken's war: the Irish Revolution, 1916–1923* (Dublin: UCD Press, 2014).
58   'The commencement of the Civil War in Dundalk', p. 3.
59   BMH, WS1,148, 'Patrick J. Casey', p. 11.
60   BMH, WS658, 'John Grant', p. 19.
61   BMH, WS647, 'Edward Boyle', pp. 15–16.
62   Frank Gallagher, railway worker, Belfast; Sergeant C. Dowson, Middlesbrough; Corporal Crosby; Trooper W.H. Telford; Pte. C.H. Harper, Canterbury.

63 British Pathé News filmed the wreckage in aftermath of the attack. The newsreel is available to view online at https://www.youtube.com/watch?v=5NJl9c4yuxQ.

64 TNA, CO 904, CICMR, Co. Louth, May 1921.

65 *Irish Times*, 21 Jun. 1921, p. 5.

66 *Irish Independent*, 21 Jun. 1921, p. 5.

67 *Irish Independent*, 6 May 1921, p. 5.

68 *Irish Independent*, 11 May 1921, p. 6.

69 *Freeman's Journal*, 8 Jun. 1921, p. 4.

70 TNA, CO 904, CICMR, Co. Louth, Armagh, Jun. 1921.

71 *Freeman's Journal*, 9 Jul. 1921, p. 5.

72 Handwritten Memoirs by Frank Aiken detailing the history and organisation of the 4th Northern Division, p. 1, P104/1,308 (Frank Aiken Papers), UCDA.

73 Ibid., p. 7.

74 Ibid., p. 3.

75 Robert Lynch, 'Frank Aiken's civil wars, 1922–1923', in Evans and Kelly, *Frank Aiken, nationalist and internationalist*, p. 83.

76 'The commencement of the Civil War in Dundalk', p. 5.

77 BMH, WS672, 'Thomas Luckie', p. 4.

78 BMH, WS890, 'Edward Fullerton', p. 27.

79 Letter from Frank Aiken to all officers and men of the 4th Northern Division, 'Position of the 4th Northern Division from Jan. 1922 to Jul. 17 1922', P104/1,247(2) (Frank Aiken papers), UCDA.

80 Robert Lynch, 'Donegal and the joint I.R.A. northern offensive, May–November 1922', *Irish Historical Studies*, 35 (2006–7), pp. 184–99.

81 BMH, WS1,148, 'Patrick J. Casey', p. 33.

82 Robert Lynch, *The Northern IRA and the early years of Partition, 1920–22* (Dublin: Irish Academic Press, 2006).

83 BMH, WS658, 'John Grant', p. 20.

84 Ibid., p. 21.

85 Feraghal McGarry, *Eoin O'Duffy*, p. 99.

86 Ibid., p. 60.

87 Robert Lynch, 'The Clones affray, 1922: massacre or invasion?', *History Ireland*, 12(3) (2004), pp. 33–7.

88 A detailed account of events leading up to the killings is contained in, Lynch, 'Explaining the Altnaveigh Massacre'.

89 *Irish Independent*, 29 Mar. 1922, p. 5.

90 *Irish Times*, 22 Jun. 1922, p. 6.

91 For an account of the shooting, see Bureau of Military History, Witness Statement, 890 (Edward Fullerton), pp. 24–5.

92 Lynch, 'Frank Aiken's civil wars, 1922–1923', p. 83.

93 'The Commencement of the Civil War in Dundalk', p. 6.

94 Michael Hopkinson, *Green against green: the Irish Civil War* (Dublin: Gill & Macmillan, 1988).

10

The Civil War in Drogheda,
January–July 1922

Mal Martin

When the British Army vacated the Military Barracks at Millmount on Monday, 23 January 1922, it was amongst one of the first barracks to be handed over to the new Irish State. The local newspapers surprisingly underplayed the affair, the following being the only mention of this historical event: 'The KOYLI [King's Own Yorkshire Light Infantry] stationed in Drogheda for some time past left on Monday last for Plymouth, and the Barracks are to be taken over by the IRA [Irish Republican Army].'[1] Six weeks later, on Wednesday, 15 March 1922, the Royal Irish Constabulary (RIC) evacuated the West Gate and South Gate Barracks in Drogheda. These were the last of the British Forces to leave the town.

From early afternoon, the people of Drogheda had gathered along the route from West Gate Barracks towards the railway station. At 2.45 p.m., the officer commanding the Irish forces, Commandant Kavanagh, along with the liaison officer, Captain O'Connor, came out from Millmount to assist at the takeover. Just before 3 p.m., the RIC emerged from West Gate Barracks. 'There was a good deal of merriment and jubilation but an impressive silence prevailed when a few minutes before 3 o'clock the RIC men evacuated the West Gate Barracks'. They marched across West Street, down Shop Street and, just as they were crossing the bridge at the bottom of Shop Street, a band of Irish pipers came into sight, followed by Irish soldiers. 'The two forces almost met at the bridge. It was certainly not a prearranged movement, but nothing more spectacular could have been contrived'. The RIC continued in silence and turned left into the South Gate Barracks. The Irish soldiers carried on proudly marching to the sound of the pipe band, up Shop Street, over West Street stopping outside West Gate Barracks.

The head constable of the RIC stayed behind to hand over control of the Barracks to Staff-Captain Grey, officially. 'This formal ceremony was attended by an interesting and almost amusing incident. While Captain O'Connor was searching through the furniture he found, of all things in the world, the flag of the local pipers' band, which had been captured by the Black and Tans in the course of hostilities'. The flag was passed to the band outside and the tricolour was raised over Drogheda's West Gate Barracks to the sound of enormous cheering from the local citizens. While all this excitement was going on, the RIC men marched out of South Gate Barracks to the railway station and made their way to Dundalk. 'The South Gate Barracks was occupied by the men of the 2nd battalion of the IRA, with Commandant Byrne in charge'.[2]

The period when the RIC evacuated was critical to what was to follow over the next few weeks. The atmosphere was one of jubilation and everybody seemed to be united but behind the scenes all was not well. Commandant Kavanagh resigned the very next day. An entry in the newly formed Irish Republican Police (IRP) daybook gives an idea of the confusion that was about. 'Brigade troubles impede work, Brigade O/C asked to resign, Brigade staff resignation accepted'.[3] There was also a 'meeting of unit at West Gate' that took place on 16 March 1922,[4] while 17 March has an interesting comment in the IRP day book: 'Rebels still hold Millmount'.[5] This is the first time the term 'rebel' was used and was the first indication of a split in the IRA. Also on that day Commandant Landers arrived in town to take command: 'Commandant Landers arrives to take command. Brigade resolved into separate and independent battalions'.[6] This appears to be the moment when the 1st battalion of the IRA in Drogheda split into two separate organisations. An agreement was reached and logged in the IRP daybook: '1st Battalion evacuates Millmount, send maintenance party to West Gate – Maintenance party from each Battalion in Millmount. Police evacuate Millmount'.[7]

A public meeting was called on Monday, 20 March 1922, to explore ways of policing Drogheda and its surrounding districts. It was attended by a large cross section of the townspeople and the outlying rural districts, including businessmen, members of the clergy both Protestant and Catholic, local politicians, doctors, solicitors and justices of the peace. The mayor, Philip Monahan, pointed out that various people were invited to attend the meeting which had been called 'at the request of the Brigade Commander of the area'. The Brigade Commander, however, was not able to attend the meeting, informing the mayor why he could not be there. The mayor began by stating the position the town was in, saying that because of 'political complications in Ireland, it was not possible for the Provisional Government to immediately establish a police force'. He went on to say that until a government, provisional or otherwise, was installed by an election or some other means, 'there would be no police force as they had known it in past years'. He said the IRA had taken on this role since the RIC had left the town, 'but unfortunately, they were not able to finance the entire scheme, and were looking for financial assistance'.

It was proposed to set up an interim police force and to employ several full-time policemen to patrol and protect the town and surrounding area. The area to be covered was the town, which would need six policemen, and a very large area that stretched north of Drogheda from Annagassan to Dromin on towards Slane and back into Drogheda, which would need another six policemen. Twelve policemen would require a payment of £40 per week and this would need to be covered for three months, meaning the total cost would be £600. The purpose of the meeting was to come up with ways of raising the money needed. 'It was not proposed to ask people to hand over such a sum of money blindly to anybody'.

The mayor suggested that a small committee should be formed from the people that were present. They would collect the money and 'that committee would hand over this money to the police officer, to pay his men every week'. If the committee were not happy with the manner in which the policing was being executed, they would have the power to withhold payment: 'the idea was to place those who subscribed absolutely in control financially, and they had an absolute guarantee that the money collected would not be expended for any other purpose'.

Several questions were asked with regard to how they would keep control of the money and if twelve men were enough to patrol such a large area. Colonel Thornhill asked if 'it will still be a voluntary contribution' and the mayor's reply was 'yes, absolutely voluntary'. It was also pointed out that it was not only property that needed to be protected and that 'the right of the citizen to walk the streets unmolested is just as sacred as the protection of property'. There was also a suggestion that maybe the corporation could 'appoint watchmen to police the town' but the mayor pointed out that 'you have a certain military body anxious to do this work'. Mr Anderson suggested that they were a self-appointed body. Mr

Pentland asked if the police force would be fully armed and the reply was 'yes of course'. The following interesting exchange then took place. Mr Montgomery of Beaulieu House enquired: 'I take it that the police would be attached to brigade headquarters for discipline and would be under the command and orders of the commandant for the district?' Mayor: 'Yes.' Mr Anderson: 'Are there not two forces?' Mayor: 'There are not two forces.'

Mr Anderson's apparently innocent question as to the presence of two IRA groups in Drogheda, and the mayor's firm denial of the fact, indicates that the public were suspicious that a split had actually occurred in the IRA in Drogheda and from the uncertain tone of Mr Anderson's question, it had occurred only recently.

The motion to form a committee was passed and it was elected from the people that were present. A record of people willing to donate immediately was taken and Lady Conyngham, Mrs Markey and Messrs Pentland, Montgomery, McKeown, McKenny along with some others, pledged £5 each. 'The meeting concluded with a vote of thanks to the Mayor for presiding' over the meeting.[8]

This was a very jovial and good-humoured gathering and there was a sense of people willing to come together and work in the best interests of the town. They were willing to make sacrifices and put their hands in their pockets and provide the money that was needed to pay for the protection of the town and to get through what they knew were some very unpredictable months ahead.

A letter from the Mayor was published in the *Drogheda Independent* on 1 April 1922, outlining the new arrangements with regard to the policing of the town and outlying districts. It stated that 'the IRA will patrol Drogheda and surrounding districts until such time as a regular police force is permanently established'. He went on to say that there had been numerous robberies recently and that 'the police may find it necessary to hold up any person found in the street after midnight'. The letter also advised the townspeople not to be 'loitering about the town after dark'. He also made an appeal 'to all to respond generously to the call for funds', as he continued, 'the demands made by committee in charge will barely be sufficient to defray the expenses of the next few months'.[9] The letter also stated that there did not seem to be any chance of having a stable government at an early date and that there was a lot of valuable property to be protected.

After this public meeting the mayor arranged a meeting of this new police fund committee and he requested the military representatives to attend: 'Police fund committee meeting 7(or 8) pm. Sheriffs room, Mayorality House Mayor desires presence of military reps'.[10] This committee was elected from the public meeting that was held on the previous Monday. From the newspaper report on what was said at that meeting, the committee was not aware of two separate forces occupying Millmount. Whether the Mayor knew or not was not clear. He stated at the beginning of the meeting that it was called at the request of the brigade commander and that the brigade commander had explained to him his reason for not attending. It is also now clear that the brigade commander had been asked to resign on 16 March and did so. Did the mayor know that a split had taken place in the local IRA? He stated clearly at the meeting that 'there are not two forces'.[11] We simply do not know, but he was a man that was immersed in the local volunteers for several years. One of his main fears was the policing of the town and he needed to raise money to fund the interim police force and he could not foresee what was to happen in the following months. This new arrangement, although very fragile, seemed to be working, with the IRP, made up of members of the IRA that took over Millmount, patrolling Drogheda and its surrounding districts.

The next few weeks saw the anti-Treaty IRA enforce the Belfast boycott. The Belfast boycott was an idea thought up by four Sinn Féin members of Belfast Corporation in response to riots that had broken out in Belfast and Derry, where it was felt that Catholics were being persecuted. Sean MacEntee, who was a TD (Teachta Dála – member of Dáil Éireann) for Monaghan, made an appeal to the Dáil for a boycott of all goods coming from Belfast to the south of Ireland and for any resident in the south to withdraw all their money from Belfast-based banks. The Dáil was divided over this but the anti-Treaty side eventually decided to enforce this boycott. In Drogheda, trains were stopped and searched for merchandise coming from Belfast. The raiding of trains started in the last week of March, and in that first week on a daily basis.

The relationship between the IRP and the anti-Treaty IRA began to deteriorate because of the Belfast boycott. On 28 March, the IRP tried to stop a van on the Dublin Road in which armed men under Commandant Murray were travelling. The van failed to stop. The next day, 'members of the Active Service Unit (ASU) were interrogated on the Dublin road. Became abusive and threatened the patrol'.[12] These men of the ASU were out putting up posters 'warning certain persons who had accounts in Ulster bank to withdraw funds under threat. These posters were found extensively posted around the town'.[13] The IRP and the mayor found themselves in a very uncomfortable position. The police force was being funded mostly by the business people of the town and yet they were being warned not to intervene in the enforcement of the Belfast boycott. On 30 March 1922, an entry was logged in the IRP daybook: 'Reports sent to GHQ O/C Brigade advises police not to interfere in these matters'.[14]

On Sunday, 3 April, Éamon de Valera, accompanied by Cathal Brugha and Erskine Childers, addressed a crowd of about 3,000 people at the Tholsel in the centre of Drogheda. The party had already been speaking at a rally in Dundalk earlier that day and this was a quick stop-off on their way to address another meeting in Balbriggan. The meeting, which was reported on in detail in the *Drogheda Independent* of 8 April 1922, took place at about 8pm. Mr P Carroll TD officiated and he was the first person to speak. He said 'that they were assembled there to preach the old policy, and stand where they stood in the 1918 election'. Cathal Brugha was next to speak. He referred derisively to parliamentarianism as the 'the reign of humbug' through which they had all lived. He asserted that the Irish people had too long depended on talk to win their freedom and that by negotiating with Westminster, the question of Irish freedom had been dramatically altered from that of an Irish struggle where the whole world had taken notice, to a domestic issue that was now to be solved by the British government. He continued:

> [If] England was allowed to continue to make the Irish question a domestic question the outside world would no longer listen to Irish voices, and by declaring a Republic and then announcing by your own free will that you are British subjects the world would say you deserve what you get and you'll get what you deserve.[15]

Éamon de Valera was next to speak. He was greeted with the sound of loud cheers. Quoting Arthur Griffith, he said: 'the cry of surrender has never been forced from the lips of Irish people – were they going to shout it out now?' He asked what the struggle had been for, for all those years. If the Irish people wanted to be British subjects there would have been no need for their ancestors to have fought for what they had now, which was a republic, which had been established by the Irish people, and to support the Treaty would mean disestablishing this republic. 'Did they want this nation of theirs to be made a subject province – nay two subject provinces – of Britain? Did they want the northern portion of their country to be cut of?'[16] If they did not want these things they could not vote for the Treaty. De Valera said the Treaty was a barrier to independence, making 'the road far more difficult than it ever was before'. Britain, he said, would not evacuate from Ireland and had never any intention of doing so. The fact that Britain had insisted on having the use of Irish ports showed this, and they would have the right 'to come back and put her forces in Ireland any time there was strained relations between herself and a foreign power'. The people themselves would have to examine this Treaty. It was not a real Treaty but a play on words to trick the 'gullible Irish people'.

Ireland, he said could not and should not accept this Treaty and if the struggle for Irish freedom needed to continue, even if that meant war, it should. 'We made it impossible for the British Government to rule Ireland (applause), and we can make it impossible for any Government working under British authority to rule Ireland'. There was no such thing as a Free State; however, there was an Irish republic and this republic was a legal one and it would 'exist until Irish people voted it away'. The Treaty would not change the overriding will in the hearts of Irishmen for full independence and 'it would be better to be fighting the British than to be at their brothers' throats'.[17]

These very provocative election speeches by Éamon de Valera and Cathal Brugha seemed to give the anti-Treaty side a new impetus and confidence and a belief that the course of action that they were engaged in was the right one to pursue. They began to stop RIC vehicles in broad daylight and, as a result, tensions in the town began to rise.

The vital time in Drogheda when the split in the IRA became visible was in April and May 1922. From mid-April, there were several incidents involving the RIC and the IRA. There was a hold up on Easter Monday, 17 April, when three RIC constables had their bicycles taken from them. A Crossley tender with three RIC constables was stopped in the main street outside the post office, when four armed men approached the vehicle and took possession of it and drove it away. On the morning of Thursday, 20 April, a car in which 'Rev R Watson, a Church of England clergyman, and two armed constables from Gormanstown was held up and seized at the South quay'.[18] This hold-up was also carried out by four armed men. Although nobody was injured in these confrontations, the tension between the republicans and the former police force was being ratcheted up.

At the centre of developments as they unfolded was Mayor of Drogheda Philip Monahan. Monahan was a republican and was central to the establishment of the Irish volunteers in Drogheda in 1914. On Easter Monday, as the Rising was taking place, Monahan was at the Fairyhouse races. When he returned to Drogheda on Easter Monday evening, he was questioned on his whereabouts. He was arrested on 5 May along with thirteen other Drogheda men and sent to Frongoch internment camp in Wales. Some of his fellow prisoners in Wales included Michael Collins, Richard Mulcahy and Sean Hales, men who would come to have major roles in the fight for Irish freedom. He was a model prisoner, but he did have one serious quarrel with Collins while he was there. The Frongoch prisoners were released in late December and Monahan was back in Drogheda by Christmas. He found himself in prison again, this time in Crumlin Road Gaol in Belfast, after he took part in and spoke at a rally in Drogheda in the summer of 1917. He continued to be a strong advocate for Irish independence and although he was not an important figure nationally 'he was clearly an influential leader in the Drogheda area and he was regarded as a threat by the British Government'.[19]

In 1918, Monahan was again arrested along with prominent members of Sinn Féin for his part in opposing the conscription bill. He ended up in Lincoln Prison, spending nine months there, and helping Éamon de Valera escape 'disguised as a priest'.[20] He was released again in 1919 and once again returned to Drogheda. Philip Monahan was elected to Drogheda Corporation in 1920, topping the poll in the St Laurence's Gate Ward. He was a respected man in Drogheda and became mayor for the first time in 1920.

Sunday, 30 April 1922, was the day that changed the military situation in Drogheda. An RIC constable was shot and killed in an ambush on the outskirts of the town. Constable Benjamin Bentley was sent to Drogheda on the morning of 30 April to collect a minister of the church to perform a religious service at Gormanstown Army Camp. He was ambushed at Stameen, about a mile and a half from the town, on the main Drogheda to Dublin road. An armed gang was waiting for him and, as he approached, they opened fire killing him. Although nobody was found responsible for this act, the anti-Treaty IRA, based at Millmount, were the chief suspects.

This action was about to have major consequences for the local IRA unit and the town of Drogheda.

In retaliation for the killing of Constable Bentley, the Black and Tans, who were stationed at Gormanstown Army Camp, made a visit to Drogheda in the early hours of the morning of 2 May.[21] There were several lorryloads of Black and Tans involved in the raid. Mayor of Drogheda, Alderman Philip Monahan, had been informed of the Black and Tans intention to seek retaliation for their colleague's death. The mayor contacted both factions of the IRA to inform them of the situation. At around 11 p.m. on the night of 1 May 1922, the mayor was contacted by the adjutant of the Gormanstown Camp to tell him there was no reason to be worried. But, despite the adjutant's reassurances, the Black and Tans invaded the town, at 1 a.m. on 2 May. Four lorry loads of Tans surrounded Millmount Barracks, trapping the IRA unit inside. The rest of the Black and Tans then drove their vehicles through the main streets of the town 'firing volley after volley indiscriminately into almost every shop and house in the three main streets'.[22] They also bombed and set fire to the republican election headquarters, putting in danger the entire block of buildings in the street. This action continued for five hours until 6 a.m., but, before they left the town, the Black and Tans left slips of paper saying 'this is in reprisal for the shooting of Constable Bentley. Further cases of murder will be more drastically avenged – Black and Tans'.[23]

As the Tans were driving out of Drogheda on the night of the attack, there was a collision between two armoured cars at the bottom of Mary's Street close to Millmount. One of the cars was burnt out and the other was commandeered by the anti-Treaty IRA and brought to Millmount.[24] A local priest, Fr McCooey, intervened and negotiated with the anti-Treaty forces in Millmount for the return of the car. He pointed out that there was a lot of bitterness and anger in Gormanstown Army Camp and that they wanted their car returned immediately.[25] He also indicated that if the car was not returned, further trouble was likely. The IRA agreed to return the car and arrangements were made for a small party along with the priest to drive the car out of Drogheda and hand it over to a contingent of Gormanstown officers.[26]

At a meeting of the Drogheda Corporation on May 2nd a letter was sent to all relevant parties: 'We express our sincere sympathy with the relatives of the late Constable Bentley shot outside Drogheda. That we are of the opinion that all sections of the Irish Army should guarantee that the truce should be rigidly preserved and that assurance be given that no further attacks would be made on English troops until the truce is officially terminated. That we strongly condemn the wanton destruction and indiscriminate shooting carried out in the town on Monday night the 1st inst, by the Gormanstown forces, and we call upon the authorities controlling these forces to take steps to prevent a repetition.'[27]

Copies of this resolution were sent to officers commanding RIC Gormanstown, IRA Millmount and Commandant Landers, IRA 1st Eastern Division.[28] A meeting was held in the South Quay Barracks to discuss the tense situation in the town. Brigade-Officer Rooney, commander of the Irish Republican Police, Mayor Philip Monahan, James Murphy TD and two RIC Officers from Gormanstown Camp attended.[29] The following statement was released to the press by the RIC, denying any part in the attack on Drogheda:

Following the publication in the press of certain reprehensible acts of misconduct in and around Drogheda on 30th ult and 1st inst, a representative meeting of head constables, sergeants and constables of the old RIC quartered at Gormanstown, desire the public to know that they disclaim any responsibility for such occurrences. On the contrary they incurred personal risk and censure to prevent it and have demanded from the Inspector-General the fullest inquiry to fix responsibility. Senders' names being forwarded through the post.

[Signed] 'OLD RIC GORMANSTOWN CAMP'.[30]

In the early hours of 3 May, a special train arrived from Dublin at Drogheda train station carrying a large force of National Army troops with armoured cars and lorries.[31] Commandants Daly and Thornton were in command. A notice was served on the anti-Treaty IRA stationed at Millmount to vacate and hand the Barracks over. The National Army troops stated that they were there at the request of the mayor and that Millmount was needed for their base and, if necessary, force would be used if the Barracks was not surrendered to them immediately. A deadline was given of 2 p.m. on 3 May to vacate Millmount. The National Army troops called on all the citizens of the town to co-operate with them.[32] This notice was posted through the town:

> To the people of Drogheda. We have come here at the invitation of the Mayor to protect the town against a repetition of Monday night's terror. For this purpose possession of Millmount Barracks is essential. We have therefore called upon those in occupation to vacate the Barracks by 2 p.m. this day, May 3rd 1922. In the event of it being necessary to employ force to secure the Barracks, we call upon all citizens to co-operate with our troops.
>
> Col. Commandant P O Daly
>
> Col. Commandant F Thornton
>
> Commandant P McCrea
>
> 3rd May 1922.[33]

Also during the morning of 3 May a further conference was held and attended by Fr Seagrave PP St Peters, Fr Nulty PP St Mary's, Fr McCooey of Mell, the mayor, Alderman Monahan and Alderman Murphy TD along with representatives of both sides of the army, pro-Treaty and anti-Treaty. At the meeting, it was stated that Millmount Barracks had been in the hands of the regular army and that the anti-Treaty side only got possession of the Barracks by deceit. It was also stated that the Irregulars admitted that they could not guarantee protection for the town and a demand was made for them to withdraw from Millmount.[34] This demand was met with the response that the IRA garrison would only vacate the Barracks on the instructions of the Army Executive.[35] As a result, Mayor Monahan believed he had no choice but to ask the National Army troops for protection for the town and its citizens.

Millmount was not evacuated by the deadline, nor was there any effort made to take it. A temporary truce was agreed between the two sides of the IRA. On 4 May, 'Truce arrived at between both sections of the Army'.[36] This was extended again on 8 May, and on 10 May the truce was 'extended indefinitely'.[37] The RIC from Gormanstown arrived back in Drogheda on Wednesday, 3 May but were stopped by a National Army officer. The officer insisted that the RIC should keep their weapons on the floor of the tender and not have them on display over the side of the vehicle.[38] The officer also stated that arrangements would have to be made for the RIC to get their supplies 'in the ordinary civilian way, and that displays of arms are not to be used in this area except by legitimate and recognised authorities, when necessary'.[39]

There were no new developments by the end of the week. The status quo remained with Millmount in the hands of the IRA and the regular National Army in control of the rest of the town. The threat of trouble from Gormanstown abated but there was now a very visible split in the IRA in Drogheda. In the months after the signing of the Anglo-Irish Treaty, Drogheda was a relatively peaceful town but the fall-out from the killing of Constable Bentley thrust Drogheda into the middle of the growing tensions between the pro and anti-Treaty sides. There was very little chance that the small number of anti-Treaty IRA supporters in Drogheda would ever be able to take control of the town and hold it for any period.

There was no real support for the anti-Treaty side. In the general election of 16 June 1922, there were six candidates in the Louth–Meath constituency: one Labour, four pro-Treaty Sinn Féin and one anti-Treaty Sinn Féin. Five were elected, with the Labour candidate, Cathal O' Shannon, heading the poll. The pro-Treaty candidates, Eamon Duggan, Peter Hughes and Alderman J.E. Murphy, along with the one anti-Treaty candidate, J.J. O' Kelly, were also elected.[40] The election of three pro-Treaty Sinn Féin candidates, to which can be added O'Shannon who supported the Treaty, indicates that support for the anti-Treaty side was minimal. Also, the election was carried out in a calm almost friendly atmosphere, in an area once renowned for political violence. 'The election was characterised by the utmost good humour, and there was much friendly rivalry in bringing up the votes'.[41] The total poll for Louth–Meath was 38,010 out of which the pro-Treaty candidates, including O'Shannon, polled 28,633 first preference votes.[42]

The commencement of the Civil War in Dublin with the shelling of the Four Courts was the trigger that initiated the opening of hostilities in Drogheda; however, it was a combination of seemingly unconnected events in Drogheda and Dublin that finally brought war to the streets of Drogheda.

The Belfast boycott, where goods destined for or sent from Northern Ireland were regularly seized and destroyed, was being enforced in

Drogheda by the IRA. Two raids were planned, one in Drogheda on 26 June at the railway station and one in Dublin, at a car dealership a day later. While the raid was in progress in Dublin, the National Army forces surrounded the premises and succeeded in arresting the leader of the raids. The commander was a man named Leo Henderson and he was also the director of the Belfast boycott. In Drogheda, the IRA were in the process of searching a train when they were arrested by National Army troops. 'Another raid on Rly station at 10 a.m. 5 men arrested in connection with same from Millmount bcks detained in West Gate Barracks pending investigations from BHQ'.[43]

In retaliation for Henderson's arrest and the five men arrested in Drogheda, General 'Ginger' O'Connell, assistant chief of staff to the National Army, was taken prisoner by the IRA. A telephone message was sent to Eoin O'Duffy, chief of staff, which stated that '[O'Connell] is being detained in the Four Courts as a hostage for Comdt. Leo Henderson and other prisoners'.[44] The Provisional Government felt that they could not ignore this act by the anti-Treaty forces and 'hence arose the ultimatum for the surrender of the Four Courts and other points of vantage held by the Executive'.[45]

The beginning of the conflict in Drogheda started in parallel with the actions in Dublin. Rumours spread of an imminent 'attack being launched on Millmount by Dáil troops'.[46] In the early hours of 28 June, when the attack on the Four Courts got underway, the prisoners that had been taken at the railway station in Drogheda escaped from West Gate Barracks: '4 Irregular troops prisoners at West Gate escaped from West Gate Barrack at 3am this morning also 5 regular guard who turned traitors and decamped to Millmount Barracks taking 9 rifles and a large amount of ammunition with them'.[47]

The citizens of the town did not want this conflict and many of them fled Drogheda in fear of their lives.[48] The tactics of the IRA at this stage was mainly confined to sniping and they were positioned in several places through the town. The first casualties of the fighting were Sergeant William Leech of the IRA and Volunteer Jack Lynch of the National Army.[49] Leech was killed by a bullet on Pitcher Hill steps, just 100 yards outside the gates of Millmount. Lynch, meanwhile, was hit in the leg and died later in the Cottage hospital.[50] By now the National Army forces had Millmount surrounded: 'Treaty broken today Regular troops surround Millmount Barracks all roads picketed with regular troops and trees felled'.[51] Reinforcements were sent to Drogheda to assist the Regular troops, 'the garrison in Drogheda was reinforced by one hundred men under Comt. Mooney'.[52]

The IRA launched an attack on West Gate Barracks with 'heavy firing all day from Grove and Millmount'.[53] The National Army cordon in place around Millmount was also attacked, 'An outpost of 4 men on the Donore side of town were disarmed and stripped of their great coats and caps'.[54] More National Army reinforcements arrived on Saturday evening, 1 July 1922. By this stage the town was 'practically deserted of local inhabitants'.[55]

Sunday saw a lull in the fighting but some sporadic firing was heard through the day.[56] By Monday, the local citizens were very annoyed with what looked like a long stand-off developing. They were in their fifth day of disturbances and several of the townspeople had been injured by stray bullets and were very lucky no innocent civilian had been killed. All that had been achieved so far was 'to terrify the civilian people and suspend all business'.[57]

The IRA was now in control of the railway station and an attempt was made to cross the Boyne viaduct bridge.[58] As the engine was about to cross over the road at Newfoundwell, a caged-in lorry in which a unit of National Army soldiers was travelling showed up. The vehicle had a machine gun mounted on it. 'Several spectators thought a battle was imminent but the engine back-pedalled and rushed back to the station.'[59] Shots were heard ringing out as the engine retreated. The lorry continued its journey and a short time later heavy machine gun fire could be heard coming from the Cartown area.

Monday, 3 July, turned out to be the decisive day in the conflict in Drogheda. On that morning, 'Commandment MacMahon arrived with a field gun and an armoured car'.[60] The IRP daybook records this simply by saying 'big gun arrives in Drogheda'. Monday was also the day when the mayor became one of the casualties. It was reported that '[At] about 2 o'clock on Monday when the Mayor of Drogheda (Ald, Monahan) and Ald. Joseph Stanley were crossing from John Street to Dominic's Bridge some shots were fired … and the Mayor received a bullet wound in the neck'.[61] He was fortunate that the wound was not serious and he was taken to the hospital on the Dublin Road for treatment. Three shots were fired, the first missed but he was hit by the second one. 'Hearing a rifle shot his worship turned around and it was then that a shot hit him. He fell and while Alderman Stanley was endeavouring to raise him a third shot passed over Alderman Stanley's head'.[62]

The next morning the Provisional Government would intensify their efforts to take control of Millmount. 'An ultimatum was sent to the Executive forces by telephone demanding unconditional surrender'.[63] No reply was received and the large eighteen pounder field gun that had been used in the shelling the Four Courts the previous week was moved into position. It was placed alongside the river beside Dominic's Bridge and the Dominician Church. It was approximately 500 yards from Millmount with a clear view of its target. At about 9.25 a.m. the first shell was fired. 'The range was obtained with the first shot and the ladder to the tower was shot away with one of the first balls.'[64] Large crowds gathered at vantage points throughout the town to observe this historic event and to 'follow the course of each shell.'[65]

The booming sound of the big gun was ear-splitting and some of the buildings of the old town shook as the shells exploded on their target: 'The roar of the big gun which was heard quite plainly so far away as Laytown and almost shook the whole town and was in each case followed by a deafening explosion as the shell struck.'[66] A total of forty shells were fired at Millmount, a cloud of smoke and debris rose as each shell landed.[67] After about one hour the IRA began to abandon the barracks. There was a large hole some twelve feet wide in the northwest face of the tower and the former officers' quarters were totally destroyed, only the walls left standing. 'At ten minutes to 4 o'clock the last shell was fired.' Shortly after 6 p.m. approximately sixty troops of the National Army marched in formation from South Quay to Millmount via John Street. They 'entered Millmount through several breaches in the back wall made by their gunner'.[68] A despatch was sent to General Headquarters from Drogheda post office at 6.35 p.m. stating:

> Some of our troops have been in the tower already, but came out again and are searching for land mines. They are ready to re-enter. They believe a number of Irregulars are still in the building, but there is no fire from them at present. There is no report as to arms and prisoners captured. The artillery firing was splendid.[69]

There was not much the men who occupied Millmount could do in the face of such an attack. They had few weapons and sniping from the tower was really their only option. Some improvised explosives in the form of land mines were discovered. At about 4.30 p.m., the IRA gave up possession of the railway station. By evening, Millmount was firmly in the hands of the National Army forces along with the Railway station. The IRA had also fled from their position at Grove Hill. Many of the IRA from Millmount were in hiding in houses on the portion of the town south of the river: 'A large number continue to occupy houses in Mary's Street where they have trenches cut across the street and mined. The general sniping tactics were to occupy a house, use it for five or ten minutes and then leave to take up another position elsewhere'.[70]

Before the IRA left Millmount, part of the Barracks was set on fire. When the National Army troops entered Millmount they conducted a search of the premises. Among the items found were ammunition, blankets and provisions and a 'complete grenade plant along with grenades'.[71] With the battle for Drogheda now over, the townspeople began to emerge to see the result of the days' encounter. The streets had been deserted for almost a week and 'hundreds visited Millmount and the vicinity to see the ruins'.[72]

Miraculously, there were no fatalities on either side during the assault. There was, however, one innocent civilian killed in the course of the events. A twenty-one-year-old woman by the name of Alice Slowey was unfortunately killed. Miss Slowey, who lived in Fair Street, entered a building across the road from her home with her brother and some other companions.[73] They entered the Boyne Wire Weaving Works, which was being refurbished at the time, to watch the unfolding drama. They had with them a pair of binoculars and as they watched the bombardment there was a knock on the door, followed by an order to open it. They responded by shouting 'all right!' and Miss Slowey, along with the owner of the premises, Peter Reilly, rushed to open it.[74] Before they reached the door there was another knock, and when the soldiers got no response one of them 'raised his rifle to shoot away the lock and fired through the door'.[75] Unfortunately, Miss Slowey was standing behind the door and about to open it when she was mortally wounded. First aid was administered immediately but she died a short time later.

On Wednesday morning, the streets of Drogheda returned to as near normal as possible. Businesses reopened and people were back in the streets. The railway lines were repaired and by evening the line between Dublin and Dundalk was back to normal.[76] There was, however, one incident on Wednesday evening. Shots were heard in the Newfoundwell area. Some of the IRA that had abandoned the railway station returned to the edge of town and fired shots into the air in an attempt to draw the national troops to that area. 'The National Forces rushed to the scene of the firing and a running battle ensued, the Irregulars retreating to the fields shooting as they went'.[77] There was great uneasiness around the town as nobody knew what was going on. It all ended in about half an hour, but the townspeople were reminded that the danger had not fully abated.

By the end of the week, Drogheda was in the hands of the National Army. The field gun had already left Drogheda and it was sent on to Passage West in Cork on board the SS *Arvonia*. The fight for Drogheda was all but over. Most of the IRA were scattered throughout the countryside. There were, however, a couple of sporadic attacks still occurring. On 7 July, the railway station was attacked but the National Army forces were in position and prevented the IRA from gaining control of the station: 'Attacked by 30 mutineers about 10 p.m. last night. Attack beaten off'.[78] The next day a unit of the National Army was patrolling the Ardee area and came across a group of IRA that had occupied Smarmore Castle. Shots were fired between both parties but the IRA surrendered almost immediately. 'The captured party was part of the garrison that succeeded in escaping from Millmount during the siege.'[79]

Drogheda had gone from being a relatively peaceful town at the beginning of March to one of the main focal points of fighting in the early days of the Civil War. In March and April, after the British forces had left the town, there was a void which was filled by the IRA. The mayor, Philip Monahan, came forward to lead the town through this turbulent and unsettling time. Drogheda Corporation set up an interim police force. But everything changed with the killing of Constable Benjamin Bentley on 30 April. By the end of April, the IRA in Millmount had aligned themselves with the anti-Treaty side. There is evidence that the split in the IRA had affected Drogheda as early as March 1922, but after the Black and Tan attack on the town in retaliation to Bentley's murder, the mayor felt that he had no choice but to ask for assistance from the pro-Treaty government as the IRA in Millmount could not guarantee protection for the town. This call from the Mayor brought the pro-Treaty forces in great numbers to Drogheda for the first time. A brief stand-off occurred in the early days of May, but after a series of negotiations brokered by the mayor, local politicians and the clergy, a truce was agreed. This truce remained until the last few days of June.

Drogheda's location on the river Boyne is key to the decision made by the Provisional Government to take such drastic action in their bid to take full control of the town. With such uncertainty throughout the country, the government could not risk Drogheda coming under control of the anti-Treaty side even though it was highly unlikely that they could gain control of Drogheda and keep it. There was limited support for the anti-Treaty side and the IRA in Millmount consisted of a small hard-core group of men with a few snipers located in several positions in the town. The danger for the Provisional Government was a prolonged confrontation. Had the anti-Treaty side been able to do that, it could have affected the situation throughout Ireland at such an early stage in the war.

The IRA in Dundalk had not declared which side they would support at this time. They eventually supported the anti-Treaty side but their decision could have been made earlier if there was a prolonged stand-off in Drogheda. The river Boyne was a natural defensive barrier between north and south, with only three crossing points in Drogheda, one very important railway bridge and two road bridges. The same rules applied to Drogheda in 1922 as applied when Oliver Cromwell attacked the town more than 250 years earlier. He needed control of Drogheda to progress north and secure the northern part of Ireland. The government needed control of Drogheda to prevent the northern part of Ireland coming under the control of the anti-Treaty side. The government could not afford to fight a war on two fronts, one in the north and one in the south where the greater support for the anti-Treaty cause was. This would have split their forces and made the fight for Ireland a much harder prospect.

NOTES

1   *Drogheda Argus*, 28 Jan. 1922.
2   All quotations are from *Freemans Journal*, 16 Mar. 1922.
3   Millmount Museum Drogheda, Irish Republican Police (IRP) Daybook.
4   Ibid.
5   Ibid.
6   Ibid.
7   Ibid.
8   All quotations are from *Drogheda Independent*, 25 Mar. 1922.

9   All quotations are from *Drogheda Independent*, 1 Apr. 1922.
10 Millmount Museum Drogheda, IRP Daybook.
11 *Drogheda Independent*, 25 Mar. 1922
12 Millmount Museum, IRP Daybook.
13 Ibid.
14 Ibid.
15 *Drogheda Independent*, 8 Apr. 1922.
16 Ibid.
17 Ibid.
18 Millmount Museum, IRP Daybook.
19 Aodh Quinlivan, *Philip Monahan, a man apart: the life and times of Ireland's first Local Authority Manager* (Dublin: IPA, 2006), p. 22.
20 Ibid., p. 24.
21 *Drogheda Argus*, 6 May 1922.
22 *Drogheda Independent*, 6 May 1922.
23 Ibid.
24 *Drogheda Argus*, 6 May 1922.
25 *Drogheda Independent*, 6 May 1922.
26 Ibid.
27 Louth County Archives, Drogheda Minute Book.
28 Ibid.
29 *Freemans Journal*, 3 May 1922.
30 *Drogheda Argus*, 6 May 1922.
31 Ibid.
32 Ibid.
33 Ibid.
34 *Freemans Journal*, 4 May 1922.
35 Ibid.
36 Millmount Museum, IRP Daybook.
37 Ibid.
38 *Drogheda Argus*, 6 May 1922.
39 Ibid.
40 *Drogheda Argus*, 24 Jun. 1922.
41 Ibid.
42 Ibid.
43 Millmount Museum, IRP Daybook.
44 *Drogheda Independent*, 1 Jul. 1922.
45 *Drogheda Argus*, 1 Jul.1922.
46 Ibid.
47 Millmount Museum, IRP Daybook.
48 *Drogheda Independent*, 8 Jul. 1922.
49 Ibid.
50 Ibid.
51 Millmount Museum, IRP Daybook.
52 University College Dublin Archives (UCDA), Mulcahy papers, P/7/B/106/189, 'Report on position in Drogheda, 26 June 1922 to 4 July 1922'.
53 Millmount Museum, IRP Daybook.
54 UCDA, Mulcahy papers, P/7/B/106/189, 'Report on position in Drogheda, 26 June 1922 to 4 July 1922'.

55   Millmount Museum, IRP Daybook.
56   *Drogheda Independent*, 8 Jul. 1922.
57   Ibid.
58   Ibid.
59   Ibid.
60   UCDA, Mulcahy papers, P/7/B/106/189, 'Report on position in Drogheda, 26 June 1922 to 4 July 1922'.
61   *Drogheda Independent*, 8 Jul. 1922.
62   *Drogheda Advertiser* (special edition), 4 Jul. 1922.
63   UCDA, Mulcahy papers, P/7/B/106/189, 'Report on position in Drogheda, 26 June 1922 to 4 July 1922'.
64   *Drogheda Independent*, 8 Jul. 1922.
65   Ibid.
66   Ibid.
67   Military Archives.
68   *Drogheda Independent*, 8 Jul. 1922.
69   UCDA, Mulcahy papers, P/7/B/106/102, 'Report received from Drogheda post office, 4 July 1922'.
70   UCDA, Mulcahy papers, P/7/B/106/189, 'Report on position in Drogheda, 26 June 1922 to 4 July 1922'.
71   Ibid.
72   *Drogheda Independent*, 8 Jul. 1922.
73   *Drogheda Independent*, 22 Jul. 1922.
74   Ibid.
75   *Drogheda Independent*, 8 Jul. 1922.
76   Ibid.
77   Ibid.
78   UCDA, Mulcahy papers, P/7/B/106/285, 'From Drogheda, 7 July 1922'.
79   UCDA, Mulcahy papers, P/7/B/106/318, 'From Divisional Adjutant Drogheda, 8 July 1922'.

11

The Civil War in Dundalk and the Case of Charles H. Gyles, 1898–1922

Don Johnston

The original Gyles family were landlords in Castletowncooley in the seventeenth century but by the beginning of the twentieth century were a case of an 'honourable come down' family.

Charles Henry Gyles was the son of a printer on William Street, Dundalk. Charles Gyles, at the age of sixteen, like many other Irishmen, joined the British Army in Dublin during the heady days of August 1914. He moved to France in September 1914 and was in the 16th Division Cyclist Company, Royal Field Artillery.[1] He joined the 5th Royal Irish Lancers first as a bugler and then served in an infantry regiment during several big engagements in France.[2] Before demobilisation from the British Army, Gyles was a shoeing smith with the 12th Lancers.[3]

In July 1922, the Dáil authorised the recruitment of an army with the establishment of 35,000 men and Michael Collins actively recruited former members of the British Army who brought useful experience and training to the new force.[4] Many old IRA men who had fought alongside Collins in the War of Independence bitterly resented their presence. Charles Gyles, aged twenty-four, joined the National Army in the troubled month of August 1922, after the Civil War had broken out.[5] He was assigned to the local intelligence unit of the Criminal Investigation Department (CID) and the Machine Gun Corps in Dundalk.[6] Gyles was a member of the local Church of Ireland community.[7] While the Civil War was raging, members of the Church of Ireland suffered raids, attacks on their property, eviction notices and murder. Their fears were sufficiently aroused for J.A.F. Gregg, the archbishop of Dublin, to lead a deputation from the General Synod to the provisional government enquiring 'if they were to be permitted to live in Ireland or if it were desired that they should leave the country'.[8]

Arthur Griffith, president of the Dáil and chairman of the Irish delegation at the negotiations in London that produced the Anglo-Irish Treaty of 1921, did his best to reassure the deputation as he had done earlier at the time of the signing of the Treaty.[9] The editor of *The Church of Ireland Gazette* congratulated the president as head of the new State, and hoped that the goodwill, which he expressed towards his fellow-countrymen of different political and religious opinions, would be reciprocated by them in the fullest possible measure.[10]

Following the sudden death in August 1922 of Arthur Griffith, Kevin O'Higgins, who emerged as one of the strongest men in the new government, declared in the Dáil:

these people [members of the minority community] are part and parcel of the nation, and we, being the majority and strength of the country … it comes well from us to show that these people are regarded, not as alien enemies, not as planters but that we regard them as part and parcel of the nation and that we wish them to take their share of its responsibilities.[11]

Nevertheless, Protestants generally kept their head well below the parapet. They felt a threat to their position from the growing intransigence of the anti-Treaty forces in the south. So, it was most unusual for somebody in Gyles' position to display such loyalty to the Provisional Government especially in the Dundalk area where republicans were very active.

For Dundalk and north Louth, generally, the period between the Truce in July 1921 and the signing of the Treaty on 7 December 1921 was one of uncertainty, accompanied by a growing tension, occasioned by the partition of Ireland. This development ushered in attacks made upon Catholics, notably in Belfast, very often by uniformed mobs of Special Constabulary. Inevitably, this led to tit-for-tat outrages, which did not leave Dundalk unscathed. The burning of the well-known Protestant-owned premises of Thomas Craig at the Market Square, Dundalk, in August 1920, was an early manifestation of this new development.[12] After firemen unearthed the charred remains of three employees from the mass of smouldering debris of Mr Craig's premises, Fr McKeone, parish priest of Dundalk, stated that 'our Protestant neighbours always lived peaceably – here they were treated with consideration and they flourished here; reprisal is a form of paganism – an eye for an eye and a tooth for a tooth'.[13]

Mr Craig had been connected with the Dundalk Presbyterian Church all his life, having been baptised in that church. He felt deeply that his thirty years in business had been taken away from him and that sad circumstances had compelled the break-up of his home and his severance from the community where he had expected to live out his life.[14] He was awarded £40,000 as compensation for his loss.[15] After five members of the McMahon family in Belfast were dragged from their beds in the dead of night and shot down in cold blood in late March 1922, a threatening notice was posted on a tree beside the Town Hall that the Protestants of Dundalk would soon meet the same fate. At the same time, several Protestants shopkeepers had received threatening notices in the post. The Protestant residents of Dundalk, who stated they had in the past lived in peace and goodwill with their Catholic neighbours, expressed their outrage at the talk of reprisals and regret that any section of those who differ in religion from them should have any doubt on their views on these matters.[16]

On the morning of Thursday, 13 April 1922, Dundalk military barracks was evacuated by the last remnants of the British army garrison. From the backs of lorries laden with clothes and stores of various kinds as they left the barracks for the last time, Union flags were flying. Barrack Street Station was the centre of the troops leaving. They did not seem down-hearted and sang 'Paddy McGinty's Goat' as they waved farewell to their late neighbours. The barracks was quietly taken over at noon by about fifty men from counties Armagh and Down all armed with rifles. Amid all the excitement they had slipped in unknown under the command of the colonel of the 4th Northern Division, Frank Aiken, acting on behalf of General Headquarters, Beggars Bush, Dublin.[17]

Following the takeover of the barracks, General Aiken moved his headquarters from Newry to Dundalk. Dundalk became a destination for some of the many displaced nationalists of east Ulster in the exodus southwards, following the pogroms leading up to the establishment of the six-county administration.[18] In May, a north Louth police force was established with headquarters in the Town Hall. They took over some of the duties formerly discharged by the Royal Irish Constabulary (RIC) and worked in conjunction with the republican courts, which with the departure of the British now began to operate openly.[19] This rough and ready law and order system was used to deal with some of the sectarian attacks made on local Protestant houses and shops. It functioned until July 1922 when it was suspended by the incoming troops of the Provisional Government in their capture of the town from Frank Aiken's anti-Treaty forces.[20]

In response to the growing rifts south of the border over the Anglo-Irish Treaty, both Michael Collins and Liam Lynch, in an attempt to avert a divisive civil war, decided to start a unifying one in the north. Aiken himself stated that he would maintain a neutral position 'until an ordered state of Government attaining in the South – we could attack the North with a chance of getting a united Ireland, which was always the immediate job to us as Northerners'.[21] Aiken was prominent in all aspects of the planning for the Ulster offensive and personally travelled to Dublin on several occasions to collect weapons and equipment for transport to his headquarters at Dundalk.[22]

The northern offensive was not generally launched as intended at the beginning of May, but on 2 May 1922, in Tyrone, which was quickly suppressed, and then again, on 19 May, in Belfast, which was again quickly suppressed. Aiken was due to take the field on 22 May. Despite causing death and destruction in Belfast and elsewhere in the north, it proved to be a catastrophic failure. It also proved to be deeply counterproductive, and inspired the Northern Ireland government to introduce internment under the draconian Special Powers Act.

For someone like Aiken, whose purported focus remained the undoing of partition, this daring offensive seemed like an ideal opportunity to, perhaps, fatally destabilise the Northern Ireland statelet. But Aiken's men took no part in the intended assault. Despite his ostensible position as commander of the northern rising, on the morning of 22 May 1922, only a matter of hours before his division was due to go into action, the attacks were called off, most probably on the instructions of Eoin O'Duffy, chief of staff.[23] Instead, in the face of the internment sweeps in the north, Aiken withdrew his men south of the border into a series of temporary camps, with his own headquarters at Dundalk. From here, his men launched a series of incursions across the border. Many of the attacks in Armagh were opportunistic, with small parties of IRA men moving across the border to await a chance to kidnap or shoot Crown forces. The attacks were effectively a resumption of the strategies of earlier campaigns of attrition, intimidation and reprisal. The victims included not only the members of the Ulster Special Constabulary but also members of the Catholic community, and innocent Protestant civilians.[24]

Aiken made it clear that even if he was ordered to do so he would not attack the forces of the Irregulars. If, however, he had to part company with Mulcahy, he would not fight against him because fighting would only ruin the country without gaining any ground for the Republic. Aiken then travelled to Limerick to meet General Liam Lynch on 8 July 1922, but his peace mission ended in failure. On his return to Dundalk, Aiken found orders awaiting him to attack the Irregular forces within his divisional area. It was now clear to him that the time for taking sides had arrived. After a meeting of his staff, he ordered that all the arms and war materials in the 4th Northern Division be concealed and arrangements made for the evacuation of military posts in the event of the break with the Beggars Bush authorities.[25]

While Aiken was absent in Limerick, General Emmet Dalton, the director of military operations of the Provisional Government, paid a brief visit to Dundalk to assess the general situation there.[26] Aiken was meanwhile ordered to report to Beggars Bush on 15 July. At the meeting with Mulcahy it must have been evident to Aiken and his colleagues that they were talking to deaf ears as by this time the Civil War had progressed beyond any point of reconciliation. That evening Aiken returned to the military barracks in Dundalk and on the following morning (16 July 1922) he was awakened, as he put it, 'with two Thompsons at my nose'. During the night, elements of the 5th Northern Division based in Co. Monaghan under General Hogan arrived in Dundalk. They took possession of the military barracks without any struggle. Some members of the garrison were in league with Hogan and facilitated his entry.[27]

Aiken's second in command, John McCoy, had participated in the earlier conference with Mulcahy but did not return with Aiken to Dundalk. On his arrival at the railway station the following morning, McCoy found the town in the possession of the Provisional Government forces and only narrowly escaped arrest. He held a divisional meeting on Sunday, 23 July 1922, in Faughart graveyard, using as a desk the flat tombstone which tradition holds covers the grave of Edward Bruce who fell in the Battle of Faughart in 1318. The unanimous verdict of the meeting was to attack without delay the pro-Treaty forces that had invaded Dundalk.[28] With men from the divisional encampments at Dungooley and Ravensdale,

McCoy planned a counter-attack to free Aiken from Dundalk Gaol. It was agreed that an ultimatum would be delivered to the Provisional Government forces first but there was no response and on 27 July an attack was launched. A mine placed against the perimeter wall on the Ardee Road was detonated and the prisoners who had been alerted to the possibility of an attempted release were ready to move. In the confusion that followed, over 100 prisoners including Aiken escaped through the breach in the wall. The division then re-grouped around their camps in Ravensdale and Omeath where plans were made for an attack to free the remaining republican prisoners held in Dundalk barracks.

Aiken directed operations from his headquarters at Ravensdale. The counter-attack on the army barracks was planned for Monday, 14 August 1922. Some men having earlier crossed the mountain from Omeath had infiltrated the town of Dundalk. They seized the post office and put the telegraph department out of action.[29] In addition, Aiken had a number of his men 'planted' in the barracks itself who were able to give him vital information regarding the defensive scheme.[30] His 300-strong force armed with small arms and explosives supplied up until a month before by the very Army they were now going to attack, commenced operations at 4am.

Aiken organised boats to ferry his men across the Castletown river from the Blue Anchor, Bellurgan, to Soldiers Point into Dundalk.[31] Having blown in the barrack gate on the Point Road, Aiken and about nine men rushed through the breach and were met with heavy fire. When bags of explosives thrown into the windows of the ground floors of the barrack rooms detonated, the inmates generally surrendered. The garrison had been completely taken by surprise. Many of the senior officers were absent in Dublin attending the funeral of Arthur Griffith who had died on 12 August. Three hundred and fifty soldiers of the Provisional Government were captured and marched through the town to the jail and more than 200 republicans imprisoned there were released. Four hundred rifles and a large volume of ammunition were captured and throughout the day lorry loads of arms, ammunition and other stores from the military barracks were conveyed northwards to dumps located along the Louth/ Armagh border. Aiken lacked trained gunners and when he captured a field gun at Dundalk on 14 August he was forced to abandon it because no one knew how operate it.[32]

Throughout Tuesday, 15 August 1922, the town was filled with rumours of the impending arrival of government troops to retake the military barracks. This gave rise to fears of many civilian casualties and widespread destruction of property. These fears were added to by a report that Aiken had placed mines under the military barracks buildings with the intention of setting them off as part of his evacuation of town. The fear of the damage this would do to adjacent civilian property prompted the administrator of the parish priest, Rev Father McKeone, to intervene. He sought a meeting with Aiken and secured a promise from him that he would not destroy the barracks.[33] Shortly afterwards the town was re-taken by the Provisional Government troops without further resistance, Frank Aiken's men having retreated northwards into the border areas of north Louth, south Armagh and south Down. The Provisional Government forces then secured the town but in the weeks and months which followed, with north Louth awash with weapons, sniping in and around Dundalk became a regular occurrence, especially at night.

During the Civil War period, Dundalk was heavily garrisoned which, in the army census of 12/13 November 1922, consisted of 756 men.[34] The Dundalk district extended throughout Co. Louth and a portion of east Monaghan. Throughout these districts the troops were attached to the 5th Northern Division, which had been incorporated into the Dublin Command. Most of the personnel in Dundalk hailed from northern counties Monaghan, Fermanagh, Armagh and Antrim. Others were from midland counties such as Meath, Westmeath, Kildare and Portlaoise, and about thirty came from the north Louth area.[35]

At the outset of the Civil War, the Republicans had control of the whole south and west of the country but by the end of August 1922 they had failed to secure the necessary degree of popular support. Following the sudden death of Arthur Griffith's and the assassination of Michael Collins ten days later on 22 August, the bitter struggle slipped into the familiar guerrilla pattern of the War of Independence two years before – flying columns, ambushes, assassinations and booby traps. It had been the custom of members of the Greenore garrison of the National Army to motor daily to headquarters in Dundalk.

On the morning of Saturday, 4 November 1922, as the convoy passed underneath the railway bridge at Rockmarshall there was a terrible explosion. The Crossley Tender in which they were travelling had got clear of the mine by a couple of feet when the explosion occurred so there was little damage to the vehicle. There followed a wild outburst of rifle shooting from Irregulars discharging volley after volley at the occupants of the car. Two of the attackers, who numbered about twenty-two, were said to have been killed. They were seen to fall along the mountain slopes – both shot through the head – and were carried away by their comrades back up the mountain. Two of the soldiers, Captain Boyle from Greenore and Sergeant Treanor from Monaghan (who was engaged to be married), were killed in the ambush. It was freely stated locally that the object of the attack on the Crossley was to 'get' local man, Captain Boyle.[36]

On 9 September 1922, almost three months after the election, the new Dáil met but the Republican deputies did not attend. Cosgrave (as President), the young Kevin O'Higgins (Home Affairs) and Richard Mulcahy (Defence) and the rest of the government were formally appointed into the positions they had effectively held since the deaths of Griffiths and Collins. In October, special emergency powers were given to the army to hold military courts and inflict the death penalty for a wide range of offences including the unauthorised possession of arms. These drastic powers would, it was hoped, help to end the breakdown of law and order, limit the widespread destruction of property and shorten the war: their effect inevitably was to aggravate further an already embittered situation.[37] At the same time in an effort to calm the situation the government offered an amnesty to the members of the IRA who would surrender by 15 October 1922, but made it clear that any person found in possession of arms was likely to be tried by court martial.[38]

On 17 November, the first executions took place. The republicans responded by threatening death to those who had voted for the emergency power resolutions and in response the government carried out a pitiless series of executions. Erskine Childers married Mary (Molly) Osgood and received the yacht, the Asgard, as a wedding present from his wife's family. He transported guns for the Irish Volunteers aboard the Asgard to Howth on 26 July 1914. He was appointed director of publicity for the First Dáil and it is believed to be around this time that Michael Collins gave Childers a small Spanish revolver for his personal use. Childers split with Collins over the Treaty and had been on the run for several months before his arrest on 10 November 1922. When found with the 'Collins' revolver, Childers was taken to Beggar's Bush, court-martialled and found guilty. There was a national outrage when he was executed on 24 November.[39]

Local factors added to tensions in the Dundalk area. On 23 July 1922, Margaret Moore, twelve years old, who was related to a well-known local IRA officer, and Minnie Connolly, twenty years old, were shot dead by members of the Royal Sussex Regiment a few hundred yards from the Free State border at Jonesborough, Co. Armagh. A sentry who was posted outside Moore's house facing the border heard footsteps coming from the direction of the Free State. In the darkness he could see no one and when his challenge went unanswered and the footsteps continued, he opened fire, killing two of the three girls coming towards the house across the fields.[40] A report of a British Army inquiry into the killings issued at the end of November 1922, decreed the soldiers had carried out their orders properly and that the shooting actually occurred after curfew.[41] The reaction amongst the wider community to the killings, and to the subsequent exoneration of the soldiers, was one of outrage.

It was in this atmosphere of heightened tension that Volunteer Charles H. Gyles was shot on Thursday night, 30 November 1922, in Clanbrassil Street, Dundalk, within a stone's throw of his family home in Bachelors Walk.[42] It was generally stated in the town that Gyles, because of his activities with the army in Dundalk, had been earmarked (he had been involved in intelligence work). Dressed in a civilian coat but with army trousers he had just turned the corner of Bachelor's Walk into Clanbrassil Street when an attempt was made to seize the revolver, which he carried in his coat pocket. He held on to the weapon and immediately a shot was heard. Within forty yards of the scene of the shooting an armed guard was on duty at the post office but refrained from firing as scores of civilians and unarmed soldiers were in the streets at the time.[43]

One of the first to arrive on the scene was Sergeant Kane who had months earlier been in charge of the guard at the post office. The sergeant rendered what aid he could to his fallen comrade and had him removed to the County Infirmary. On his way to hospital the wounded soldier handed over his revolver to his sergeant.[44] Dr O'Hagan said he had operated on the accused who did not improve and died on Friday, 1 December about 11 a.m. The cause of death was internal haemorrhage, shock and perforation of his intestines caused by bullet wounds to the abdomen.[45]

Startling disclosures were made at Charles Gyles' inquest, which was held in the Louth County Infirmary on the evening of the following day, 2 December 1922. A sergeant in the National Army who was on duty on the night of the shooting at the Central Hotel in Clanbrassil Street identified the remains of Charles Gyles, aged twenty-two, unmarried and a private and a machine gunner in Dundalk. The sergeant stated he heard revolver shots and a man shouting 'Oh my God, I'm shot!' He proceeded to the scene of the shooting and saw the injured man being helped into Rice's public house in Clanbrassil Street. He then saw two men running down Bachelors Walk, they were about sixty yards in front of him. He called on them to halt and then fired his revolver twice but the distance was too great and did not hit them. They disappeared down an alleyway on the left-hand side. He searched the houses in the vicinity but did not find any of the fellows that fired.

Another Volunteer in the National Army called Peter McCaffrey told the inquest that the deceased was shot just outside Rice's public house. He was speaking to Gyles moments before his assassination. He swore that two men passed them at the start of the conversation and that when they had finished the two men, whom he knew, returned. As soon as he turned away he heard revolver shots. The Volunteer swore that the two youths who shot Gyles were named Alfred Heaney of Union Street and Mulholland of Quay Street. It was stated in evidence that they were both about eighteen years old. The Coroner inquired, 'you have no doubt these were the men who fired the shots?' The Volunteer replied, 'the two men I mentioned were the men who fired the shots'.

The coroner told the jury that it was a sad duty for him to have to ask an Irish jury to return a verdict of murder against the two Irish boys but 'you have a duty to perform as citizens of this country and I know you will do that duty and return a verdict of murder against the two men whose names have been mentioned. Your duty is to find that they were guilty of the murder of this soldier of Ireland, Charles Gyles'. The coroner went on to say that this crime was a very serious stain on the character of the town and that it was a terrible thing that soldiers were not able to walk the streets of Dundalk without being at the mercy of armed assassins and that even if this man had been on duty – and they had evidence that he was not – he was deliberately killed and there was no getting away from the fact that it was murder. He concluded with the hope 'that very shortly retribution will fall on the people who are responsible for shooting this unfortunate man'. The jury having deliberated for about fifteen minutes returned a unanimous verdict that

The deceased died from internal haemorrhage and shock and perforation of his intestines, caused by bullet wounds in the abdomen.

That the shots were deliberately fired by two men named Heaney and Mulholland, who are guilty of wilful murder. We condemn in the strongest manner the present turmoil in Dundalk and we offer our sincerest sympathy to the deceased's mother and relatives.

Fr McKeone, speaking in St Nicholas Catholic church, Dundalk, the Sunday after the shooting, condemned the shooting of Volunteer Gyles and appealed to parents to exercise more control over their children, many of whom had received instruction of a certain class in school when it would have been better if they had been taught their Catechism, and in the past some of these children had been unwillingly forced into certain organisations.[46]

On the same Sunday, 2 December, as Fr McKeone made his comments, the funeral of Volunteer Charles Gyles made its way from his mother's residence in Bachelor's Walk for burial in an isolated plot in the Protestant section of St Patrick's Cemetery, Dowdallshill. A tremendous crowd, representative of all creeds in the community, attended the funeral in tribute to the memory of the young soldier who lost his life so tragically. Free State soldiers with rifles at the reverse immediately preceded the hearse along with 100 members of the Ex-Servicemen's Legion, while a large detachment of his comrades in the 5th Northern Division of the army of the provisional government followed.[47] The coffin was draped with the tricolour and surrounded by a profusion of beautiful wreaths. The firing party of Free State soldiers included several from his formers comrades in the Great War and his more recent comrades in the army of the Provisional Government.

Headed by their officers, a large contingent of Free State troops marched immediately behind the chief mourners. The remainder of the procession was made up of carriages and an armoured car, while hundreds of the general public occupied the sidewalks en route. Reverend Canon Hamilton MA, Rector of St Nicholas Church of Ireland Parish, Dundalk, officiated at the graveside. After three volleys were fired over the grave, the Last Post was sounded.

> Softly a look of peace
> Over the dying soldier came.
> The roll was called in Heaven,
> And he answered to his name.[48]

Heeney and Mulholland were arrested by a National Army patrol on 28 February 1923. Mrs Kathleen Bonner, sister of the late Charles Gyles, wrote on 5 April 1923, from No. 7 Napier Barracks, married quarters, Shorncliffe, Kent, to Collins Barracks.[49] She noted that it was over three weeks since the men who murdered her brother had been captured and that she has been waiting every day to hear of their execution as there was ample proof of their involvement and pointed out that Volunteer McCaffrey had seen them and given that evidence at the inquest. On the morning of 1 December, she accompanied her mother to the infirmary and she claimed that her brother Charles in his dying moments confirmed that Heaney and Mulholland had shot him, and he commented that there had been men shot for only having arms on them.

She wondered why there was no sign of the execution of the men that wilfully shot 'my darling brother'. She wanted to see justice done and her brother's death avenged: 'if he had been killed in a fight or ambush they would not have felt it so much'. The letter continued:

My poor mother is left alone now by his death as he was her youngest boy and only support … my mother wrote and told me there was a petition being made for them [Heaney and Mulholland] owing to their youth but they were not too young to take a young man's life, the smartest and bravest soldier that was in Dundalk barracks.[50]

A reply from the office of the Assistant Adjutant General, Collins Barracks of the Dublin Command, confirmed on 20 April 1923, that J. Mulholland, Quay Street, Dundalk, and 'Hick' Heaney, The Courts, Dundalk, were both found guilty by the Coroner's Jury of the murder of Volunteer Gyles on the unsubstantiated evidence of one witness; that both men were captured during a round-up in Ardee some weeks earlier and that efforts had been made to bring them to trial by a military court but were not pursued, owing to the lack of evidence. If Mrs Bonner was prepared to come forward to give evidence of her brother's dying statement, the authorities would be in a position to proceed with the trial, otherwise it was simply waste of time trying to obtain a conviction.[51]

Mrs Bonner replied on 3 May 1923 that none of the relations was summoned to the inquest of her brother to give evidence, that Heaney lived at the back of their family home and every night he was at the back of their house making a nuisance of himself, if she were to come forward now with the dying statement of her brother, they would shoot her or her husband and it would not be safe for her to put her foot in Dundalk again. She concluded, 'My poor mother is heart-broken to think they are not being punished for the great loss she has sustained; she is alone now'.[52]

Robert Gyles, Millstream, Castlebellingham, wrote on 9 May 1923 to the adjutant general at Portobello Barracks wondering why Heaney and Mulholland deserted their homes on the night his brother was assassinated and remained in hiding until they were run to earth at Kellystown (between Dunleer and Clogher Head) thirteen weeks later, noting that 'innocent men can always stand their ground'. He went on to state that people were willing to give evidence if they could be sure they would not meet the same fate as their late brother; that the medical officers and men of the jury got their death warning if anything befell either Heaney or Mulholland, and this had some bearing on the case. He hoped that in the near future those seeking justice can do so without the fear of reprisal.[53]

A memorandum from Dublin Command, dated 31 May 1923, stated that, regarding the non-notification of relatives about the inquest, the Presbyterian Minister was acting for the Gyles family and knew all the arrangements from the Military Barracks, that at the inquest of Charles Gyles, Volunteer Peter McCaffrey stated that he was standing in Clanbrassil Street, some distance away from Gyles and that he saw Heaney and Mulholland pass by Gyles and then return. He then heard a shot, saw Gyles lying on pavement, and Heaney and Mulholland running away. As he did not witness the actual shooting, a good barrister would make holes through McCaffrey's evidence and make it impossible to obtain a murder verdict. The memorandum concluded that the considered opinion was that Heaney and Mulholland were scouts for the party who murdered Gyles and that bringing in new witnesses would be a doubtful legal matter.[54]

The Dáil passed the Irish Free State Constitution Bill on 6 December 1922, exactly one strife-torn year after the signing of the Anglo-Irish Treaty. The provisional government ceased to exist and the Irish Free State came into existence.[55] An editorial in the *Irish Times* painted a dismal picture:

> Only a year ago the outlook was more than encouraging. Southern Ireland credit stood high and with the coming of stable government a long period of prosperity and progress seemed to be in sight. Since that time the land has been devastated by a cruel warfare. Many of the

best Irishmen are in exile. A huge bill of damages has been compiled and still is being compiled, against the State. The national settlement continues to be resisted by Irishmen who have rejected all possible overtures of peace. We do not doubt that the Free State armed henceforward with the panoply of self-government and based upon the people's will, has before it a great and fortunate career. We cannot question the courage or sincerity of the men who will be responsible for its administration in the early stages. Nevertheless, the making of the new State will be no easy matter. Freedom comes to us at the last, not blithe or smiling but with a countenance severe and even tragic. Therefore, we greet her cordially, indeed and hopefully, but without exultation. Whatever comfort her cornucopia may hold, she comes to a sad abode.[56]

The Free State government ruthlessly set about breaking the resistance of the Irregulars and commenced a series of pitiless executions. Rory O'Connor, Liam Mellows, Joseph McKelvey and Dick Barrett, without even the pretext of a trial, were executed on 8 December 1922, in reprisal for the killing of Sean Hales, a pro-Treaty Dáil deputy, outside Leinster House the previous day. In one respect reprisals worked, as attacks on TDs ceased.[57] General Mulcahy addressed the following Christmas message to the Irish Army:

of those who have fallen by our sides since last Christmas our minds are filled with fondness and gratitude ... to their relatives we tender again our sincerest sympathy with an assurance that their example shall strengthen us to serve our country's needs with strength, patience and denying festival and relaxation, to oppose the injustices and oppressions of today as we opposed the injustices and oppressions of yesterday and till a place is realised for our people from which they may go to greatness.[58]

In January 1923, three people were executed in the Dundalk Gaol: Thomas McKeown of Cooley; John McNulty (alias Joseph Murphy) of Belleek; and Thomas Murray, Kilcairn, Co. Meath. Later that month Messrs Thomas Lennon, Dowdallshill; James Melia, Bridge Street; and Joseph (Josie) Ferguson, Gyles Quay, were executed by firing squad in the military barracks.[59] Josie, whose family had long connections with herring fishing at the quay, was the owner of a number of boats there. He was on the run from the Free State forces. A boat with a cargo of coal had arrived at Gyles Quay and arrangements were made for Josie to take passage via Liverpool to the United States but he refused to run away.[60] Ferguson was arrested on 7 January 1923 near Lordship and sentenced to death. His execution at the age of twenty-seven in the military barracks in Dundalk on 22 January 1923 brought great sorrow and sadness to the closely knit community of Gyles Quay.

In his final letter home, Ferguson, a former captain of Cooley Kickhams Senior Football team, wrote:

> [G]ive Mary one of my photos. Tell Dannie to make the drills for Owen as I promised I would. Get him to make them … Be proud that you have a son that you will meet in Heaven that died for Ireland like a man. I will meet death as many a brave Irishman did before so be proud of my death, not sorry. Let Dannie take my bicycle down from Toners and keep it in remembrance of me … I am getting a happy death, better than some boys that died on the mountain and no priest near them. So be of good heart Mother. It is all God's will.[61]

By January 1923, over fifty Republicans had been executed and twenty-seven more were to die in the same way before the end of hostilities. The public at large recognised that stern measures were necessary to end the Civil War. Hostilities continued right up to the termination of the Civil War on 27 April 1923, following orders given by de Valera and Frank Aiken. The latter had succeeded as chief of staff of the anti-Treaty forces after the death of Liam Lynch in a shoot-out with Free State forces in the mountains of Co. Waterford on 10 April 1923. De Valera tried to secure a ceasefire on favourable terms but the government refused. Republican arms were accordingly dumped in safe places, the Irregulars ceased to resist, they were accorded no amnesty and had to go on the run to evade arrest. De Valera issued a proclamation to his followers on 24 May 1923: 'Soldiers of the Republic, Legion of the Rearguard: The Republic can no longer be defended successfully by your arms … military victory must be allowed to rest for the moment with those who have destroyed the Republic.'[62]

Ernest Dixon, Church of Ireland clergyman of 4 Faughart Terrace, Dundalk, helped Mrs Gyles on 27 November 1923 to fill out the application form for a dependant's allowance under the Army Pensions Acts, which covered the dependants of those killed or injured on or after 1 April 1922 in the course of duty while on active service. The solicitors, Dickie Coulter and Hamill of Roden Place, Dundalk, also helped Mrs Gyles with her claim. Charles' wages were 42 shillings a week.[63] A dependant's allowance was paid for the period 19 August 1922 to 27 October 1923 at 28 shillings a week, 435 days at 4 shillings a day. Payment of dependant's allowance was suspended as the case was referred to the Pensions Board for attention.[64]

A member of the Garda Síochána reported that Mrs Elizabeth Gyles was sixty-two-and-a-half years old with no income and no visible means of support. About two years prior to her son's death she was earning an annual wage of £20. Her late son was the sole support of his mother. Her other children being married and having families of their own were unable to contribute anything to her upkeep. They were all labourers. A further report stated that Mrs Elizabeth Gyles had £26 on hand at the time of her son's death. Canon Hamilton, Dundalk, contributed ten shillings per month towards her upkeep from 27 October 1923. [65]

On 10 June 1924, an allowance of 15 shillings per week was recommended by the Army Pensions board for Mrs Elizabeth Gyles. This was to be paid retrospectively from 1 November 1923, the first anniversary of her son's death. Further application forms were filled out in 1924 with the assistance of Goodlett Hamill, solicitor, Dundalk, and later in 1925 by W.A. White, Principal, St Nicholas National School, Dundalk, who lived at 32 Dublin Street, Dundalk.[66] Mrs Elizabeth Gyles continued to receive fifteen shillings a week until her death on 14 July 1938.[67] Her daughter, Kathleen, advised the pension board that her mother had died at Old Hill, Drogheda and to cease paying the weekly pension of fifteen shillings she received for the loss of her son who was 'a Free State soldier and was killed by the Republicans'.[68] Elizabeth's final resting place was along with her son, Charles, in his isolated grave in the Protestant section of St Patrick's cemetery, Dowdallshill, Dundalk.

NOTES

1   *Tempest's Annual*, 1916, p. 6.
2   The 5th Royal Irish Lancers was a cavalry regiment of the British army. The regiment was originally formed in 1689 as James Wynne's Regiment of Dragoons. They fought in the Battle of the Boyne and at the Battle of Aughrim for the forces of William of Orange.

3   Military Archives, Cathal Brugha Barracks, Dublin (henceforth MA) Army Dependents Claim, undated, W2D61, Charles Gyles.
4   Peter Cottrell (ed.), *The War for Ireland*, 1913–1923 (Oxford: Osprey Publishing, 2009), pp. 148, 173.
5   *Irish Times*, 2 Dec. 1922.
6   MA, W2D61, Charles Gyles, 'Memo to Adjutant General, 31 December 1923', p. 46.
7   *Dundalk Democrat*, 2 Dec. 1922; *Dundalk Democrat*, 9 Dec. 1922.
8   *Irish Times*, 8 Dec. 1922.
9   Ibid., 30 Apr. 1922.
10   *The Church of Ireland Gazette*, 8 Dec. 1922.
11   Jack White, *Minority report: the Protestant Community in the Irish Republic* (Dublin: Gill & Macmillan, 1975), p. 91.
12   *Dundalk Democrat*, 14 Aug. 1920.
13   Ibid., 4 Sept. 1920.
14   Ibid., 27 Aug. 1921.
15   Ibid., 16 Dec. 1922.
16   Ibid., 1 Apr. 1922.
17   Ibid., 15 Apr. 1922.
18   MA, BMH, WS492, 'John McCoy', p. 125.
19   Joseph Gavin and Harold O'Sullivan, *Dundalk: a military history* (Dundalk, 1987), p. 102; *Dundalk Democrat*, 13 May 1922;
20   Gavin and O'Sullivan, *Dundalk: a military history*, (Dundalk, 1987), p. 102.
21   Frank Aiken 'Position of the 4th Northern Division from January 1922 to July 18th 1922, 3 p.m.', Ibid., p. 257.
22   Bryce Evans and Stephen Kelly (eds), *Frank Aiken, nationalist and internationalist* (Dublin: Irish Academic Press, 2014), p. 85.
23   Matthew Lewis, *Frank Aiken's war: the Irish Revolution, 1916–1923* (Dublin, UCD Press, 2014), pp. 142–5.
24   Evans and Kelly, *Frank Aiken, nationalist and internationalist*, p. 86.
25   Lewis, *Frank Aiken's war*, p. 178.
26   Calton Younger, *Ireland's Civil War* (London: Muller, 1969), p. 348.
27   Evans and Kelly, *Frank Aiken, nationalist and internationalist*, p. 93.
28   MA, BMH, WS492, 'John McCoy, p149.
29   *Dundalk Democrat*, 19 Aug. 1922.
30   Ibid.
31   Gavin and O'Sullivan, *Dundalk: a military history*, p. 122.
32   Cottrell (ed.), *The War for Ireland*, p. 173.
33   *Dundalk Democrat*, 19 Aug. 1922.
34   MA, 'Army Census Report', 12/13 Nov. 1922.
35   Gavin and O'Sullivan, *Dundalk: a military history*, pp. 135–7. The National Army had four major garrisons, in Greenore, Dundalk, Ardee and Drogheda, of whom just under 100 men were from Co. Louth.
36   *Dundalk Democrat*, 11 Nov. 1922. No mention was made in the paper of Captain Boyle's place of burial, Kilwirra cemetery. A headstone was placed by his family over his burial place in 2012.
37   John A. Murphy, *Ireland in the twentieth century* (Dublin: Gill & Macmillan, 1975), p. 57.
38   *Dundalk Democrat*, 14 Oct. 1922.
39   *Irish Times*, 3 Sept. 2015.
40   *Dundalk Democrat*, 25 Nov. 1922.

41 *Dundalk Examiner*, 25 Nov. 1922.

42 *Dundalk Democrat*, 2 Dec. 1922.

43 *Irish Times*, 2 and 9 Dec. 1922.

44 *Dundalk Democrat*, 2 Dec. 1922.

45 The following account of the inquest is taken from *Dundalk Examiner*, 9 Dec. 1922.

46 *Dundalk Examiner*, 9 Dec. 1922 Ibid.

47 *Dundalk Democrat*, 20 Aug. 1922. There were something like 1,000 ex-servicemen living in Dundalk district.

48 *Dundalk Democrat*, 9 Dec. 1922; *Frontier Sentinel*, 9 Dec. 1922.

49 Kathleen and her husband Henry Victor Bonner – his last known job was sexton, possibly at St Nicholas – emigrated with their family to Australia after the death of Mrs Elizabeth Gyles in 1938.

50 MA, W2D61, Charles Gyles, 'C Bonner to Adjutant General', undated, received 5 Apr. 1923, pp. 6–7.

51 MA, W2D61, Charles Gyles, 'Office of Adjutant General to Mrs C Bonner', 21 Apr. 1923, p. 13.

52 MA, W2D61, Charles Gyles 'C Bonner to Adjutant General', 2 May 1923, pp. 15–16.

53 MA, W2D61, Charles Gyles, 'Robert Gyles to Adjutant General', 9 May 1923, pp. 21–4.

54 MA, W2D61, Charles Gyles, 'Dublin Command HQ to Assistant Adjutant Headquarters', 31 May 1923, pp. 27–9. The memorandum also noted that 'handing them over to civil authorities would be the easiest way out for Heaney and Mulholland … and that on the occasion of the funeral of Gyles, his Mother did not desire a soldiers' funeral for him and objected to the Tricolour on the coffin – and now they are thirsting for revenge'.

55 Murphy, *Ireland in the twentieth century*, p. 57.

56 *Irish Times*, 4 Dec. 1922.

57 Cottrell (ed.), *The war for Ireland*, p. 185.

58 *Frontier Sentinel*, 30 Dec.1922.

59 Gavin and O'Sullivan, *Gyles Quay, the early and the later years*, p. 135.

60 Tony McDonnell, *Gyles Quay the Early and the Later Years* (Dundalk, 1995), p. 21.

61 Sean Boyle, *Cooley Kickham GFC, 1887–1987* (Cooley Co. Louth: The Club, 1987), p. 53.

62 Murphy, *Ireland in the twentieth century*, p. 57.

63 MA, W2D61, Charles Gyles, 'Dependant's allowance Gratuity application', 27 Nov. 1923, pp. 35–8.

64 MA, W2D61, Charles Gyles, 'Quartermaster General to Adjutant General', 21 Mar. 1924, p. 56.

65 MA, W2D61, Charles Gyles, 'Garda Siochana reports', Apr. 1924, pp. 64–85.

66 MA, WD44, Charles Gyles,'Recommendation of Army Pensions Board', 10 Jun. 1924, p. 4.

67 *Dundalk Democrat*, 23 Jul. 1938.

68 MA, W2D61, 'Charles Gyles', 'Letter from K Bonner', n.d., p. 94.

12

War of Independence and Civil War Memorial Inscriptions in County Louth, 1916–1923

Séamus Bellew

O ne of the enduring marks of civilization are the ceremonies and symbols relating to death and burial. Since the foundation of the state, various kinds of memorials and gravestones in Co. Louth have been a focus for commemoration. War memorials are places where people grieve collectively or individually.[1] These visible signs of collective bereavement are sometimes decorative or sacred and are to be found in streets, roadsides and graveyards. In Ireland, Celtic crosses were particularly popular.[2] Some of the well-known memorials in the county were constructed within a decade of the founding of the state. The fiftieth anniversary of 1916 marked a period of renewed interest. More recently, the lead-up to the 'Decade of Commemoration' has seen the erection of memorials to some of the dead not previously remembered in Co. Louth. This essay narrates the period 1916–23 in the county through memorial or monument.

Even though there are very few specific '1916 memorials' in the county, the annual commemorations are in effect a remembrance of the service of Co. Louth's Volunteers from 1916 to 1923.[3] The past decade has seen a more open acknowledgement by families of those Irish who fought abroad with British forces and of those who actively took part in the Rising (1916) and later in the War of Independence (1919–21). A narrative has yet to emerge on how those who died in the Civil War will be 'officially' commemorated.[4] Monuments pertaining to the 1919–23 period are described in the first section (The Monuments). Brief details of those commemorated and also others who are interred locally and who died as a result of the conflict are given in the second section (Volunteers).

The Monuments

The 'Soloheadbeg Ambush' in Co. Tipperary occurred on 21 January 1919 and marked the start of the War of Independence that ended on 11 July 1921 with a truce. The Anglo-Irish Treaty was negotiated during the truce and signed on 6 December 1921. Those who died in Louth during the period (1919–21) included IRA Volunteers and members of the Royal Irish Constabulary (RIC) – including those known as Black and Tans. A number of civilians died in circumstances either accidentally or that were unexplained.

The early months of 1922 saw the emergence of divisions on the Treaty. The shooting of Field Marshall Sir Henry Wilson in London on 22 June resulted in British pressure on the Provisional Government to take action against the anti-Treaty leadership in occupation of the Four Courts and other strongpoints in Dublin. The subsequent bombardment of the Four Courts by the National Army on 28 June 1922 marked the beginning of the Civil War. It was to last eleven months until the opponents of the Treaty called a ceasefire on 24 May 1923. Members of both the National Army and the anti-Treaty forces died in battle in Drogheda with the shelling of Millmount and also in sporadic ambushes or raids in rural parts of the county. In Dundalk, anti-Treaty republicans were executed in the Military Barracks.

The four main republican monuments in Co. Louth are located at Drogheda, Dundalk, Ardee and Knockbridge. The earliest monument to be constructed is that on the Marsh Road, Drogheda.[5] It marks the location where the bodies of Alderman Thomas Halpin and John (Seán) Moran were found following their deaths. They were killed by Black and Tan forces on 9 February 1921.[6] The home of a third man, Thomas Grogan, on the Marsh Road, was also raided but he had made good his escape before their arrival.[7] A first-anniversary Mass for Halpin and Moran was celebrated in St Peter's Church (RC) and afterwards Cumann na mBan members 'marched to the new cemetery' and laid wreaths on Mr Halpin's grave.[8] In 1931, by which time the monument at the Marsh Road had been erected, the Drogheda annual commemoration had become well established. That year hundreds marched from St Peter's to the memorial cross and the procession included Drogheda's mayor, several Corporation members and various football teams and political organisations in the town.[9] The details of the others named on the monument are given later in the essay. The inscription on the monument reads:

> I gcuimhne díl na sair-fear Tomas Ó h-Ailpin & An Caiptín S. Ó Móráin a dunmharbhuigead le saighdiúirí d'arm Sásana ar an 9adh Feabhra '21. An Caiptín S. Ó Flannagáin a thuit a troid ar an 29adh Bealtaine '22. F' O Líam Ó Laodhóg ar an 29adh Meithimh '22 a fuair bas d'en 9adh briogaid i lugmaid teas i seirbhis na hEireann. Ar deas-laimh Dé go raibh a n-anamna![10] [Moss] An Ceannphort P. Ó Mainnín, An Caiptín Pádraig Ó Cuanaigh, An Caiptín Bearnárd Ó Dalaigh.

National Graves Assoc.

Translated, this reads:

> In loving memory of the heroic men Thomas Halpin and Captain S. Moran who were murdered by soldiers of the British Army on the 9th of February 1921. Captain S. Flanagan who died in combat on the 29th May 1922. [Sec Ldr] Liam Leech who died on the 29th June 1922, a member of the 9th Brigade of South Louth, in the service of Ireland. May their souls be at God's right hand. Commandant P. Mannion, Captain Patrick Cooney, Captain Bernard Daly.

Parallels are to be found between republican monuments and those memorials commemorating the Great War (1914–18) dead. Donal Hall has detailed the Great War monuments, plaques and headstones.[11] The Marsh Road Republican monument is a Celtic Cross and it bears similarities to the Great War memorial cross at St Mary's Square, Drogheda. The latter monument cut from local limestone from the Sheephouse quarries, Oldbridge, was unveiled in 1925.[12] The design of these crosses makes an intentional and significant political statement by deliberately linking those commemorated with Gaelic, if not Catholic, antiquity.[13] An obvious difference between republican and Great War memorials in Louth is the use of Irish-language inscriptions on the republican monuments. The Irish seanchló lettering that remained in use until the 1960s was often used.

The 'Dundalk Erection Committee' under the chairmanship of John Toal was established to raise funds for the erection of wayside crosses in memory of Irish Republican Army (IRA) men killed in action in North Louth.[14] It was also the intention to erect a permanent memorial to those IRA members who died 'in the fight for freedom'.[15] The memorial was duly completed and erected in St Patrick's Cemetery (Dowdallshill) on the republican plot and unveiled on Easter Sunday, 1935, by Miss Mary McSwiney.[16] The monument at Dundalk, in contrast to that at Drogheda, is of an obelisk or cenotaph form. The inscriptions appear on the north, east and south-facing sides of the monument. The east-facing side reads:

I mbuan-chuimhne ar thréan-saighdiúirí an 1adh bridgaide de'n 4adh Roinn Tuaisceartaigh d'arm poblacht na h-Éireann a thug a n-anam ar son na hÉireann i gcúis naomhtha na Saoirse 1916-1923 a thógadh an leacht so. Cuireadh chun báis iad so leanas taobh amuigh d'ar dtighthibh Féin:- Seán MagAoid i gCuailgne 13-5-1921. Seán MacUaitéir & Pádraig MacUaitéir i nDúndealgan 18-6-1921. Seán Mac an Ultaigh, Tomás MacEoin, Tomás Ó Muireadhaigh i bpríosún Dúindealgan 13-1-1923. Seámus Ó Maoildhia, Tomás Ó Lionnáin, Seosamh MacFearghusa i mbearraic Dúindealgan 22-1-1923 agus Sailbheastar Ó hÉinigh i bpríosún Mhontseoidh i mBaile Átha Cliath 11-12-1922. Go mairigh a n-iodhbairt go deo i gcuimhne Ghaedheal agus go ndéanaidh Dia trócaire ar a n-anam. A.D. 1935.

Translated, this reads:

This memorial was erected in everlasting memory of the strong soldiers of the 1st Brigade in the 4th Northern Division of the Republican Army of Ireland who gave their souls for Ireland in the sacred cause of freedom (1916-1923). The following were put to death outside of our own homes:- John Magee in Cooley 13-5-1921. John Watters & Patrick Watters in Dundalk 18-6-1921. John McNulty, Thomas McKeown, Thomas Murray in Dundalk Prison 13-1-1923. James Melia, Thomas Lennon, Joseph Ferguson in Dundalk Barracks 22-1-1923 and Sylvester Heaney in Mountjoy Prison in Dublin 11-12-1922. May their sacrifice live for ever in the memory of the Irish and may God have mercy on their souls.

The north-facing side reads:

> I gcuimhne freisin ar na h-Óglaigh seo leanas a marbhuigheadh i gcath Tomás Ó Maolchallann 16-4-1920. Seán Ó Coigligh 3-9-1921. Tomás MacCathmhaoil 14-7-1922. Pádraig MacCionaodha 14-8-1922. Seán Ó h-Ailpín 8-10-1922. Brian Ó Muirgheasa 1-4-1923. Seán Ó Cuinn 22-5-1923. Dia libh a bhráithre, Fuair bás dúinn gan géilleadh go raibh agaibh sámh shuan i láthair an aoin mhic.
>
> Mac an t-Saoir, Dúndealgan.[17]

Translated, this reads:

> Also in memory of the following Volunteers who were killed in battle Thomas Mulholland 16-4-1920, John Quigley 3-9-1921, Thomas Campbell 14-7-1922, Patrick McKenna 14-8-1922, Sean Halpin 8-10-1922, Bernard Morris 1-4-1923, John Quinn 22-5-1923. God be with you, brothers, who died for us without surrendering, may you sleep peacefully in the presence of the only son [of God].

The south-facing side reads:

> I n-onoir freisin dos na h-Óglaigh eile ó'n gceanntar so a d'fhan dílís don Phoblacht agus gur thrúig bháis dóibh an pháirt a ghlacadar i gCogadh na Saoirse agus do: Brian Ó h-Annluain 14-3-1921, Tomás Ó Marcaigh 30-6-1922 a marbhuigheadh sa troid i mBaile Átha Cliath. Ar dheis Dé go raibh a n-anam.

Translated, this reads:

> Also in honour of the other Volunteers from this locality who remained loyal to the Republic and whose participation in the War of Independence brought about their deaths and of Brian O'Hanlon 14-3-1921, Thomas Markey 30-6-1922 who were killed in the fighting in Dublin. May their souls be at God's right hand.

A smaller, separate, flat gravestone contains eighteen names, ten of which are repeated from above. Five of the eight additional names date from later periods and the other three date from the Civil War period. These latter three are Donnchadh Ó Laodha, Séamus Ó Maoildhia and Domhnall Ó Maoldomnaigh, which translated are Denis Leahy, James Meegan and Daniel Downey. The inscription on the gravestone reads:

> Tá adhlactha fé'n leacht so na h-Óglaigh seo leannas d'arm poblacht na h-Éireann. Sailbheastar Ó hÉinigh 22-1-1923, Tomás Mac Eoin 13-1-1923, Seán Mac an Ultaigh 13-1-1923, Séamus Ó Maoildhia, Tomás Ó Lionnáin 22-1-1923, Seosamh MacFearghusa, Tomás MacCathmhaoil 14-7-1922, Pádraig MacCionaodh 14-8-1922, Seamas Ó Miodhgain 2-9-1922, Seán Ó h-Ailpín 8-10-1922, Donnchadh Ó Laodha 21-12-1922, Domhnall Ó Maoldomnaigh 31-7-1923.[18]

Translated, this reads:

> Buried beneath this memorial are the following volunteers of the Irish Republican Army. Sylvester Heaney 22-1-1923, Thomas McKeown 13-1-1923, John McNulty 13-1-1923, James Melia, Thomas Lennon 22-1-1923, Joseph Ferguson, Thomas Campbell 14-7-1922, Patrick McKenna 14-8-1922, James Meegan 2-9-1922, John Halpin 8-10-1922, Denis Leahy 21-12-1922, Daniel Downey 31-7-1923.

Separately a smaller stone reads: 'Renovated by National Graves Association'. The stone mason was McAteer, Dundalk.

The Ardee monument, known locally as the 'Soldier's Monument', was the work of the Dublin-based sculptor, Leo Broe. It was unveiled by Eugene Kavanagh on 18 September 1955 and was dedicated to Patrick Tierney and Sean O'Carroll, shot by the Black and Tans on 30 November 1920.[19] The impressive thirteen-foot high memorial is now at John Street, Ardee, opposite St Mary's Church, on a plot of ground made available by the County Council.[20] It is a statue of a typical Irish Volunteer, fashioned in limestone. Much of Broe's work was associated with ecclesiastical commissions for Dublin churches, along with many IRA memorials in provincial districts. The inscription at Ardee reads:

> I gcaoin-chuimhne ar an Captaen Sean Ó Cearbhaill agus ar an Ceatrunac Padraig Ó Tighearnaigh a fuair bás ar son na hÉireann

30ú Samhain 1920. Solas na bFlatas da n-anam. Aonad Áth Fhirdia Sean-Óglaigh na hÉireann do thóg.

On the other side of the monument, an English translation appears.

> In proud memory of Capt Sean O'Carroll and Q.M. Patrick Tierney who died for Ireland 30th November 1920. May they rest in peace. Erected by Ardee Unit Old I.R.A.

Smaller roadside monuments also honour these men at Tierney Street and O'Carroll Street in Ardee. The older Tierney family gravestone at Ballapousta graveyard is recumbent and part of the inscription reads 'Also John Tierney died 28th May 1924. And his son Patrick Q.M. IRA shot 30th Nov. 1920'.

The Republican memorial at Knockbridge Graveyard was erected in 1966 to coincide with the fiftieth anniversary of 1916. A tall rectangular-shaped undecorated monument was inserted into the graveyard wall and the inscription on a separate panel was then attached, it reads:

> Erected to commemorate members of the Fourth Northern Division (I.R.A. Veterans) and Fianna Éireann who are buried in this graveyard. May they rest in peace.

The panel also contains the depiction of two crossed tricolours. A new bilingual plaque added to the monument was unveiled on 24 April 2016 when Mrs Mary McCann, daughter of Paddy Hughes, was present. The English inscription on the plaque reads:

> Easter 1916-2016 Rising Centenary. Dundalk & District Old I.R.A. Commemoration Committee remembers the men and women buried in Knockbridge Cemetery who participated in the fight for freedom during the 1916-1921 period.

Volunteers

In this section, brief details are provided in relation to those commemorated on the Drogheda and Dundalk monuments. Additional memorials and inscriptions from around the county are also included.

Drogheda monument

Captain James Flanagan, Magdalen Street, Drogheda, one of the Irregular IRA garrisons stationed at Millmount Barracks was shot at Gormanston Train Station by the RIC.[21] The monument at the station reads:

> Erec in memory of Cpt. James (Tim) Flanagan 1st Bat. 9th Brg. IRA who died here 29 May 1922 in defence of the Republic. R.I.P. Erec by his comrades.[22]

Thomas Halpin is also commemorated on the Leech family gravestone at St Peter's graveyard, Drogheda:

> I.H.S. Erected by Mary Leech North Road, in loving memory of her husband John 6th November 1912. Also in sad and ever loving memory of her son-in-law Alderman Thomas J. Halpin Georges Street who was shot on Ash Wednesday 9 Feb. 1921 and his wife Agnes who died 15th June 1973. R.I.P. Moss.

William Leech (d. 1922) is interred in St Peter's graveyard and the inscription reads:

> In loving memory of William Leech died 19th Dec. 1916. His son William killed 29th June 1922 aged 21 years. His wife Kate died 26th Nov. 1951.

A marble plaque marks the location at Pitcher's Lane, Drogheda, where William (Liam) was shot by a sniper from the National Army.[23] That inscription reads:

> Erec. in memory of Sec. Ldr. Liam Leech 1st Bat. 9th Brg. IRA who died here 29 June 1922. In defence of the Republic. R.I.P. Erec. by his comrades.

Liam Leech was credited with saving the life of his friend, Harry Fairtlough, by pushing him to one side while under gunfire. 'Liam took the bullet for Harry and died. Harry would pass the spot where his comrade died and raise his cap to the man who saved his life.'[24] On his way home from Mass in 1984, Harry Fairclough 'stopped at the plaque ... he again raised his cap, said a little prayer and collapsed' on the same spot. His headstone at Calvary Cemetery, Drogheda, reads:

> In loving memory of Harry Fairtlough died 21st December 1984 aged 83 years. O.C. Engineers 1st Battalion 9th Brigade 1st Eastern Division I.R.A. 1918-1924. R.I.P.

Bernard Daly is buried in St Mary's Church of Ireland Churchyard, Drogheda, and his memorial reads:

> I ndíl chuimhne Captaen B Ó Dálaigh an chead chat Bridgáid Átha Cliath arm poblachta na h-Éireann a dunmharbhuighead 26adh de Lughnasa 1922. Erected by his comrades of the I.R.A.

Translated, this reads:

> In loving memory of Captain B. Daly, 1st Division of the Dublin Brigade of the Irish Republican Army who was murdered on 26th of August 1922.

The memorial is of an obelisk design and has cross-rifles depicted on it. It was unveiled on 17 September 1933.[25] A native of Drogheda, there is also a memorial to him at Sampson's Lane.

Captain Patrick Cooney, a native of Monasterboice, who is also named on the Marsh Road monument, was one of four Anti-Treaty IRA killed during a raid in Bantry, Co. Cork, on 30 August 1922. He was buried locally in Co. Cork. The family gravestone at Monasterboice reads:

> Erected by Nicholas Cooney Slate Hill who died Sep. 23rd 1924 aged 54 years. His wife Julia who died 24 April 1952 aged 88 and their son Patrick who died 13 Aug. 1922 aged 25.[26]

Commandant Patrick Mannion from Co. Mayo, who is also named on the Marsh Road monument, took the anti-Treaty side in the Civil War when he was attached to the Louth Brigade, 1st Eastern Division, IRA. 'By his daring, coolness and courage Commandant Mannion became the idol of the Republican Forces who were shelled out of the position in Drogheda, and who were forced to act as guerrilla columns'.[27] He was killed on 17 September 1922 following an attack on the Free State Army headquarters at Westland Row, Dublin.

Dundalk

Seven of those twenty-one listed on the republican monument at Dundalk are buried locally in their family graves, the locations and headstone or memorial inscriptions are given as follows:

John Watters and Patrick Watters, Dowdallshill:

Vita Mutatur Non Tollitur [Life is changed, not taken away] Of your charity pray for the repose of the souls of John Watters, Seatown Place, Dundalk who died 13th April 1919 aged 59 years. Also his two sons John aged 22 years. Patrick aged 18 years. Who died for Ireland's Freedom 18th June 1921. On whose souls sweet Jesus have Mercy. R.I.P. This stone was erected by Annie, widow of John Watters.

I do not grudge them Lord I do not grudge my two strong sons, that I have seen go out to break their strength and die, they and a few in bloody protest for a glorious thing, they shall be spoken of among their people. The generations shall remember them, and call them blessed. 'The Mother' – Pearse. His wife Annie who died 29th January 1947 aged 87 years. Their daughter Annie who died 5 Aug. 1958. McAteer, Dundalk.[28]

Bernard O'Hanlon, Dowdallshill:

In loving memory of Rosie Theresa O'Hanlon St Mary's Road who died 8th Feb. 1921 aged 14 years. Patrick O'Hanlon who died 11th Feb. 1921 aged 2[5?] years. Bernard Malachi O'Hanlon Dublin Brigade I.R.A. who fell in action Ct. Brunswick St 14th March 1921 aged 17 years ... and their beloved mother Rose O'Hanlon who died 23rd Nov. 1921 aged 61 years.

Thomas Markey, Dowdallshill:[29]

In loving memory of Thomas Markey C. Coy. 1st Batt. Dublin Brigade I.R.A. Killed in Action in Dublin 1st July 1922. R.I.P.

The headstone contains the I.R.A. motif.

Thomas Mulholland, Castletown graveyard:[30]

IHS Pray for the repose of the soul of Thomas Mulholland, Qr. Master 1st. Batt. Louth Brigade I.R.A. who was shot by forces of the British Crown in Dundalk 16th April 1920. R.I.P. McAteer DK.

John Joseph Magee, Cill Mhuire Graveyard, Templetown:

Public Memorial. Erected to the memory of Sec.-Com. John Joseph Magee I.R.A. Cooley who nobly gave his young life in the cause of Irish Independence May 13th 1921. Go dtugaidh Dia Trocaire ar a anam.[31]

The others listed on the Dundalk monument are briefly accounted for: John Quigley, whose family headstone is at Knockbridge, was killed on 4 September 1921. Thomas Campbell, IRA (known also as John Joseph), from Crossmaglen, was killed on 14 July 1922 at Anne Street Barracks when General Dan Hogan invaded and captured the town. Patrick McKenna, IRA, died on 14 August 1922, at the Military Barracks, Dundalk, as it was being taken by anti-Treaty forces. John Halpin of Moira Castle was killed on 8 October 1922 at Ravensdale by National Army soldiers. James Meegan died on 2 September 1922 from pneumonia. He had been active in the IRA and served a long term of imprisonment prior to the truce. Later he joined the Civic Police force. He was buried in the republican plot at Dowdallshill.[32] Denis Leahy was wounded in 1922 in an attack on Dundalk Military Barracks. He died on 22 December 1922 at Crooksling Sanatorium, Co. Dublin.[33]

During the Civil War, the Provisional Government adopted special powers and executed seventy-seven prisoners. On 13 January 1923 at Dundalk Prison, Thomas McKeown, John McNulty and Thomas Murray were shot on a charge of being in possession of firearms. At the Military Barracks, James Melia, Thomas Lennon and Joseph Ferguson were executed on 22 January 1923.[34]

Sylvester Heaney of Dillonstown was one of five soldiers of the National Army executed by firing squad on 8 January 1923 at Portobello Barracks. They were the first National Army troops to be executed and they were charged with treachery on 1 December 1922 at Leixlip, Co. Kildare, for assisting armed persons to use force against the National Army.[35] The remains of Sylvester Heaney and of five of those executed at Dundalk were reinterred in Dowdallshill on 30 October 1924.[36] As the coffins were laid into their graves at the republican plot, there followed an armed clash between Free State forces and anti-Treaty supporters. One person died from injuries received in the crossfire.[37]

Bernard Morris a native of Culloville, Co. Armagh, was shot on 1 April 1923 at Ballybinaby. John Quinn was shot at Springhill, Tallanstown, on 22 April 1923. The Quinn gravestone inscription at St Mary's, Newry, includes that to John Francis Quinn, 'Commandant General I.R.A. died of wounds 22nd May 1923 aged 22 years'. The republican monument at Newry includes the name of John Francis Quinn, Dromalane Park, 22 May 1923.

Daniel Downey, born in 1890, was the son of Patrick and Rose Downey of Barrack Street, Dundalk. By 1911 he was recorded at the boys' boarding school in Rathdrum, Co. Wicklow, along with Patrick Downey (aged six), presumably his brother. His sister, May, was recorded in 1911 at St Joseph's Orphanage, Seatown, along with Hannah Downey (aged eight). Daniel Downey was in prison in the Curragh and he probably died from the ill-effects of an earlier hunger strike there.[38] His burial date is recorded in the Dowdallshill burial book of 1923 as 2 August and his date of death on the monument is given as 31 July 1923. The burial of Patrick Downey is also recorded along with the names of Patrick McKenna and James Meegan as being buried in the republican plot.

The Great War dead and those republicans who died over the period (1916–23) have been commemorated by their families on public memorials as discussed in the first section. The one group who have not been commemorated in Co. Louth are those members of the Black and Tans or Auxiliaries who were killed during the War of Independence. One such member was Constable William Campbell who was shot at Dowdallshill, Dundalk, on the night of 17 June 1921. He was accorded a full ceremonial funeral and was buried in St Patrick's Cemetery, Dowdallshill, in an unmarked grave which is simply concreted over.[39]

The National Graves Association is mentioned on both the Drogheda and Dundalk memorials. It originated after the rising of 1867 when a memorial committee was formed in Dublin.[40] In 1926, the committee became known as Cumann Uaigheann na Laochra Gael or the National Graves Association. Historian Anne Dolan notes the low morale after the Civil War that contributed to the 'disgraceful neglect' of the graves of the men of 1922 and 1923.[41] She states that The National Graves Association was founded in 1926 by Sinn Féin in an effort to stake its claim to the republican dead. Celtic crosses, statues or other monuments were chosen as memorials. Civil War names were added to the lists of War of Independence dead. Dolan suggests that names included in the ecumenism of an 'all who died for Ireland' never seemed to include the Free State dead. For many years, the association refused to recognise the legitimacy of the Free State.[42]

The gravestones at Dowdallshill of Joseph O'Higgins, the Rogers brothers and members of the McGuill family allow brief mention of their contributions during the War of Independence and the Civil War. Joseph O'Higgins died on 25 October 1976 and is buried along with other family members, the most recent being his son Fr Brian O'Higgins, who died in 2009. Joseph was born in Boherboy near Kells, Co. Meath. In 1920, he was appointed Adjutant of the Drogheda Battalion by which time he worked in Austin's Shop, a 'safe house', in West Street. His witness statement to the Bureau of Military History offers interesting insights into activities around Drogheda, including the order in April 1921 from General Headquarters (GHQ) to raid the rate collectors in the Drogheda area (this was part of a national strategy).[43] His brother Brian, the well-known poet, took part in the Rising and was also the publisher of the Wolfe Tone Annual.

On 14 August 1922, Dundalk was recaptured by the Irregulars under the command of Frank Aiken. The only Irregular reported injured at the barracks on that occasion was Thomas Rogers, Divisional Quartermaster of the 4th Northern Division. He had been noted as an All-Ireland cycle champion.[44] Thomas's brother, Frank Rogers, also participated in the War of Independence. He was sent to the Crumlin Road Prison in Belfast and it appears that he got hold of a missal from the prison library and he had all the inmates in the prison with him sign their names and their home town or county.[45] Frank Rogers was again imprisoned during the Civil War and was sent first to Mountjoy, then to Dundalk. However, he escaped and was on the run until the end of the war before returning to Dundalk. The two brothers are buried side by side. Thomas died on 21 October 1969 aged seventy-five and Frank died on 7 June 1988 aged ninety-six.

The three McGuill brothers, James, John (Seán) and Joseph, are recorded as having 'mobilised' at Dundalk in 1916.[46] James McGuill noted that three McGuill brothers – himself, John, and Joseph – were rounded up as active republicans in January 1920 and were imprisoned in Crumlin Road, Belfast. James was elected to Dundalk Urban District Council and to Louth County Council in 1920. However, he maintained connections with the 4th Northern Division. James stated that he was imprisoned eight times, and was the only one tried by courts martial in Belfast arising from the German Plot scare. The McGuill property in Bridge Street was burnt down by the Black and Tans in 1920.[47] John stated that he was arrested several times and had been on hunger strike in Dundalk and Mountjoy prisons. James, who is buried in Dowdallshill, died on 3 June 1953. His funeral notice described him as Brigadier, 4th Northern Division IRA. John McGuill died in Belfast on 24 March 1989.[48] (Patrick) Joseph McGuill, who had been interned in 1916 at Frongoch, died on 28 October 1949, and he is buried in Dowdallshill in a grave that simply carries the 'McGuill' family name.

The 1949 burial book at Dowdallshill notes that the grave was reopened for the burial of Joseph. His wife Mary (née O'Driscoll) had died on 21 November 1937.[49] She was a niece of Michael Collins on her maternal side. Among those attending her funeral were William Cosgrave and General O'Duffy as well as her uncle Seán Collins.[50]

The final McGuill headstone of interest at Dowdallshill is that of Annie McGuill who died on 10 July 1962. She was among those 100 men and women who received certificates at the Tostal held in Dundalk.[51] Other gravestones at Dowdallshill that have mention of 'Old I.R.A.' or membership of the 4th Northern Division include those of Edward Carolan (d. 1924), John Garvey (d. 1966), Daniel O'Hare (d. 1977), Joseph Lennon (d. 1983), John White (d. 1985) and Edward (Eddie) Lawless (d. 1990).

Knockbridge

Among those buried in Knockbridge is Paddy Hughes who was the 'acknowledged leader of the Co. Louth Irish Volunteers'.[52] The family gravestone inscription reads:

In loving memory of Commandant Patrick Hughes, o/c Louth - Meath Areas, Easter Week Rising 1916, died 2nd February 1936, and his wife Elizabeth Christina died 28th December 1963. Go ndeanfaí Dia trócaire ortha.

Also buried in Knockbridge is John (Jack) Quigley and the family headstone reads:

IHS In loving memory of John Quigley I.R.A. Cavanore who died 4th Sep. 1921. His mother Bridget who died 14th Feb. 1922. His father Patrick who died 5th Dec. 1902. R.I.P.[53]

The headstone in memory of Samuel Hughes (Little Ash) who died on 9 July 1899, commemorates among other family members his son, 'John Hughes (Frongoch Internee 1917-1919) who died 10th March 1951'. The Walsh headstone, also at Knockbridge, includes Bernard Walsh of Annaghs who died on 31 January 1968 and his wife Annie (née Hughes) who died on 3 August 1964. Annie was brother of John Hughes. Bernard's nephew was Jack Quigley, mentioned above, who was 'waked' at Walsh's in Annaghs.[54] The Walshs' house at Annaghs 'was at one time the headquarters of the Fourth Northern Division, I.R.A., where many men prominent in the national movement found refuge, including Mr. Frank Aiken, who was OC of the division. His house was also used as a dispersal point on the occasion of the big break-out from Dundalk Jail'.[55]

Finally, a mention of streets named in honour of some of those who died during this period. These include O'Carroll Street and Tierney Street in Ardee; Flanagan Terrace, Halpin Terrace, Liam Leech Terrace and Moran Terrace in Drogheda; and Hughes Park, Lennon/Melia Terrace and Mulholland Avenue, Dundalk. Culhane Street, Dundalk, was named in 1932 to honour Patrick Culhane of Castletown Mount who died on 19 September 1920.[56] A prominent Sinn Féin member, he was raised to the rank of commander of the 1st Battalion of the Dundalk Volunteers and was buried in Urney Graveyard.[57] In 1966, the Railway Stations were renamed MacBride Station (Drogheda) and Clarke Station (Dundalk) after Major John McBride and Thomas J. Clarke, both of whom were executed after the 1916 Rising.

Government Forces and others

The commemoration of National Army (1922–3) members occurs mainly on family headstones. Unlike those who died during the War of Independence, they are not remembered on public memorials. Those on the anti-Treaty side who died during the Civil War are not commemorated on specific public memorials either, but some of their names are included on the Drogheda and Dundalk memorials. Attention is drawn to six of those members of the National Army who are remembered on family headstones.

Volunteer Charles Gyles, a member of the National Army, was shot in Clanbrassil Street, Dundalk on 30 November 1922. He previously had served in France during the Great War. His military funeral at St Patrick's Cemetery, Dundalk was attended by members of the National Army, the British Legion and former comrades with whom he had previously served.[58] His headstone, in the Protestant section, is similar to those in the graveyard commemorating the Great War dead, but it does not bear any insignia. The inscription reads:

> In cherished memory of Vol. Charles Gyles F.S.A. who died from Gunshot wounds 1st December 1922 and his sorrowing mother Elizabeth Johnston Gyles died 14th July 1938.

Commandant Frank Byrne was killed by anti-Treaty forces in the attack on the Military Barracks in Dundalk on 14 August 1922. The family headstone in Louth Village includes him as follows 'Pray for the soul of Thomas Byrne who died 22nd June 1912. Also his son Francis Irish National Army who died of wounds 14th Aug. 1922 at Dundalk'. A recently erected headstone at Kilwirra graveyard, Templetown, for Captain James Boyle OC of Greenore National Army Barracks, who was killed in an ambush at Rockmarshall reads:

> In memory of Captain James Boyle, Muchgrange, Greenore of The Irish Free State Army, 5th Northern Division ambushed and killed at Rockmarshall, Jenkinstown on 4th November 1922 aged 24 Years. A thiarna déan trócaire air.[59]

Two National Soldiers from Drogheda were killed in action in Co. Cork and both are buried in St Peter's cemetery. The remains of Private

Michael Woods (aged 20) of Nun's Walk, Drogheda, were interred with full military honours in the family burial at St Peter's Cemetery.[60] He is simply remembered on another Leech family gravestone as follows:

> IHS In loving memory of Willie Leech[61] Pearse Park died 8th May 2006. Patrick Woods Nun's Walk, his wife Margaret, their son Michael. Rest in Peace.

Part of the inscription for the second soldier, Patrick Breen reads:

> Erected by Patrick Breen in loving memory of his son Patrick Breen first National Soldier from Drogheda killed in action Aug. 18 1922 at Kildorrery Co Cork aged 19 years.

Sergeant George Laverty, who was shot at Bridge Street, Dundalk, on 17 July 1922, died from his injuries on 7 August at the Louth Infirmary. His funeral took place from the Military Barracks to St Patrick's Cemetery.[62] His grave does not appear to be marked.

At the height of the civil war in 1922, An Garda Síochána were posted to Dundalk and Drogheda. A unique memorial erected in 1995 at Ice House Hill Park, Dundalk commemorating Garda Martin Naughton and all members of the Garda Síochána who served in Dundalk since the foundation of the State.[63]

Finally, attention is drawn to Volunteers who subsequently were prominent in local or national politics. Peter Hughes, brother of Paddy Hughes, followed the more constitutional political path and was elected for Sinn Féin to Dáil Éireann in the 1921 general election. He supported the Treaty in 1921 on the opposite side to his brother Paddy. He later joined Cumann nGaedheal and served as Minister of Defence from 1924 to 1927. Peter died on 24 June 1954 and is buried at Dowdallshill along with his wife Lucy (née McKevitt). Other Volunteers of note were Laurence (Larry) Walsh, who was first elected as a TD (Teachta Dála – member of Dáil Éireann) in 1937. He died on 11 August 1962 and is buried in Calvary Cemetery, Drogheda. Tom Burke, was prominent in the GAA. A noted athlete, he acted as Louth County Secretary from 1918 to 1923 at the request of Michael Collins.[64] He also has the distinction of refereeing the All-Ireland in 1928 when the 'Sam Maguire' Cup was first presented. He died on 26 August 1967 and is also buried in Calvary

Cemetery. Frank Necy, who mobilised in 1916, was subsequently editor of the *Dundalk Democrat* (1941–66). He died on 28 February 1970 and is buried at Kilsaran.

The 1916 Rising and the Louth connections

The only death relating to the Rising in Co. Louth took place on Easter Monday, 24 April 1916, when Constable Charles McGee was killed at Castlebellingham as Volunteers made their way through the village on their way to Dublin.[65]

The Irish Police and Constabulary Recognition Fund in 1917 provided funding for the provision of headstones for Easter Rising police casualties that included Constable McGee, who was buried in Gortahork, Co. Donegal.[66] Very few monuments in Co. Louth relate specifically to the Rising. The plaque erected in 1956 on the John Boyle O'Reilly Hall, Clanbrassil Street, Dundalk commemorates the Dundalk contingent of Volunteers who left the hall on Easter Sunday to take part in the 1916 Rising. However, some of those from Co. Louth who died in Dublin during Easter Week are locally remembered on family gravestones. Those who were killed in the 'Louth Dairy' in North King Street, Dublin, merit attention as their Louth connections and Stanley family relationships have largely been undocumented. The 'North King Street Massacre'[67] took place in Dublin towards the end of the Easter Week. This involved the largest loss of civilian life during the Rising and followed the death of fourteen officers of the South Staffordshire Regiment. On 30 April 2016, to mark the 100th anniversary of the North King Street massacre, the Stoneybatter and Smithfield People's History Project unveiled a plaque at the junction of North King Street and Church Street commemorating the sixteen civilians who died.[68] Part of the inscription reads:

> On the night of Friday/Saturday 28th/29th April 1916 during some of the fiercest fighting of the Rising sixteen innocent civilians, who were sheltering in their homes, were brutally murdered by British crown forces.

That night four civilians were shot at No. 27 North King Street, known as the 'Louth Dairy', the residence of Mrs Bridget Lawless. They were James Finnegan, Pakie Hoey, Peter Lawless and James McCartney.[69] Two of the four were from Co. Louth and the third was Mrs Lawless' son. A letter from M. (Michael) McGrath, 9 Linenhall Street, Dublin, to Joseph Dolan, 30 April 1916, details the Louth Dairy occurrence:

> The sadest [sic] thing of the whole war was the Louth Dairy ocurrence [sic] ... where four young men were shot dead by the soldiers in their room. One James Finegan born in Stickillen [and] Paddy Hoey from above Dunleer. I was speaking to them on Thursday and they were wishing they had gone to the country while they could get away. Hoey was home for Easter and came home Easter Monday. Another the son of the proprietress only 21 years [and] a young man who leaves a young widow the[y] came from Exchange St for safety. The military buryed [sic] them in the yard but thank God wee [sic] removed them and gave them [a] Christian buryal [sic]... I think all the other Ardee people came safe. [70]

Patrick Hoey was born in June 1887 at Cruicetown, Clogherhead, to Bernard Hoey and Julia Connor. The inscription on the family gravestone at Mayne (near Clogherhead) reads:

> Erected by Julia Hoey Cruisetown in loving memory of her husband Bernard Hoey who died 8th Dec. 1903 aged 63. Also her son Patrick who died 29th April 1916 aged 28. Interred in Glasnevin. Also her son Thomas who died 30th Jan. 1917 aged 37. Also the above named Julia Hoey who died 18th April 1926 aged 74.

Patrick Hoey and James Finegan are buried in the same grave at Glasnevin but there is no headstone. Peter Joseph Lawless was buried in the Stanley family plot that existed prior to 1916. The inscription on his uncle's headstone reads:

> Erected by Mrs Stanley 36 Parnell St. in memory of her beloved husband John who departed this life 8th Nov. 1915, aged 55 years also his daughter Kathleen M. aged 6 months and Peter J. Lawless nephew of the above aged 21 years. Also her beloved daughter Josephine Markey who died Nov. 1st 1924 aged 25 years. R.I.P.[71]

Bridget Lawless (née Stanley) married in the USA. She died on 14 August 1950 and her death notice referred to her husband, Anthony Lawless of Togher, and to her son, Peadar Lawless of the 'Louth Dairy'.[72] In her witness statement she stated that Peter was born on 27 November 1894 in New York and that they returned to Ireland in 1899.[73] The birth place of James Finnegan has been given as both Philipstown, Dunleer, and Stickillin, Ardee.[74] This points to the family of Patrick Finnegan and Elizabeth Nevin (of Cliven) who were married in July 1873. The first three children including James were born in Cliven/Philipstown (in Dunleer parish) and their next three children were born in Stickillin (in Ardee parish).

James's baptismal date was 24 May 1874. In 1916, his elderly parents were granted an award by the Rebellion (Victims) Committee as they were deemed dependent on their son.[75] The name Stanley carries strong 1916 associations. Joseph Stanley, a printer, served as Press Agent to Pádraig Pearse at the GPO where he delivered copies of a handbill entitled 'The Provisional Government to the Citizens of Dublin' on Easter Tuesday. In 1918, he started printing *An tOglach* for Michael Collins. In 1919, frustrated by the confiscation of his presses, he moved with his family to Drogheda where he opened a cinema. In 1920, he was elected to Louth County Council. When the Civil War started in 1922, he resigned his position in the IRA.[76]

Joseph Stanley, who born in Dublin, was a son of John Stanley mentioned above, thus Joseph and Peter Lawless, who were killed at the 'Louth Dairy', were first cousins. In 1901, James Finnegan, who was also killed at the 'Louth Dairy', was a resident in the Stanley Household at Great Britain Street, Dublin. Part of Joseph Stanley's gravestone at St Peter's, Drogheda reads:

In fond and loving memory of Joseph M. Stanley Mill Lane died 2 June 1950. His wife Teresa died 20 July 1960. Their son Colbert died 18 Dec. 1965. Cuimhnigh a Ghaedhil.

A commemorative garden was opened on 24 April 2016 in Drogheda in honour of Joseph Stanley. A copy of the Proclamation is cast in stone. Probably no greater honour could be attributed to its original printer. Also of interest is the in-law relationship between the

Stanleys and Pakie Hoey who was killed at the 'Louth Dairy'. Lizzie Hoey is listed as a niece and resident with Mathew Stanley at St Joseph's Place, Inn's Quay, Dublin. She was, in fact, a first cousin of Mathew's wife, Annie, daughter of Laurence Verdon of Cruisetown.[77] Another member of the Stanley family associated with the period was Laurence Stanley who served as Mayor of Drogheda in 1916. He is recorded as also being related to Peter Lawless.[78] Those Drogheda Volunteers who 'mobilised' in 1916 appear to have trained and performed manoeuvres in Stanley's yard in Narrow West Street.[79] His family headstone is at St Peter's graveyard. Laurence himself died on 18 April 1947, aged eighty-seven.

Apart from those who were killed at the 'Louth Dairy' there are others with Louth connections who were killed in Dublin during the Rising. Fr Felix Watters SM from Dundalk died on 8 May 1916 as the result of a gunshot wound while on a mission of duty and charity during the Rising in Dublin.[80] He was a member of the Marist Community in Leeson Street. His name appears on the commemorative wall recently erected at Glasnevin where he is buried.

The gravestone at Kilsaran of Mrs Jane Tuite (née Kelly), who died in November 1976, provides a link with the Rising. She married first in 1911 to John Mallon (39 South King Street, Dublin), a civilian who was killed during the Rising. She married again in 1919 to Thomas Tuite of Sunnyside, Drogheda.[81]

The plaque, on Rossin Bridge over the river Mattock that borders Counties Louth and Meath, was erected in 1964 to commemorate Philip Clarke. During the Rising he was assigned to St Stephen's Green and to the Royal College of Surgeons where he was shot. His family moved to Monknewtown in 1876 where Philip went to school.[82] The plaque is bilingual and reads, 'In loving memory of Philip Clarke who died for Ireland in Dublin 26th April 1916 Easter Week. May the Lord have mercy on his soul.'

The recently erected monument commemorating the Thornton family of Drogheda reflects their contribution to the Rising in Dublin. The Thorntons were a prominent Drogheda family during the Rising; a plaque was unveiled to commemorate them on Easter Sunday, 27 March 2016, at 33 Peter Street, Drogheda, that reads: 'Birthplace of Frank, Hugh, Patrick and Nora Thornton who took part in the Easter Rising 1916 in the G.P.O. Dublin. Erected by the Drogheda Civic Trust 2016.'

Frank Thornton was leader of the 26th Battalion of the Volunteers and during the Rising he saw action at Liberty Hall and the Imperial Hotel, now the Gresham.[83] His brother Paddy was with him in Liberty Hall until Easter Monday afternoon, when he was sent to Fairview. He was subsequently wounded and discharged after the surrender for being under age. Frank was buried with full military honours in Glasnevin in 1965. Captain Hugh Thornton was killed by anti-Treaty forces on 27 August 1922 at Clonakilty, Co. Cork. His body was returned to Dublin in the Steamship Minerva and he was buried in the Irish Army plot at Glasnevin cemetery on 1 September 1922.[84] Their brother 'Paddy was taken out of Joe Stanley's Picturehouse ... and brutally murdered by the Black and Tans'.[85] He was buried in St Peter's, Drogheda, in 1921 but there is no memorial to him.[86]

The purchase of Ballymascanlan House in the early 1940s by George Plunkett, brother of Joseph Mary Plunkett, provides a Louth connection with the Plunkett family. George Plunkett took part in the 1916 Rising at GPO, and was active during the War of Independence but was imprisoned early in the Civil War. His father, Count George Noble Plunkett (1851–1948), is buried in Glasnevin, but his mother, Countess Mary Josephine (née Cranny), who died on 6 March 1944, is buried in Ravensdale. George died in 1944 in Dundalk when he was accidentally thrown from a pony trap. The inscription on the Plunkett gravestone at Ravensdale reads:

> Curtha annso tá Seóirse Ó Pluingceid Captaen i n-arm poblachta na h-Éireann ó 1913 go dtí na bás ar 21adh d'Eanair 1944; agus a shearc-bhean Maire[87] a fuair bás ar 1adh Deireadh Foghmhair 1951; A mhathair Iósephín bean Cúnta Uí Pluingcéid a cailleadh ar 6adh Márta 1944; agus a mhac ba sinne Ióseph Cúnta Ó Pluingcéid a d'éag ar 18aadh Bealtaine 1966. Ar dheis Dé go raibh a n-anmanna. Kelly.

Translated, this reads:

> Buried here are George Plunkett, Captain in the Irish Republican Army from 1913 until his death on 21st January 1944; and his beloved wife Mary who died on 1st October 1951; his mother Josephine, Countess Plunkett, who died 6th March 1944 and his eldest son,

Joseph, Count Plunkett, who died 18th May 1966. May their souls be at God's right hand.

The McDermott/Darcy gravestone at Haggardstown commemorates 'William Darcy died 24th Dec. 1918. Head Centre of the I.R.B. for County Louth o/c 2nd floor G.P.O. Easter Week Rising 1916. Born in Dublin St Dundalk 1875'. The son of Joseph Darcy and Anne McDermott, he was the first president of the Dundalk branch of Sinn Féin. John Devoy in a letter (dated 9 September 1929) stated that he met William Darcy for the first time in Kilmainham Gaol after the surrender.[88]

Cumann Staire Óméith unveiled a memorial plaque to seventeen named locals who took part in the Easter Rising and in the events of subsequent years. The unveiling took place on 24 April 2016 at the old graveyard in Omeath.

Joseph Larrissey, aged fifteen, of Ladywell Terrace, Dundalk, who 'mobilised' in 1916, had got as far as Ardee when he was ordered home after he was deemed too young. He took the anti-Treaty side in the Civil War. In his pension statement, he stated that he was on active service until his capture at the end of August 1922. He was released in September 1923 for health reasons.[89] He died on 17 July 1963 and his grave is in Dowdallshill. Family members have placed a small tricolour at his grave in recent times, a practice that was reflected throughout the county in the centenary year of 2016. It is poignant that his brother, Andrew Larrissey, was killed on 7 July 1916 at the Battle of the Somme.[90] Mass was celebrated on Andrew's 100th anniversary at the Dominican Church, Dundalk, on 7 July 2016. Family members were present and sheaves of wheat or barley from the battlefield were taken to the altar for the offertory. Finally, it is noted that a plaque marks the birthplace of the Gaelic scholar and historian, Joseph Dolan (1872–1930) at Main Street, Ardee. He helped fund Pearse's school at St Enda's, Rathfarnham, with a loan.

Cumann na mBan

The first Co. Louth branch of Cumann na mBan was founded in November 1915. Its founder and first president was Angela Mathews who ran a stationery shop at Clanbrassil Street, Dundalk. She played a key role in the mobilisation of the Volunteers during Easter Week.[91] The family headstone at Castletown graveyard has now fallen. Part of the inscription from an earlier recording reads:

> Erected to the memory of John Mathews, printer Dundalk, who died 30th August 1883, aged 53 years. His daughter Margaret, who died 28th Jan 1923. And Angela who died 1st Oct. 1938.[92]

In St Patrick's Cemetery, Dowdallshill, Lily Adair, who died on 4 February 1980, aged eighty, is named on the family headstone as 'Section Comdt Cumann na mBan'. Two gravestones at Drogheda commemorate members of Cumann na mBan. The Carroll headstone at St Peter's reads, 'In loving memory of James Carroll Oulster Lane, died March 1940, His daughter Kitty Grogan August 1933. Cumann na mban.' She had been a founder member of the Cumann na mBan in Drogheda and helped form the first union at Boyne Mills.[93] At Calvary Cemetery, Mrs Kathleen Tiernan of 23 Moran Terrace, who died on 25 December 1988, is recorded on her headstone as the last surviving member of Drogheda Cumann na mBan.[94] The Kelly (of Grangebellew) headstone at Dysart graveyard records three family members who were involved in 1916. These were Mary Bridget Kelly, and her brothers Thomas J. Kelly, Grangebellew, died 27 Dec. 1970, aged seventy-six, and James Kelly Capt. BCoy. 4th Northern Div., died 1 May 1967.[95]

Conscription

The need for further manpower in the British forces had become inevitable in 1918 as the Great War by then had entered its fourth year. British Prime Minister David Lloyd George presented his plans to raise half a million men of which 150,000 were expected to come from Ireland. In the light of intense opposition that almost certainly would have led to violence, the British government did not implement conscription in Ireland. Two plaques erected in thanksgiving are recorded in Co. Louth. A brass plaque in Collon Catholic Church carries the inscription:

> 1918 Chum glóire Dé agus mbuíochas do Maighdean Lourdes as sona coimirce le linn baoghail mhóir d'ár dtír. To the Glory of God and in Thanksgiving to Our Lady of Lourdes for her loving protection in a time of National danger.

The grotto at Togher Church was built by Paddy Maguire in 1919 in thanksgiving for Ireland having been saved from conscription. The idea came from a photograph of Lourdes shown to him by Fr Finnegan.[96] An inscription dated 8 December 1919 is inscribed at the grotto in thanksgiving to Our Lady of Lourdes.

In Ireland, the National Day of Commemoration of all those Irishmen and Irishwomen who died in past wars or on service with the United Nations occurs on the Sunday nearest July 11. It marks the anniversary of the date in 1921 that the truce was signed ending the Irish War of Independence. The principal ceremony is normally held at the Royal Hospital Kilmainham, Dublin. The memorials and graves of those who were casualties in the 1916–23 period provided a local focus for the bereaved. Commemoration of the republican dead commenced immediately after the events of 1916, continuing through the War of Independence and the Civil War and for the century afterwards. If anything, these commemorations have further evolved in recent years.

Commemoration can, however, be selective, in common with most of the country, no public ceremonies occur in Co. Louth to honour those members of the National Army who were killed in the Civil War. The narrative in relation to the commemoration of the War of Independence and the Civil War will emerge in due course as did that of the centenary of the Rising. President Michael D. Higgins in his address to the Michael Collins Béal na Bláth gathering on Sunday, 21 August 2016, has begun that narrative in relation to the forthcoming centenaries.[97] He opined:

> when the time comes, very soon, to commemorate those events of the early 1920s, we will need to display courage and honesty as we seek to speak the truth of the period, and in recognising that, during the War of Independence, and particularly during the Civil War, no single side had the monopoly of either atrocity or virtue.[98]

NOTES

1   Jay Winter, *Sites of memory, sites of mourning: the Great War in European cultural history* (Cambridge: CUP, 1995), p. 79.
2   Ibid., p. 92.
3   Those named on the monuments from periods after 1923 are listed but not discussed in this essay.

4   Anne Dolan, *Commemorating the Irish Civil War: history and memory, 1923–2000* (Cambridge: CUP, 2003).

5   The monument is located on the river side of the Marsh Road, 400 m east of the railway viaduct.

6   Liam Reilly, 'Account of Drogheda's part in the 1916 Rising', *Reflections on the 1916 Rising* (Drogheda: Old Drogheda Society, 2016), pp. 179–90.

7   http://www.independent.ie/regionals/droghedaindependent/news/90th-anniversary-of-halpin-and-moran-27153404.html.

8   *Irish Independent*, 10 Feb. 1922, p. 6, John Moran was buried in his native Enniscorthy.

9   *Irish Independent*, 6 Apr. 1931, p. 8.

10 Also included from a later period is 'Labhras Ó Gruagáin (1898–1979) Caith sé a shaoil ar son na h-Eireann', which translates as 'Laurence Grogan (1898–1979) He dedicated his life to Ireland'. The Grogan family gravestones are in Calvary Cemetery.

11 Donal Hall, *The unreturned army: County Louth dead in the Great War, 1914–1918* (Dundalk: County Louth Archaeological and Historical Society, 2005), pp. 24–5. A list of headstones is given ibid., Appendix 3, pp. 233–5.

12 *Irish Independent*, 6 Nov. 1925.

13 Hall, *The unreturned army*, p. 24, citing Keith Jeffrey, *Ireland and the Great War* (Cambridge: CUP, 2000), p. 131.

14 John Toal was a founder member of the IRA Veterans Association and he was honoured on the 25th anniversary of foundation in December 1968. He died on 20 Jan. 1975 and is buried in Dowdallshill.

15 *Irish Press*, 27 Jan. 1934, p. 6.

16 *Irish Independent*, 22 Apr. 1935, p. 9.

17 The final name on the north facing side is Risteard Ó Gosáin (Richard Goss), 9 Aug. 1941.

18 The additional names on the gravestone are from a later period, 9 Aug. 1941, Risteard Ó Gosáin (Richard Goss) and 11 Nov. 1957: Micheal MacUaither, Olibhear MacCramum, Pol MacGabhann, Seomso MacAodhagain, Padraig MacPartlin (Michael Watters, Oliver Craven, Paul Smith, George Keegan, Patrick Parle).

19 *Irish Press*, 19 Sept. 1955, p. 5.

20 http://www.independent.ie/regionals/droghedaindependent/lifestyle/memorial-to-black-and-tan-victims-27161669.html.

21 *Freeman's Journal*, 31 May 1922, p. 5, see also: http://www.irishmedals.org/anti-treaty-killed.html.

22 http://www.irishwarmemorials.ie/pdf/269.pdf.

23 This was just days prior to the shelling of Millmount by the National Army.

24 *Drogheda Independent*, 8 Jan. 2012.

25 *Irish Press*, 18 Sept. 1933.

26 It should be 30 Aug.1922.

27 *The Last Post, Glasnevin Cemetery* (Dublin: National Graves Association, 1932), pp. 71–2.

28 Pearse's poem 'The Mother' sets the background for the sacrifice of Mrs Watters of her two sons whose faces are also represented on the monument. Two angels are depicted offering grapes and bread symbolising the bread and wine offered at Mass. Above this is the crucified Christ, reflecting the theme of sacrifice in a Christian context. There are roadside monuments to the Watters brothers at Quay Street, Dundalk, where they were killed.

29 Thomas Markey died when he was shot at the Four Courts during the 'Battle of Dublin'.

30   There is also a monument to Thomas Mulholland at Bridge St opposite St Nicholas Church and near John Street.

31   In 2009, the 'Green' or the Park at Millgrange was dedicated in memory of John Joseph Magee Millgrange, 16 May 1897–13 May 1921. A holy water font in memory of John Joseph Magee was erected at Grange Church by his parents.

32   Eamonn O Huallachain (ed.), *The Time of the Trouble* (Dundalk: FeedARead.com, 2014), p. 539. Extract quotes *Dundalk Democrat*, 9 Sept. 1922.

33   MA, Military Service Pensions Collection (MSPC), DP5335, 'Denis Leahy'.

34   A monument in memory of Tommy McKeown (Piedmont) and Josie Ferguson (Maddoxland) was erected by Dundalk and District Old IRA along the main Dundalk–Carlingford road (R173) where the road serves as a boundary between the townlands mentioned above. The monument was unveiled on 10 December 2016.

35   Breen Timothy Murphy, 'The government's executions policy during the Irish Civil War 1922–1923' (PhD thesis, 2010, NUI Maynooth), pp. 21, 180–1.

36   The remains of Thomas Murray were taken back to Co. Meath.

37   *Dundalk Democrat*, 1 Nov. 1924.

38   James Durney, 'The Curragh internees 1921–24: from defiance to defeat'; see http://www.kildarearchsoc.ie/wp-content/uploads/2015/11/Internees.pdf, p. 20.

39   O Huallachain, *The time of the trouble*, p. 328, quotes *Dundalk Democrat*, 25 Jun. 1921.

40   http://www.nga.ie/history.php.

41   Dolan, *Commemorating the Irish Civil War*, p. 137.

42   Ibid., p. 138.

43   Military Archives Cathal Brugha Barracks (MA) Bureau of Military History (BMH) Witness Statement (WS).507, 'Joseph O'Higgins'.

44   O Huallachain, *The time of the trouble*, pp. 527–8, quotes *Newry Reporter*, 17 Aug. 1922.

45   The missal is now in the care of the County Museum at Dundalk.

46   See MA, BMH, WS.353 'James McGuill'.

47   Harold O'Sullivan, *A history of local government in the County of Louth: from earliest times to the present time* (Dublin: IPA, 2000), p.131.

48   MA, BMH, WS353, 'James McGuill', p. 64.

49   They were married in Dublin in 1930.

50   *Irish Independent*, 25 Nov. 1937.

51   *Irish Press*, 9 Nov. 1953.

52   Donal Hall, 'Blood Brothers: The Story of Dundalk Siblings Paddy and Peter Hughes', in *The Centenary Magazine: The Rising Centenary: Louth 1916–2016* (*Drogheda Independent & The Argus*, 2016), pp. 37–9.

53   Jack Quigley died in an accident while handling firearms. The correct spelling is Cavanaore.

54   Personal communication from Colm Breathnach.

55   *Irish Independent*, 3 Feb. 1968.

56   *Irish Press*, 14 Jan. 1932.

57   *Dundalk Democrat*, 25 Sept. 1920.

58   Donal Hall, 'Violence and political factionalism and their effects on North Louth 1874–1943' (PhD thesis, 2009, NUI Maynooth).

59   O' Huallachain, *The time of the trouble*, p. 558, quotes *Frontier Sentinel*, 11 Nov. 1922.

60   *Irish Independent*, 13 Nov. 1922.

61   It would appear that William Leech was a nephew of Michael Woods.

62   O' Huallachain, *The time of the trouble*, p. 522, quotes *Dundalk Democrat*, 12 Aug. 1922.

63   Garda Martin Naughton died on 19 March 1988 and is buried in Dowdallshill.
64   Liam Reilly, 'Account of Drogheda's part in the 1916 Rising', 'Reflections on The 1916 Rising' (Drogheda: Old Drogheda Society, 2016), pp. 179–88; Tom Burke, 'Burke family played big role in fight for freedom', *Centenary Magazine*, pp. 42–3.
65   BMH, WS236, 'Frank Martin'.
66   http://theirishrevolution.ie/recognising-contribution-police-fell-1916-fighting/.
67   http://www.theirishstory.com/2012/04/13/the-north-king-street-massacre-dublin-1916/.
68   http://www.decadeofcentenaries.com/30-april-1916-commemoration-of-north-king-street-massacre-dublin-7/.
69   James McCartney was buried at Glasnevin. A headstone marks his grave.
70   Louth County Archives, PP00118/ 'Letter dated 30 April 1916 from M. McGrath to Joseph Dolan'.
71   See gravestone number 745 on the following website: http://www.igpweb.com/IGPArchives/ire/dublin/photos/tombstones/1headstones/glasnevin05.txt.
72   *Irish Press*, 16 Aug. 1950, p. 10.
73   From a witness statement, taken from Mrs Lawless now in the Austin Stack Papers at the National Library of Ireland, see: http://www.easter1916.ie/index.php/rising/witnesses/.
74   Hubert Murphy, 'Louth men murdered in the centre of Dublin', *Centenary Magazine*, pp. 60–1; Letter from M. McGrath to Joseph Dolan.
75   The Finnegans (spelt Finnigan in the 1911 census returns) were living in Ballough, Lusk, Co. Dublin. Relatives still reside near Dunleer; *HC Debates*, 2 Aug. 1917, col. 2241.
76   https://gaelicpress.files.wordpress.com/2010/12/joe-stanley-printer-to-the-rising-information-leaflet1.pdf.
77   Mathew was brother of John Stanley and Mrs Lawless. The mother of Pakie and Lizzie Hoey was Julia Connor and the mother of Annie Verdon was Mary Connor, both children of Thomas Connor and Mary Norris.
78   Hubert Murphy, 'Louth men murdered in the centre of Dublin', *Centenary Magazine*, pp. 60–1.
79   Hubert Murphy, 'Drogheda's Connection', *Centenary Magazine*, pp. 48–9.
80   *The Tablet*, 20 May 1916, see http://archive.thetablet.co.uk/article/20th-may-1916/29/ obituary.
81   *Freeman's Journal*, 8 May 1916.
82   A commemorative handout by the Philip Clarke Commemoration Committee, 2015.
83   Liam Reilly 'Frank Thornton – A Drogheda man's contribution to the 1916 Rising', *Reflections on The 1916 Rising* (Drogheda: Old Drogheda Society, 2016), p. 27.
84   Information per communication from Liam Reilly. http://www.irishmedals.org/black-and-tan-medal.html.
85   MA, BMH, WS.510, 'Frank Thornton'.
86   *Freeman's Journal*, 8 Feb. 1921.
87   Mrs Mary Plunkett (née McCarthy, wife of George) died on 1 Oct. 1951. Her son Eoghan, third Count Plunkett, died on 7 Mar. 2016 and is buried in Ravensdale.
88   MA, MSPC,1D332 'William Darcy'.
89   MA, MSPC, MSP34REF2656, 'Joseph Larrissey'.
90   Hall, *The unreturned army*, p. 115.
91   Ailbhe Rogers, 'Women played their part in the Rising', *Centenary Magazine*, pp. 65–7.
92   Noel Ross and Maureen Wilson, *Tombstone Inscriptions in Castletown Graveyard, Dundalk* (Dundalk: Old Dundalk Society, 1992), p. 49.

93 http://www.independent.ie/regionals/droghedaindependent/localnotes/difficult-days-for-a--drogheda-girl-28972197.html.

94 James Garry, *Calvary cemetery: history and tombstone inscriptions* (Drogheda: Old Drogheda Society, 2002), p. 178.

95 The Kelly brothers were among those who 'mobilised' in the Dunleer area and who after the Rising 'retreated' to the Bellew (Moonveagh) Tower in the townland of Windmill.

96 Rose Corrigan (ed.), *Togher through the years: reflections and reminisences* (Togher Co. Louth: ICA Togher Guild, [1993] 2010), p. 97.

97 http://www.president.ie/en/media-library/speeches/remembering-michael-collins-in-2016-oration-at-beal-na-mblath-commemoration.

98 Acknowledgement is due to Kiera Hall for the Irish translations; Lorraine McCann at the County Archive; Colm Breathnach, Don Johnston, John McCullen, Róisín Mulligan, Peter Kavanagh, Conor Keelan, Stephen O'Donnell, John Rafferty, Aidan Rogers, Bryan Rogers and Noel Ross for helpful conversations and recollections; and finally, to the editors of the volume, Martin Maguire and Donal Hall.

13

Compiling the Names of the County Louth Volunteers Who Mobilised, Easter Week 1916

Lorraine McCann

As part of Louth's 2016 centenary programme of events, an archival exhibition, 'The Louth Volunteers 1914–1918', was developed by Louth County Archives Service. The exhibition highlighted the local perspective by narrating the story of the county's Volunteers in this period of the nation's history: from their formation in February 1914 to the general election of late 1918. Included in the exhibition was a list of names of those Volunteers who mobilised in Co. Louth during Easter Week 1916, the compilation of which is the subject of this essay.

The list of names of those who mobilised is primarily based on two main sources: the Bureau of Military History witness statements 1913–1923 (BMH WS) and the Military Service Pensions Collection (MSPC) as available from December 2015 through the website of the Military Archives.[1] Other sources included a 1966 oral history archive interview entitled 'Memories of 1916', a copy of which is available in Louth County Archives Service;[2] various Frongoch records including the 'Frongoch Roll',[3] which at the time of compiling the list of names (late 2015) were available in the Allen Library, Dublin, but are now held in the Military Archives; an account by former Volunteer James Kelly, first published in *Togher Topics*, June 1991;[4] and letters in the Joseph Dolan papers[5] held in Louth County Archives.

It was decided from the outset that as well as the Volunteer's name, the list would include the Volunteer's address at the time of mobilisation by way of town or townland and an indication if the Volunteer was one of the

Louth/Meath group that occupied Tyrrelstown House during Easter Week, in addition to the archive reference if the name was found in any of the two main sources aforementioned, and any explanatory notes if required. At the end of the list of Co. Louth Volunteers who mobilised during Easter Week 1916 is a summary list of the relevant Bureau of Military History witness statements that were consulted; also a list of names of those – as far as could be established – who were originally from Co. Louth but who had moved to Dublin or England who also took part in the Rising; and a list of names of Co. Louth people who were killed during the Rising.

The assemblage of the list of names commenced with compiling a list of witness statements made by witnesses from County Louth that are available in the BMH. The County Archives was assisted in this task by Stephen O'Donnell who had a list available from previous research.[6] The BMH collection contains some 1,773 witness statements that were collected between 1947 and 1957 in an attempt by the State to compile a history of the 1913–21 revolutionary period in Ireland. The collection was released to public access in 2003 and is now available to search online free of charge through the Military Archives website.[7] In compiling the list of names, one essential witness statement was that of Patrick McHugh, a former Lieutenant in the Irish Volunteers, Dundalk, during 1916 as at the end of his statement is an addendum containing a comprehensive list of men, largely from the Dundalk area, who took part in the Rising.

However, whilst this provided quite a lengthy list of names, it was thought necessary to check other sources for verification, and for any possible further names, in addition to the local addresses of Volunteers at the time of mobilisation in 1916. McHugh gave some addresses that were correct at the time of his witness statement (May 1952), including addresses in Dublin and the USA. McHugh's list provided the County Archives with further names to search for additional witness statements in the BMH. A simple database table was set up by the County Archives to keep track of names and witness statement reference numbers or other sources that confirmed the Volunteer.

The second archival source that was utilised was that of the MSPC. The MSPC derives from the Oireachtas resolution in 1923 to compensate wounded members and dependants of deceased members of Óglaigh na hÉireann (Irish Volunteers) and other Irish military bodies in the 1916–23 period through payment of allowances and pensions. Various legislation was subsequently introduced from 1923 to 1953 to allow for this. In December 2015, the pension files of some 2,447 veterans of Easter Week 1916 with recognised military service had been processed and were available online via the Military Archives website. As the MSPC project is ongoing, the files of further 1916 veterans have since been added.

On the Military Archives website, the search facility for the Pensions Collection allows the user to choose 'Louth' for the county within Ireland. (It is important to note that the website includes pensions and awards for other recognised military service, such as during the Civil War period or during the post-Civil War period with the National Forces, in addition to Easter Rising service.) The results give a comprehensive list of names of those who had applied for a pension or award and clicking on a name subsequently gives quite a thorough level of detail on the applicant, with information pertaining to their address, if any Easter Rising service, location of Easter Rising service, organisation company/unit/brigade details, pension summary details, the subject's scanned pension application file and 'subject information', which is a summary description of the file.

When performing this type of search (i.e. choosing 'Louth' as the county within Ireland), it is important to check the location of Easter Rising service, as an applicant with Easter Rising service and with 'Louth' included in their address detail does not necessarily mean that they served in Louth: they may have lived in Louth in later years, for example, at the time of their application. When searching the MSPC, it is also necessary to perform a second search leaving the 'county within Ireland' blank and typing 'Louth' or other variables, such as Ardee or Drogheda, into the 'subject information' field. This will yield a different list containing names of applicants who do not have 'Louth' included in their address detail, as they may only have provided their residential address such as one in Dublin at the time of their pension application. However, once this search is performed, clicking on a name to check the location of Easter Rising service or reading the file summary description will clarify if they mobilised in Louth during Easter 1916. An example is Patrick McHugh,[8] who was a section commander in the Dundalk Battalion during Easter 1916 and who subsequently moved to Dublin where he continued to be active in the Irish Volunteers and later in the Irish Republican Army. As the searches on the Pensions Collection were performed, the database table was updated with the corresponding MSPC reference number and with any new names.

In the meantime, the Dundalk Relatives Association Committee[9] provided the County Archives with a copy of their research to date, as they too were in the process of compiling the names of those who mobilised, to present commemorative medals to surviving relatives of the Easter 1916 Louth Volunteers for the 2016 centenary programme.

Other smaller sources that were subsequently examined included several archival documents contained in the Allen Library's Brother Allen Collection from Frongoch internment camp, including the Frongoch Roll,[10] which comprises handwritten names and home addresses of the Irish Volunteers from around Ireland that were interned in Frongoch after the Easter Rising, the minute book of the Irish Volunteers' Committee of Management in Frongoch Internment Camp for June 1916,[11] several prisoner autograph books,[12] and the 'Names of the Irish Prisoners Deported after the Insurrection 1916'.[13] Another source that was studied for further names was the 'Memories of 1916' oral history archive interview that was originally made by the Drogheda 1916 Commemoration Committee during the fiftieth anniversary commemorations in 1966. Those interviewed included Paddy Myles of Marsh House, Drogheda, David Blood of Sandyford Terrace, Drogheda, Joe Carr of Chord Road, Drogheda, Tom Kelly of Beech Grove Terrace, Drogheda, who read a letter on behalf of James O'Meara of Athlone who was living in Drogheda at the time of the Rising, and Nicholas Butterly of Milltown, Dunleer. The oral history interviews contain many names of those who were involved in the Volunteers in the Drogheda region in the years leading up to the Rising but who did not mobilise at Easter 1916, so only a small number of new names were found. However, it helped with clarification on several names found previously (see Table 1: Co. Louth Volunteers who mobilised Easter Week 1916).

The Annagassan and District Historical Society provided the County Archives with a copy of 'Ten in the Tower', which was an article published in *Togher Topics* for the seventy-fifth anniversary of the Easter Rising in 1991. It dealt with the Grangebellew Volunteers and included two accounts of events before, during and after the Rising. One account was that of Nicholas Butterly, which was a transcription of the aforementioned oral history interview produced in 1966. The second account, originally written during the period 1945 to 1959, was a first-hand report by former Volunteer James Kelly that provided a detailed insight into the activities of the Grangebellew Volunteers at the time. A further source was the

Joseph Dolan Papers.[14] Whilst there is an interesting group of letters that relate to Irish nationalism and independence in this collection, there are only a couple of letters from Louth Volunteers and no further names were provided; although the letters assisted with clarification in William Rynne's name, which is recorded in Edward Bailey's witness statement with the spelling Wrenn.[15]

In the same collection, a letter written from Michael McGrath of 9 Linenhall Street, Dublin, to Joseph Dolan, Ardee on 30 April 1916, which provides a witness account of the suffering and devastation during the Rising, contains the names of three men from Co. Louth who had been working in the Louth Dairy and were killed in the North King Street massacre on 28 April 1916. The fourth person from Co. Louth that was killed was a Dundalk-born priest[16] (see Table 4: Co. Louth people killed during the Rising).

When examining the witness statements (see Table 2: Bureau of Military History Witness Statements), one of the main challenges in compiling the list of men was correctly distinguishing those men with identical or similar names. For example, there were two men by the name of Patrick Hughes and both were sometimes referred to as Paddy Hughes. Whilst it was already clear from the witness statements that one Patrick Hughes was the commandant of the Louth Brigade, Thomas McCrave's witness statement clarified that the other Patrick Hughes was a brother of Vincent Hughes and acted as a messenger.[17] There were also two men by the name of James Kelly. One was from Dundalk and the other was from Grangebellew. Patrick McHugh's witness statement named the latter as Joseph;[18] although Nicholas Butterly referred to him as 'Jimmy' in his oral history account.[19] Patrick Donnelly and Peadar Donnelly also caused some initial confusion: the former resided in Cooley and the latter in Dundalk (though also from Cooley originally). As the witness statements contained many names, including those who were involved in the Volunteers in the period leading up to the Rising, it was difficult at times to ascertain whether several individual names had mobilised during Easter Week. Assistance in answering queries was provided by the Dundalk Relatives Association Committee and by several individual relatives.

Whilst the names of the leaders of the 1916 Rising are well documented, it was felt that it was important to identify and collate the local names of those from Co. Louth who were committed to securing independence for Ireland through mobilising in 1916 (see Table 3: Those originally from Co. Louth who also took part in the Rising). It is also hoped that this list of names will assist future researchers who are pursuing further investigation into the Louth Volunteers. To date, there are 131 names on the list. As stated earlier, the Military Service Pensions Collection is an ongoing project, and it is possible that through this excellent resource or through relatives or undiscovered archives that more names may come to light. If you become aware of any other names and a verifying source, please inform Louth County Archives Service.

Table 1. Co. Louth Volunteers who mobilised Easter Week 1916

No	Volunteer Name	Volunteer Address	Tyrrelstown House	Witness Statement	MSPC Reference	Explanatory Notes
1	Agnew, James	Dundalk		231; 677		Ordered to commandeer cars near Castlebellingham.
2	Atkinson, William	Dundalk		494; 677		
3	Bailey, Edward	Dundalk	Yes	232; 233; 238; 677	MSP34 REF15785	
4	Barrett, John	Dundalk		231; 677		Ordered to commandeer cars near Castlebellingham.
5	Bateson, Francis	Drogheda		1504; 1748		Sometimes referred to as 'Bates'.
6	Berrill, Joseph	Dundalk		161; 237; 238; 494; 507; 677	MSP9709	Mobilised for Dundalk arms raid. Joined main body with countermanding order, then sent to Dublin.
7	Bishop, Patrick	Dundalk		677		
8	Boyd, Patrick	Dundalk		677		
9	Bradley, Dr William	Drogheda		507; 1504; 1748		Informed Drogheda Volunteers of countermanding order.

10	Brannigan, William	Drogheda		1504; 1748		Started to walk to Dublin on Tuesday.
11	Butterly, Nicholas	Milltown		232; 238; 677		Brother of Sean. Occupied Barmeath Tower.
12	Butterly, Sean	Milltown		232; 238; 677		Brother of Nicholas. Occupied Barmeath Tower.
13	Butterly, Thomas	Gallagh				Cousin of Nicholas and Sean. Occupied Barmeath Tower.
14	Byrne, Thomas	Dundalk		677		
15	Callan, Thomas	Dundalk		494		Met for boat journey on Thursday 27 April 1916.
16	Casey, Patrick	Dundalk		231; 238; 338		Ordered to commandeer cars near Castlebellingham.
17	Clifford, Ed	Dundalk		677		
18	Clifford, Owen	Dundalk	Yes	233; 260; 677	MSP34 REF52470	
19	Clifford, Peter	Dundalk		231; 233; 238; 677	MSP34 REF4759	Ordered to commandeer cars near Castlebellingham.
20	Coburn, Francis	Dundalk	Yes	677	MSP34 REF52265	
21	Conlon James	Dundalk		677		
22	Corcoran, James	Dundalk		353		Drove horse drawn brake.
23	Corcoran, Thomas	Dundalk				Service verified by Hughes, Hannigan and MacEntee in pension application.
24	Deary, Henry	Dundalk		677		
25	Devin, Mathew	Dunleer				Hack Car Driver. Occupied Barmeath Tower.
26	Dillon, John	Brownstown, Monasterboice				Occupied Barmeath Tower.

27	Donnelly, Michael	[Armagh] / Dundalk		494; 677		Mobilised for Dundalk arms raid. Sent as messenger with countermanding order. Met for boat journey on Thursday, 27 April 1916.
28	Donnelly, Patrick	Cooley		239; 353		
29	Donnelly, Peadar	Dundalk		494; 677		
30	Duffy, Joseph	Dundalk		237; 677		Met for boat journey on Thursday, 27 April 1916.
31	Duffy, Patrick	Dundalk		237; 494		Met for boat journey on Thursday, 27 April 1916.
32	Dullaghan, Owen	Dundalk		677		
33	Dunne, James	Dundalk	Yes	231; 233; 238; 260; 677	MSP34 REF16092	
34	Durnin, James	Dundalk	Yes	677	24SP6330	
35	Farrelly, Patrick	Dundalk		677		Mobilised for Dundalk arms raid.
36	Feely,	Drogheda		695		May not be from Drogheda. However, they did meet at Feelys shop on James St, Drogheda.
37	Ferguson, Michael	Cooley		239; 353; 677	MSP34 REF4732	
38	Finn, Patrick	Dundalk	Yes	231; 233; 238; 677	MSP34 REF54570	
39	Finnegan, John	Dundalk		337; 238; 494; 677		Met for boat journey on Thursday, 27 April 1916.
40	Finnegan, Joseph	Drogheda		1748		

41	Flynn, John	Dundalk		494; 677		Met for boat journey on Thursday, 27 April 1916.
42	Garvey, John	Dundalk		353		Met for boat journey on Thursday, 27 April 1916.
43	Garvey, Patrick	Dundalk	Yes	260; 677		
44	Gavin, Thomas	Drogheda		1748		
45	Grant, Owen	Dundalk		677		
46	Greene, Arthur	Dundalk	Yes	231; 233; 238; 260; 677	MSP34 REF1387	
47	Halfpenny, Peter	Dundalk		677	MSP34 REF15902	Also used Halpin. Birth cert. states Halfpenny.
48	Hall, Samuel	Dundalk	Yes	231; 677; 695	MSP34 REF20788	
49	Hamill, Thomas	Dundalk		233; 232; 237; 677	MSP34 REF16105	Sent to Dublin with MacEntee to gather information.
50	Hand, Michael	[Dundalk]		677		Mobilised for Dundalk arms raid. Sent to O'Hannigan with countermanding order.
51	Hanratty, James	Dundalk		677; 695	MSP34 REF16107	Sometimes recorded as 'Seamus'.
52	Harkin, Michael	Drogheda / Donegal		1748		
53	Hearty, John	Dundalk		338; 677		
54	Hearty, Thomas	Dundalk		231; 233; 238; 260; 353; 677		Older IRB member. Joined at Castlebellingham. Drove horse and cart.
55	Hoey, P	Dundalk		677		
56	Hughes, Eugene	Dundalk		1052		Telegraphist in Dundalk post office on duty Easter Monday - intercepted messages.

57	Hughes, James	[Dundalk]	Yes	161; 677	MSP34 REF16156	
58	Hughes, Patrick	Dundalk (Park Street)	Yes	161; 231; 232; 233; 236; 237; 238; 260; 337; 338; 353; 494; 677; 695; 1052	MSP34 REF17680	Commandant; sometimes referred to as Paddy.
59	Hughes, Patrick	Dundalk		[677]; 695		Vincent's brother, sometimes referred to as Paddy (later in USA). Sent by O'Hannigan with Denis O'Neill to locate Thomas Ashe.
60	Hughes, Vincent	Dundalk		677; 695; 1052		Mobilised for Dundalk arms raid. Sent to O'Hannigan with countermanding order.
61	Jameson, Richard	Dundalk	Yes	233; 237; 677; 695	DP9613	
62	Jennings, James	Dundalk		238; 677; 695		
63	Kearney, Hugh	Dundalk	Yes	231; 233; 238; 260; 677	MSP34 REF2794	
64	Keenan, Michael	Drogheda/ Monaghan		1748		
65	Kelly, James	Grangebellew		238; 677		Named as Joseph in WS677; and 'Jimmy' in OHA/009. Occupied Barmeath Tower.
66	Kelly, James	Dundalk	Yes	238; 677		
67	Kelly, Thomas	Grangebellew		677		James' Brother. Occupied Barmeath Tower.
68	Kerr, Patrick	Dundalk		677		
69	Kieran, Ed	Dundalk	Yes	237; 677		
70	Kieran, John	Dundalk	Yes	233; 238; 260; 494; 677	MSP34 REF16149	

71	Kieran, Peter	Dundalk		494; 677		Met for boat journey on Thursday, 27 April 1916.
72	Kieran, Thomas	Dublin		677		Met for boat journey on Thursday, 27 April 1916.
73	Kiley, Sean	Drogheda / Waterford		1748		
74	Larrissey, Joseph	Dundalk		677		
75	Lawler, Fintan	Drogheda		1748		
76	Layng, James	Dunleer / Galway		232; 238; 677		Occupied Barmeath Tower.
77	Leahy, Denis	Dundalk		236; 353; 677	DP5335	Court-martialled for the killing of Constable McGee.
78	Litchfield, Ben	Dundalk	Yes	233		Brother of Harry Litchfield.
79	Litchfield, Henry	Dundalk	Yes	677	MSP34 REF16084	Kilcurry company; from Newtownbalregan, Dundalk.
80	Lynch, Matthew	Dundalk		677		
81	MacEntee, Seán	Dundalk / Dublin		494; 161; 231; 232; 233; 236; 260; 337; 353	MSP34 REF16538	Court-martialled for the killing of Constable McGee.
82	Malone, Frank	Drogheda		1504; 1748		
83	Malone, James	Drogheda		1504; 1748		
84	Martin, Frank	Dundalk	Yes	233; 236; 353; 677; 695	MSP34 REF15918	Court-martialled for the killing of Constable McGee.
85	Matthews, Thomas	Ardee		260; 494		Handed over weapons in Ardee with Phil McMahon.
86	McArdle, Patrick	Knockbridge		677		

87	McCrave, Thomas	Dundalk	Yes	231; 233; 677; 695	MSP34 REF697	
88	McEnteggart, John	Dundalk		677		
89	McGeough, Owen	Castleblaney		237; 677		
90	McGuill, John	Dundalk		353		Mobilised for Dundalk arms raid. Met for boat journey on Thursday, 27 April 1916.
91	McGuill, Joseph	Dundalk		353; 494; 677		Met for boat journey on Thursday, 27 April 1916.
92	McGuill, Seamus	Dundalk		353		Mobilised for Dundalk arms raid.
93	McHugh, Patrick	Dundalk	Yes	161; 223; 238; 260; 353; 337; 677	MSP34 REF12512	
94	McKenna, Patrick	Dundalk		677		
95	McMahon, Philip	Ardee		161; 232; 233; 238; 260; 677; 695		O/C Ardee. Supplied guns at Ardee.
96	McManus, James	Grangebellew				Occupied Barmeath Tower.
97	McQuillan, Felix	Dundalk		494		Met for boat journey on Thursday, 27 April 1916.
98	McQuillan, Frank	Dundalk		677		
99	McQuillan, Philip	Dundalk		231; 677		
100	McTeggart, Thomas	Dundalk	Yes	677		Down as McEntiggart in WS677. Family advised it is McTeggart. John McEnteggart was his wife's brother.

101	Monaghan, Philip	Drogheda / Dublin		507; 1504; 1748		O/C Drogheda. Went to Dublin Easter Sunday night after receiving countermanding orders.
102	Mulholland, Patrick	Kilkerley	Yes	233; 677	MSP34 REF17985	
103	Mulholland, Thomas	Dundalk	Yes	233; 677	DP23383	
104	Murtagh, Christopher	Dundalk		353		Drove horse drawn brake.
105	Murtagh, James	Dundalk		353		Drove horse drawn brake.
106	Myles, Patrick	Drogheda		1504		Sometimes recorded as 'Miles'. Agreed to go to Dublin with O'Meara but surrender notice already posted.
107	Necy, Francis	Dundalk		237; 353; 494; 677		Met for boat journey on Thursday, 27 April 1916.
108	Norton, Gerry	Dundalk		353		Provided boat for boat journey to Dublin.
109	O'Dowd, Owen	Dundalk	Yes	233; 677		
110	O'Dowd, Richard	Dundalk	Yes	237; 233; 677	MSP34 REF2649	
111	O'Hanlon, James	Cooley		239; 677		
112	O'Hannigan, Donal	Dublin / Dundalk	Yes	337; 231; 232; 233; 236; 238; 260; 337; 353; 677; 695	MSP34 REF16541	Sent by Pearse to direct military operations in Louth, Meath and Monaghan. In command during Easter.
113	O'Higgins, Joseph	Drogheda		507; 1504		Agreed to go to Dublin with O'Meara but surrender notice already posted.

114	O'Meara, James	Drogheda / Athlone			1504; 1748		Also referred to as Seamus. Tried to organise a group to go to Dublin but surrender notice already posted.
115	O'Neill, Arthur	Dundalk			260; 353; 494; 677		Met for boat journey on Thursday, 27 April 1916.
116	O'Neill, Denis		Yes		695		
117	O'Neill, Felix	[Dundalk]	Yes		677	MSP34 REF48905	
118	Quigley, Patrick	Dundalk			494; 677		Met for boat journey on Thursday, 27 April 1916.
119	Quinn, Hugh	Dublin	Yes		677	1924A25	
120	Quinn, John	Armagh			231; 238; 353; 677	MSP34 REF59165	Sometimes referred to as Jack or Sean. Court-martialled for the killing of Constable McGee.
121	Reilly, James	Kilkerley	Yes		231; 260; 677	MSP34 REF3698	
122	Reynolds, Michael	Dysart			232; 238; 677		Occupied Barmeath Tower.
123	Rynne, [William]	Dundalk / Clare			233		Noted as William Rynne in PP118/; as Wrenn in WS233. Handed over weapons in Ardee with Phil McMahon.
124	Sally, James	Dundalk			236; 353; 677; 695	MSP34 REF17725	Court-martialled for the killing of Constable McGee.
125	Sharkey, Thomas	Dundalk			677; 231		Ordered to commandeer cars near Castlebellingham.
126	Tierney, Bertie	Dublin / Grangebellew					Visitor from Dublin. Part of Grangebellew / Dunleer group.
127	Toal, James	Dundalk			161; 232; 233; 337; 494; 677		Met for boat journey on Thursday, 27 April 1916.

128	Tuite,	Tullyallen		1504		Not believed to have been a member but assembled in Drogheda with the others on Easter Sunday.
129	Tuite, Daniel	Dundalk	Yes	231; 233; 677	MSP34 REF2743	
130	Waller, Joseph	Dundalk		677		
131	Walsh, Larry	Drogheda		1504; 1748		Third in command, Drogheda.

The list of names of those who mobilised is mainly based on the Bureau of Military History witness statements (BMHWS) and the Military Service Pensions Collection (MSPC), as available at December 2015. Other sources include a 1966 oral history archive interview entitled 'Memories of 1916' (reference OHA/009); the Frongoch Roll and other Frongoch records; an account by former Volunteer James Kelly, reproduced in *Togher Topics*, June 1991; and letters in the Joseph Dolan Papers (reference PP00118/). If you know of any other names and verifying sources, please inform Archive staff.

Table 2. Bureau of Military History witness statements

WS No	Name
161	O'Hannigan, Donal
231	Clifford, Peter
232	Hamill, Thomas
233	Bailey, Edward
236	Martin, Frank
237	Duffy, Patrick
238	Greene, Arthur
239	Necy, Frank
260	Kearney, Hugh
337	Tuite, Daniel
338	McQuillan, Francis
353	McGuill, James
494	Kiernan, Peter

507	Higgins, Joseph
664	McHugh, Patrick
677	McHugh, Patrick*
695	McCrave, Thomas
1052	McEntee, Sean
1748	Walsh, Sen Larry
1504	O'Meara, James

Table 3. Those originally from Co. Louth who also took part in the Rising

Volunteer Name	Volunteer Address	Notes
Darcy, William	Dublin / Dundalk	Darcy was involved in setting up Sinn Féin in Dundalk. He left Dundalk about 1912 and became involved with the Volunteers in Dublin. He was in the GPO during the Rising. He is buried in Haggardstown. (MSPC: 1D332)
Hastings, John	Dublin / Drogheda	Recorded in 'List of Irishmen deported, without trial, to English prisons between 1 May and 15 June 1916'.
McGarvey, Michael	England / Dundalk	McGarvey was involved in setting up Sinn Féin in Dundalk. He went to England and came back to fight in the Rising. He died in the USA. (MSP34REF23881)
Munster, T.	Dublin / Drogheda	Recorded in 'List of Irishmen deported, without trial, to English prisons between 1 May 1 and 15 June 1916'.
Thornton, Frank	Drogheda/ Liverpool/ Dublin	From Drogheda but worked in Liverpool. IRB member and one of the principal Volunteer organisers in Liverpool. Returned to Dublin with Liverpool Volunteer Companies before Rising and based at Kimmage. O/C Imperial Hotel O'Connell Street during Rising. (24SP1302)
Thornton, Hugh	Drogheda/ Liverpool/ Dublin	Brother of Frank. Returned from Liverpool before Rising. GPO during Rising. (2D477)
Thornton, Nora	Drogheda/ Liverpool/ Dublin	Sister of Frank. Cumann na mBan. (MSP34REF51015)
Thornton, Patrick	Drogheda/ Liverpool/ Dublin	Brother of Frank. Returned from Liverpool before Rising. Liberty Hall and Fairview during Rising.

Table 4. Co. Louth people killed during the Rising

Name	Address	Notes
Finnegan, James	Born in Stickillen	All worked in the Louth Dairy in Dublin. Along with James McCartney, they were killed by soldiers in the North King Street Massacre where fifteen civilians were shot or bayoneted to death by soldiers from the South Staffordshire regiment on Friday, 28 April 1916.
Hoey, Paddy	Clogherhead	
Lawless, Peter	Born in New York, mother Co. Louth, connected with the Stanley family of Togher	
Watters, The Very Revd Felix Joseph, SM	Dublin / Dundalk	Born in Dundalk, 1851, Fr Watters was President of the Catholic University School, Lower Leeson Street, and was hit by a bullet in the Mount Street Bridge area. He died on 8 May 1916. (*Dundalk Democrat*)

Constable Charles McGee of Gilbertstown Barracks, Co. Louth, was the first RIC Officer to die in the 1916 Rising. He died as the result of a fatal shooting at Castlebellingham on 24 April 1916. He was a native of Co. Donegal. Volunteers Seán MacEntee, Frank Martin, Denis Leahy and James Sally were later tried by court martial and all but Sally were convicted of the murder and received death sentences, which was later commuted.

NOTES

1   http://www.militaryarchives.ie.
2   Louth County Archives, IE LHA OHA/009, Oral History Archive collection.
3   Allen Library, Dublin, IE AL 1916/201, Brother Allen collection.
4   Annagassan and District Historical Society, '*Ten in the Tower*', *The Grangebellew Volunteers 75th Anniversary 1916–1991* (Togher Topics, June 1991). The account was written during the period 1945–59.
5   Louth County Archives, IE LHA PP00118/, Joseph Dolan papers.
6   Author of *The Royal Irish Constabulary and the Black and Tans in County Louth 1919–1922* (Dundalk, 2004) and co-author (with Joseph Gavin) of *The military barracks Dundalk: a brief history* (Dundalk, 1999).
7   http://www.militaryarchives.ie.
8   Military Archives, Military Service Pensions, MSP34REF12512.
9   Committee members included: Alan Bogan, Pádraic Agnew, Noel Agnew and Marcus Howard.
10   Allen Library, Dublin, IE AL 1916/20.
11   Allen Library, Dublin, IE AL 1916/70/1.

12   Allen Library, Dublin, IE AL 1916/99, 101, 102.
13   A typescript list (in alphabetical order by surname) of Irishmen deported, without trial, to English prisons between 1 May and 15 June 1916 that was compiled and rearranged from the seventeen lists officially issued to the press for publication by the British military authorities.
14   Louth County Archives, IE LHA PP00118/, Joseph Dolan Papers.
15   BMH, WS238, 'Edward Bailey'.
16   Fr Michael Murtagh, CC, *St Patrick's Dundalk – An Anniversary Account* (Dundalk, 1997), p. 200.
17   BMH, WS695', Thomas McCrave', p. 8.
18   Ibid., BMH, WS677, 'Patrick McHugh', addendum, p. 3.
19   Louth County Archives, IE LHA OHA/009.

Contributors

Donal Hall was awarded a PhD by NUI Maynooth in 2010 for his thesis, 'Violence and political factionalism and their effects on North Louth 1874–1943'. His publications include the books *World War I and Nationalist politics in County Louth, 1914–1920*, published by Four Courts Press, and *The unreturned army: County Louth Dead in the Great War, 1914–1918*, published by the County Louth Archaeological and Historical Society. He is currently researching and writing the County Louth volume of the *Irish Revolution, 1912–1923* series edited by Dr Mary Anne Lyons and Dr Daiti Ó Corráin and published by Four Courts Press.

Ailbhe Rogers is a native of Co. Louth. She holds a BA and an MA in Irish history from NUI Maynooth. She is a recipient of the John and Pat Hume Scholarship and is currently working on her PhD thesis entitled 'Irish Revolutionary Women in Counties Louth, Armagh and Down, 1900–1924' under the supervision of Professor Terence Dooley. Ailbhe has delivered several lectures on the role of women in the Irish revolution and has contributed to 'Ireland 2016: The Women of the 1916 Rising Exhibition', the '77 Women of Richmond Barracks Project' and also the 'Louth Volunteers 1914–1918 Exhibition'. For the past three seasons, she has worked as a tour guide in Kilmainham Gaol Museum, Dublin.

Martin Maguire is senior lecturer and director of the BA (Hons.) Digital Humanities Programme in the Department of Humanities, Dundalk Institute of Technology. He has extensive publications on the history of civil service trade unions and state-building, including *The Civil Service and the revolution in Ireland 1912–1938: 'Shaking the blood-stained hand of Mr Collins'*, published by Manchester University Press. He has also published many articles on the history of Irish working-class Protestantism.

Brendan McAvinue is a graduate of the extra-mural certificate course in local history from NUI Maynooth. He has lectured on the history of policing in Co. Louth and is currently researching the career of his grandfather, Patrick McAvinue, who was a member of the Royal Irish Constabulary, the Irish Republican Police and the first ordinary member of the Garda Síochána.

Fiona Fearon is a lecturer in drama and theatre studies at Dundalk Institute of Technology, Ireland. She completed her PhD at the University of Sheffield entitled, 'The selection, production and reception of European Plays at the National Theatre

of Great Britain, 1963–1997'. Her principal areas of interest are audience and performance studies, and she has published on audience ethnography and the performance of grief in contemporary society. Recently, she has been working on the 'Revival Irish Theatre and grief in early twentieth-century Ireland'. Fiona is a former member of the executive committee of the Irish Society for Theatre Research.

Peter Rigney is industrial officer of the Irish Congress of Trade Unions. He completed his PhD at the Centre for Contemporary Irish History, TCD. His book *Trains, coal and turf – transport in emergency Ireland* is published by Irish Academic Press. He co-authored, with Shay Cody and John O'Dowd, *The Parliament of Labour, a history of the Dublin Council of Trade Unions* (Dublin Council of Trade Unions, 1986). His articles can be found at https://tcd.academia.edu/PeterRigney. He is assistant archivist of the Irish Railway Record Society.

Jean Young is originally from Dublin but now lives in Louth. She was recently awarded an MA in Irish history at NUI Maynooth for her thesis on the life of Sir John Stephen Robinson of Rokeby Hall in Louth. She has a particular interest in the affairs of the Big Houses and estates of Louth and is planning to continue research in this area for her PhD.

John McCullen is a farmer, historian and writer and a former president of both Louth and Meath Archaeological and Historical Societies. He was a columnist for the *Farmers Journal* for twenty-five years and then eight years with the *Drogheda Independent*. He has published ten books and written over thirty articles in the *Journal of the Louth Archaeological and Historical Society, Ríocht na Midhe* and the *Old Drogheda Journal* and lectures at An Grianán Adult Education Centre, Co. Louth.

Conor McNamara was senior researcher on the Notre Dame University 1916 Project. He is the 1916 Scholar in Residence at the Moore Institute at NUI Galway. He is joint editor of *The West of Ireland: New perspectives on the nineteenth century*, published by History Press, and *Easter 1916: A new illustrated history*, published by Collins Press. He has written extensively about the history of the Irish revolution and the intersection between political violence and criminality in twentieth-century Ireland.

Mal Martin is a graduate of the extra-mural certificate course in local history from NUI Maynooth, where his special area of study was the Civil War in Drogheda. For the last few years, Mal has worked as a tour guide for the Office of Public Works at Brú na Bóinne World Heritage Site.

Don Johnston has a Master's degree in local history from NUI Maynooth, and is currently President of the Co. Louth Archaeological and Historical Society. He has a special interest in the industrial heritage of Dundalk and north Louth, with particular reference to the linen industry, and has written a number of essays on the subject for the society's journal. He has recently published a detailed study on the rise and fall of the linen industry in one locality of the Cooley peninsula, *The Flurry Valley, Ravensdale, North Louth*. His latest book, *From Faughart Hill to Faughart House*, outlines the strategic importance of Faughart from the earliest times.

Séamus Bellew is from Co. Galway and is presently joint secretary of the County Louth Archaeological and Historical Society. He teaches mathematics at Dundalk Institute of Technology. His interests include heraldry, psephology and local history.

Lorraine McCann is the county archivist at Louth County Archives Services (since 2000). She manages, preserves and makes archives of public and private origin relating to the history of Co. Louth accessible to the public, in addition to providing records management services to Louth County Council. Her interest in emphasising the importance of the County Archives to the community both as a repository for historical documents and as a resource for research led to the organisation of a highly successful exhibition in 2016 on the role of the Irish Volunteers 1914–18 in Co. Louth, for which she drew on public contributions and documents already housed in the archives. Lorraine is a member of the Archives and Records Association UK & Ireland, the Local Authority Archivists' Group and the Records Management Policy Working Group for local authorities.

Index

pension files of Volunteers, 282–3
Pentland, George Charles, 154
Pentland, George Henry, 154, 158
Petty Sessions courts, 100
Plaster ambush, the, 10–11, 102, 195, 202
Plunkett, Count George Noble, 273–4
Plunkett, Countess, 51, 273
Plunkett, George, 273
police raids on homes and businesses, 51, 52, 53, 98, 100–1
policing in Drogheda after the RIC handover, 215–19
Powell, Baden, 113
press coverage, 3, 4, 5, 44, 182 *see also* *Dundalk Democrat* (newspaper)
prisoners' dependants, financial support, 44–5, 50–1
pro-Treatyite Sinn Féin, 15–16
Proclamation of the Irish Republic, the, 271
Provisional Government, 14, 16, 55, 77–8, 79, 137, 142, 216, 226, 231, 237, 262
Protestant dressmakers Dundalk, death of, 199–201
PRSTV (proportional representation single transferable vote system), 13, 15
Public Safety Act (1922), 55

Queen's Royal Theatre, Dublin, 111
Quigley, James, 183
Quigley, John, 256, 262, 266
Quinn, John, 256, 263
Quinn, Maire, 120
Quinn, Peter, 204

rail system, attacks on, 136, 137, 138–9, **142–4**, 226, 240–1, 267
Railway Gazette, The (newspaper), 137, 141
railways, the, 60–1, 81, 131–42, **142–4**
Rankin, Patrick, 198, 202
Rathdonnell, Lord, 149
Rathescar demesne, 149, 158
Ravensdale Park, 103, 148–9, 155–7, 164
Reaghstown Temperance Solidarity Dramatic Class, 122
Reddan, Denis, 87
Redmond, John, 1, 4, 5, 9, 176, 178, 179, 182
refugees, Ulster, 205–6, 236, 237
Reilly, Thomas, 204

republican courts, the, 75, 96, 97, 103, 104, 186, 237
republican monuments and memorials, 254–66
revolutionary fervour across Europe, 70–1
RIC, the, 11, 13, 39, 43, 46, 49, 86, 137, 179, 259; attacks on, 11, 95–6, 98, 101, 102, 105, 196, 197–8, 202, 253; barracks in Co. Louth, 87, **106**, 214–15; during the Civil War, 220, 224–5; and County Inspector reports, 67, 87–8, 89, 90, 93–4, 95, 103–4, 194, 197, 198, 204; and Cumann na mBan, 38, 51, 53; and industrial unrest, 67, 69, 71, 72, 74, 89; raids by, 46, 51, 52, 53, 98, 100–1; and the Republican courts, 97, 103; and the Volunteers, 7, 8, 35, 45, 90, 91, 92, 94, 193, 195 *see also* ADRIC (Auxiliary Division of the RIC); Black and Tans (Special Reserves of the RIC), the
Rice, Georgina, 200
Riders to the Sea (play), 122
Ridgeway, Charles F., 72
rifle theft at Greenore Point, 98
road competition on rail business, 135–6, 141–2
road maintenance, 77
Robert Emmet (play), 110, 111, 119–20, 123–4
Robinson, Seamus, 95
Roche, Augustine, 1
Rockmarshall railway bridge attack, the, 240–1, 267
Roden, Earl of, 147
Rogers, Frank, 264–5
Rogers, Thomas, 264–5
Rokeby Hall estate, 149–50, 158
Rolsea atrocity, the, 208
Rooney, Eamonn, 69, 71, 72, 76, 79–80, 223
route marches and drilling, 6–8, 40, 90, 91, 179–80
rural local elections (June 1920), 10, 76, 194
Russell, John J., 161
Russian Revolution, the, 60, 70–1
Ryan, Min, 51

Saint-Mihiel, France, 152
Sally, James, 93, 297
seanchló lettering on monuments, 254